Remembering Augustine

VERITAS
Series Introduction

"... the truth will set you free" (John 8:32)

In much contemporary discourse, Pilate's question has been taken to mark the absolute boundary of human thought. Beyond this boundary, it is often suggested, is an intellectual hinterland into which we must not venture. This terrain is an agnosticism of thought: because truth cannot be possessed, it must not be spoken. Thus, it is argued that the defenders of "truth" in our day are often traffickers in ideology, merchants of counterfeits, or anti-liberal. They are, because it is somewhat taken for granted that Nietzsche's word is final: truth is the domain of tyranny.

Is this indeed the case, or might another vision of truth offer itself? The ancient Greeks named the love of wisdom as *philia*, or friendship. The one who would become wise, they argued, would be a "friend of truth." For both philosophy and theology might be conceived as schools in the friendship of truth, as a kind of relation. For like friendship, truth is as much discovered as it is made. If truth is then so elusive, if its domain is *terra incognita*, perhaps this is because it arrives to us—unannounced—as gift, as a person, and not some thing.

The aim of the Veritas book series is to publish incisive and original current scholarly work that inhabits "the between" and "the beyond" of theology and philosophy. These volumes will all share a common aspiration to transcend the institutional divorce in which these two disciplines often find themselves, and to engage questions of pressing concern to both philosophers and theologians in such a way as to reinvigorate both disciplines with a kind of interdisciplinary desire, often so absent in contemporary academe. In a word, these volumes represent collective efforts in the befriending of truth, doing so beyond the simulacra of pretend tolerance, the violent, yet insipid reasoning of liberalism that asks with Pilate, "What is truth?"—expecting a consensus of non-commitment; one that encourages the commodification of the mind, now sedated by the civil service of career, ministered by the frightened patrons of position.

The series will therefore consist of two wings: (1) original monographs; and (2) essay collections on a range of topics in theology and philosophy. The latter will principally be the products of the annual conferences of the Centre of Theology and Philosophy (www.theologyphilosophycentre.co.uk).

Conor Cunningham and Joseph Terry, *Veritas Series Editors*

Available from Cascade Books

Anthony D. Baker	*Diagonal Advance: Perfection in Christian Theology*
D. C. Schindler	*The Perfection of Freedom: Schiller, Schelling, and Hegel between the Ancients and the Moderns*
Rustin Brian	*Covering Up Luther: How Barth's Christology Challenged the* Deus Absconditus *that Haunts Modernity*
Timothy Stanley	*Protestant Metaphysics After Karl Barth and Martin Heidegger*
Christopher Ben Simpson	*The Truth Is the Way: Kierkegaard's* Theologia Viatorum
Richard H. Bell	*Wagner's Parsifal: An Appreciation in the Light of His Theological Journey*
Antonio Lopez	*Gift and the Unity of Being*
Toyohiko Kagawa	*Cosmic Purpose*, translated and introduced by Thomas John Hastings
Nigel Zimmerman	*Facing the Other: John Paul II, Levinas, and the Body*
Conor Sweeney	*Sacramental Presence after Heidegger: Onto-theology, Sacraments, and the Mother's Smile*
John Behr et al. (eds.)	*The Role of Death in Life: A Multidisciplinary Examination of the Relation between Life and Death*
Eric Austin Lee et al. (eds.)	*The Resounding Soul: Reflection on the Metaphysics and Vivacity of the Human Person*
Orion Edgar	*Things Seen and Unseen: The Logic of Incarnation in Merleau-Ponty's Metaphysics of Flesh*
Duncan B. Reyburn	*Seeing Things as They Are: G. K. Chesterton and the Drama of Meaning*
Lyndon Shakespeare	*Being the Body of Christ in the Age of Management*
Michael V. Di Fuccia	*Owen Barfield: Philosophy, Poetry, and Theology*
John McNerney	*Wealth of Persons: Economics with a Human Face*
Norm Klassen	*The Fellowship of the Beatific Vision: Chaucer on Overcoming Tyranny and Becoming Ourselves*
Donald Wallenfang	*Human and Divine Being: A Study of the Theological Anthropology of Edith Stein*
Sotiris Mitralexis	*Ever-Moving Repose: A Contemporary Reading of Maximus the Confessor's Theory of Time*
Sotiris Mitralexis et al. (eds.)	*Maximus the Confessor as a European Philosopher*
Kevin Corrigan	*Love, Friendship, Beauty, and the Good: Plato, Aristotle, and the Later Tradition*
Andrew Brower Latz	*The Social Philosophy of Gillian Rose*

1. Note: Nathan Kerr, *Christ, History, and Apocalyptic*, although volume 3 of the original SCM Veritas series, is available from Cascade as part of the Theopolitical Visions series.

D. C. Schindler	*Love and the Postmodern Predicament: Rediscovering the Real in Beauty, Goodness, and Truth*
Stephen Kampowski	*Embracing Our Finitude: Exercises in a Christian Anthropology between Dependence and Gratitude*
William Desmond	*The Gift of Beauty and the Passion of Being: On the Threshold between the Aesthetic and the Religious*
Charles Péguy	*Notes on Bergson and Descartes*
David Alcalde	*Cosmology without God: The Problematic Theology Inherent in Modern Cosmology*
Benson P. Fraser	*Hide and Seek: The Sacred Art of Indirect Communication*
Philip John Paul Gonzales	*Exorcising Philosophical Modernity: Cyril O'Regan and Christian Discourse after Modernity*
Caitlin Smith Gilson	*Subordinated Ethics: Natural Law and Moral Miscellany in Aquinas and Dostoyevsky*
Michael Dominic Taylor	*The Foundations of Nature: Metaphysics of Gift for an Integral Ecological Ethic*
David W. Opderbeck	*The End of the Law? Law, Theology, and Neuroscience*
Caitlin Smith Gilson	*As It Is in Heaven: Some Christian Questions on the Nature of Paradise*
Andrew T. J. Kaethler	*The Eschatological Person: Alexander Schemann and Joseph Ratzinger in Dialogue*
Emmanuel Falque	*By Way of Obstacles: A Pathway through a Work*
Paul Tyson (ed.)	*Astonishment in Science: Engagements with William Desmond*
Darren Dyk	*Will & Love: Shakespeare and the Motion of the Soul*
Matthew Vest	*Ethics Lost in Modernity: Reflections on Wittgenstein and Bioethics*
Hanna Lucas	*Sensing the Sacred: Recovering a Mystagogical Vision of Knowledge and Salvation*
Philip Gonzales et al. (eds.)	*Finitude's Wounded Praise: Responses to Jean-Louis Crétien*
Martin Koci et al. (eds.)	*God and Phenomenology: Thinking with Jean-Yves Lacoste*
Steven E. Knepper (ed.)	*A Heart of Flesh: William Desmond and the Bible*
James Madden	*Thinking About Thinking: Mind and Meaning in the Era of Techno-Nihilism*
Tyler Dalton McNabb	*An Analytic Theology of Evangelism: A Classical Theist's Approach*
John Milbank et al. (eds.)	*New Trinitarian Ontologies, Volume 1*
Duncan Reyburn	*The Roots of the World: The Remarkable Prescience of G. K. Chesterton*
Pablo Irizar et al. (eds.)	*To Die of Not Writing: Doing Philosophy of Religion with Emmanuel Falque*
Rachel M. Coleman	*Matter as an Image of the Good: Ferdinand Ulrich's Metaphysics of Creation*

Remembering Augustine

The Symphonic Forms and Fundamental Affordances of Memory in His Theology of *Memoria*

CHRISTINE F. STEPHENSON

CASCADE *Books* • Eugene, Oregon

REMEMBERING AUGUSTINE
The Symphonic Forms and Fundamental Affordances of Memory in His Theology of *Memoria*

Veritas

Copyright © 2025 Christine F. Stephenson. All rights reserved. Except for brief quotations in critical publications or reviews, no part of this book may be reproduced in any manner without prior written permission from the publisher. Write: Permissions, Wipf and Stock Publishers, 199 W. 8th Ave., Suite 3, Eugene, OR 97401.

Cascade Books
An Imprint of Wipf and Stock Publishers
199 W. 8th Ave., Suite 3
Eugene, OR 97401

www.wipfandstock.com

PAPERBACK ISBN: 979-8-3852-4986-2
HARDCOVER ISBN: 979-8-3852-4987-9
EBOOK ISBN: 979-8-3852-4988-6

Cataloguing-in-Publication data:

Names: Stephenson, Christine F. [author]

Title: Remembering Augustine : the symphonic forms and fundamental affordanaces of memory in his theology of *memoria* / Christine F. Stephenson.

Description: Eugene, OR: Cascade Books, 2025 | Series: Veritas | Includes bibliographical references.

Identifiers: ISBN 979-8-3852-4986-2 (paperback) | ISBN 979-8-3852-4987-9 (hardcover) | ISBN 979-8-3852-4988-6 (ebook)

Subjects: LCSH: Augustine, of Hippo, Saint, 354–430. | Memory—Religious aspects—Christianity. | Memory (Philosophy). | Memory. | Christianity—Psychology. | Genetics. | Religion and science.

Classification: BR65.A9 S747 2025 (print) | BR65.A9 (ebook)

Scripture quotations are from New Revised Standard Bible, copyright © 1989 National Council of the Churches of Christ in the U.S.A. Used by permission. All rights reserved.

Dedicated to

Victoria April Stephenson
(Vicki)

in aeternum amandus, in aeternum recordatus

You conferred this honour on my memory that you should dwell in it.

Conf. X.25.36.

Contents

List of Tables and Illustrations x

Preface xi

Acknowledgements xiii

Abbreviations xiv

1: Introduction 1
2: The Architectonics and Beginnings of Augustine's Theology of *Memoria* 10
3: The First Decade of Augustine's Interrogation of *Memoria*: 386–395 AD 35
4: Augustine's Theology of *Memoria* in *Confessiones* 66
5: *Memoria* Through the Lens of Augustinian *Scientia* and *Sapientia* 98
6: Re-collecting Memory: Old Wine, New Skins 116
7: Enigmatic Arc-tectonics of Time and Memory 159
8: The Archaeology of Memory by Recalling Creation 196
9: Re-Thinking Augustine's Theology of *Memoria* 266

Bibliography 295

Tables

Table 3.1: The symphonic forms of memory

Table 4.1: *Ordo* of *memoria* in *Confessiones* X

Table 6.1: Summary of the Arc Gene

Table 8.1: Side-by-side comparison of the texts in Books XIII and I.

Table 8.2: Creation in XIII recapitulates creation from I–XII

Table 8.3a: Memory/memories regarding teaching and learning as documented in XIII, X, and I–IX, XI–XII.

Table 8.3b: Memory/memories regarding recollection and forgetfulness as documented in XIII, X, and I–IX, XI–XII.

Table 8.3c: Images, *Phantasiae*, and *Phantasmata* as documented in XIII, X, and III, IV, VI, VII, VIII, IX, and XII

Table 8.3d: Memory/Memories regarding senses and sense-perception as documented in XIII, X, and I–IX, XI–XII.

Table 8.4a: Part 1: The *beata vita* in XIII and I–XII.

Table 8.4b: Part 2: Fallenness that hinders attainment of the *beata vita*.

Table 8.5: Temporality and time in XIII and its correlatives in I–XII.

Table 8.6: A brief survey through *Confessiones* from I–XIII regarding the connecting theme of *Confessio*

Illustrations

Figure 7.1: The Architectonics of Time and Memory

Figure 7.2: Physical time as exemplified by the Arc gene.

Preface

MY INTEREST IN AUGUSTINE was piqued when I read his theory on memory and the theology of *memoria* that he consequently developed. To my surprise I discovered that despite the enormous volume of publications on Augustine, Augustinian memory was vastly underrepresented within this caucus. Memory was of the utmost importance to Augustine because he believed that within his soul there was a memory of God. He recognized memory to be pivotal in his journey to know and understand God and in his remembrance of God. His burning desire to understand memory is evident in his writings on memory, and specifically, in *Confessiones*, especially Book X. The research presented in this book is adapted from my doctoral thesis which examined Augustine's early writings and *Confessiones* to understand how he developed his theology of *memoria*. I decided to utilize architectonics to determine if there was a structure, logic, and particular methodology to Augustinian memory. This architectonic examination revealed in greater depth Augustine's logical, profound, and multi-faceted approach in his interrogation of memory and in the development of his theology. Architectonics is not just a dry, structural, physical analysis of memory for it also reveals the metaphysics of memory and the inner heart of Augustine as evident in his narrative within *Confessiones*. This narrative skillfully draws the reader into Augustine's text and invites them to join him on his journey to know God and the fulfilment of the *beata vita*. All facets of *memoria* and, even Augustine himself, are elucidated through the architectonic interrogation of Augustinian memory.

This architectonic investigation of Augustinian memory unveiled four main neoteric discoveries. First, there are eight symphonic forms of memory and their fundamental affordances in *Conf.* X and Augustine's earlier writings: location of *memoria*, power of memory, sense-perception, teaching/learning, recollection and forgetfulness, images, *phantasiae* and *phantasmata*, transiency of memory, the *beata vita*. Second, genetic analysis of the physical dimension of memory via a unique memory gene called Arc, identified a potential genomic memory process that provided knowledge

PREFACE

regarding the inner workings of memory. This genetic analysis is not meant to be a distinct and separate interrogation aside from the theology of Augustinian memory. It does not pitch science against theology. They are one and the same thing. Imagine a tree that consists of roots, trunk, branches, leaves, chlorophyll, biochemical pathways, and water absorption from the earth. Whether one describes the leaves, roots, biochemical pathways, water absorption, or the sun's action on chlorophyll, one is describing one and the same thing, the tree and the symphonic forms and fundamental affordances that make up that tree. The diverse disciplines—science, theology, narrative, etc.—each undergird the other. The science in this book undergirds Augustinian memory and his theology of *memoria* and reveals how Augustinian *scientia*, in turn, undergirds the genetics and his theology of *memoria*. Third, is the development of a model resulting from the examination of architectonics, time, and memory that describes the simultaneity of the three cardinal "moments" of time (creation, incarnation, eternity), with temporal time (past, present, future), and physical time illustrated by the Arc gene. Arc in physical time intercalates with eternity and temporal time. For Augustine time and memory could not exist without one another. Fourth, I develop a theory of recapitulation where XIII recapitulates I–XII as viewed through creation, memory, time, and other motifs present in *Confessiones*. This theory of recapitulation is formulated by considering *Confessiones* to be one united volume where all thirteen books are written as a whole and where XIII reiterates and recapitulates Augustine's theology of creation and memory. There are many motifs within *Confessiones* and the unity and recapitulation comes not from just one motif, e.g., *exidus-reditus*, *confessio*, or literary narrative, but from considering all motifs in a holistic explication. When viewed in this manner, XIII recapitulates I–XII.

It is my hope that this book provokes a new way of thinking about Augustinian memory and *Confessiones* and, indeed, a re-thinking of Augustine's theology of *memoria*.

Acknowledgements

My deepest gratitude is to God for he has sustained me, lifted me up, encouraged me, and inspired me, in a deep and profound way along this journey. To the many people who have supported and encouraged me, thank you! I am enormously indebted to my mother, no longer with us, but forever in my memory. Thank you for the wisdom you imparted. I am beyond fortunate to have a dear and very close family, John and Julie, Pedro, Charlotte, all their kids and grandkids who cheer me on. My godson James continues to inspire me by his passion for knowledge. Dr. Conor Cunningham, my deepest gratitude, you revealed to me the universe of patristics and patrology and there I discovered Augustine. Thank you for your insights and informative discussions. Last but not least, I am thankful to, and for, Augustine, who inspires me, encourages me, and pushes me to think beyond my cerebration.

Abbreviations

Primary sources

An. et Or.	*de anima et eius Origine*
Beata V.	*de beata vita*
C. Acad.	*contra academicos*
Conf.	*confessiones*
Civ. Dei	*de civitate dei*
Doc. Chr.	*de doctrina christiana*
En. Ps.	*enarrationes in Psalmos*
Ench.	*enchiridion ad Laurentium de fide et spe et caritate*
Ep.	*epistula*
Ep. Gal.	*Epistolae ad Galatas expositio*
Gn. Litt.	*de Genesi ad litteram*
Gn. Man.	*de Genesi contra manichaeos*
Imm. An.	*de immortalitate animae*
Io. Ev. Tr.	*tractatus in evangelium Iohannis*
Lib. Arb.	*de libero arbitrio*
Mag.	*de magistro*
Mor. Eccl.	*de moribus ecclesiae catholicae et de moribus manichaeorum*
Mus.	*de musica*
Ord.	*de ordine*
Orig. An.	*de anima et eius origine*
Quant. An.	*de quantitate animae*

Retr.	*retractationes*
Serm.	*sermones*
Sol.	*soliloquia*
Trin.	*de trinitate*
Util. Cred.	*de utilitate credendi*
V. Rel.	*de vera religione*

General abbreviations

ARN	*Annual Review of Neuroscience*
ARP	*Annual Review of Psychology*
AugStud	*Augustinian Studies*
CCSL	Corpus Christianorum Series Latina
CSEL	Corpus Scriptorum Ecclesiasticorum Latinorum
EB	*Encyclopedia Britannica*
FoC	The Fathers of the Church
LCL	Loeb Classical Library
NCP	*New Century Press*
NLM	*Neurobiology of Learning and Memory*
NN	*Nature Neuroscience*
NP	*Neural Plasticity*
NRN	*Nature Reviews Neuroscience*
PL	*Patrologia Latina*
SP	*Studia Patristica*
TM	*Trends in Neuroscience*

1

Introduction

"Great is the power of memory, an awe-inspiring mystery, my God, a power of profound and infinite multiplicity."[1]

Augustine was in awe of memory. He understood the power, significance, and importance of memory in his journey to know and understand God. Augustine discerned the memory of God (*memoria Dei*)[2] within *memoria*.[3] There, he discovered the place where he encountered the Divine. Without memory nothing would exist for Augustine, not the past, nor the present, nor the future. Augustine's inherent inquisitiveness drove his desire to understand the inner workings of *memoria*. He first started to interrogate *memoria* and memory at Cassiciacum in 386 AD. A decade later, he wrote his most famous treatise on memory, *Confessiones* X, which contains his detailed account of *memoria*, including the description of the different types of memory, their function and operation. Here, Augustine's interrogation of memory was with a specific end goal in mind. He wanted to know how it was that he remembered God as he searched to know

---

1. *Conf.* X.17.26.

2. *Memoria Dei* is infrequently used by Augustine in *Confessiones*; however, it is implicit in his writings. *Conf.* X recapitulates *Conf.* I–IX and shows how Augustine goes from *memoria sui* to *memoria Dei* with memory of God present to the soul. Mourant, *Saint*, 68. *Conf.* X.12.30–31, 23.33, 24.35–25.36.

3. In this book, "*memoria*" is used to depict the palaces or storehouse that houses actual memories. "Memory" depicts images, memories of events, things, and realities.

and understand God and achieve the *beata vita* (the happy life). How did memory work in this process? How was *memoria* the gateway to the Divine? Augustine was acutely aware of the significance of memory in his life; it had first become a reality at his conversion.

Augustine approached his interrogation of memory from many angles—taxonomy of memory, anatomical operation of sense perception in forming images, creation of images, the formation, storage, remembrance, and retrieval of memory, and science, to mention a few. Augustine did not make a distinction between any of the above. It is we who tend to lapse into making such distinctions. Augustine's blending of disciplines is reminiscent of the seamless curtain in the temple, a representation of what this blending results in. When considered as separate entities, the curtain rips into different pieces much like when it ripped into two upon Christ's death on the cross (Matt 27:50–51). The torn curtain is a reminder of all that is wrong and dis-membered. This results in the distortion and division of specialisms when in reality they should be considered together and accepted just like the seamless curtain, which epitomized the unity God has intended. Augustine's thought process regarding the interrelatedness of disciplines was like the seamless curtain. Reflecting on his conversation with Faustus, Augustine recognized that several truths cannot contradict one another; rather, all truth comes from God regardless of the discipline that truth comes from.[4] Like Augustine, I have blended the disciplines into one seamless curtain. It is not theology versus science; it is not a defense of the compatibility of science and theology, as if there is a bifurcation of the two. It views them as the metaphysical and physical unified, much in the same manner as the metaphysical soul and the physical body. They assist each other and one discipline is not superior to the other.

Important to Augustine was his theology of *creatio ex nihilo*. According to Augustine's interpretation of Gen 1, as exemplified in *Confessiones* and *Gn. Litt.*, nothing existed before creation, and everything was made from nothing, and in a specific sequence and *ordo*. Augustine writes, "in the beginning, that is from yourself, in your wisdom which is begotten of your substance, you made something and made it out of nothing."[5] This was true of memory and time, both of which would not exist without each other, and as an act of creation, both are creatures. Creation *ex nihilo* informed Augustine's theology of *memoria*. It is also an important foundation for the research represented in this book. Memory becomes the basis for bringing back memory (present time from time past) and forms the memory of the

---

4. *Conf.* V.6.10.
5. *Conf.* XII.7.7.

INTRODUCTION

future time through anticipation of eternity. In the same manner, movement in time is a re-enactment of creation in time; it is a re-calling of time itself. It is a re-enactment of time from creation *ex nihilo* to the incarnation of Christ to his resurrection and the eschatological realization of eternity.

Augustine believed there was an *ordo* to creation, and in like fashion, he thought there was of memory. This can be observed through an architectonic analysis of his theology of *memoria*. Architectonics is a "tool" used to examine the physical structure and function of memory in order to identify any logical structure behind Augustinian memory. This would be limiting and reductionist if this was all that an architectonic study did. Architectonics is revelatory regarding the understanding of memory as dynamic and fluidic with provision of knowledge of the inner workings of memory both at the physical and metaphysical levels. An important aspect of architectonics is that it brings value to the metaphysical realm because it allows for an improved understanding of memory and its role in the rational soul's ability to return to its origins.[6] Architectonics helps to identify relationships between parts and the whole, and the whole that is composed of parts (i.e., unity). It provides insight into Augustine's relationship with *memoria*, memory, and the Divine in his journey to know and understand God, and how he manages to cleverly draw the reader into his narrative. As Falconer asserts, architectonic theology seeks to draw the reader into its narrative rather than being removed from it and unengaged.[7] Architectonics allows for knowledge to become well-ordered (cf. *ordo* of creation *ex nihilo*) and thus, more easily recollected and retrieved in memory.[8] Parker writes regarding the importance of architectonics and its role in memory:

> New experiences can be more easily catalogued and located in the relevance and meaningfulness. The ordering framework becomes more vivid and thus more stable and less easily forgotten. Importance of this is attested to by the fact that, if the memory content of a locus is forgotten, extra effort will often retrieve it. But if the organizing structure of memory loci collapses, all of its contents also fall into oblivion.[9]

---

6. Greer discusses the architectonic value that comes from architectonic analysis. I adapt this to the architectonics of memory where the same value is ascribed to the information that architectonics reveals. Greer, "Architectonics," 72.

7. Falconer, "Architectonic," 2.

8. Parker, "Architectonics," 150.

9. Parker, "Architectonics," 150.

Ultimately, architectonics challenges one to expand the ways in which one thinks about *memoria* and memory and to recognize that it can provide a new way of thinking about Augustinian memory.

This book includes the scientific investigation of memory via a genomic memory process, much like Augustine, who used scientific knowledge (*scientia*) to interrogate memory. This is the physical arm of architectonics where physical matter, e.g., the human body and its parts, is examined to reveal information regarding memory. Investigation of a gene called Arc[10]—known to be involved in the regulation of memory formation, consolidation, storage, and recollection—was undertaken to determine if its role in a genomic memory process could further delineate Augustinian memory. The study of Arc should not be perceived as a purely scientific endeavor but rather, as research that provides additional information regarding the inner workings of memory, including innate memory. How does Arc fit into Augustinian memory, what does it tells us of Augustine and his theology, and does Arc have similar parallels with his theory of memory? These questions are addressed in chapter 6.

Arc is also an exemplar of physical time working in conjunction with temporal time and eternity. Genomic study is important as the genome remembers how genes operate and regulate systems such as a genomic memory process. Arc recalls creation in this manner. It is because of creation that Arc has a conserved nature and unique expression and has survived through generations without "changing" its regulatory function and operation. The architectonics of Arc brings together the physical and the metaphysical through the unity of body (physical memory) and the metaphysical (rational soul's ability to remember its origins). Arc like creation has an *ordo*, a sequence of the genome and its regulation of memory; it also brings *ordo* to memory by bringing together memories that are disordered in the deep recesses of *memoria* in the mind.

Many scholars view a theological topic through a pinhole, e.g., just one aspect or one motif of an entire book or doctrine. This is true of Augustinian memory where some scholars limit Augustinian memory in *Confessiones* to the study of literary, Christological, Trinitarian, *exidus-reditus*, or praise motifs, to name a few, to the exclusion of all else. Memory cannot be viewed through a pinhole, for in doing so, memory's cyclical remembrance of eternity to temporality to creation and vice versa becomes a diminution

---

10. This book does not claim that Arc is the one and only gene associated with, and involved in, Augustinian memory. The investigation of this particular memory gene is apt since it has specific features that correlate with Augustinian memory and which provide insights to some of Augustine's paradoxes regarding memory. Herein onwards, "Arc" will be used when referring to the "Arc gene."

of Augustine's theology of *memoria*. A more holistic reading of his theology of *memoria* and a co-option of a transdisciplinary approach similar to that which Augustine used seems pivotal. Augustine used the knowledge he had of various disciplines to find answers to his questions regarding *memoria*. We need to "re-program" ourselves to read Augustine correctly as he develops his theology of *memoria* utilizing different spheres of knowledge. There is a cultural bias against this. However, we need not be allergic to the synergism of Augustine's methodology. I propose, through a multi-faceted approach to memory, a more fertile way of thinking and an attempt to provide a hermeneutical corrective to modern anachronism.

To understand Augustine's approach and interrogation of *memoria*, it is crucial to discover Augustine the man and when memory became important to him. Augustinian interiority was central to Augustine discovering himself, his journey towards knowledge and understanding of God, and indeed, his interrogation of memory. Chapter 2 presents Augustinian interiority in the context of *memoria* and introduces the use of architectonics in the development of his theology of *memoria*. It describes how architectonics applies to the study of Augustinian memory and includes a discussion regarding Augustine's palaces of memory. Architectonics is shown to be a multi-factorial investigation of memory utilizing all available knowledge that contributes towards an understanding of memory. This is a performative laying out of my premises; however, this approach did lead to a detailed investigation into, and profound understanding of, *memoria* and memory. According to Geertz, this type of analysis sorts out the structures of signification.[11] Architectonics provides a logical, structural approach to deciphering what Augustine is communicating regarding *memoria*. It reveals specific insight into how Augustine seeks to know and understand God.

Chapter 3 discusses the development of Augustine's theology of *memoria* in his writings on memory from his time at Cassiciacum to *Confessiones*, since it was at Cassiciacum that the earnest development of his theology of *memoria* started. This chapter aims to understand the architectonic structure present in the early development, and the structure, of Augustinian memory. Due to the enormity of this endeavor, this survey, while comprehensive, is limited to his major early works from 386 to 395 AD.[12] It required a logical analysis of the different structures and patterns that emerged and a non-reductionist approach to reading Augustine. This also required engaging with Augustine as he journeyed towards the Divine and fulfillment of the *beata vita*. Augustine has a strategy to his inquiry

---

11. Geertz, *Thick Description*, 314.

12. This survey excludes most letters and sermons that Augustine wrote.

of memory, including how he taught his readers and students on memory. The architectonic structure that unfolds reveals seven symphonic forms and fundamental affordances[13] of memory that occur in a particular sequence: the location of memory, sense perception, teaching/learning, recollection and forgetfulness, images, *phantasia* and *phantasmata*, transiency of memory, and the *beata vita*.

Chapter 4 investigates Augustine theology of *memoria* in *Confessiones* with an in-depth focus on X, XI, and XIII. The symphonic forms and fundamental affordances of memory are discovered to occur in the same sequence identified in chapter 3; however, *Conf.* X reveals one more symphonic form, the power of memory. The architectonics of the inner workings of memory is discovered and expounded by Augustine in such a manner that his reader can gain insight into Augustine's own struggles, perplexities, and growing understanding of God. This investigation unveils in part an understanding of how Augustine's ingenious mind worked. To the best of my knowledge, this identification of the symphonic forms of memory in *Conf.* X (and in his earlier works) has not been previously identified in this particular structure and sequence with all its ramifications in understanding Augustine's theology of *memoria*.

Chapter 5 discusses the extensive knowledge Augustine had of medical and scientific matters and assists in understanding Augustine's philosophy in using this knowledge in his probing of memory. It is an examination of *scientia* and how it evolves towards *sapientia* when *scientia* provides knowledge that informs the rational soul. Augustine's knowledge and use of *scientia* undergirds his theology as he did not view medicine, science, or theology as independent disciplines.

Chapter 6 investigates the role of a specific memory gene called Arc, which is centrally involved in a neuronal communication system. Arc regulates, through its expression, memory formation, consolidation, storage, and recollection. Arc is proposed as an exemplar of a gene involved in a genomic memory process that mirrors Augustine's operational dynamics

---

13. The definition of symphonic form is given by the Merriam-Webster dictionary as suggestive of a symphony, especially in form, interweaving of themes, or harmonious arrangement. Musical compositions consist of several sections of movements. Augustine often talked of memory in terms of music, song, poems, and numbers, which were essential in understanding memory and types of memory. Symphonic forms also represent order, a specific sequence, and movement, which aligns with Augustine's theology of creation *ex nihilo* and the logic and order behind his theory of memory. Fundamental affordances are the fundamental quality or property of an object [memory] that defines its possible uses or makes clear how it can or should be used. *Merriam-Webster Dictionary*, s.v. "Affordance," https://www.merriam-webster.com/dictionary/affordance.

INTRODUCTION

of memory and time, provides some insights into Augustine's own paradoxes regarding memory, and is significant and congruent with Augustine's theology of *memoria*. Arc was selected as a prime candidate because of its unique structure and highly conserved nature. Its role in memory and time is an exemplar of creation, physical time, and movement towards eternity. Arc is also involved in the spatio-temporal dimension of memory and the metaphysical in context of its role in the achievement of the *beata vita*. The necessity to investigate memory in terms of Arc is important as Arc is not simply a gene in the physical sense, but it is a gene that provides information regarding memory and can assist the soul in its remembrance of its origin. Arc is an example of how *scientia* works in unison and cooperates with *sapientia*; in doing so it generates a biological wisdom[14] that informs divine *sapientia*. The biological wisdom that comes from Arc expression and regulation of memory demonstrates how Arc operates in both physical (body) and metaphysical (soul) realities. The use of Arc to investigate Augustinian memory is not inconsistent with Augustine's modus operandi given that Augustine employed multiple disciplines in his endeavors to understand memory and time. I suspect too, that Augustine, being the man who used all knowledge available to him to decipher memory, would have used this information had it been available to him. Arc presents a new way of thinking about the same Augustinian ideas pertaining to memory.

Chapter 7 investigates memory and time. Augustine knew that without time there could be no memory and without memory there could be no time. The interconnectedness of the two was important to Augustine, especially since both are creatures of creation *ex nihilio*. The question is asked whether time has an architectonic breakdown in structure analogous to that of memory. How does time relate to memory, creation, eternity, and even Arc? The relationship between the Arc-hitectonics (Arc) of time and memory, where Arc is a gene representative of physical time and which intercalates with temporal time and eternity, is described. Temporal time includes the role of the *historia sacra* of Christ in terms of creation, the incarnation, eternity, Augustine's life, and Arc since the *historia sacra* is the temporal dispersion of God's action in time. Through the *historia sacra* of Christ, Augustine recognizes his journey through creation and the incarnation and in his perpetual anticipation of future time in eternity. Time is an experience of the soul and memory, one of the reasons why Augustine felt memory and time were closely linked. This is an important motif in

---

14. Biological wisdom: a term I formulated to describe the sapiential knowledge that is derived and developed from *scientia*. It informs *sapientia* and the rational soul. This aligns with Augustine's belief that *scientia* can be a temporal evolution towards divine wisdom (*sapientia*).

the comprehension of time. Hence, Augustine's compulsion to write *Conf.* XI. Moreover, this chapter has three main sections regarding time: eternity, temporal time, and physical time, all with their own Augustinian enigmas of memory and time. A model for eternity, temporal time, and physical time is described, where creation, the incarnation, and eternity, correspond to temporal time, past, present, and future, and physical time as represented by Arc past, Arc present, and Arc future. All three modes of time—eternity, temporal time, and physical time—are interconnected, flow bidirectionally and in a cyclical manner, all the while recognizing the eternal "timelessness" of eternity. These dynamic, fluidic interactions and their relationships provide insight and new knowledge with regard to the understanding of physical time (via Arc) in conjunction with memory, eternity, and temporal time. I propose Arc as an exemplar of physical time and present how it relates to eternity and temporal time.

Chapter 8 describes the architectonic structure in *Conf.* XIII, which is similar to that of memory in *Conf.* X but viewed through the lens of creation; it investigates this archaeology of memory by recalling creation. This sheds light on Augustine's creation *ex nihilo* theology in the context of memory; creation *ex nihilo* is the foundation for all his theological thinking and doctrines. The architectonic structure of *Conf.* XIII aligns with the symphonic forms of memory in *Conf.* X and throughout *Conf.* I–XII. *Confessiones* XIII has a similar structure and *ordo* of memory (symphonic forms) as identified in chapters 3 and 4. These symphonic forms and the motifs of memory, time, and creation are compared in parallel between *Conf.* XIII and I–XII. There is a clear structure that emerges along with multiple motifs that together support a unity of *Conf.* I–XIII. I propose a theory of recapitulation whereby *Conf.* XIII is a recapitulation of *Conf.* I–XII. This theory of recapitulation reveals five distinct categories regarding Augustine and his writings. These are Augustine's cerebration, creation theology, pedagogy, recapitulation, and unity of *Confessiones*. This theory of recapitulation was developed from a multi-faceted architectonic investigation of memory in *Conf.* XIII and X, and then in *Conf.* I–IX, XI–XII. It reveals a multiplicity of layers and motifs that when taken together are non-reductionist and support a holistic, non-limiting account of the unity to *Conf.* I–XIII and recapitulation of *Conf.* I–XII in *Conf.* XIII. The theory of recapitulation provides insight into the inner workings of Augustine's mind and the deeper, profound, archaeological excavation of memory that allows for a rethinking of Augustinian memory.

Chapter 9 proposes a "re-thinking" of Augustine's theology of *memoria*. All the propositions and theories in the previous chapters add insight and revelatory information that furthers the understanding of how memory functions and operates in the physical, spiritual, and metaphysical realities. Such a "re-thinking" is possible because of the knowledge gained through the architectonic investigation of *memoria* and memory. Four categories were identified in this rethinking of Augustinian memory, the architectonic structure of memory, Arc-hitectonics (Arc) and memory, architectonics of time and memory, and the theory of recapitulation. The architectonic structure of memory brings together the symphonic forms and their fundamental affordances in the light of the various components of Augustine's theory of memory, the theology of creation *ex nihilo*, and sacramental remembrance of God. The arc-hitectonics (Arc) and memory is an unveiling of Arc as an exemplar of a gene involved in a genomic memory system. Arc provides supporting evidence for a physical structure to memory, and even time, which aligns with, and augments, Augustine's theory of memory. The investigation of Arc's role in memory is informative in five aspects of memory: the symphonic forms, creation *ex nihilo*, the unity of body and soul, temporality, and memory of the Divine. The third category pertains to the architectonics of time and memory. Augustine's view of time in temporality is conditioned by his views of eternity. Time is temporal only in that the present time passes into the past, and present time is expectation of the eschatological hope of achieving the *beata vita*. It is God in Christ who integrates both past and present, and memory and expectation. The *historia sacra* of Christ expands knowledge and experience of the present time since the present time always includes the memory of God's activity, and knowledge of future time, which includes the eschatological expectation of the *beata vita* in eternity. The final category regards the theory of recapitulation which formulates the findings from the architectonic investigation of *memoria*, the symphonic forms of memory, Augustine's theology of creation *ex nihilo*, and multiple motifs within *Confessiones* that together support a unity of *Conf*. I–XIII and a recapitulation of memory.

In conclusion, the use of architectonics as an investigatory tool in the study of Augustinian memory has provided neoteric insights that allow for a "re-thinking" of Augustine's theology of *memoria*. It is my hope that this book provokes a new way of thinking, of telling the same story, of what has always been.

2

The Architectonics and Beginnings of Augustine's Theology of *Memoria*

"Memory itself is a form of architecture."

—LOUISE JOSÉPHINE BOURGEOIS[1]

AUGUSTINE'S THEOLOGY OF *MEMORIA* is quite complex, with many seemingly perplexing elements. Yet, Augustinian memory has an architectonic[2] structure revealed in his metaphysics of memory; memory resides in *memoria*, which resides in the mind, which is located in the rational soul. Augustine describes vast palaces or storehouse of *memoria* that are cavernous, with indescribable secret nooks and crannies.[3] This alludes to an architectonic structure similar to that of an architect's design for a building. The housing of memories in the different "nooks and

---

1. French-American artist.

2. Architectonics is a term derived from the Greek *architecton* meaning "master craftsman." Architectonics is defined as relating to, or characteristic of architecture, design, and construction. It is essentially a logical, structural approach, adopted here in the study of Augustinian memory. There is a difference between the terms "architecture" and "architectonics." Architecture is both the process and product of planning, designing, and constructing a building or structure. Architectonics is the study of architecture itself. Greer, "Architectonics," 71.

3. *Conf.* X.8.13.

crannies" is metaphorically similar to the occupants of a house with people in different rooms and locations. Memory itself also has an architectonic structure when one thinks of the different types of memory, the anatomical functioning of memory, and the operation of memory recollection and retrieval. The logic of Augustine's theology materializes as he explains *memoria*, as does the mode of teaching that he uses in *Confessiones*. Both have an inbuilt architectonic configuration.

Architecture has a long tradition of evoking memory; to imagine an architecture of memory is to understand the relationship that can exist between physical reality and mental meanings.[4] Augustine says the same thing but in a somewhat different manner. He writes about remembering Carthage and the faces he has seen (X.16.25). In this context, Carthage is the physical reality of an object that was seen, and the memory of Carthage is the "mental meaning." He continues, "for the image of an object to be impressed upon the memory, it is first necessary for the object to be present, so that an impression of the image becomes possible."[5] Augustine remembers the "physical reality" of Carthage and recollects the images formed in memory and located in *memoria*. Remizova asserts that the concept of architectural memory has many shades and forms and manifests itself in a variety of different forms of professional consciousness.[6] There are traces of memory in the theory, history, language, fantasy, and practice of architecture.[7] Augustine too presents the distinct aspects of memory, including historical, in terms of creation *ex nihilo*, the incarnation, eternity, temporality, and his personal life. He wrote about learning the liberal arts, the differences between *phantasiae* and *phantasmata* (true verses false images), imagination, and time and memory. All these are mentioned in *Conf.* X–XI. These categories of Augustinian memory illustrate that memory is the common denominator in the processing and storing of images and information (memories) that can be retrieved at a later date. In the architectural profession memory is also the main way of storing information and skills.[8] Ar-

---

4. Some authors like Jo and Remizova do not differentiate between architecture and architectonics. Both Remizova and Jo believe that architectural memory is a mental phenomenon. Jo, "Aldo," 231–37; Remizova, "Architectural," 97–108.

5. *Conf.* X.16.25.

6. In some explanations of consciousness, consciousness is synonymous with the mind and, at other times, an aspect of mind. In the past, it was defined as one's "inner life," the world of introspection, of private thought, imagination, and volition. Jaynes, *Origin*; Remizova, "Architectural," 97; Wikipedia, s.v. "Consciousness," https://en.wikipedia.org/wiki/Consciousness.

7. Remizova, "Architectural," 97.

8. Remizova, "Architectural," 98.

chitecture is a form of art that through its buildings and monuments stores information about the important phenomena of the spiritual and material culture of humankind.[9] The same is true of Augustinian memory. *Memoria* is the building or monument (palaces/storehouse) that contains the images and memories of spiritual practices and experiences. Through the *memoria Dei* located in the vast palaces of *memoria* and the remembrance of the incarnation, Augustine is not only able to participate in Eucharistic moments of union with the Divine, but he can also convey the truth of God to others; he uses memory to do both.

Within the Augustinian corpus, *memoria* and memory have architectonic structures. How does this impact or change what Augustine said about memory? In reality, it did not affect what he said. However, knowledge of the architectonics of memory reveals several truths. First, there is a logic and structure to the way Augustine thought and wrote about memory. Second, there are hints of how he himself was taught in his Roman Latin education and how this underlies his exposition on memory. Third, architectonics reveals relationships that exist between parts and the whole (e.g., individual images together make a narrative of speech) and the whole with its parts. Fourth, it reveals the meaning of the memories. Fifth, it draws Augustine's reader into his narrative. Finally, it reveals much about Augustine's own journey as he sought to know and understand God and progress towards the *beata vita*. Yet the study of the architectonics of memory in relation to Augustinian memory is, to the best of my knowledge, virtually non-existent.

House of Memory, Palaces of Memory

The house of memory is an architectonic trope that describes the intimate relationship between architecture and memory.[10] The historical development of this mnemonic technique is important in understanding how Augustine developed his initial thought processes regarding memory. The concept of a "building" to explain memory and how it worked is thought to have originated with Simonides of Ceos (556–468 BC), who is often credited with formalizing the relationship between architecture and memory by associating image (memory) with place (architecture).[11] This association describes a memory system with an architectonic format. Years later, Aristotle (384–322 BC) was interested in the mental processes involved in

---

9. Remizova, "Architectural," 98.
10. Spagnolo, "Memory," V-1.
11. Yates, *Art*, 1.

understanding and thinking in association with knowledge and memory.[12] He believed memory to be located in the same area of the soul as imagination. This suggests an architectonic format whereby memory is found in a specific location within a given structure, in this case, the soul. The anonymous author of *Rhetorica ad Herennium* (written in 90s BC) wrote a famous section on memory and the method of loci.[13] The *Rhetorica ad Herennium* depicts memory as the guardian of all parts of rhetoric and describes "ideas" that are contained in the "treasure-house."[14] However, it was the Roman rhetoricians Cicero (106–43 BC) and Quintilian (35–100 AD) who both invoked the use of architecture as an aid for memory; both were also skeptical of Simonide's being credited as the originator of this technique.[15] They advised their students to construct a mental storage space in order to remember the many facts and stories that one needed to draw upon in public speaking.[16] This storage space could be a real or idealized building. Quintilian suggested using a spacious house with many rooms.[17] Purdy writes that the analogy between a house and memory appears in Roman rhetorical treatises in order to spur recollection; thus, an orator could quickly pull information from his mind as he spoke.[18] This system allowed knowledge to be contained in a logical sequence, i.e., a correct order of memories, and retained for a long period of time.

Latin rhetoricians repeated the trope that memory was a treasure-house.[19] Purdy describes the stability of containers that preserved memories until they were needed. In this setting, spatialized memory is arranged in the present moment into distinct entities and then placed within this stable container. Within this concept of a stable container, architecture was presumed to be the stable component; here the mind flowed, perceptions rolled into consciousness, but the house of memory, within which these were contained, remained unaltered. Within this context, temporal time also came into play; past, present, and future time. Thus, time and space also existed in a single architectonic structure in which past memories

---

12. Jo, "Aldo," 233.

13. Caplan, *Rhetorica ad Herennium* 3.16–24.

14. Caplan, *Rhetorica ad Herennium* 3.16.

15. Purdy, "House," 146, 149.

16. Cicero, *De Orate* II.lxxxvi.351–lxxxix.361; Quintilian, *Institutio* XI.ii; Purdy, "House," 146.

17. Quintilian, *Institutio* XI.ii.20.

18. Purdy, "House," 146.

19. Quintilian, *Institutio* XI.ii.2; Caplan, *Rhetorica ad Herennium* 3.16.28; Purdy, "House," 147.

were integrated, interpreted, and modified.[20] A key element of Augustine's philosophy of time is the dimensionality of time (*Conf.* X–XI). Memory remembers within an architectonic structure.

It would seem unlikely that the idea of an architectonic memory system with a storehouse that had many caverns was novel to Augustine. He was familiar with Aristotle, Cicero, and Quintilian, and their writings.[21] O'Donnell "tentatively" disagrees, arguing that the most that can be said is that Augustine draws from a "store of imagery congruent with the technique."[22] Nevertheless, it appears that Augustine may have adapted the concept of the "houses of memory." "Houses of memory" became the "palaces of memory." Augustine adapted "palaces of memory" to include memory of God, *memoria* as the gateway to the Divine, and the operations of memory.

Augustine described *memoria* as "vast palaces of memory" where there were treasuries, including secret "nooks and crannies," storing innumerable images of all kinds of objects brought in by sense perception.[23] Augustine described how when he wanted to retrieve something from memory, he went into the storehouse and asked to retrieve the memories.[24] Some were retrieved easily but others were not, and he had to go in search for the memory he wanted until it "emerges from its hiding places."[25] Augustine wrote that this was what happened when he wanted to recount a narrative from memory.[26] Here is a visual of Augustine metaphorically using the image of his "vast palaces of memory" and the different storage spaces within to find memories and retrieve them in order to recount a narrative.

When Augustine uses the phrase "palaces of memory" he elevates the phrase "house of memory." The *Collins English Dictionary* defines the word palace as "a very large, impressive house, especially one which is the official home of a king, queen, or president."[27] The "house of memory" is no longer just a "house"; it is now the "palaces of memory." Interestingly, Augustine uses the plural "palaces" (*praetoria*),[28] suggesting that there is such

---

20. Jo, "Aldo," 236.
21. Purdy, "House," 146, 149.
22. O'Donnell, *Augustine*, 177.
23. *Conf.* X.8.12–13; cf. X.8.13–14; X.17.26.
24. *Conf.* X.8.12.
25. *Conf.* X.8.12.
26. *Conf.* X.8.12.
27. *Collins English Dictionary*, s.v. "Palace," https://www.collinsdictionary.com/dictionary/english/palace.
28. *Praetorium* originally identified the tent of a general within a Roman *castrum* (encampment). Smith, "*Praetorium*."

an abundance of memories that they cannot be stored in only one palace. Augustine was correct; the human brain memory storage is 2.5 petabytes (2,500 terabytes).[29] The elevation to "palaces" suggests there is a change in how Augustine conceives of their function. He recognizes the "palaces of memory" as the place where memory in *memoria* leads him to the Divine through recollection of the *memoria Dei*. It is not just a place where memories are stored but where a meaningful and transformative experience can take place.

The Beginnings of Augustine's Theology of *Memoria*

How did Augustine reach the point of his prodigious inquisitiveness and the start of his extensive interrogation of *memoria* and memory? To answer this question one must return to Augustine's conversion as described in *Conf.* VII, VIII, and IX, and discover when memory became important to him. *Confessiones* VII relates Augustine's struggle between his desire to know and be with God and the temptations and sins of his flesh. In this struggle, he finally discovered that he loved God and was caught up to him by his beauty.[30] But just as suddenly, Augustine was quickly torn away from God by the weight of his flesh. After discovering the transitory experience of participation, Augustine mentions for the first time the memory of God within. He declared, "but with me there remained a memory of you" (VII.17.23). Here is the first inklings of Augustine's realization of the importance of memory. Earlier in *Conf.* II.9.17 Augustine did declare that God was the source of his memory ("the living memory of my soul"), but it was here in Book VII where he began to realize the significance of memory. *Confessiones* VIII reveals how Augustine's conversion was a tormented affair. He would vacillate between the desires of his flesh and that of his soul. He was certain of eternal life in God but he acknowledged that in his "temporal life everything was in a state of uncertainty."[31] One day, in desperation, Augustine cried out imploring God, "Why not now? Why not an end to my impure life in this very hour?"[32] It was then that Augustine heard the voice of a child who brought his attention to read Scripture, whereupon he was told "to put on Christ" (Rom 13:13–14). Augustine's shadows of doubt

---

29. This is equivalent to three million hours of TV shows that would take three hundred years of continuous TV running. Reber, "What Is?," 70.

30. *Conf.* VII.17.23.

31. *Conf.* VIII.1.1.

32. *Conf.* VIII.12.28.

were dispelled. His mother Monica was overjoyed at the news, for she had spent many years praying for this moment.³³

Augustine in his conversion to Christ and post conversion saw a movement of memory that went from the moment of his conversion (memory of God within) through to his baptism, the Eucharist, and on to eternal life. This was Augustine's movement through memory in his life (his *historia*). Breyfogle posits that his conversion is the start of "the ordering of memory" and "an understanding of the meaning of his past, and consequently of his present."³⁴ This "ordering of memory" leads Augustine to Christ. His recollection of God brought him to the fields and vast palaces of memory. It was the start of his interrogation of memory.³⁵ To get a better idea of how Augustine started his actual journey searching for answers regarding how memory functioned in drawing him towards God and how memory operated in the physical realm, it is important to examine Augustine's practice of interiority through which he came to know the pathway to the Divine via *memoria* in his soul.

In conversion, Augustine recollected many "beginnings." There was the beginning of new life in Christ. Fox describes this beginning as consisting of two components, first, an *aversio*, a turning away from God (*aversio ad Deo*), and second, a *conversio*, a turning towards God (*conversio ad Deum*).³⁶ Augustine's temporal rebelliousness was the denial of relationship with God, a turning away (*aversio*). There was also the beginnings of creation in his life, for Augustine believed creation *ex nihilo* to be essential in his life orientated towards God; all creatures were created from nothing and they only found their happiness in their creator and not in themselves.³⁷ Thus, Augustine recollected the beginnings of creation where God had created from nothing; he understood creation *ex nihilo* to be an ongoing work of the Creator. He only had to look at the universe around him to recognize God as the Creator. In doing so, Augustine also recollected his own beginnings, acknowledging that God had created him in his mother's womb.³⁸ Augustine remembered his own growth in his creation, eventually leading to his conversion, which ratified a coming into relationship of consummate intimacy with God. There was the beginning of hope for the *beata vita* and life eternal. The vision at Ostia where Augustine and Monica were lifted

---

33. *Conf.* VIII.12.30.
34. Breyfogle, "Memory," 217.
35. *Conf.* X.8.12.
36. Fox, *Augustine*, 7.
37. Chambers, *Reconsidering*, 82.
38. *Conf.* IX.9.21.

beyond the physical realm into momentary union with the "eternal being" filled Augustine with an "ardent affection" towards God and longing for eternal life.[39] Finally, there was the beginning of understanding and remembering God in memory. In *Conf.* X.24.35, Augustine declares, "For I have found nothing coming from you which I have not stored in my memory since the time I first learnt of you" and in X.25.36, "you conferred this honour on my memory that you should dwell in it."

Augustine thought it was inadequate for memory to be just a mnemonic function of the mind. He recognized memory as having three broad functions. First, memory was a reminder of God's creative act and of the ongoing of creation through him. His firm belief in creation *ex nihilo* meant he could look back on creation and remember how God created being from non-being; how in himself he could not find happiness but through his creator he could.[40] Creation *ex nihilo* was the starting point towards a life orientated towards God, one of intimacy with God, and ontological dependence. Augustine recalled how God was manifest through his creation. Further, the incarnation was a continuation of God's creation. Robinette declares that through the incarnate Christ, creaturely reality is shepherded into its fullest fruition.[41] Creation *ex nihilo* and the incarnation, while historically different events, are two aspects of one self-communicating act.[42] According to Robinette, the inmost content of creation *ex nihilo* is that beings are created to participate in divine life and are created *in* Christ. God also calls Augustine to participate in his own creation, and thus to be truly created.[43] Additionally, the incarnation brings forth the eschatological promise of creation *ex nihilo* in the beginning. Thus, for Augustine, memory was pivotal, since creation *ex nihilo* was the start of an ontologically dependent relationship with God. Second, memory was very much involved in knowing and understanding God and fulfillment of the *beata vita*. However, to discover the true pathway to God, Augustine realized that he first had to know himself. The contemplation and memory of God in creation was where Augustine saw the starting point in the creation of his new life as a Christian. Contemplation allowed Augustine to let go of his defenses and, as Robinette would say, "live into" his creaturely contingency with progressive freedom and deepest acceptance.[44] This, involved a step-by-step process of

---

39. *Conf.* IX.10.24–25.
40. *Civ. Dei* 12.1.
41. Robinette, *Difference*, xv.
42. Robinette, *Difference*, xv.
43. Anderson and Bockmuehl, *Creation*, 169.
44. Robinette, *Difference*, xiv.

interior examination, i.e., the important exercise of Augustinian interiority. Contemplative practice allowed Augustine to recollect his dependence on God, the one who brought human being (and thus him) into being *ex nihilo*. Third, Augustine's interrogations of memory recognized the complexity of the mechanics of memory, i.e., the complexity of the operation and function of different types of memory, all of which assisted the soul in remembering its origins and the human being in remembering the Divine. Augustinian interiority is, therefore, important in understanding Augustine's interrogation of memory and the development of his theology of *memoria*.

Augustinian Interiority

"I entered into my innermost citadel and was given the power to do so because you had become my helper."[45]

Augustine's background in Neoplatonism is important in understanding the development of his practice of interiority and interrogation of memory. Augustine the orator and rhetor was acquainted with Platonic philosophy, particularly the works of Plotinus and Porphyry.[46] He had read the *libri platonicorum* in his search for a way that would deepen his self-knowledge and understanding of how to attain true happiness; he believed that the true end of *philosophia* was the attainment of wisdom and the *beata vita*.[47] These Platonic books admonished Augustine to "return into myself."[48] Plotinus understood the Delphic maxim "know thyself" as a command to "withdraw within yourself, and examine yourself."[49] He had developed Plato's philosophy of interiority, describing the return of the soul to intellect and the One from whom the soul proceeded. This conception of interiority to search for the Divine within was a central feature of the Roman school of epistemology, advocated by both Plotinus and Porphyry.[50] This Neoplatonic influence

---

45. *Conf.* VII.10.16.

46. *Conf.* VII.9.13. Augustine had read "certain books of the Platonists (*libri platonicorum*)."

47. *Conf.* VII.9.13. Regarding the happy life: *Conf.* X.20.29–23.33. Gilson, *Christian*, 3.

48. *Conf.* VII.10.16.

49. Guthrie, *Plotinus* I.6.9.

50. Augustine developed a practice of interiority followed by an upward movement to participation in the Divine based on Plotinian philosophy. Both Plotinus and Augustine believed that the movement was from the material to the immaterial, and then from within the immaterial, from the mutable to the immutable. Unlike Plotinus,

18

on Augustine is important because he did not know where to find God. He assumed this was due to his lack of self-knowledge. The Neoplatonists, Augustine believed, had succeeded in reaching the natural knowledge of God. They had beheld the inner Truth that is God, and therefore, could tell him where to look to find it.[51]

Augustine turned inwardly to examine his "inner man,"[52] where he could acquire "self-knowledge" and ultimately, according to Bonner, become like god.[53] Augustine believed that through interior cognition the incorporeal soul understood the material world. This was controversial in his day as Platonists, Manicheans, Stoics, and Epicureans all believed the soul and mind and everything within were corporeal.[54] Augustine believed it was through divine illumination[55] that the soul was allowed to understand the corporeal; God was known to the mind in the same way as the sunlight was shown to the corporeal eye.[56] Augustine encountered the phrase "inner man" after he began reading the Pauline literature first introduced to him in the sermons of Ambrose, bishop of Milan.[57] Ambrose had preached on the introspective turn towards the "inner man."[58] However, it is Augustine who

---

interiority for Augustine became a journey to the intelligible nature of being. As Pegis says, "it is within us that we reach more intimately the reality and the truth of human being and the Divine Being." Pegis, "Mind," 1–61; Brown, *Augustine*, 79–92; Kenney, "Faith," 278.

51. Cary, "Plotinus," 232; Beatrice, "Quosdam," 252.

52. This term "inner man" was not a common phrase in Augustine's time nor in ancient philosophy. There is no record of its use until its appearance in the Pauline writings in the New Testament. It is a term adopted by Augustine. Cary, *Augustine's Invention*, 47.

53. *Trin.* IX.11.16. "We are like God inasmuch as we know Him." Per Bonner, interiority is a way of achieving deification. Augustinian deification (*deificare*) is the process of the soul becoming immutably good through increasing our knowledge of God and loving him, made possible by adopting us as his sons "through participating in our humanity in the person of Jesus Christ." Bonner, "*Deificare*," 226.

54. Cary, "Plotinus," 231.

55. Augustine's theory of divine illumination includes at least three major points: (1) God is light and illuminates all humans to different degrees, (2) there are intelligible truths, the *rationes aeternae*, which God illumines, (3) human minds can know the divine truths only as God illumines them. Nash, "Illumination," 438.

56. *Sol.* I.8.15.

57. The three occurrences of the term "inner man" are in Rom 7:22, 2 Cor 4:16, and Eph 3:16. The Greek is ἔσω ἄνθρωπος, translated as "inner man." The noun is the general word for "human being," not "man," but most translations interpret it as "inner man." Following the lead of Cary, this phrase "inner man" is used to preserve integrity with the discussions in the literature. Cary, *Augustine's Invention*, 162n4.

58. Per Madec, Ambrose used this phrase purely exegetically and from a pastoral

is credited by various authors as the discoverer of the "inner man," although he is often perceived as individualistic in his orientation and discovery of interiority.[59] However, amongst these authors there seems to be a disconnect regarding their discussions of Augustinian interiority, with many gravitating to one particular aspect of interiority. Some focus on interiority as an examination of the inner man, some consider it purely an intellectual process, and others consider it a contemplative process.[60] There is a tendency to use these terms interchangeably and often, with the same meaning of an inward movement to the inner man. However, Augustinian interiority is really a movement within Augustine that developed into a spiritual exercise that he practiced throughout his life. Madec, writing on *Conf.* III.6.11, comments that interiority was not an introspection in Augustine's life that went instantly from flesh into his mind and to transcendence.[61] Interiority was a movement that started with the introspection of the inner man but then developed to include an exercise of the mind followed by a meditative and contemplative process. There is an architectonic pattern in interiority that was expressed in this movement within Augustine. Gilson supports a progressive movement to Augustine's thought and meditation towards reaching God: "Every step must be made in its proper place and time if the mind is to arrive at its goal."[62] With this movement, Augustine no longer saw interiority as just an examination for self-knowledge, but rather a movement towards participation[63] with God where his soul transcended

---

not philosophical, perspective. Augustine took the phrase and developed the philosophical concept of the "inner space of the self." Madec, "L'homme."

59. Cary claims Augustine invented the "inner self." He describes this as a Christian idea that originated in the Platonic tradition. What Cary claims is new from Augustine and different from Platonism is that the inward in turn creates an inner space that is private; this private nature of the inner self is a consequence of the sinful nature of man. Cary, *Augustine's Invention*, 5.

60. Cary focuses on Augustinian interiority as an invention of the inner self. Kenney describes interiority as a contemplative process. Marrou argues that interiority is a philosophical exercise of the mind to gain intellectual comprehension of objects of faith. Grove views interiority somewhat differently; he describes interiority in terms of memory, which is the place of Augustine's *interior intimo meo* and which reflects Augustine's recalling of his life in *Conf.* I–X. He asserts that memory is the most interiorizing aspect of the human person and results in an outward movement towards God and neighbor. Cary, *Augustine's Invention*; Kenney, *Contemplation*; Marrou, *Saint Augustin*, 297–327; Grove, *Augustine*, 1–2, 9–10.

61. Madec, *Saint*, 91.

62. Gilson, *Christian*, 26–27.

63. Augustine uses *participatio* to describe the fact that humans exist only by the sharing of God's being with humans, i.e., participation in God. God is both Being

temporal reality and encountered eternal truth through *memoria* located in the mind of the rational soul. Within *memoria* he found a remembrance of God (*memoria Dei*), which was the fulcrum between Augustine's inner man and the Divine. The presence of *memoria Dei*, and consequently the possibility of knowledge of God, fueled his growing and fervent desire to understand how a remembrance of God facilitated his rational soul's ability to experience God. Augustinian interiority in *Confessiones* has three movements: turning inward (*interior examen*), turning outward (*exercitatio animi*), and turning upward (*meditatio/ingressio* [to *(ad)* God] *et contemplatio* [in *(apud)* God]),[64] each with specific roles in the acquisition of self-knowledge, the discovery of *memoria Dei*, the knowledge and transcendence of the soul, divine illumination, and experience of participation in the Divine.

Interior Examen

"And so step by step I ascended from bodies to the soul which perceives through the body, and from there to its inward force, to which bodily senses report external sensations."[65]

In *Ord.*, Augustine wrote of the first step in the inward turn of interiority, *interior examen*. He said, "man does not know himself. Now, for acquiring this self-knowledge, he needs a constant habit of withdrawing from the things of the senses and of concentrating his thought within himself and holding it there."[66] Augustine's inability to control his carnal temptations made him desperate to find the truth, as he was so afraid of dying before

---

and the source of Being. Creatures have being because God freely shared or bestowed this on them by creating them *ex nihilo*. To be at all is to participate in God. Meconi describes how *participatio* "represents creation's need to partake of the perfect and immutable source of Being." *Conf.* VII.9.14, VII.18.24–19.25; Bonner, "Augustine's Conception," 373; Ortiz, *You Made*, 14, 17; Meconi, "Incarnation," 68.

64. In Augustine's interiority, *meditatio* is the upward turn to God (*ad Deus*). *Ingressio* can be used interchangeably with *meditatio* and is used, in this context, to further define *meditatio*. It is translated as "entry" to God's presence. *Contemplatio* is the upward turn toward being in/with God (*apud Deus*). Kenney, *Contemplation*, 61–92, 99–100.

65. *Conf.* VII.17.23.

66. *Ord.* I.1.3; also, *Trin.* X.5.7 (so then it is one thing not to know oneself, another not to think about oneself).

the truth was found.⁶⁷ He firmly believed the lack of self-knowledge was the source of his lack of discipline.

Augustine, through *interior examen*, entered his inner space, and there he discovered himself within memory.⁶⁸ According to Kohut, remembering is an engagement "that enables the individual to recognize himself in his recalled past and facilitates healing the discontinuity of the self—caused . . . by myriad interactions with others and the larger world."⁶⁹ As Augustine's soul looked inwards, it discovered rationality and a remembrance of God, and it perceived the intelligible and immutable. Yet Augustine did not retreat into himself and withdraw from his senses with the intention of staying within the intellect of his mind struggling with his demons, his self, and self-knowledge. He saw the reality of truth and the encounter with the Divine that went beyond the intellect of the mind. This is unlike the Cartesian interiorism of modern philosophy where Descartes went into his consciousness and was unable to build a way out from his mind back into the world.⁷⁰ The trace, the tenuous remembrance of the incorporeal God present in Augustine, went beyond his soul, and lured him outwards and upwards to the Divine.

Through *interior examen*, Augustine's inward turning into his inner man allowed him to develop a growing awareness of the *spiritalis substantia* and the need to reject the *carnalium cognitationum figmenta* in this process.⁷¹ Despite his decision to live a chaste life, his struggles continued to torment him, particularly, his inability to stop the images in his memory of his past sexual exploits, which influenced his nightly dreams causing "carnal emissions."⁷² Augustine began to see that he had been searching through eyes that viewed the world and a body that looked out to the wrong external stimuli due to the soul's detachment from its Creator. However, God, by his grace, used internal goading (*stimulis internis*) so that Augustine, through

---

67. *Conf.* VII.5.7.

68. *Conf.* X.18.14.

69. Kohut, *Restoration*, 82.

70. Pegis, "Mind," 38. Cottingham said Descartes was conscious of the finite but aware of the infinity placed by God in his mind. God placed the idea of God himself in Descartes' mind. Since God created him, his mind must be a reliable instrument. Stróżyński also points out that self-knowledge as simple awareness of the mind's existence is not a Cartesian introspection. Stróżyński writes that *De Trinitate* attempts to suggests an ontological dimension of the self and self-knowledge, but in a non-Cartesian way. Cottingham, "Descartes' I"; Stróżyński, "There," 288.

71. *Conf.* VI.3.4; Reid, "Patrician," 19.

72. *Sol* I.10.17; *Conf.* VII.17.23; X.30.41–42.

an interior sight (*interiorem aspectum*), could see God's manifest presence.[73] Only God could reveal to Augustine his true self, as his memories of his past were self-deceiving. They tended to take Augustine in a direction he struggled with, one that satisfied only his ego.[74] Augustine worked hard not to focus on the body and lower, sensitive soul but rather to delight in the truth he had discovered.[75]

Augustine needed to transcend the self to discover the rational soul and find the immutable God who was present to his self.[76] In this regard, Luke 15:17 was an important text for Augustine. The prodigal son "came to himself" at the lowest moment of his existence.[77] Augustine understood this to mean that in a moment of realization the soul came back to itself; it was also simultaneously a coming to God who was within and above.[78] This gave Augustine hope. He discovered God was intimately present in the depths of his rational soul: "But you were more inward than my most inward part and higher that the highest element in me" (*interior intimo meo et superior summo meo*).[79] It was this recognition and acceptance of the truth that enabled Augustine to move forward. Augustine had become more aware of himself, and his inner man had begun attending to his soul, which he had discovered was not divine.

Augustine realized in his interiority that he had shifted in awareness from "I am" to "I know that I am," a more intuitive move of the illuminated mind and a step towards its ultimate goal of perfect wisdom and the *beata vita*.[80] In this process Augustine also shifted from an awareness of "God is" to "I know that God is." He came to know God is Being, "I AM WHO I AM," and "truth . . . not diffused through space, either finite or infinite."[81] With these understandings of the truth, Augustine's inner man also discovered that the rational soul, as Reid describes, "was the resonant zone of contact with God."[82] The Creator is the God who spoke to Moses and to whom Moses could speak to. Faur writes that, "this means God is semiologically

---

73. *Conf.* VII.8.12; Reid, "Patrician," 21.
74. *Conf.* X.40.65.
75. *Retr.* 1.1.3; 1.3.2; *Conf.* I.20.31.
76. Sweeney, "God," 682, 685.
77. Sweeney, "God," 683.
78. Sweeney, "God," 683, 685.
79. *Conf.* III.6.11.
80. Coughlan, "*Si Fallor*," 149.
81. *Conf.* VII.10.16. Stróżyński also discusses this realization of Augustine. Stróżyński, "There," 288.
82. Reid, "Patrician," 19.

accessible."[83] Augustine recognized he could therefore speak of, and to, God since God had first spoken to him, much like Moses. Augustine identified God as *the* God who speaks to his people, and the God who allows his people to speak to their God.

Augustine began to comprehend that when he ushered God "into his inner self," God permitted him to transcend his mind and see the "immutable light."[84] This inward journey of discovery took Augustine to the very depth of his being to find the Source of his being.[85] This required Augustine to dig deeper, turn outward from his inner self, and embrace *exercitatio animi*, an exercise of the soul and mind.

Exercitatio Animi

*"I entered into the very seat of my mind,
which is located in my memory."*[86]

The mind (*mens*), the highest part of the rational soul,[87] was the logical place for Augustine to go deeper and evaluate the truths he had unearthed during his *interior examen*. Consequently, he developed an exercise of the soul and mind, *exercitatio animi*.[88] Marrou asserts that *exercitatio animi* began as a philosophical exercise of the mind.[89] However, this evolved from merely a philosophical exercise for Augustine when he realized he had to confront both the metaphysical and physical realities of his rational soul by turning outwards rather than remaining within his inner self. Augustine's adaptation of *exercitatio animi* had two important goals. The first was to train the mind to purge materialistic concepts from the mind.[90] The second, to transfer the affections "from the things of this world to God via an

---

83. Faur, *Golden*, 38.

84. *Conf.* VII.10.16.

85. Sweeney, "God," 687.

86. *Conf.* X.25.36.

87. Gilson has a detailed explanation of *mens* and *animus* (rational soul). *Mens* is the higher part of the soul that "clings to things intelligible and to God ... the mind contains reason and intelligence." Gilson, *Christian*, 64n3.

88. Teske, "Augustine's," 148–58. See also *Conf.* X.1.1–43.70; *En. Ps.* 145.5; *Trin.* XIV.3.5.

89. Marrou defines *exercitatio animi* as a philosophical exercise of the mind or soul where the mind is trained to attain an intellectual comprehension of objects of faith. Marrou, *Saint*, 297–327.

90. Hochschild, *Memory*, 149.

incorporeal rational soul."⁹¹ Ayres defines Augustine's use of *exercitatio mentis* in *De Trinitate* as "a training in modes of thinking increasingly interior, and increasingly free from images, a gradual intellectual movement from the material to the immaterial, fundamentally Neoplatonic in character."⁹²

It was through the practice of *exercitatio animi* that Augustine recognized that memory located in the mind was the gateway to the Divine.⁹³ Memory was the place where Augustine was able to come to peace with his demons and see beyond himself and towards God. He discovered that memory and mind were intricately connected: "We call memory itself the mind" and "Memory is . . . the stomach of the mind."⁹⁴ Hochschild describes memory as the power of the soul that "looks down" or outwards to the sensible, and "up" or inwards to the intelligible.⁹⁵ This was Augustine's discovery. Further, an *a priori* knowledge of God resided in memory, albeit a "tenuous consciousness of the truth."⁹⁶ Chadwick explains how, to Augustine, memory had a far deeper and wider meaning than what we currently understand memory to be.⁹⁷ Memory was understood to mean that the mind knew things it did not know it knew, a remembrance/knowledge of God that was embedded in the mind. This *a priori* knowledge caused a seeking of God through *memoria* in the rational soul. Therefore, God could only be sought if there was a remembrance of God through which Augustine was able to desire God and the *beata vita*.⁹⁸ This *memoria Dei* was recognizable to his rational soul.

What emerges from Augustine's *exercitatio animi* is an interiority that paved the way for Augustine's soul to re-member, seek, and know God through memory. *Exercitatio animi* prepared the mind and the soul for its encounter with the Divine as it actively engaged and participated in seeking the Divine; this could only happen with the help of divine illumination.⁹⁹

---

91. Ayres, "Christological," 114.

92. Ayres uses *"mentis"* in the same context as *"animi."* In Latin, these two words can be used interchangeably. *Mentis* tends to be related solely with the mind whereas *animi* can also be used as soul. My use of *animi* reflects the development of an exercise that trains both soul and mind. Ayres, "Christological," 128.

93. *Conf*. X.24.35; X.25.36.

94. *Conf*. X.14.21.

95. Hochschild, *Memory*, 145.

96. *Conf*. X.24.35.

97. Chadwick, *Saint*, 185n12; *Conf*. X.21.31–26.37.

98. *Sol*. I.4.9; II.20.34.

99. Zwollo states that it is precisely because of Augustine's *imago Dei* doctrine that the intellect's inherent capacity for obtaining knowledge of God results in the turning to the Source. This contact with divine Light effectuates a spiritual renewal

Meditatio and *Contemplatio*

"The soul ... is led to the house of God by following a certain sweetness, an indescribable interior pleasure. It is as if a musical instrument sweetly sounded from the house of God, and while walking in the tabernacle she heard the interior sound, and, led by its sweetness, followed it."[100]

At this stage of interiority, Augustine realized an upward movement to see "the face of God" was imperative.[101] The innate presence of the *memoria Dei* lay at the heart of this upward turn to God and was at the center of both *meditatio* (*ingressio*) and *contemplatio*.[102] It was that sacred space between seeker and the sought, the homecoming between the *peregrinus*[103] and the Father, and that sacramental encounter between the lost and the God who saves. *Meditatio* and *contemplatio* are closely related and in the Christian setting must both be practiced if an encounter with God is desired. Through *meditatio* and *contemplatio* Augustine made himself radically available to the presence of God so that he could ascend to, and participate with, God.

Meditatio

"You alone are great, and you alone dwell on high in the silence."[104]

Meditatio was the very first step in approaching God and knowing God after the discovery of the *memoria Dei*. It was in the silence and solitude of *meditatio* that Augustine created a space that emboldened the emergence of "words from my soul and a cry from my mind, which is known to your

---

or "re-creation" of the human being that ultimately leads to perfect knowledge and intellectual vision. This dynamic process requires divine illumination, which results in the potential to participate in the infinity of the Creator and to encounter God by a direct experience of divine Light. Zwollo, "St. Augustine," 88–91.

100. *En. Ps.* 41.9.

101. *Ord.* I.8.23.

102. Kenney, *Contemplation*, 61–92, 99–100.

103. Sweeney describes Augustine's journey from looking within to the soul looking outwards and upwards to God as the journey from the self as *spiritus ambulans* (wandering spirit) to a *peregrinus* (foreigner in a strange land striving to return home). He is on a journey from being a homeless wanderer to a foreigner realizing he has a home. E.g., the prodigal son becomes a *peregrinus* when he comes to himself and starts to return home. Sweeney, "God," 686.

104. *Conf.* I.18.29.

ear."[105] At the start of *Confessiones*, Augustine writes, "Who then are you, my God? . . . What am I to you . . . ?"[106] This was the relational uncovering in his interiority. Through *meditatio* Augustine looked to and called upon God. As Hochschild says, "the invocation brings a God perceived as distant (transcendent) into the heart (*cor*) of a person."[107] Kenney writes that *contemplatio*[108] "as a form of interior knowledge, is the natural expression of the soul's station in the hierarchy of being and its exercise allows the soul to recover the native dignity of its created nature proximate to God."[109] *Meditatio* secured for the soul knowledge that is both *a priori* and indubitable; it situated the soul by revealing its transcendent source, opening it up to an ontological vista previously unknown to Augustine.[110] In the interior depth of his soul, Augustine could discern the divine presence. Pegis writes, "at the moment we discover ourselves as minds, we are freed from the life of sense, but at this moment we discover the presence of God."[111] Madec describes this as "an exercise in accommodating the mind to the radiance of spiritual light."[112] The upward turn to the Divine (*ad Deus*) through *meditatio* or *ingressio* was necessary so that the Creator of the rational soul could transcend the created soul even in the spatio-temporal world.[113] Augustine through *ingressio* entered into God's presence.

Contemplatio

Contemplatio was the movement of God toward Augustine that accorded Augustine a temporal moment of being in/with (*apud Deus*) the Eternal Being. It was inherently temporal due to the soul's separation from its Creator, a result of its prelapsarian state.[114] The omnipresent God (*ubique totus*), however, presented himself to Augustine's soul, for God knew his soul directly and intimately.[115] Boersma suggests that Augustine's conception of

---

105. *Conf.* X.2.2; Niño, "Spiritual," 90.
106. *Conf.* I.4.4–5.5.
107. Hochschild, *Memory*, 149.
108. Kenney uses contemplation and meditation interchangeably.
109. Kenney, *Contemplation*, 85.
110. Kenney, *Contemplation*, 85, 87; Kenney, "Faith," 282.
111. Pegis, "Mind," 46.
112. Madec, "Analyse," 65.
113. Kenney, *Contemplation*, 90.
114. Kenney, *Contemplation*, 88, 111.
115. *Conf.* I.3.3; VI.3.4. Boersma and O'Donnell translate *ubique totus* as "whole

ubique totus revealed a continuity between how Augustine saw God in this life and in the next.[116]

Contemplatio was that place where Augustine sought to ascend to, and participate with, God. The limitation of *contemplatio* was the temporary nature of ascent and participation. It was a transient reality that allowed a momentary glimpse of the eternal realm and of immortality. Permanent participation in the Divine was an eschatological reality fulfilled only in eternity. However, participation, though momentary, was a revelatory process.[117] Augustine was left with the certainty of the truth, the reality of the innate presence of the *memoria Dei*, the knowledge that ascent of the soul was possible, but also a deep sense of regret that ascension and participation were transient realities. Augustine and his soul had to come to terms with the "episodic character of contemplative knowledge"[118] and the infinitude of temporality. The forte of *contemplatio* was that there remained with Augustine a memory of the Divine and of these experiential encounters. Augustine could say, "yet the memory of you remained in me."[119] In the end, *contemplatio* was, as Hankey states, "a return to that gaze of eternal being which belongs to memory and to the fundamental structure of our minds."[120] The remembrance of God was the anchor of this transient reality of ascent; it was the lynchpin in the linking of heaven and earth, eternal and temporal, human being and Divine Being. *Contemplatio* provided Augustine with hope, for the remembrance of God constantly drew Augustine's soul back to its origins and the eschatological expectation of that final union with the Divine in the eternal realm. In fact, transcendence "transformed Augustine's understanding of God and gave wings to his soul."[121] His soul was led to the house of God by following a certain sweetness and an indescribable interior pleasure.[122] This emphasized to Augustine the constant need to practice interiority and the importance of memory in this practice. This fueled his insatiable desire to know more of God.

---

and everywhere" to articulate the divine presence in Augustine's works, especially in *Confessiones*. Both offer detailed overviews on Augustine's use of this phrase. Boersma, "Augustine," 2, 16; O'Donnell, *Augustine*.

116. Boersma, "Augustine," 2, 16.
117. Milbank, "Confession," 30.
118. Kenney, *Contemplation*, 88.
119. *Conf.* VII.17.23.
120. Hankey, "Self-Knowledge," 107; *Trin.* XIII.9.13; XI.7.11; XII.2.2–3.3.
121. Kenney, *Contemplation*, 168–69.
122. *En. Ps.* 41.9.

Christological Complicity

The Christological complicity in Augustinian interiority, memory, and *participatio* cannot be underestimated nor left undiscussed. Augustine understood Christ to be the source of participatory wisdom, the one who was immutable, and the Logos who participated in the created and the mutable.[123] The created soul recognized the ontological distance between itself and its Creator due to its prelapsarian condition. It was acutely aware of the need for a divine intervention, as there was no salvific efficacy in Augustinian interiority, not even in the *contemplatio* stage where ascent of the soul was possible. Augustine realized that with the upward turn and the ascent of the soul there was also a downward turn, a divine descent, of God himself. As Milbank describes, "God himself descends all the way to actual and personal incarnation of human flesh."[124] Le Blond describes so profoundly the incarnation as the insertion of the eternal into temporality.[125] It was simultaneously a descent of the Divine and an act that facilitated the ascent of the temporal rational soul. Augustine writes, "God's only son . . . laid down his majesty to the level of the human and exalted human lowliness to the level of the divine . . . in order that he—a human being who through God was beyond human beings—might be the mediator between God and human beings."[126] As Meconi writes,

> It is the paradox of Christ which allows Augustine to see how the perfect and immutable is able to participate in lesser things: namely our humanity. The Divine, born of a woman, participates in our nature so that we might more fully participate in Him as brothers and sisters. Christ came to partake of our fallen humanity not out of His greatness but on account of our wretchedness.[127]

In the incarnation, God did not relinquish divinity in order to become creaturely but rather became creaturely to reveal what creation is really like. Through Christ, the redemptive act of creation becomes apparent. Christ reveals the heart of the God–creation relationship; to Augustine the reality of the inmost content of creation *ex nihilo* is that he is created *in* Christ.[128]

---

123. Meconi, "Incarnation," 68.

124. Milbank, "Confession," 13.

125. "L'Incarnation, insertion de l'éternel dans le temps." Le Blond, *Conversions*, 19.

126. *Ep. Gal.* 24.8.

127. Meconi, "Incarnation," 71.

128. Robinette, *Difference*, xv.

Augustine, through Christ, understands that it is possible to participate (*participatio*),[129] in God and the eschatological journey towards achieving the *beata vita*. Bonner recognizes this relationship between participation and Christ when he writes, "Christ, then, is the theological datum; the philosophical conception is that of participation by man in God."[130] Furthermore, it was through the incarnate Christ that Augustine realizes the way to knowledge of God; this was the intellectual Augustine who through reason acquired knowledge. Yet, the profundity of the Divine becoming incarnate, and divine grace achieved through the incarnation of Christ, was not lost on Augustine. He believed that the soul had no way home without the divine grace; the fallen nature of the soul could not be healed by *contemplatio* alone but required divine assistance to overcome its prelapsarian condition.[131] The incarnation became the pivotal moment in the *historia sacra* of Christ to Augustine; through the incarnation he could escape the temporal constraints of creation *ex nihilo* and through Christ's mediation, anticipate eternity.[132] The incarnate Christ meant that nothing stood in-between God and his creation.

Implicit in the contemplative practice of Augustine was the lifelong need for the external authority of the incarnate Christ.[133] Augustine describes how in submission to Christ, Christ "raises those submissive to him" and "carries them across to himself."[134] In the practice of *contemplatio*, Augustine remembered the incarnation where in the intersection of divine descent and the ascent of the soul, an existential sacramental moment occurred. This bidirectional participation "exacerbated the soul's sense of eschatological longing."[135] According to Ayres, Augustine developed a "theological" *exercitatio* through Christology; "Fallen humanity needs to undergo a certain *exercitatio* . . . and such *exercitatio* is provided by the

---

129. In *Confessiones*, *participatio* is found three times, and only in Book VII, where Augustine is struggling to properly understand Christ's incarnation. Augustine uses *participatio* to explain how man exists by participating in God who is both Being and the source of being. Meconi, "Incarnation," 62.

Conf. VII.18.24 is where the downward participation of the Divine becomes formative in Augustine's conversion and where he is able to conceive of participation in terms of the higher partaking of the lower. Meconi, "Incarnation," 70.

130. Bonner, "Augustine's Conception," 373.
131. Kenney, *Contemplation*, 91–92.
132. Chadwick, *Saint*, 227n14. Clemmons, "Time," 9.
133. Cary, *Soul*, 236.
134. *Conf.* VII.18.24.
135. Kenney, *Contemplation*, 92.

Incarnation."¹³⁶ *Contemplatio* thus became an instrument of grace, and the remembrance of God located deep within the rational soul became the driver in the search to seek the "face of God."¹³⁷ Grove asserts that Augustine's mediatory Christology culminates in the ascended Christ who continues to mediate the Divine to the human in present time; this mediation remains ongoing even though Christ is resurrected and no longer an embodied temporal Christ.¹³⁸ He posits that human memory fails to mediate, but Christ continues to succeed. Grove continues, "Christ's mediation has been made possible and sustained the shift from the individual to the whole Christ" (*totus Christus*).¹³⁹ Christ is thus central to Augustinian *mediatatio* and *contemplatio*.

Memoria Dei

During 1954–66, Cilleruelo, Morán, and Madec were at the center of the debate regarding the inclusion of a *memoria Dei* within Augustinian thought, particularly relating to *Confessiones* X and *De Trinitate*.¹⁴⁰ The debate was never resolved and continues to this day.¹⁴¹ Grove argues that the imposition of the phrase "*memoria Dei*" limits the discussion, with scholars restricting themselves to specific texts at the exclusion of others, and restricts the remembering of God as an action or work within the created order.¹⁴² Grove considers the term *memoria Dei* to be a "narrow recalling of an external content." He is correct regarding the imposition of a "sweeping philosophical concept" based on the term *memoria Dei*.¹⁴³ However, a holistic approach to the study of *memoria* where this terminology is not limited to one interpretation and discipline shows that while Augustine may not have specifically used the phrase "*memoria Dei*," he does speak of an

---

136. Ayres, "Christological," 125.

137. *Contemplatio* as an instrument of grace is explained more clearly in the final ascent narrative from *Doc. Christ.* 2.VII.9–11. Kenney, *Contemplation*, 120. *Ord.* I.8.23 (Face of God). The total dependence on God's grace is necessary for the transcendence of the mind and going beyond self-knowledge. Stróżyński, "There," 299–300.

138. Grove, *Augustine*, 63, 71.

139. Grove, *Augustine*, 82.

140. Cilleruelo, "'Memoria,'" 499–509; Cilleruelo, "Por qué?," 289–94; Morán, "Sobre," 205–9. The positions of these scholars are summarized by Madec, "Pour," 89–92; O'Donnell, *Augustine*, 176–77.

141. Grove, *Augustine*, 5–6.

142. Grove, *Augustine*, 5–6.

143. Grove, *Augustine*, 5.

innate knowledge of God.¹⁴⁴ It is logical that *memoria* is the place where the *memoria Dei* resided and where Augustine would go to look for God. The phrase "*memoria Dei*" may not be explicitly mentioned, but it is implicit in the text of *Conf.* X. The discovery of the *memoria Dei* was profound to Augustine in its revelation that there was an actual memory of God within his (Augustine's) mind which linked his rational soul and the Divine. The *memoria Dei* was embedded in the deepest core of his *memoria*, and it was through this *memoria Dei* that Augustine was able to remember God. In the act of creating the rational soul, God made himself known in *memoria* via an innate *memoria Dei*. Augustine declared to God, "You remain in my consciousness."¹⁴⁵ Breyfogle suggests that Augustine believed that God was always present innately in memory and emphasized this truth by using a strange mixture of verb tenses in *Conf.* X.24.35.¹⁴⁶

Memoria Dei was a trace memory or *vestigium* of the Divine that existed in Augustine's soul.¹⁴⁷ The memory of God was an essential prerequisite for seeking (*quaerere*) the face of God,¹⁴⁸ and it was the cause of Augustine's desire for God and knowledge of God.¹⁴⁹ God resided innately in *memoria* waiting to be discovered. Moreover, God was accessed via the *memoria Dei*, which galvanized Augustine's desire to interrogate and understand *memoria* and memory. It was interior intellection that had helped Augustine remember God and achieve recognition of the eternal Being who spoke in a language his soul could understand. Hochschild writes, "God contains human memory and in doing so fills it, illumines it, and speaks to it in a language it comprehends."¹⁵⁰ *Memoria* was where Augustine recognized his ontological dependence on God and God's grace, necessary to know God and achieve the *beata vita*.¹⁵¹

Kenney writes that the soul, and specifically the mind, had to be trained to actualize its *memoria Dei* because actualization of this latent connection

---

144. *Conf.* X.12.30–31; 23.33; 24.35; 25.36.

145. *Conf.* X.24.35. Consciousness can be translated as memory. See O'Donnell, *Augustine*, 132.

146. Augustine conceded earlier in *Conf.* X that truth was innately present in memory. He goes on to state that when truth is found, God is found, because God resides in memory and is sought in memory. Breyfogle, "Memory," 214.

147. *Gn. Litt.* XII.24.51; Sweeney, "God," 686.

148. *Sol.* II.20.34; *Ord.* I.8.23; Kenney, *Contemplation*, 120.

149. *Sol.* I.4.9.

150. Hochschild, *Memory*, 149.

151. Sweeney, "God," 686.

to God was essential for knowledge of God to emerge.¹⁵² Augustine contends that unless he remembers God through the *memoria Dei*, he could not endeavor to understand him, love him, and know him perfectly, and he required divine assistance to do this.¹⁵³ The mind's self-awareness could not be eliminated as it was the presence of *memoria Dei* that allowed the self to act. *Confessiones* VII shows that Augustine succeeded in remembering God through interior cognition and acknowledging that an *a priori* knowledge existed.¹⁵⁴ Augustine describes in *Enarrationes in Psalmos* how *memoria Dei* was not a residing "with" God but an understanding that God "is" since "whatever understands God is with (*cum*) God."¹⁵⁵ *Memoria Dei* was both the pointer and connector to the Divine and a gateway to the recovery of life and sustenance in the Divine.¹⁵⁶

Concluding Remarks

Augustine's fervid desire to know the intricate details of *memoria* and memory compelled him to investigate memory, from this investigation he developed his theology of *memoria*. Augustine realized through memory that interiority was a discovery that finite creaturely existence and memory ultimately participated in God who lovingly upholds all in and for Christ.¹⁵⁷ His theological concept of connecting the rational soul with the mind (*mens*) and *memoria* is a central reality in his theology of *memoria* (*Conf.* X.14.21). The rational soul did have a trace of the Divine within; the soul, made in the image and likeness of God, had the *imago Dei* imprinted in the mind in *memoria*.¹⁵⁸ It was, therefore, logical that *memoria* was the place where a remembrance of God resided and where Augustine would go to look for God. Human beings were created with the capacity to discover the *memoria Dei* in the inner space of memory and, consequently, were able to search for the unchanging Truth, the Creator God.

---

152. Kenney, "Faith," 275. However, Matthews believes Augustine had explicitly rejected the belief that there was a "time when *memoria* was empty, wholly 'potential' and in need of actualization." Matthews, "Augustinian," 199.

153. *Trin.* IX.11.16; XIV.12.15; 14.18.

154. Kenney, *Contemplation*, 90.

155. *En. Ps.* 41.10; *Ord.* II.2.4. "quasi ego quod sapiens facit dixerim esse *cum* Deo, *cum* Deo est."

156. *Conf.* XII.10.10: "In you I am recovering life." *Conf.* X.28.39: "You lift up the person whom you fill."

157. Wu, "End,'" 11.

158. Drever, *Image*, 114–18. *Conf.* X.25.36; *Trin.* XII.7.12.

It is important to know the beginnings of Augustine's intellectual exploration and his personal journey if we are to understand his interrogation of memory and the development of his theology of *memoria*. Augustine's inward turn to understand himself through the practice of interiority was found to follow a particular sequence of steps: *interior examen, exercitatio animi, meditatio,* and *contemplatio*. This architectonic structure to interiority is not one typically ascribed to interiority as most authors tend to focus on one aspect or combine all steps. Interiority and its ordered structure revealed to Augustine the memory of God within his soul. Williams writes that Augustine's introspective methodology interrogates and demythologizes the solitary human ego by establishing the self firmly in relation to God.[159] Augustine, through his practice of interiority, discovered what he required for his journey to know and understand God. The importance of this journey was not lost on Augustine and his inquisitive mind. He understood the constraints of temporality, yet through interiority Augustine discovered how to pursue the Divine. He also recognized the centrality of memory in his search to know and understand God.

---

159. Williams, *On Augustine*, 186.

3

The First Decade of Augustine's Interrogation of *Memoria*: 386–395 AD

"I desire to know God and the soul."[1]

AUGUSTINE'S THEOLOGY OF *MEMORIA* cannot be understood without a grasp of how his own questions and ruminations evolved from his early writings. This chapter, a survey of these works from 386–395 AD, demonstrates that his questions regarding *memoria* are prevalent in his early works; some references to *memoria* are explicit in the text while others are implicit. Augustine's writings might, at first, seem disjointed, aporetic, and even confusing. However, the study of his works on *memoria* reveals a visualization and unfolding of Augustine's mind and thought process that demonstrates the ingenuity of his thinking, and a hidden logic in his meanderings. There was a constant swirl of ideas percolating through Augustine's thought, some to be put down in ink and others settling into the recesses of his mind to be remembered and retrieved at the appropriate time. Augustine's interrogation of *memoria* came about because he believed memory was centrally involved in every aspect of life, both physical and spiritual, including his soul's desire to know, understand, and participate in the Divine. His hunger to find answers regarding how memory and *memoria Dei* functioned became more fervent and intense when he realized the central role of memory in this process.[2] Augustine's concept of

---

1. *Sol.* I.2.7.

2. In his Cassiciacum writings, Augustine appears to be less expressive about his

memoria, i.e., it is in memory that God is first sought, was extraordinarily radical for his times; his conceptuality of *memoria* incredible even for his contemporaries. In fact, it is amazing to realize that it took sixteen hundred years before the first taxonomy of memory was proposed by Tulving in the 1970s; it is astonishing to realize how similar Tulving's multisystem model of memory is to Augustine's own model of memory.[3]

Memoria in Augustine's Cassiciacum Writings: 386–387 AD

According to O'Daly, the earliest accounts of *memoria* are found in *De Ordine* II.2.6–7, recorded in Augustine's debate with his interlocuter Licentius.[4] However, all four books written at Cassiciacum (*Contra Academicos, De Beata Vita, De Ordine, Soliloquia*) have accounts of *memoria*. They were written over a period of six months between August 386 and the beginning of 387.[5] In these books the most extensive discussion is found in *Soliloquia*.[6] Other books written in the first decade post conversion have detailed interrogations of *memoria*: *De Immortalitate Animae, De Libero Arbitrio, De Magistro*, and *De Vera Religione*. Augustine's earliest predominant questions regarding *memoria* are documented primarily in *De Musica, Soliloquia, De Genesi ad Litteram, De Ordine, Epistula 7*, and *Retractationes*.[7] Augustine's interrogations disclose to him and his audience that memory has an architectonic structure where key features of memory interconnect and weave together throughout his writings.

---

desire to search for God perhaps because these books are more philosophical in nature. However, in *Sol.* I.2.7 Augustine expresses his desire to know God, and a sense of fervency is becoming evident. The fervent nature of Augustine's search is noted more profusely throughout his writings in *Confessiones*. Notable examples: *Conf.* III.4.7 "I longed for the immortality of wisdom with an incredible ardour in my heart"; *Conf.* III.4.8 "My God, how I burned, how I burned with longing"; *Conf.* XI.22.28 "My mind is on fire to solve this very intricate enigma."

3. Tulving, "Multiple," 67–80; Cassel et al., "From," 21–41.

4. O'Daly, "III: Memory," 461.

5. Di Berardino, "Cassiciacum," 135.

6. *Soliloquia* discusses *memoria* in Book I and II, specifically regarding recollection, forgetting, and the Platonic theory of *anamnesis*.

7. Mourant, *Saint*, 9.

Contra Academicos

In *Contra Academicos* Augustine stresses the need to have a stenographer record the words of his debates with his entourage. He writes in II.9.22:

> Nevertheless, because memory is an unreliable custodian of our reasonings, I was anxious to have our frequent disputations committed to writing, so that those boys might learn to apply their minds to those questions and might attempt to attack and pursue them.[8]

Memories can settle in the dark recesses of *memoria* causing a forgetfulness of memory. Writing preserves memory and assists in remembering, especially when something that is truthful might need to be remembered.[9] Socrates also saw a connection between writing and forgetfulness, although his perspective was different, and his words were written down by his student Plato. Plato in *Phaedrus* discusses with Socrates the significance of written words and forgetfulness.[10] Socrates did think some good could come out of written words but, in general, he was against writing because he thought that it caused a complacency and forgetfulness of what was written:

> It will implant forgetfulness in their souls: they will cease to exercise memory because they rely on that which is written, calling things to remembrance no longer from within themselves, but by means of external marks.[11]

In *Contra Academicos* Augustine engages with the combination of *memoria* and *doctrina* and explores its implication for the teacher, not the pupil. Augustine was convinced that a wise teacher needed memory in order to impart his wisdom to others.[12] This feature of memory is also discussed in *De Ordine* when Licentius questions Augustine, and also in *Soliloquia*.[13] His teachings on memory did not go unnoticed by his students. Alypius, commented on memory and teaching saying, "For if nothing escapes me,

---

8. *Sol.* I.1.1 also mentions the memory's incapacity to retain everything. *Reason*: "Is memory so great that it can accurately hold on to everything that has been conceived?" *Augustine*: "That is difficult to do, indeed, it is impossible." *Reason*: "Therefore, it must be written down."
9. Cf. *Sol.* II.20.34–35.
10. Plato, *Phaedrus*.
11. Plato, *Phaedrus*, 274e–275a.
12. *C. Acad.* II.6.14.
13. *Ord.* II.2.6–7; *Sol.* I.1.1.

I shall be grateful not only for your teaching (*doctrina*), but also for my memory."[14]

In *Contra Academicos* there are also the first inklings of Augustinian interiority. Augustine questions whether the possession of truth or the simple search for truth is necessary and sufficient for happiness.[15] His answer is that truth arises through redirecting the inquiry from a disputation on the outside to one within oneself.[16] The significance of *interior examen* in remembering truth is implicit in *Contra Academicos*.

De Beata Vita

Augustine wrote *De Beata Vita* as he questioned what constituted the happy life and how it could be attained. He also wanted to know how it equated solely with the God who alone is unchangeable and eternal.[17] The knowledge of God as unchangeable and eternal is something absolutely knowable and yet incomprehensible. Augustine wrote that it was necessary to lead a good life in order to attain God and true happiness.[18] This good life was identified with God and not just contemplation; this was unlike Aristotle's belief that contemplation alone was sufficient.[19] In fact, Augustine, in *De Beata Vita*, takes Plato's theory of recollection and adapts it to explain how there is first the recollection of God, a result of an emanation from God that causes one to remember.[20] This in turn ought to lead to the desire to seek God and develop a yearning for the Divine. *De Beata Vita* describes the dialectical discourse of the *beata vita* with his students and his mother. Augustine explains the things that do not facilitate a happy life (e.g., fear, earthly riches, and false happiness) derived from worldly pleasure.[21] He leads them to the point where there is a recognition that God is eternal and ever remaining, and that whoever possesses God is happy.

---

14. *C. Acad.* II.6.14.

15. Per Kavanagh "possession of truth" does not mean possession of the totality of all knowable truth but the gradual discovery and combination of fragments of truth to attain an increasingly perfect knowledge without reaching an exhaustive grasp of its totality. Kavanagh, "Answers," 89n6.

16. *C. Acad.* I.2.5; Stock, *Augustine*, 226.

17. Mourant, *Saint*, 42.

18. *Beata V.* 2.11.

19. Mourant, *Saint*, 42.

20. Vandermark Lowe, "Platonic," 32.

21. *Beata V.* 2.11.

Augustine's immediate objective in his search for the *beata vita* was the possibility of achieving a "state of ontological plenitude."[22] Try as he might, Augustine found it hard to attain the true happy life and so began to believe that it could not be achieved here on earth. His spiritual practice of interiority allowed him to work on putting aside his corporeal temptations and develop healthy habits that were focused on encountering the Divine in his journey towards fulfillment of the *beata vita*. Augustine was starting to realize that through *memoria* he was "beginning to know (*recognoscere*)" the God that he sought.[23] In *Beata V.* 4.35 Augustine summarizes the true happy life, "to recognize piously and completely the One through whom you are led into the truth, the nature of the truth you enjoy, and the bond that connects you with the supreme measure."

De Ordine

The interrogation of *memoria* centers on the question regarding the location, quality, and association of memory with the transient. It is here in *De Ordine* that Augustine begins to doubt some aspects of Plato's theory of memory and reminiscence.[24]

Augustine tells Zenobius (I.2.5) that he is writing down his words so that "*nec aliter dicendi necessitas nec labor **recordationis** esset.*" *Recordatio* is the word Augustine tends to use for Platonic recollection; however, he often uses it in a much broader sense; in *De Ordine*, *recordationis* refers to the recollection of ordinary memory.[25] Interestingly, as in *Contra Academicos*, Augustine requests that his words be written down. Further, as in *C. Acad.* II.6.14, Augustine brings up the Wise Man's need of *memoria* to teach, "for honorable and necessary sorts of teaching" ("*propter honestas ac necessarias disciplinas*").[26]

In Book II, Licentius explicates his view regarding the location and nature of *memoria*: "I am of the opinion that memory is one of these subservient parts."[27] He believes that *memoria* plays a role in the lower soul's use of the senses and he associates memory with the transient. Memory is used to

---

22. Stock, *Augustine*, 224.

23. Cf. *C. Acad.* II.2.4.

24. O'Daly "III: Memory," 461–69 has an extensive discussion of the influence of Plato and Plotinus on Augustine and the differences that emerge as Augustine's theory of memory evolves.

25. Lowe, "Platonic," 33.

26. *Ord.* II.2.7; O'Daly, "III: Memory," 465.

27. *Ord.* II.2.6.

remember fluctuating things and is therefore itself unreliable, inferior, and transient: "Fleeting realities also belong to this lower part. What is memory for, if not for such impermanent realities?"[28] This transiency of memory is also mentioned in *Sol.* I.1.1 where, as Conybeare writes, memory is presented as "a part of the *anima* but a *vilissima pars*—an extremely inferior part . . . that deals with the transient."[29] Licentius' argument was based on his Plotinian view of the role and location of *memoria* in the lower soul; "memory is of things that have happened and passed away."[30] He also had a dualistic view of human nature, and the body and soul. For Augustine, there could be no separation of the mind and the body in remembering. Further, the soul detached from the body was mutable. It needed the body where with mutual co-operation it could identify truth and adhere to God.[31] Augustine sensed that memory had a more important role than realized by his interlocutor. He believed the soul was comprised of a lower and higher constituent with *memoria* not only associated with images of transitory things but also the immutable and divine. Since the higher part of the soul, the rational soul, was not tainted by sense perception, and was permanent and immutable, it could be called wise and be with God.[32] It is evident that Augustine's own thoughts of *memoria* are evolving. Winkler writes that the evolution of Augustine's own theory of *memoria* is evidenced in *De Ordine* by his refutation of Licentius' views regarding *memoria*:

> Returning to these previous opinions, which take precedence over the words of Licentius, Saint Augustine has arrived at the starting point of the future development of his theory of memory. The first stage of his personal thought on this subject is therefore characterized by doubt and reservations about Plotinian doctrines which he had adopted before. Thus, the discussion of *De Ordine* prepares the way rather than announcing a direction.[33]

I concur with Winkler.

---

28. *Ord.* II.2.6; Conybeare, "Duty," 55; *Sol.* I.1.1.

29. Conybeare, "Duty," 55.

30. Conybeare, "Duty," 55; *Enneads* 4.4.6. Licentius' view is that there could be two souls or two parts of the soul. The two parts of the soul may be what he eventually leans towards when referring to the Plotinian view of *memoria* located in the lower soul.

31. *Ord.* II.13.38.

32. *Ord.* II.2.7. Conybeare, "Duty," 55.

33. My translation of a quote from Winkler's French text. Winkler, "Théorie," 519.

Soliloquia

Of all the books written at Cassiciacum, *Soliloquia* has the most extensive discussion on *memoria*, in particular, on recollection and forgetting, and the Platonic theory of *anamnesis*. It is an important book because there is a shift from *memoria* as just a recollection of perceived physical things to recollection of the metaphysical. Book I is a search for intellectual and moral self-knowledge, and Book II is a discussion on the nature of truth, the soul's immortality, and memory as recollection and forgetfulness.[34] The search for God in *memoria* is more evident in *Soliloquia*, a crucial development in Augustine's theology. *Soliloquia* is a debate between Reason (*Ratio*)[35] and Augustine written in a Platonic philosophical dialogue format but unprecedented in that the entire work was a dialogue between Augustine *and himself*; indeed, Augustine had to invent a new word to describe this dialogical book—*soliloquium*.[36]

The beginnings of Augustine's shift from full to partial acceptance of the Platonic theory of *anamnesis* is evident in *Soliloquia*. Anamnesis involved the recollection of memories that one had never experienced; it also meant not-forgetting.[37] From the time of Plato, philosophical discussions of recollection often included its contrast with *oblivio* (forgetting).[38] Augustine also considered the phenomena of remembering and forgetting to be closely related. Augustine's theory of recollection is closest in resemblance to Plato's *Meno* where Plato equates learning with recollection. Yet, despite the similarities to Plato's theory of *anamnesis*, it is evident in *Soliloquia* that Augustine's thinking had already begun to diverge from Plato.[39] Augustine connects the subject of the liberal arts[40] with recollection and with learning; this is a concept observed throughout his works. Unlike Plato, Augustine believed in a two-stage recollection; first the liberal arts that have been learnt are recollected as such, i.e., a bringing forth of only the liberal arts themselves.[41] In an ideal situation, some truth is discern, generating a desire

---

34. Augustine, *Soliloquies*, 10–14.

35. *Ratio* depicts Augustine's Reason and interlocutor.

36. Foley, *Soliloquies*, xxix, 3.

37. Per Bourke, the Greeks had a word for forgetting, *amnesis*, and for recollection they used the term *anamnesis* which can mean either not forgetting or remembering. Bourke, *Augustine's*, 167.

38. Bourke, *Augustine's*, 167.

39. Lowe, "Platonic," 54.

40. In *Retr.* 1.5.3 Augustine lists seven liberal arts: grammar, dialectic, rhetoric, music, geometry, arithmetic, and philosophy.

41. Lowe, "Platonic," 52.

to see the truth in full (*totam facies veritatis*).⁴² Second, the truth from the liberal arts is recollected such that there is a total recollection of the truth as described by the phrase *recordationi revisendaeque veritati* in II.20.34,⁴³ and this invites the student into a metaphysical encounter with memory and recollection. *Soliloquia* explains this digression from Plato's *anamnesis*.⁴⁴

There are three types of forgetfulness (*oblivio*) and recollection (*recordationis*) that can be delineated in *Sol.* II.20.34. The first type of forgetfulness and recollection is "partial forgetfulness" and "partial recollection" (*pars quaedam recordationis*).⁴⁵ Here, "something" is forgotten and cannot be recollected even when prompted by false reminders; yet, through these suggestions there is a recollection of what "something" is not. Augustine would say that this type of recollection "is, itself, a certain part of remembering," i.e., "partial recollection."⁴⁶ Augustine refers to this type of forgetfulness in *Conf.* X, illustrated by the parable of the woman and her lost drachma.⁴⁷ The second type of forgetfulness/recollection is a complete forgetfulness (*validissima oblivione*) with no recollection.⁴⁸ Here a memory is unable to be recalled at all, "buried in the most profound oblivion,"⁴⁹ due to the distance in time from the actual event. It cannot be recalled even upon suggestion; instead of recollection there is a belief that the event occurred based on the evidence provided by others. The third type of forgetfulness and recollection is "forgetful remembrance."⁵⁰ Reason defines this type as "recollection of reminiscent truth" (*recordationi revisendaeque veritati*).⁵¹ This Augustine describes as:

> Such a type of forgetfulness occurs when we see something, recognize for certain that we have seen it at some time, and declare that we know it. But, where or when or how or in whose company it came to our attention, we struggle to review and remember. As, for example, if this were to happen to us in the case of a man, we ask him where it was we made his acquaintance. When

---

42. Lowe, "Platonic," 52.
43. Lowe, "Platonic," 52.
44. *Sol.* II.20.34–35 describes Augustinian recollection of memory.
45. Lowe, "Platonic," 48.
46. *Sol.* II.20.34.
47. *Conf.* X.18.27; Luke 15:8.
48. Lowe, "Platonic," 48.
49. *Sol.* II.20.34.
50. I use this phrase to describe a memory forgotten but remembered in its entirety when reminded.
51. *Sol.* II.20.34; Lowe, "Platonic," 52.

he has reminded us of it, all at once the whole affair floods back to our memory like a light and we no longer have difficulty in remembering.⁵²

This is a full recollection or a total non-forgetfulness recalling a certain memory and the circumstances around that memory (*ubi, quanto, quamodo*).⁵³ Importantly, full recollection is triggered by something,⁵⁴ e.g., a particular object has meaning, and recollection is triggered by observation of some aspect of the object. This type of forgetfulness and recollection is different from the first type in that the recollection is both of the memory itself and the associated circumstances, i.e., the where, when, and how. In the first type of forgetfulness and recollection, the remembrance is what the memory is *not* rather than what it actually is.

Augustine's venture into recollection as described in *Sol.* II.20.34 has been primarily in the physical and perceptible world. According to Lowe, one phrase, *recordationi revisendaeque veritati* (recollection and recollection of the truth) and specifically the word *veritati*, may invite a metaphysical interpretation.⁵⁵ While it is true that the rest of the passage (II.20.35) is anchored in the perceptible world,⁵⁶ the phrase "recollection of the truth" perhaps provides the first glimpse of the involvement of recollection in both the physical and the metaphysical.

Section II.20.34 is connected to II.20.35 by "*tales*," a linguistic link whereby Augustine establishes a relation between non-physical recollection and the third type of forgetfulness (forgetful reminiscence) in II.20.34.⁵⁷ Students who have learnt the liberal arts can suffer from this type of forgetfulness if they detect only a glimmer of truth in recollection (II.20.35).⁵⁸ However, if they can behold all of the truth then they are like those (*tales*) who have not only recalled a piece of knowledge but have also recalled all the associated memory-data; the final goal is the "full countenance of truth" (*totam facies veritatis*).⁵⁹ According to Lowe, if the liberal arts are learnt and recollected as liberal arts only and no truth discerned in them, then

---

52. *Sol.* II.20.34.
53. (Where, how much, how). Lowe, "Platonic," 50.
54. This triggering of a memory is reminiscent of Proust's involuntary memory. Eating tea-soaked Madeleine cakes triggers Proust's memory of eating madeleine cakes with his aunt, and memories of his childhood home. Proust, *In Search*.
55. Lowe, "Platonic," 51.
56. Lowe, "Platonic," 51.
57. Lowe, "Platonic," 51–52.
58. Lowe, "Platonic," 52.
59. Lowe, "Platonic," 52.

recollection is only partial, leading to a forgetfulness of what the liberal arts point to.⁶⁰

Reality is contorted by the perils of deception from images that invade the mind. Augustine warns of these "false colours and forms" that distort truth, thereby deceiving the well-learned in the liberal arts:⁶¹

> Such imaginations as these are to be shunned with great precaution. There falsity is detected when they vary with the varying so-called mirror of thought, whereas that countenance of truth is ever one and changeless.⁶²

The phrase "mirror of thought" is used by Plotinus in relation to imagination; he also stated that visible "colours and shapes" were "but reproductions of the Reason-Principle."⁶³ Augustine may have had these phrases in mind as he warned about the infiltration of false images that contaminate the truth. Augustinian recollection also facilitates the discovery of truth since *ratio* was regarded as the contemplation of truth.⁶⁴ In *Soliloquia*, *ratio* is described by Augustine as "the mind's act of looking."⁶⁵ For Nash, *ratio* used in this context is related to the mind in the same way as sight is to the eye and so the mind must look to find truth.⁶⁶ Augustine is beginning to recognize that there is more to the intellectual soul than sense knowledge, for the soul also searches for truth and discovers it. Upon discovery, the soul realizes that truth is actually recollection of a known unchangeable truth so obscure that it is buried deep within *memoria*.⁶⁷

Undoubtedly, *memoria* is clearly central to the soul's search for truth. The outcome of this search is God himself. Augustine writes, "the gaze is followed by the very vision of God, who is the final end of our gazing, not because the gaze no longer exists, but because it has nothing further toward which to strive."⁶⁸ *Soliloquia* is where the first indications are found that memory is more than just remembering experiences, learning, and images of things perceived. In the language of interiority, memory can be an outward remembrance of physical things, or an upward journey of recollection

---

60. Lowe, "Platonic," 52.
61. Lowe, "Platonic," 52–53.
62. *Sol.* II.20.35.
63. *Enneads* 1.4.10; 4.3.12; 6.3.15; Foley, *Soliloquies*, 306n137.
64. *Sol.* I.6.13; Bourke, *Augustine*, 170.
65. *Sol.* I.6.13.
66. *Sol.* I.6.13; *Imm. An.* 6.10; Nash, *Light*, 64.
67. Cf. *Sol.* II.20.35.
68. *Sol.* I.6.13.

through sensible things to the intelligible. It is through recollection that knowledge can be attained. Hochschild writes:

> The possibility of recollection proves that knowledge can come into being thanks to explicit logical connections, even where there is no full and conscious apprehension. Thus memory contains a horizon of rational coherence, which is itself the ground for knowledge. This points to Augustine's emerging sense that knowledge must include other aspects of the activity of the intellectual soul and cannot be reduced to a simple propositional certainty.[69]

A defining role of memory is the discovery in *Soliloquia* that memory is the vehicle that facilitates the discovery of truth and encounter with the Divine.

Memoria in Augustine's Writings from 387–395 AD

Augustine's writings post Cassiciacum and prior to *Confessiones* develop in more detail the characteristics of *memoria*. The following survey is of some of the key books that contain references to *memoria*.

De Immortalitate Animae

Augustine wrote *De Immortalitate Animae* shortly after he had left Cassiciacum; it was written between Ash Wednesday in March and Easter Sunday in April of 387 AD.[70] It is an unfinished work written by a man eager to acquire wisdom regarding his new faith. His ideas are rather immature compared to later writings. In *Retractationes*, Augustine would look back on this book and called it a reminder (*commonitorium*) to himself to complete the *Soliloquia*; he declared, "because of the intricacy and brevity of its reasoning, it is so obscure that even my attention flags as I read it and I myself, can scarcely understand it."[71] Nevertheless, Augustine was able to provide some insight into the complexities of the immortality of the soul he was seeking to understand. He concludes that the unchanging existence of the truth in his mind can only exist in an incorporeal substance that is alive, the soul, and thus the rational soul, which is inseparably connected to this truth, is immortal.[72] Augustine also associates temporality with his theology of

---

69. Hochschild, *Memory*, 101.
70. Schopp, "Immortality," 9.
71. *Retr.* 1.5.1.
72. Schopp, "Immortality," 8.

memoria, believing it is necessary for memory to be able to conceive of time as past, present, and future.[73]

Augustine writes that an action, such as speaking the shortest syllable and hearing the beginning and end of that syllable, requires memory to complete that action.[74] There is also the expectation that it will be finished; "Moreover, what is done in this manner must be accompanied once by the expectation (*expectatio*) that it can be completed and also by memory, in order to comprehend the measure of its capacity."[75] Here is the Augustinian link between temporality and memory which is developed further in *Imm. An.* 3.3-4, where time consists of the past, present, and future:

> Expectation pertains to future events, memory to past events, the intention to act, however, belongs to the present through which the future passes into the past; neither can we anticipate the end of a commenced movement of a body without any memory.

Augustine elaborates further, "the intention to act lies in the present through which the future lapses into the past, and the outcome of the motion of a body, once started, cannot be expected without memory."[76] While actions are constrained by time and space, memory is required to understand the action and its completion. All three aspects of time—past, present, and future—are important in *memoria*. For Augustine, the past, present, and future of temporality cannot exist together in the physical realm; however, they can in the mind. The example of speech has already demonstrated this fact. Though a spoken word has a distinct past, present, and future (beginning, middle, and end), the mind must transcend time in order to understand the word; a person must simultaneously remember the first part of the word, attend to the middle, and anticipate the last part.[77] Memory is

---

73. *Imm. An.* 3.3-4.

74. *Imm. An.* 3.3. This concept of the temporality of speaking and *memoria* is brought out in more detail in *Conf.* XI.6.8.

75. *Imm. An.* 3.3. This is reminiscent of both Aristotle and Plato who use the same argument. Plato in *Phaedo* compares himself to the swans of Apollo who sing most beautifully before they die. Birds sing of the not-present future, poets use rhythm and melodies to make present the images of memory, and the birds sing about what they did before. Poets, musician, and birds are incited to sing because of what is absent through memory. There is the same need of memory in the requirement to sing words and a continuity of past, present, and future. Plato, *Phaedo*, 84e-85b. For a more elaborate discussion, see Wiskus, "On Song," 917-34.

76. *Imm. An.* 3.3. Time past, present, and future is discussed in greater detail in *Conf.* XI.

77. Lowe, "Platonic," 59-60.

crucial in remembering the past; if the past is forgotten, it is lost forever. Remembering the present is also important; the present is lost when the past is forgotten as the present moment cannot be recalled again. Memory is important in remembering the future because it is in memory that the outcome or end of an action is retained. Additionally, present in the mind is the existence of the unknown. Augustine states that "in the one who intends to carry out something, there can exist something that really [still] belongs in the realm of things not yet in existence."[78] Augustine writes:

> There is something in the mind that is not actual in present thought[;] . . . the mind is not aware it possesses something, except what has entered its thought. Therefore, something may be in the mind of whose presence there the mind itself is not aware.[79]

Augustine's theology is still very immature, but he is beginning to develop his theory of the rational soul and innate knowledge.

In *Imm. An.* 4.6., the liberal arts, the trained mind, and forgetfulness are brought together in a manner reminiscent of *Contra Academicos* and *Soliloquia*.[80] When the arts are forgotten because the mind has been preoccupied with "other things," recollection of these forgotten arts is still possible, according to Augustine. Augustine has added another dimension to the recollection process. As Lowe explains, "instead of recollecting the forgotten data, we find it: the usual verb *recorder* does not appear, because Augustine is again looking at the process of recollection as a remedy to forgetfulness."[81] It is, therefore, possible to reason with ourselves or through clever questioning, recollect forgotten arts. In other words, it is possible to induce recollection.

It would appear that initially in *De Immortalitate Animae* Augustine uses the basis of Plato's theory of recollection to support his arguments. In *Imm. An.* 4.6., the Platonic echoes are evident. According to Lowe, the reference to the questioner who tries to help a person remember the forgotten arts, refers specifically to the *Meno* version of recollection; the choice of *ars geometrica* calls to mind *Soliloquia* and may also reflect the example Socrates uses in the *Meno*.[82] Augustine differs from Plato in stating that recollection can be induced by the person themselves. Recollection involves the metaphysical since the existence of things unknown and the

---

78. *Imm. An.* 3.3.
79. *Imm. An.* 4.6.
80. *C. Acad.* I.1.4; II.6.14; *Sol.* II.20.35.
81. Lowe, "Platonic," 63.
82. Lowe, "Platonic," 64.

recollection of things temporal and eternal are in memory, and memory is able to transcend time. Augustine saw memory as a physical faculty with metaphysical powers, unlike Plato who thought memory was related only to the physical.[83]

De Quantitate Animae

De Quantitate Animae was written in Rome between 387 and 388 AD. Augustine, in dialogue with Evodius, explains the origins, nature, and magnitude of the soul, and the concept of body/soul union and separation. The text describes how the soul passes through three stages: the power of the soul in the body (matter), the soul's power in itself (spirit), and its power before God (God).[84] Buried throughout are scattered references to *memoria*. Chapter 5 is the exception with a significant section devoted to Augustine's discussion with Evodius regarding the location of memory.

The first reference to *memoria* and the soul is found in 5.8–9. Augustine asks the question, "does memory, in your opinion, belong to the soul or the body?" Evodius finds it hard to accept that the soul can contain images within the confines of its space. Augustine also says that the soul, while lacking quantity, can contain what is great by virtue of memory.[85] He explains that it is the mind that retains and sees the images, size, and character of a city (e.g., Milan) even though the eyes themselves do not see the city (5.8). The mind can recognize temporal space as it can see the intervening distance. The mind and memory are also vast and located within the soul. Augustine writes, "I wish you to consider somewhat more carefully how great and how many objects our memory contains; all of these, of course, are contained in the soul" (5.9). Later in 14.24 Augustine explains that reason (*ratio*) is the sight of the soul; the eye is actually the *ratio inferior* by which the mind sees sense images that are stored in the memory.[86] Augustine is speaking of memory working with imagination; arising from experience in time and the gathering and retention of images, which in turn give rise to natures that are understood.[87] The soul, "a rational substance made to rule the body,"[88] is present to the body through memory.

---

83. Lowe, "Platonic," 61.

84. Schopp, *Fathers*, 54.

85. *Quant. An.* 14.23.

86. Cf. *Sol.* I.6.13. See *Imm. An.* 6.10; 7.23; Nash, *Light*, 64, 75.

87. On memory and imagination, see the correspondence between Augustine and Nebridius, especially *Ep.* VI and VII. Breyfogle, "Memory," 139–54.

88. *Quant. An.* 13.22.

While Augustine held a non-dualistic view of the unity of the body and soul; the soul always maintained its superiority.[89] The union of the physical with the spiritual is, according to Hochschild, explained by Augustine through an anthropological lens; since God "never abandons the soul," the physical itself is firmly held under divine providence by virtue of its subordination to a particular soul.[90] The body itself limits the soul only with respect to present perception;[91] however, memory enables the soul to overcome this limitation by the activity of memory, particularly recollection and expectation.[92]

De Musica

Augustine started writing *De Musica* prior to his baptism in 387 AD and finished it sometime in 391 AD in Africa. It follows a dialogic format between the student (*discipulus*) and the teacher (*magister*, i.e., Augustine). It is an unfinished work intended to be a series on music, with the first six books comprising the section that "pertain to that part called Rhythm."[93] The first five books are on rhythm and meter in music, while the sixth book is on the hierarchy of numbers as constitutive of the soul, the universe, and the angels.[94] Hochschild has researched *memoria* in *De Musica* and concludes that in Book VI Augustine develops a twofold sense of memory pertaining to the sensible and the intelligible.[95] This twofold sense has a moral character (more strongly than for Plotinus) which must be incorporated into the life of the virtues according to the higher truth. There is also a rhythm and order to memory; first, there is rhythm in the perception and second, rhythm in the memory.[96] *De Musica* is demonstrative of the architectonics of memory

---

89. *Quant. An.* 14.23.

90. *Quant. An.* 36.80; Hochschild, *Memory*, 109.

91. *Quant. An.* 25.48. Sense perception is defined by Augustine as "a bodily experience of which the soul is not unaware." According to Hochschild, the Augustinian model of perception is Aristotelian with regard to the passage of time in that sense perception in itself is instantaneous, but the intelligibility of what is experienced, the collection of what is taken in through the various senses, presupposes a synthesis of data. Hochschild, *Memory*, 105.

92. Hochschild, *Memory*, 104.

93. *Retr.* 1.5.3.

94. Saint Augustine, *On Music*, 154.

95. Hochschild's article "Unity of Memory in *De Musica*" is a comprehensive treatise. She discusses the same ideas in her book *Memory in Augustine's Theological Anthropology*, 117–31. Hochschild, "Unity," 611–17. *Mus.* VI.

96. Hochschild, "Unity," 611.

that exists through the rhythm and meter of music and the hierarchy of numbers. Further, *De Musica* presents for the first time the central role *memoria* has in the mind's knowledge of God, although it is barely developed.[97]

An insight into Augustine's theory of *memoria* actually starts in Book I where the association of memory with imitation is observed. This is an important association which sets up the discussion of *memoria* in Book VI. In I.5.10, the *magister* describes the flute player who remembers from memory the tunes that he plays. Through practice his fingers become better at playing flawlessly. The flute player plays whether he learns tunes himself or learns them from others thereby, imitating them. This, however, is the type of memory that humans have in common with the beasts.[98] Nevertheless, the salient connection between imitation and memory is apparent. What slowly becomes evident to the *discipulus* is that there are those actors and musicians who have no grasp of the principle of acting or music; they strive only for an imitation that will earn them the mob's applause and coins.[99] Augustine considers the distinction between good and bad art, and notes the role of memory in bad art. The artist who learns by imitation instead of learning through new creative discovery fabricates bad art.[100] To Augustine, this is an abuse of memory.

The exposition of memory in Book VI is quite extensive; it broadly falls into two categories: memory pertaining to the sensible, and memory pertaining to the spiritual, where memory is central in the soul's knowledge of God.[101] The Augustinian movement from memory just relating to the sensible to becoming the vehicle by which he remembers and can encounter the Divine can be seen most clearly in Book VI. In VI.3.4 the *magister* discusses the association between *memoria* and recollection specifically with regard to audible things. Lowe writes that the most salient point made in this passage is "the connection of memory-data (memory-rhythms) with the sensations (perceptible rhythms) that give rise to them."[102] He goes on to say that in this passage, "there is a brief description of the process of memory." Here, however, *memoria* is only associated with perceptible and

---

97. Hochschild, *Memory*, 110, 229.

98. In I.1–5, the similarities between a flute player and birds making music are described. In both, memory has the same function in learning and imitation of music. Both humans and beasts have rhythm and order in music and execution. At this point Augustine associates memory with imitation to explain how both the flute player and the bird can produce music.

99. *Mus.* V.10–6.11.

100. Cf. *Imm. An.* 3.3.

101. *Mus.* VI.5.10; Mourant, *Saint*, 13; Hochschild, "Unity," 611.

102. Lowe, "Platonic," 88.

sensible things. VI.4.6 deals with the issue of deciding which is superior, the imitation of memory or the use of numbers in the memory verses numbers that are imprinted in the mind.[103] Augustine connects memory and forgetting; "numbers in the memory, although they remain longer than those numbers they are imprinted by . . . both pass away, one by cessation, others by forgetting." Imitation is deemed superior because forgetting occurs by cessation whereas memory that forgets numbers is inferior because it is the purpose of memory to remember.[104] This is a more negative dynamic to memory because it is a memory that is forgotten as opposed to a recollection of memory. The ensuing section VI.4.7–5.14 considers the nature of sense perception and the involvement of the soul. According to Lowe, this is where Augustine formulates a theory of sensation in which the soul plays an active part; sensation (*sentire*) becomes an action of the soul and the sense itself (*sensus*) becomes a "tool" of the body whereby the soul becomes aware of the external stimuli affecting the body.[105] In this manner the soul retains superiority over the body.[106] The vital role of memory in the soul's focus on returning to God begins at VI.5.14. The soul struggles with the "push of carnal pleasures," yielding to their attention despite trying to overcome them. Peace comes though when one turns back to God. As the *magister* writes in VI.5.14: "But a greater unquiet arises for one turning back to God . . . and it is so until the push of carnal business, excited by daily habit and inserting itself into the heart of the conversion by disorderly memories, comes to rest." Memory can and does play a role in distracting the soul's focus from esteeming "the body's pleasure" (VI.5.14). Augustine declares that it is the grace of God through Jesus Christ that can deliver him from his body of death.[107] The soul, when it turns back to God, does so through a movement in memory as it remembers by the grace of God. The dialogue at this point reverts back to sensible memory and temporal spatial memory.[108] The beginning and end of a syllable, stretched over time, has defined spatial and temporal intervals. Memory is necessary to remember what is heard, otherwise the first part of the syllable disappears into the unheard.[109] *Memoria* also judges the diversity in different sounds and their respective time

---

103. Hochschild, *Memory*, 121.
104. Hochschild, *Memory*, 121.
105. Lowe, "Platonic," 90.
106. *Mus.* VI.5.9.
107. *Mus.* VI.5.14.
108. *Mus.* VI.8.21.
109. *Mus.* VI.8.21.

intervals. As Hochschild states, memory is a tool that operates in a twofold manner; she writes:

> The judicial numbers bring a superior order to the lower kinds of number through the memory, effectively referring reason to what comes through the senses. Conversely, memory assists the judgement in comprehending as an inarticulate whole the seemingly boundless "diversity" (*varietas*) of what occurs in time.[110]

The concept of temporality and *ordo* now becomes important in the dialogue. The two in Book VI are not exclusive of each other. Musical measure imposes *ordo*, and time implies spatiality creating "temporal spaces" (*temporalium spatium*) where the unintelligible can become the intelligible.[111] According to Hochschild, memory reveals the ability of the mind to express and discern *ordo* in the whole of creation; it does this by its dual function of linking the mind to the intelligible reasons and opening the mind to the sensible world as something possessing an intrinsic *ordo*.[112] Hochschild asserts that "*Mus.* deepens this interpretation by making memory into the moral filter . . . through which the mind selectively chooses to attend to what is taken in through the senses, purging images that correspond to the ill-considered use of physical goods."[113]

Augustine observes that memory serves to order the soul with respect to what is lesser, and it does this by mediating a higher *ordo* that is perceived through the mind and reason; this higher *ordo* is called *aequalitas* (equality) and mediated by memory, it is able to discern the *ordo* present in creation.[114] In this discernment, the soul realizes that it has already, through recollection, access to this *ordo*. *Ordo* does not pass before the eyes in temporal succession, but is present, immediately, when it is remembered. It is in the soul, but not *of* the soul, coming from a principle that transcends the soul itself.[115] Hochschild writes that memory is what links the temporality of the soul's mode of perceiving to the transcendence of the soul's mode of being of truth.[116] What Augustine is developing in VI.11 is the concept that there are two types of memory. One is associated with the sensible, temporal,

---

110. Hochschild, *Memory*, 125.
111. Hochschild, "Unity," 615.
112. Hochschild, *Memory*, 230. Architectonic structure also has an *ordo*.
113. Hochschild, *Memory*, 230.
114. *Mus.* VI.13.37; Hochschild, *Memory*, 125.
115. Hochschild, "Unity," 615.
116. Hochschild, *Memory*, 230.

and unintelligible while the other is associated with the intelligible and eternal.[117]

VI.11 has an extended discussion on *phantasiae* and *phantasmata*.[118] Augustine describes the difference between the two as follows:

> For my father I have often seen I know, in one way, and my grandfather I have never seen, another way. The first of these is a phantasia, the other phantasm. The first I find in my memory, the last in that motion of my mind born of those the memory has.[119]

Phantasia is thus a memory created from images that are retained based on known and perceived physical sense interactions while *phantasmata* are images that have not been perceived but are created from the images or memories already present in *memoria*; *phantasmata* may not be dependable or even true. *Phantasmata* are concerned with the active imagination. Memory plays a different role in the distinction between *phantasiae* and *phantasmata*. Augustine explains:

> But what I make from what I've seen, I make by memory. Yet it's one thing to find a phantasia in the memory and another to make a phantasm out of the memory. And a power of the soul can do all these things.[120]

Phantasia is found in *memoria* itself while the *phantasmata* are the product of mental labor. Thonnard argues that *phantasmata* are more often than not perverse in nature and burden the mind with the weight of its own vacuity.[121] *Phantasmata* are second-order memory images voluntarily induced in the mind that can impair the proper functioning of the intellect and hamper its efforts to find truth.[122] Augustine advises "it is the greatest error to

---

117. Hochschild, *Memory*, 127.

118. These terms appear to be of Stoic origin. Augustine's demarcation of *phantasia* from *phantasma* does not correspond to the Stoic distinction between *phantasia* as the making of an impression or alteration in the mind to the perceived object and *phantasma* as the product of an "empty attraction" or "appearance of thinking" without any direct external thought. Augustine's definition of the difference between these terms is in *Mus.* VI.11.22. When Augustine uses the term *phantasia*, he has no ambiguity assigned to it unlike Porphyry who adapted the Stoic definition and uses the term interchangeably with *phantasma*. Augustine may have been influenced by Cicero's use of *phantasia*. O'Daly, *Augustine's Philosophy*, 107–8.

119. *Mus.* VI.11.32.
120. *Mus.* VI.11.32.
121. *Mus.* VI.11.32; Finaert and Thonnard, *Oeuvres*, 523–24.
122. Djuth, "Veiled," 80.

hold even true phantasms for things known," and counsels that one should resist *phantasmata* lest one falls into the trap of being deceived by them.[123]

De Musica is a complex work that can be difficult and even confusing to read; however, this complexity arises from Augustine's search for God through *memoria*. VI.12.34 opens in the same manner as VI.5.14 with the following concept, "but the memory not only takes in the carnal motions of the mind . . . but also the spiritual motions." The two types of memory compete against each other and can find no peace. This struggle between the soul's desire to turn to God and succumbing to carnal desires is constant. *Memoria* does have what Lowe describes as vestigial "shadowy remains of past perceptions,"[124] however, *memoria* is also the soul's means of turning back to God as it remembers truth. And this kind of truth, Augustine concludes, is properly *in* the soul, though *from* God who is truth most supremely.[125] The soul, which is superior to the body when subordinate to God, can discern what it takes to turn back to God. Hochschild elaborates on what Augustine writes regarding "to live in *memoria*."[126] She writes, "living 'in memory' requires a strict discernment of *ordo* in the sensible, and an almost clinical attention with discipline, avoiding pleasure simply for its own sake."

Augustine in *De Musica* has introduced the role of memory in association with the Divine and not just with perceptible, sensible things. This is a far superior concept of memory which includes a metaphysical recollection and pursuit of God.[127]

De Moribus Ecclesiae Catholicae de Moribus Manichoraeorum

This book was written to refute the false claims of the Manichaeans and their belief that they were superior to the Christians. It was written in 388 AD and revised in 390 AD.[128] There is a brief section in I.6.9–10, titled "Virtue Gives Perfection to the Soul; The Soul Obtains Virtue by Following God; Following God is the Happy Life." This is in effect a quick summary, in a few sentences, of the happy life described in the *De Beata Vita*. Augustine writes that "Only God remains, therefore, if we follow after Him, we live well; if we reach Him, we live not only well but happily."[129] Although memory or

---

123. *Mus.* VI.11.32.
124. Lowe, "Platonic," 102.
125. Hochschild, *Memory*, 129.
126. Hochschild, "Unity," 615.
127. *Mus.* VI.12.35.
128. Gallagher, "Introduction," xi–xx.
129. *Mor. Eccl.* I.6.10.

its role is not specifically mentioned in *De Moribus Ecclesiae* memory is fundamental in the achievement of the happy life as noted in *De Beata Vita*. Augustine, also in chapter 11.18, encourages his readers to strive after God, "To strive after God, then, is to desire happiness; to reach God is happiness itself."

De Libero Arbitrio

Augustine started writing *De Libero Arbitrio* in Rome in 388 AD and finished it in 395 AD, several years after his ordination as bishop of Hippo.[130] The first book is believed to be written early on, with Books II and III written when he was a presbyter, consequently, there is a clear distinction in the maturity of his theology between the "early" and "late" Augustine.[131] The book, written in the form of a dialogue with his student Evodius,[132] was written as a refutation of the dualistic Manichaean belief of the eternal and conflicting forces of Light (Good) and Darkness (Evil); conflict in man between good and evil represented the universal conflict between these ultimate cosmic forces.[133] The main themes of *De Libero Arbitrio* are the freedom of the will and the nature and origin of moral evil. There is no detailed explicit dialogue about memory, but it is evident in certain sections that memory is pertinent if not central to the arguments that are debated.

In chapter II.12.34 the dialogue centers on finding truth and the happy life, a concept first present in *De Beata Vita*. Augustine writes in II.13.35:

> I had promised to show you, if you recall, that there is something higher than our mind and reason. There you have it—truth itself! . . . And who is happier than the man who finds joy in the firm, changeless, and most excellent truth? . . . When truth steals into our minds with a kind of eloquent silence without, as it were, the noisy intrusion of words, shall we look for another happy life and not enjoy that which is so sure and intimately present to us?

Gilson asserts that when the soul sees truth in its own mind (of which it is certain it has) it does not see God's essence; however, it recognizes what it

---

130. Russell, *Teacher*, 66.

131. Authors such as Séjourné and O'Connell claim that Book II is a retraction of the first. Séjourné, "Conversions," 243–64; O'Connell, "*De Libero*," 49–68.

132. Evodius is not mentioned by name in *De Libero Arbitrio*; however, Augustine's letter to Evodius in 415 AD leaves no doubt that Evodius is the interlocutor (162.2). Russell, *Teacher*, 70.

133. Russell, *Teacher*, 66.

must do to enjoy happiness.¹³⁴ Truth is independent, and transcendent of the mind it rules.¹³⁵ In discovering the transcendence of truth, the mind discovers God's existence.¹³⁶

Augustine discusses the origin of the soul (III.20.56–21.62); however, more important to Augustine is the soul's future destination. III.20–21 introduces the concept of temporality and remembering/recollection of memories regarding the soul and truth. The first mention is in III.21.59 where "a path through temporal things has been marked out . . . that we accept on faith past and future events so far as this suffices for men on their journey towards things eternal." In III.21.61 Augustine writes, "within the order of temporal events, our expectation of the things to come [*futurorum exspectatio*] should certainly occupy our attention more than an inquiry into things of the past." This concept of temporality of past, present, and future was also evident in *De Immortalitate Animae* and *De Musica*.¹³⁷ The course of the present is dependent on understanding the role of temporality as it pertains to recollection and forgetfulness of the past, and expectation of the future outcome or end, a result of present actions.

Lib. Arb. has definitive contributions to the understanding of *memoria*.

Epistola VII

Epistola VII is a letter Augustine wrote in 389 AD¹³⁸ in response to Nebridius (*Ep.* VI.1.), who had argued that there can be no memory without *phantasia* (*omnis . . . memoria sine phantasia esse non possit*).¹³⁹ The overriding

---

134. Gilson, *Christian*, 67, 22; *Lib. Arb.* II.13.35.

135. *Lib. Arb.* II.12.34.

136. Gilson, *Christian*, 21.

137. *Imm. An.* 3.3–4: time consists of past, present, and future. The same phrase *futurorum expectatio* (future expectation) occurs in 3.3 and *Lib. Arb.* III.21.61. In *De Immortalitate Animae*, expectation is associated with the future, memory with the past, and intention to act within the present. In *De Libero Arbitrio*, Augustine writes that it is not helpful to recollect the past if in the present he errs by not remembering (knowing) the end where he will find rest. In *Mus.* VI.8.21, temporality is associated with time intervals where sound in the present becomes past and there is expectation of the sound continuing into the future. The *ordo* that exists in temporality is evident in *De Libero Arbitrio*.

138. *Ep.* VII is generally believed to have been written in 389, but some translators like Teske give a range of 388–391. Teske, *Letters*, 26.

139. *Ep.* VI.1.1. O'Daly believes that Nebridius' position on memory was influenced by the Aristotelian tradition of memory. Augustine disagrees with Nebridius' position in *Ep.* VII.1.1, "You think that there can be no memory without images or

theme in *Ep.* VII is the power of memory with particular reference to the role of imagination. Augustine categorizes mental images into three types: those based on actual impressions of the things obtained via our senses (e.g., Carthage), things we think of (e.g., fantasies), and things we reason to (e.g., numbers and dimensions).[140] Mourant categorizes the response of Augustine in *Ep.* VII into three characteristics regarding memory: *phantasia* not conditioned by time and space, validity of memory in the present, and Augustine's developing objections to *anamnesis*.[141]

One theme that stands out is the Augustinian concept that memory is not just a remembrance of past things but of things still in existence. Here, the association of the temporality of memory with the remembrance of past *and* present memories is laid out for Nebridius. Augustine asserts that past memories are those that have in part "left us behind and partly... those we have left behind."[142] He cites the memory of Carthage as something that still exists but that he has left behind. This is a memory of past time. In VII.1.2., Augustine describes how memory can be of things that have not passed out of existence. Eternity, for example, lasts forever, and does not need a product of the imagination to enter the mind. Nevertheless, eternity cannot enter the mind unless it is remembered. Augustine concludes that "there can be a memory of certain things without imagination."[143] According to O'Daly, this recollection of the memory of eternity is necessary because human beings are distracted from the knowledge of eternity.[144] This recollection of eternity occurs in the present.[145] Memory is capable of recollection and remembrance of the past in the present because of the memory that exists in the present.[146] The validity of present memory is just as valid to Augustine as memory of the past. O'Daly writes, "what Augustine is insisting upon is the validity of a memory which does not need the aid of any *phantasia* conditioned by space or time."[147] However, he does warn in VII.2.4–5 of the dangers of creating false images.

---

representations of imagination, which you chose to call '*phantasia*.' I disagree." Gerard O'Daly, "III: Memory," 466.

140. *Ep.* VII.2.4; VII.3.6–7. Mourant, *Saint*, 16–17.

141. Mourant, *Saint*, 16–17.

142. *Ep.* VII.1.1.

143. *Ep.* VII.1.2.

144. O'Daly, "III: Memory," 466.

145. Here one can see the development of Augustine's theory of temporality in his theology of *memoria*. Temporality and memory are inseparable and cannot be understood without the other. His detailed analysis is recorded in *Conf.* XI.

146. *Ep.* VII.1.2.

147. O'Daly, "III: Memory," 466.

Finally, Augustine informs Nebridius that the soul has the power (*vim*) to remember things it has not seen.[148] This power (*vis*) is particularly noticeable in regard to numbers or imagining something the soul has seen in a transformed state, like a raven that is turned into a different image by adding elements to it.[149] Imagination alters data that is brought in by the senses and is able to create images that have not been experienced by any of the senses in their totality.[150]

In this letter, Augustine's association of memories with past recollections is reminiscent of Plato's theory of *anamnesis* because it is a recollection of something in the past that exists in the past. O'Daly writes that O'Connell[151] is correct when he states that "to justify using the term *memoria*, there must be reference to the past."[152] He continues on to say that "Augustine distinguishes formally between the "pastness" of the act of apprehension and of the object apprehended." There are definitely Platonian overtones to Augustine's language (e.g., *memoria, oblivio*) and concepts regarding memory throughout *Ep*. VII. It is true, as O'Daly states, that *Ep*. VII does defend *anamnesis* against an invalid objection; however, when Augustine realizes the implications of the constant presence of truth to the mind, he deliberately dissociated himself from the Platonic theory of *anamnesis* because of its concept of past acquisition of knowledge.[153] Perhaps Augustine saw that the memory of history had become memory of the present in the incarnation of Christ. Memory of the past was indisputably so important to memory in the present for God had entered into the present of history. In *Retr*. 1.4.4 Augustine writes that the unchangeable truths become evident to human beings because of the light of eternal reason that is present in them.[154] Knowledge of things in the past were not forgotten as Plato thought.

---

148. *Ep.* VII.3.6; Teske, *Works*, 29.

149. *Ep.* VII.3.6.

150. *Ep.* VII.3.6.

151. O'Connell, "Pre-existence," 71.

152. O'Daly, "Did?," 232.

153. O'Daly writes that *Ep.* VII marks this progressive abandonment of Platonic *anamnesis*. O'Daly, "III: Memory," 467.

154. Aquinas, years later, follows Augustine is his use of the phrase "light of natural reason." Aquinas associates this light as the divine light, which is imprinted on us. "The light of Thy countenance, O Lord, is signed upon us: thus implying that the *light of natural reason*, whereby we discern what is good and what is evil, which is the function of the natural law, is nothing else than an imprint on us of the Divine light." Aquinas, *Summa*, I–II. Q90. A1. ad 1.

De Magistro

De Magistro (389 AD) is a dialogue between Augustine and his interlocutor, his son Adeodatus.[155] Augustine described the contents of this book as having "a discussion, an investigation, and the discovery that there is no teacher who teaches men knowledge except God" (*Retr.* 1.11). According to Hochschild, *De Magistro* "opens up the conceptual space for memory to become the foundation of knowledge as a dialectical mode of presence."[156] She also argues that *De Magistro* does not use a "theory of memory." While it is true that there is no specific theory of memory described in *De Magistro*, it is contended here that there are indeed some important sections (e.g., chapter 12) that provide significant contributions towards the formulation of Augustine's theology of *memoria*.

Augustine is concerned about how one succeeds in learning.[157] He understands how the ability to recognize a sound provides meaning to the knowledge of words. However, recognition of that sound is *only* possible if there is some retention of that sound as a memory in *memoria*:

> It is perfectly logical and true to conclude that whenever words are spoken, we either know what they mean or we do not. If we know, they recall rather than teach something to us; if we do not know, they cannot even recall something, though they may lead us to inquire.[158]

The reality of understanding meaning is not from the words themselves, but the truth which presides over the mind itself from within.[159] Truth resides within *memoria*; this is a foundational characteristic of memory.

Chapter 12 is more specific in the discussion of images and recollection. In 12.39–40, Augustine, as in *Ord.* II.2.7, stresses the necessary involvement of memory in instruction and learning, both on the part of the teacher and student. However, he now elaborates on the role of images in recollection and sense perception. Augustine presents an interesting point regarding memory; he writes:

---

155. Russell, *Teacher*, 3.
156. Hochschild, *Memory*, 110.
157. *Mag.* 11.36–38; 14.45–46; Matthews, "Augustine," 158.
158. *Mag.* 11.36.
159. *Mag.* 11.38. Per Russell, "presides" is a favorite term Augustine used to describe the action of the "inner light" upon the soul in its perception of truth. Russell, *Teacher*, 51.

> But when questions are asked, not about those which our senses perceived on former occasions, then our words do not refer to the things themselves, but to the images impressed by them upon the senses and stored away in the memory.[160]

Matthews contends there is a tendency to change the subject when asked about familiar but absent sensible things by deferring to memory images instead.[161] He claims that this is a peculiar thing for Augustine to say given that its meaning is hard to understand. Perhaps what Augustine might be thinking is akin to the example of when a person is asked to describe an object like a lamp of particular shape and color present before them and they exclaim that it reminds them of a similar lamp they saw some years earlier. When they start to describe the lamp before them, they really are resorting to the past images and memory of the earlier lamp stored in the recesses of *memoria*. These images are "witnesses, so to speak, of things previously experienced by the senses" but, as Augustine writes, "these images are only witnesses for ourselves."[162]

Augustine also acknowledges the action of God in the role of learning and understanding the veracity of what is true. He writes:

> But when it is a question of things which we behold the mind, namely, with our intellect and reason, we give verbal expression to realities which we directly perceive as in that inner light of truth[163] by which the inner man, as he is called, is enlightened and made happy. But, here again, if the one who hears my words sees those things himself with that clear and inner eye of the soul, he knows the things whereof I speak by contemplating them himself, and not by my words. Therefore, even when I say what is true, and he sees what is true, it is not I who teach him. For he is being taught, not by my words, but by the realities themselves made manifest to him by the enlightening action of God from within.[164]

In this excerpt, an extrapolation of what Paul says in Ephesians 3:16 can be observed; Paul writes, "I pray that out of his glorious riches he may strengthen you with power through his Spirit in your inner being." This passage is also reminiscent of the happy life described in *De Beata Vita* where

---

160. *Mag.* 12.39. Matthews, "Augustine," 157.

161. Matthews, "Augustine," 157.

162. *Mag.* 12.40.

163. The "inner light of truth" is a phrase that Augustine uses for "divine illumination."

164. *Mag.* 12.40.

the "inner light of truth" reveals to the soul what is necessary to achieve the *beata vita*. In chapter 14.46, it is the Teacher who directs the inward turn to him for instruction in the acquisition of the happy life, which is defined by Augustine in this text as "to love Him and to know Him, that is the happy life." There is also reference to the realities made manifest by the action of God via what Augustine would later describe as "divine illumination." This is a recurrent theme in Augustine's theology of *memoria*; it is through God's action via *memoria* that one can know and understand the realities of truth and the Divine.

Hochschild, in *De Magistro*, asserts that the only explicit function accorded to memory is the retention of images of things sensed in the past; hence, memory can become the foundation of knowledge.[165] This is paradoxical. How is it possible to learn something unless one already has some anterior knowledge? What is learnt can only be affirmed as true if there is anterior knowledge. This is the same question seen in Plato's *Meno* where Plato provides an answer through his theory of recollection. Augustine accepts this theory, but with modifications, e.g., not embracing pre-existence.[166] The link between temporality and memory is noted; recollection pertains to past images. Augustine says it is through judgment that we see past images as "certain attestations of things sensed previously."[167] Our mind can therefore consider them and take them as truthful in the limited manner in which anything can be truthful that is based on sense perception.[168]

It is true that *De Magistro* may not have many explicit references to memory; it does, however, have crucial insights regarding the function and characteristics of memory that are key to Augustine's theology of *memoria* and that cannot be overlooked. Even Adeodatus, Augustine's son, recognized the central role of *memoria* in the discussions. Adeodatus in 14.46 acknowledges, "but as to the truth of what is said, I have also learned that He alone teaches who made use of external words to remind us that He dwells within us." The most significant role of *memoria* is when it is invoked in remembering the indwelling God.

---

165. Hochschild, *Memory*, 110–17.
166. Hochschild, *Memory*, 113.
167. *Mag.* 12.39.
168. *Mag.* 12.39. Hochschild, *Memory*, 117.

De Vera Religione

De Vera Religione (390 AD) was addressed to Romanianus, Augustine's patron and his principal student at Cassiciacum.[169] It was the last book he wrote before he was ordained as a priest at Hippo. Augustine writes that he repeatedly and at length argues that the one true God is to be worshipped by the true religion (*Retr.* XII.1). He also notes that this book addresses the Manichaeans and their "two natures." There are just a few specific references to memory that demonstrate the underlying role of memory and images. The first mention related to memory is in III.3:

> Nothing hinders the perception of truth more than a life devoted to lusts, and the false images[170] of sensible things, derived from the sensible world and impressed on us by the agency of the body, which beget various opinions and errors.

False images distract from the true worship of God by creating fantasies. The soul should, according to Augustine, accept the "temporal condition of human society" but at the same time, it should have "directed its regard to eternal things."[171] Augustine describes *phantasmata* as "nothing but figments of corporeal shapes appearing to bodily senses" declaring that it is the "easiest thing in the world to commit them to memory."[172] Images committed to memory are easy to manipulate; they form different shapes, they can expand or minimize, decrease or multiply in number, and/or the order of images can be disturbed and reset.[173] Augustine warns that it is difficult to guard against *phantasmata* as one seeks the truth; he encourages the reader to not serve the creature but to serve the Creator.[174]

XXXIV.64 has the most content regarding imagination. Early on, Augustine did not have a theory of imagination. A shift in his understanding of *imaginatio* is noted over time, including variations in the definition of the word *imaginatio*.[175] Indeed, according to Breyfogle, in this section, *imaginatio* is used in the sense of the "vain imaginations" (Rom 1:21); *imaginatione* are derived from things perceived by the senses and are barriers to proper

---

169. Burleigh, *Augustine*, 222.

170. The words for false images in this text is *"falsas imagines"* and not *phantasmata* which can be the source of false images.

171. *V. Rel.* X.18.

172. *V. Rel.* X.18.

173. *V. Rel.* X.18.

174. *V. Rel.* X.18–19.

175. Breyfogle, "Memory," 214.

contemplation.¹⁷⁶ The influence of imagination persuades Augustine to do what he desires, for these imaginations cloud the mind with illusions and fantasies:¹⁷⁷

> Obstinate souls! Give me a single man who can see without being influenced by imaginations derived from things seen in the flesh (*sine ulla imaginatione visorm carnalium*). . . . And in imagination (*figmento cogitationis*) I go where I like, and speak to whom I like. These imaginary things are false, and what is false cannot be known. When I contemplate them and believe in them, I do not have knowledge, because what I contemplate with the intelligence must be true, and not by any possibility what are commonly called phantasms (*phantasmata*).¹⁷⁸

Imaginatio through the formation of *phantasmata* seeks via falsehoods to distract and hinder the ability to worship the true God.¹⁷⁹

The Symphonic Forms and Fundamental Affordances of Augustinian Memory

Augustine's writings in his first decade post conversion illustrate the extent to which *memoria* was deeply embedded in his desire to know God and the *beata vita*. The details regarding *memoria* and memory were substantial in these books and sufficient to identify and extrapolate an architectonic structure to memory. Seven symphonic forms and fundamental affordances of memory were identified that are key to his theology of *memoria*. The term "symphonic form" is appropriated from Augustine's conceptualization of memory and music, and how rhythm and order of different words sung together form the whole of a song in a movement from beginning to end through past, present, and future time. The symphonic forms of memory, while they have their own independent characteristics and fundamental affordances, work in relation to each other creating an *ordo* and rhythm. Wiskus goes as far as to say that it is through rhythm that memory is studied.¹⁸⁰ *Ordo* is embedded in the symphonic forms, and together with the

---

176. Breyfogle states the most explicit use of *imaginatio* as vain imaginations is found in *De Vera Religione*. Breyfogle, "Memory," 214.

177. Breyfogle, "Memory," 214.

178. *V. Rel.* XXXIV.64.

179. Breyfogle, "Memory," 215.

180. Wiskus writes that Augustine has an exhaustive exploration of music, rhythm, order, and numbers in *De Musica* because he is searching for God in his memory.

relational component, allow for an understanding of how *memoria* and memory function both at the spiritual and physical level. Wiskus writes, "In his performance of language, therefore, Augustine confirms the kind of memory in which he finds God—it is the same kind of memory (he confirms at the end of *Conf.* XI) that we engage in when we sing."[181]

Of note, is the fact that the four books written at Cassiciacum, all, to one degree or another, discuss these symphonic forms of memory. The later books between 387–396 AD also include and develop these aspects of memory. The symphonic forms and fundamental affordances of memory and the books in which they appear are listed in Table 3.1. These symphonic forms create an architectonic structure to *memoria* and Augustine's theology.

Table 3.1: The symphonic forms of memory

Symphonic Forms	Cassiciacum Writings	Works: 387–395 AD
Location of *Memoria*	Ord.	Imm. An., Quant. An., Lib. Arb.
Sense perception	Sol.	Quant. An., Mus., V. Rel.
Teaching/Learning	C. Acad., Ord., Sol.	Imm. An., Mag.
Recollection and Forgetfulness	C. Acad., Ord.	Imm. An., Quant. An., Mus., Ep. VII, Mag.
Images, *Phantasiae*, *Phantasmata*	Sol., Beata V.	Quant. An., Mus., Ep. VII, Mag., V. Rel.
Transiency of Memory	Sol., Ord.	Imm. An., Mus., Ep. VII, Lib. Arb., Mag., V. Rel.
The *Beata Vita*	C. Acad., Ord., Beata V., Sol.	Imm. An., Mus., Ep. VII, Mag., Mor. Eccl., Lib. Arb., V. Rel.

Table 3.1 demonstrates the following facts:

1. All symphonic forms are found in Augustine's books written at Cassiciacum. It would seem therefore that Augustine already had

---

Beneath the memory of events, of things, or capacities is a memory of a whole, a memory of order, of number. Wiskus, "On Music," 276.

181. Wiskus, "On Music," 283.

developed in his own mind the sequence of these symphonic forms of memory.

2. Augustine's writings from 387–395 AD also included these symphonic forms. They were further developed compared to the Cassiciacum books. However, comparatively, they were still considered immature compared to *Confessiones* and *De Trinitate*.

3. Important to note, is that the *beata vita* is discussed in eleven out of the twelve books surveyed in this chapter. The desire to know and possess God and thus know the happy life was, in a sense, not just a symphonic form but a fundamental principle of his theology of *memoria*.

4. From the very beginning Augustine understood the significance of memory not just in a physical temporal sense but also within a metaphysical dimension.

Concluding Remarks

Close analysis of Augustinian memory in these earlier works reveals an architectonic structure behind Augustine's questions, discussions, and presentations of *memoria*. This structure is based on the seven symphonic forms and fundamental affordances of memory that serve, or at least attempt, to understand Augustine's interrogations of memory. This assists in understanding Augustine's logic as he developed his theology regarding the types of memory and their functions. Such an architectonic structure with the identification of the seven symphonic forms of memory in Augustine's earlier works has not been previously reported. This uncovers the complexity of Augustine's theology of *memoria* and provides for an in-depth appreciation of Augustine himself, his logical mind, and the evolution of his theology.

The symphonic forms of memory discovered in this survey of Augustine's early works lay the groundwork for understanding memory in *Confessiones* X–XI.

4

Augustine's Theology of *Memoria* in *Confessiones*

"I come to the fields and vast palaces of memory . . ."[1]

AUGUSTINE WROTE *CONFESSIONES* BETWEEN 397 and 401 AD. It can be said that *Confessiones* is the most famous of all his writings. Book X has the most comprehensive description of *memoria*; here Augustine's theology of *memoria* reaches it apotheosis. There is also further delineation of *memoria* in Books XI–XIII. Yet, of the numerous academic articles and books written on *Confessiones*, very few tackle the topic of memory; when they do, it is often in passing or written with a specific focus on a particular aspect of *memoria*.[2] Lacking in the literature is a comprehensive, logical examination and correlation of the various aspects of memory from his early writings to his later writings to determine if there is a specific pattern or structure to Augustine's interrogation of memory and consequent development of his theology of *memoria*. An in-depth investigation of Augustine's writings reveals that a pattern does indeed exist. An architectonic structure starts to emerge revealing the symphonic forms and fundamental affordances of

---

1. *Conf.* X.8.12.

2. Hochschild writes from an anthropological perspective, focusing on *Conf.* X. Ayres explores the Trinitarian aspect of *memoria*. O'Daly's focus is empirical memory. Nash's focus is knowledge coming from the mind and thus memory. Mourant has a nice synopsis of *memoria* that, while comprehensive in its discussion of the different aspects of *memoria*, lacks in detail. Grove examines *memoria* from a Christological perspective. Hochschild, *Memory*; Ayres, *Augustine*; O'Daly, *Augustine's*; Nash, *Light*; Mourant, *Saint Augustine*; Grove, *Augustine*.

memory. The logic of his theology materializes as he explains *memoria*. As Augustine explores various aspects of *memoria* it becomes evident that he discusses *memoria* with three specific end goals: to understand how it is that he remembers God; to understand how memory aides in the search for, and understanding of, God; and to understand how to achieve the *beata vita*.

The Symphonic Forms and Fundamental Affordances of *Memoria*

The blueprint of Augustine's theology of *memoria* in *Conf.* X is logically laid out into eight distinct and sequential symphonic forms. It includes an additional symphonic form that is not present in the previous chapter, the power of memory. To the best of my knowledge this presentation of *memoria* as independent symphonic forms occurring in a sequential architectonic structure with theological implications has not been previously reported. The eight symphonic forms of memory and the order in which they appear are as follows in Table 4.1:

Table 4.1: *Ordo* **of** *memoria* **in** *Confessiones* **X**

Symphonic Forms of *Memoria*	Key References: Book X
Location of *Memoria*	8.11–14
Power of Memory	8.11; 8.15; 17.26
Sense perception	8.13–14; 9.16; 12.19; 14.22; 33.49; 35.54–55; 40.65
Teaching/Learning	9.16; 10.17; 13.20; 15.23
Recollection and Forgetfulness	9.16; 10.17; 11.18; 13.20; 14.21–22; 16.24–25; 18.27; 19.28; 20.29; 24.22–25.23, (8.13)*
Images, *Phantasiae*, *Phantasmata*	9.16; 10.17; 11.18; 16.24–25; 17.26; 8.15 (8.12–13)*
Temporal Dimension (Transiency) of Memory	10.17; 15.19; 18.23; 28.38
The *Beata Vita*	20.29–43.68, (8.13–14)*
* Mentioned in synopsis of *memoria* (8.11–14)	

Augustine's recounting of *memoria* commences in X.8.11–14 where there is a brief synopsis of memory followed by a more detailed exposition in the following chapters where the symphonic forms and fundamental affordances of memory are described.

Location of *Memoria*

Knowledge of the location of *memoria* was not inconsequential to Augustine. This knowledge was necessary in fulfilling his aspiration to acquire the *beata vita* and ascend to God. At the time he wrote *Confessiones*, Augustine knew with certainty that *memoria* resided in the mind, which in turn was located in the rational soul. It was Augustine's aim to rise above the natural capacity of the body in a step-by-step fashion to ascend, via the soul, to the God who made him.[3] In doing so, he comes to the "fields and vast palaces of memory" where the numerous memories and images are stored in the "mysterious, secret, and indescribable nooks and crannies."[4] Augustine metaphorically describes in X.14.21 the "stomach of the mind" as the location of memory, having earlier stated that mind is the very memory itself. The point is that the location of *memoria* is situated in the mind itself and the two cannot be separated, and memories are stored in the "stomach" or the "nooks and crannies." The operation of *memoria* within its vast palaces and fields is such that memories are not "swallowed up and buried in oblivion (*oblivio*)" but are available even to the point of pouring "out to crowd the mind."[5] The great vastness and hidden spaces of *memoria* reveal a great fluidity and movement of images in and out of the deep recesses of *memoria*.[6] There is the implication of a disordered and ordered organization of memory which is later confirmed in XI.11.18. The idea of a fluidic and dynamic operation of *memoria* is thus seen from the beginning of Augustine's discussion of memory in Book X continuing into Book XI with its association with temporality.

Augustine starts his remarkable elaboration on memory in *Conf.* X with the visualization of the location of *memoria* as fields and vast palaces, and the storage of memories within *memoria*. Right from the beginning he wants his readers to grasp the enormity of *memoria* and memories by describing the location. Augustine is defining an architectonic structure to *memoria* and memory.

---

3. *Conf.* X.8.12.
4. *Conf.* X.8.12–13.
5. *Conf.* X.8.12.
6. *Conf.* X.8.12–13.

Power of *Memoria*

As Augustine writes about the complexities and intricacies of the structure and function of memory, his words are infiltrated with his sense of wonderment and amazement, his perplexities, his incomprehension, and his understanding. The power of memory is referenced only eight times in *Conf.* X, however, the underlying thread of all of Augustine's discussions on *memoria* is its power.

Augustine's illustrates the significance of the power of *memoria* by emphasizing the magnitude of the power at the start of two important sections of *Conf.* X. The power of memory is emphasized at the start of the discussion of the role of *memoria* in the formation, retention, recollection, and remembrance of memories, images, and skills (X.8.12). The second section (X.17.26) is the start of the discussion of the happy life and the role of *memoria* in Augustine's journey to achieve the *beata vita*. Both these sections start with the same phrase. The Latin and English translations are as follows:

X.8.15	*magna ista **vis** est memoriae*	The power of memory is great
X.17.26	*magna **vis** est memoriae*	Great is the power of memory
X.17.26	*tanta **vis** est memoriae*	So great is the power of memory

Starting these two sections with the same acknowledgement of the greatness of the power of memory, suggests that Augustine wanted to emphasize the two significant aspects of memory and was genuinely astounded by the functioning of memory. Both are important and have the same goal of searching for God, finding him, and the *beata vita*.

The other five mentions of the power of memory regard specific functions of memory. In X.7.11, Augustine describes the power of the soul that gives life to the body and the senses to perceive (*est alia **vis**, non solum qua vivifico sed etiam qua sensificio carnem meam*). In X.13.20, the recollection of memories is possible due to the power of memory (*utique per **vim** memoriae recordabor*). The ability to hold memories in *memoria* is made possible due to the power of memory in X.14.21 (*sicut sese habet **vis** memoriae*). The presence in memory of objects as opposed to their image (e.g., numbers and not images of numbers) is because of the power of memory in X.15.23 (*nisi eadem imago **vi** memoriae*). Finally in X.16.25, Augustine admits that the power of memory is something he does not understand, "*et ecce memoriae meae **vis** non comprehenditur.*"

In his earlier writings Augustine seems to prefer to talk about the power of the *soul* with regard to memory as opposed to the power of *memory*. In *Mus.* VI, Augustine uses the phrase "power of the soul" (*quae omnia **vis** animae potest*)[7] to describe how the soul can find a *phantasia* in *memoria* and also create *phantasmata*. This phrase is used only once in Book VI. In *Ep.* VII.3.6 Nebridius states that the soul has an innate power to remember things it has not seen (imagination).[8] The Latin translation for the context of power are as follows, "*nisi esse **vim** quamdam minuendi et augendi animae*[9] *insitam*" (but by a diminishing and increasing power [*force*] innate in the soul) and "*quae **vis** in numeris praecipue animadverti potest*" (the power [*force*] can be noticed especially in regard to numbers.) The term *vim/vis* is used in the soul's association with function of the mind and is the same term used in *Conf.* X for power; however, this has a different meaning from that used to describe the "great power of *memoria*." The earlier use of *vis* might be better translated as "force" as force implies an active, intense action compelled by physical, moral, or intellectual means and with a final end result while power implies the possession of control, authority, or influence with a vast capacity.[10] The use of *vis* in *Conf.* X is associated with *memoria* while in the earlier writings it appears to be more often associated with the soul.[11] This differentiation in the use of *vim/vis* would also fit with the other five mentions of *vis* in *Conf.* X where *vim/vis* pertains to a function of memory.

Sense Perception

The role of sense perception and memory is the first principle of *memoria* that Augustine establishes in *Conf.* X.8.13 before he describes what sense

---

7. *Mus.* VI.11.32.

8. Teske, *Works*, 18.

9. Some translators translate *animae* as mind, others as soul. Gilson points out that Augustine at times uses *animus* and *anima* to mean the soul, but *anima* is most often used by Augustine to refer to the animating principle of bodies considered in the vital function it exercises in them while Augustine preferably designates animus to mean the soul, i.e., a vital principle that is at the same time a rational substance. Parsons and Cunningham translate *anima* as mind. Gilson, *Christian*, 269n1a; Cunningham, *From Nicene*; Parsons, *Saint*, 18.

10. Definitions of power and force from *Merriam-Webster Dictionary*.

11. A more detailed examination of the use of *vis* in Augustine's writings, and a comprehensive linguistic analysis, would be needed to augment this interpretation; however, this is outside the scope of this work. Therefore, it is recognized that my interpretation may have an element of presumption based on the texts examined in this section.

perception is and how it works. He says, "Memory preserves in distinct particulars and general categories all the perceptions which have penetrated, each by its own route of entry." Hochschild describes the significance of the preservation of knowledge acquired through sense perception as a foundational role of memory.[12] The five senses all produce perceptions that are stored in the memory of the mind; sight, sound, smell, taste, and touch, all of which demonstrate the power of sensation.[13] Years earlier in *De Quantitate Animae*, Augustine informed Evodius, who had chosen to describe the five senses in this manner, that his description was "very ancient and commonly used by the old masters of rhetoric."[14] He preferred to define sensation as "a bodily experience of which the soul is not unaware."[15]

Sense perception does utilize all five senses. Augustine describes how the pleasures of the ears have a "tenacious hold" on him and "subjugated" him.[16] His ears hear when the words of numbers are spoken or songs are sung.[17] Augustine is aware of how ears can cause temptation but how moved he is when he hears songs in which sacred words are chanted well.[18] The eyes see and are entrapped by the various arts and crafts men make; these men follow what they have made and abandon the God who made them.[19] It is the contrast between what men create verses the creation of humankind *ex nihilo* by the Divine. Augustine is grateful that God rescues him from these temptations when he succumbs.[20] The sense of smell is not a temptation to Augustine, even as he remembers perfumes; he is indifferent to the presence of perfumes.[21] Augustine does struggle every day with uncontrolled desires in eating and drinking. He cannot give up the pleasures of eating and drinking but realizes he must moderate between "laxity and austerity."[22] Finally, Augustine warns of a temptation that is "manifold in its danger."[23] It is the "lust of the flesh which inheres in the delight given by all pleasures of the senses (those who are enslaved to it perish by putting themselves far

---

12. Hochschild, *Memory*, 13.
13. *Conf.* X.8.13.
14. *Quant. An.* 23.41.
15. *Quant. An.* 23.41.
16. *Conf.* X.33.49.
17. *Conf.* X.8–13; 33.49.
18. *Conf.* X.33.49.
19. *Conf.* X.34.53.
20. *Conf.* X.34.53.
21. *Conf.* X.32.48.
22. *Conf.* X.31.47.
23. *Conf.* X.34.53.

from you)."[24] Fortunately, "in the soul there exists, through the medium of the same bodily senses, a cupidity which does not take delight in carnal pleasures but in perceptions acquired through the flesh."[25] Augustine is aware that he does not use the senses for the proper acquisition of knowledge when succumbing to temptations of the flesh. He is also aware of his ability to distinguish the activity of the senses of pleasure verses that of the senses of curiosity.[26] Augustine acknowledges that God walks beside him, teaching and helping him regarding the senses and their proper use. It is the "abiding light of God" that enabled an understanding and insight into these matters.[27] The result was that Augustine was drawn by God who sometimes caused him "to enter into an extraordinary depth of feeling marked by a strange sweetness."[28]

Sense perception is the first step in understanding how memory works in the physical sense.

Teaching and Learning

Confessiones brings to its apex the dialectical debate regarding learning and teaching that started at Cassiciacum. Augustine had initially approached the debate of the association of memory with learning and teaching very much from a philosophical viewpoint.[29] In *C. Acad.* I.1.3, Augustine writes how he was "compelled to flee to the bosom of philosophy." However, by the time Augustine wrote *Confessiones*, this philosophical approach had evolved to extricate the underlying reason for trying to understand *memoria*, its role in his search to know and understand God and achieve the *beata vita*. Augustine had purposed this from the start, but the role of *memoria* in this capacity became more prominent in his thought process throughout the years. *Confessiones* X approaches teaching and learning from a somewhat different angle to Augustine's earlier works where memory involved committing his words to writing for his students to remember and the wise teachers to teach properly. Here the discussion centers on the liberal arts, skills learnt, and memory having knowledge of skills and memories within its deep recesses. The actual skills themselves, acquired via the liberal arts,

---

24. *Conf.* X.35.54.
25. *Conf.* X.35.54.
26. *Conf.* X.35.55.
27. *Conf.* X.40.65.
28. *Conf.* X.40.65.
29. *C. Acad.* I.1.3–4.

are carried in the interior space of *memoria*.[30] They are not just carried into these interior spaces; they are pushed back into the *deep* recesses of *memoria*.

Augustine explains the difference between sense perception and the learning of skills acquired through the liberal arts. The realities of the liberal arts contained in *memoria* are different from the images of actions that pass and fade created by sense perception, e.g., a voice makes an impression through the ears and leaves behind a trace allowing it to be recalled.[31] The object itself has no entry into *memoria*, only the images that are created, unlike the actual skills acquired through the liberal arts. Augustine concludes that these skills must already be in his memory "but so remote and pushed into the background, as if in most secret caverns, that unless they were dug out by someone drawing attention to them, perhaps I could not have thought of them."[32] With these stored skills, Augustine defines learning as this:

> We find that the process of learning is simply this: by thinking we, as it were, gather together ideas which the memory contains in a dispersed and disordered way, and by concentrating our attention we arrange them in order as if ready to hand, stored in the very memory where previously they lay hidden, scattered, and neglected. Now they easily come forward under the direction of the mind familiar with them.[33]

When Augustine then elaborates on memory containing the "innumerable principles and laws of numbers and dimensions" he also describes how these are different from the numbers that are thought of mathematically or that are images of numbers.[34] Numbers are ideas held in his memory in the way that he learnt them.[35] These ideas pertain not just to the skills learnt from the liberal arts but also the "notions" of the four perturbations of the mind.[36] The images might be imprinted by the physical senses, but the "notions" are not received through bodily senses, they are perceived by

---

30. *Conf.* X.9.16.
31. *Conf.* X.9.16.
32. *Conf.* X.10.17. Augustine echoes Plato that learning is remembering, bringing to the conscious mind something already present. Chadwick, *Saint*, 189.
33. *Conf.* X.11.18.
34. *Conf.* X.12.19.
35. *Conf.* X.13.20.
36. *Conf.* X.14.22. Four perturbations: cupidity, gladness, fear, sadness.

the mind through memory.[37] Augustine concludes that memory enables the recognition of these skills and notions allowing them to be both learnt and taught.

Recollection and Forgetfulness

As Augustine's theology matures, he is less inclined to be completely accepting of Plato's influences regarding the concept that recollection is of memories not yet experienced. Recollection meant far more, leading Augustine to dissociate from Plato's *anamnesis*. *Confessiones* X illustrates this when Augustine developed his theory that recollection was a two-stage process: (i) recollection of learnt arts and of truth from the liberal arts[38] and (ii) recollection of present memories. For recollection to occur, the mind must have the ability to retain not only the "images imprinted by the physical senses" (e.g., the sounds of names) but also the "notions themselves."[39] The act of recollecting the "image" and its "notion" led Augustine to note that in his act of remembering, the image was available to him. This might at first seem obvious, however, Augustine's insight was that remembrance and recognition of the image is located in memory itself.[40] Augustine asserts that "surely memory is present to itself through itself, and not through its own image."[41] This claim of Augustine brings forth another aspect of *memoria* that intrigues him and prompts further interrogation of *memoria*. This is the idea of memory associated with forgetfulness and the ability to remember forgetfulness. Augustine writes:

> If I had forgotten what the force of the sound was, I would be incapable of recognizing it. So when I remember memory, memory is available to itself through itself. But when I remember forgetfulness, both memory and forgetfulness are present—memory by means of which I could remember, forgetfulness which I did remember.[42]

This is a remarkably interesting concept of forgetfulness. Forgetfulness can be recalled, allowing recognition of a hidden memory, and forgetfulness itself can be remembered. How is this so? Is this recollection of forgetfulness

---

37. *Conf.* X.14.22–25.23.
38. *Sol.* II.20.34.
39. *Conf.* X.14.22.
40. *Conf.* X.15.23.
41. *Conf.* X.15.23.
42. *Conf.* X.16.24.

a remembrance of its actual presence in memory or is it remembering through its image?[43] This perplexes Augustine, and he acknowledges the difficulty he has in resolving this mystery. He concedes, "Yet in some way, though incomprehensible and inexplicable, I am certain that I remember forgetfulness itself, and yet forgetfulness destroys what we remember."[44]

Confessiones X confirms what Augustine presented in *Soliloquia* regarding the delineation of different types of forgetfulness and recollection (*recordationis*).[45] *Confessiones* X.18.27 illustrates the concept of partial forgetfulness through the woman in Luke 15:8 who lost her drachma and searched for it. Augustine's point is that she would not have searched for the coin had she not remembered it; it had to be in her memory because otherwise she would not have recognized the drachma when she found it. And here Augustine comes back to the point that "the object was lost to the eyes but held in the memory"[46] because the image of the object was retained within memory. Complete forgetfulness where memory is totally effaced from the mind, described in *Sol.* II.20.34 as *validissima oblivion*, is reiterated in *Conf.* X.19.28. Memory is unable to recall anything pertaining to a particular memory, and therefore, memory cannot even be searched when prompted. Additionally, Augustine declares that "when at least we remember ourselves to have completely forgotten, we have not totally forgotten."[47] It is interesting to note that Augustine presents the concept that it is memory itself that contains these three different types of memory; memory is the source of forgetfulness.[48] This paradoxical debate regarding remembering, forgetfulness, and remembering forgetfulness finds no solid answers from Augustine; he asks of God:

> How then am I to seek for you, Lord? . . . but then I ought to say how my request proceeds; is it by remembering, as if I had forgotten it and still recall that I had forgotten? Or is through an urge to learn something quite unknown, whether I never had known it or had so forgotten it that I do not even remember having forgotten it?[49]

---

43. *Conf.* X.16.24.
44. *Conf.* X.16.25.
45. *Sol.* II.20.34.
46. *Conf.* X.18.27.
47. *Conf.* X.19.28.
48. *Conf.* X.18.27–19.28.
49. *Conf.* X.20.29.

Images, Phantasiae, Phantasmata

Augustine asks the following question, "But who can say how images are created?"[50] By this time, Augustine would have assumed that most of his readers would have some understanding of memory in particular with regard to the skills of the liberal arts, notions of objects, true or false images, and fantasies.[51] Consequently, Augustine's discussions on images centers more on memory-image processes and the effect of images rather than on in-depth definition of what an image is or is not. The key references to images in Book X are presented sequentially from X.8.12 to X.30.41. How the formation of images (*imaginum*) happens is unclear to Augustine, but he knows for certain that they are a result of sense perceptions; as O'Daly puts it, incorporeal sense impression leads to incorporeal memory-image.[52] Images of every kind are stored and hidden in the deep recesses of *memoria*. Images are continuously being formed while our perceptive processes are taking place. However, they are not formed spontaneously but their formation is a willed one, i.e., a selective process.[53] These images can be recalled even if the things that left them behind are no longer present just like temporarily forgotten words.[54]

Augustine, at this point, interjects his discussion of *memoria* with an expression of wonder at the power of memory, its vastness, and its profoundness.[55] His awe of memory and images is conspicuous in X.8.14. He communicates that images can be of past events, yet they are futuristic in that they are foundational in thinking of future events and actions. They are also images of the present because the imagining of the future occurs in the present. The vast recesses of *memoria* holds all these images. Further, it can be said that some images are imprinted on the mind. Images of objects are presented to Augustine's mind when he thinks about, for example, the sky or the ocean.[56] He can "see" the sky or ocean when not directly looking at

---

50. *Conf.* X.8.13.

51. By the time *Confessiones* was written, Augustine had acquired a large group of followers and students who were well read and knew his works. His books were widely circulated throughout the Mediterranean and he had corresponded to others in Gaul, Spain, Italy, and the Middle East. So anxious were some to get new material from Augustine, that some of his friends stole a copy of Chapter 12 of *De Trinitate* before it was completed. McKenna, *Saint*, viii; O'Donnell, "St. Augustine."

52. *Conf.* X.8.12–13; O'Daly, *Augustine's Philosophy*, 132.

53. O'Daly, *Augustine's Philosophy*, 132.

54. *Conf.* X.8.12–13.

55. *Conf.* X.8.15.

56. *Conf.* X.8.15.

them because of the images in his mind. This concept is mentioned in *De Musica* with regard to numbers and objects and in *Confessiones*.[57] Sounds and names also have images imprinted by the physical senses that enable recognition of the sound or name.[58]

Confessiones X.9.16–10.17 discusses the difference between images and the skills acquired through the liberal arts, their realities that are in memory itself as opposed to their image. Augustine describes these as truth of realities that are already in memory, but so remote and pushed into the background, as if in most secret caverns.[59] Images that constitute innate memories in *Confessiones* emerge as a memory process whereby images and memories further Augustine's pursuit of God. God is not found among the images of physical objects stored in *memoria* yet these images allow him to realize this fact. God can be found in the discovery of truth in *memoria*. "Where I discovered the truth, there I found my God, truth itself.... [Y]ou remain in my consciousness, and there I find you when I recall you and delight in you."[60]

Images, which are present in an orderly or disorderly fashion, are discerned inwardly not through the senses. It is by "concentrating our attention we arrange them in order (*ordo*) as if ready to hand, stored in the very memory where previously they lay hidden, scattered, and neglected."[61] These images are brought together (*cogenda*) and gathered (*colligenda*) so that they are capable of being known.[62] They are preserved to be available to the thought that recalls them (*sed rerum sensarum imagines illic praesto sunt **cogitationi** reminiscenti eas*).[63] From a negative perspective, the power of images is such that images of past acts (e.g., lust and sexual habits) remain and are forcibly imposed on Augustine's mind even when Augustine has no control of his consciousness during his sleep.[64] He calls these "illusionary images" that cause "false dreams" a sickness of the soul.[65]

---

57. *Mus.* VI.4.6. In *Conf.* X.10.17 Augustine also calls images of objects "realities." "I hid in my memory not their images but the realities."

58. *Conf.* X.26.25.

59. *Conf.* X.10.17.

60. *Conf.* X.24.35.

61. *Conf.* X.11.18.

62. *Conf.* X.11.18.

63. *Conf.* X.8.13. *Cogitationi* translated as thought.

64. *Conf.* X.30.41.

65. *Conf.* X.30.41–42.

Imaginatio

Augustine's conception of *imaginatio* is inextricably bound up with his understandings of memory and the role that memory plays in storing, reproducing, and arranging the images generated in it on the basis of sense experience.[66] Augustine appears to have a threefold use of the word *imaginatio*.[67] The three interpretations are fantasy, simple mental image, or a mental image produced by an intentional creative act. *De Vera Religione* has the most explicit use of *imaginatio* perceived by senses and that create *phantasmata*.[68] According to Breyfogle, Augustine modified his distinction between *phantasiae* and *imaginatio* somewhere between *De Vera Religione* and *Confessiones*.[69] Augustine accords a strong degree of reality to images present in memory in *Confessiones*; this was not something he was willing to commit to in *De Vera Religione*. In *Confessiones*, *imaginatio* pertains to a second sense in the formulation of more general mental images; the mind can imagine the sun rising and the memory can contain "images" of the happy life or of truth.[70] Breyfogle asserts that, in this sense, *imaginatio* can have a positive connotation, mental images of the happy life.[71]

Augustine also uses *imaginatio* in terms of "vain fantasies" which cause images to deviate from their reality.[72] This is because imagination constitutes the locus of the mind's struggle to liberate itself from the ill effects of memory images that orient it toward the world rather than God.[73] Truth cannot come forward in memory until the things stored there are arranged by "close attention."[74] Imagination thus becomes central to the whole of Augustine's endeavors. To ascend to God by means of memory means memory must be rightly ordered by imagination in accordance with the truth.[75] Imagination poses a threat in these circumstances when it is disordered and distracted from its focus on the Divine. Indeed, when

---

66. Djuth, "Veiled," 79.

67. Breyfogle, "Memory," 214.

68. *V. Rel.* LXIV. *Phantasia* implies an image that is stored and intact in *memoria*. *Phantasma* refers to an invented image that is derived from *phantasia*.

69. Breyfogle, "Memory," 215.

70. Breyfogle, "Memory," 215.

71. Breyfogle, "Memory," 215.

72. *Conf.* XIII.6.7 (Rom 1:21).

73. Djuth, "Veiled," 82.

74. Breyfogle, "Memory," 217.

75. Breyfogle, "Memory," 217.

images in memory are disordered, memory is in a state of sin.[76] However, imagination does not need to pose a threat because it is also by means of the memory that Augustine has a "knowledge of his good conscience."[77]

Another function of *imaginatio* is its association with future expectation and time. This development is new in *Confessiones*.[78] Imagination, through its creative power, can provide images of what can be expected in the future since images in memory can create new images. Imagination impacts both the temporal now and the eternal future. In the present, it can remember the future through recollection of the incarnation and the Word of God.[79]

Phantasiae, Phantasmata

When Augustine considered the role of imagination, he identified two types of images: *phantasiae* and *phantasmata*. *Phantasiae* are images that reproduce the sensory *visio* of the soul; they are created from the interaction of the soul and body senses which create images built from reality.[80] According to Park, Augustine in *Confessiones* calls the sensory *visio* the *imago* of the soul which is stored and intact in memory.[81] *Phantasiae* are thus true images whereas *phantasmata* are invented images derived from *phantasiae*.[82] *Imaginatio* has the ability to form both *phantasiae* and *phantasmata*; they share a common feature in that they are both images, but they differ in the way they are formed.[83] It was important to Augustine that his readers saw the distinction between *phantasiae* and *phantasmata* since it could lead them to truth, the Truth, or deception.

The word *phantasiae* appears only twice in *Confessiones* but *phantasmata* occurs on significantly more occasions.[84] There must be some significance as to why Augustine used this specific word *phantasiae* only twice in *Confessiones*. Understanding the context in which *phantasiae* occurs in both

---

76. Breyfogle, "Memory," 217.
77. *Conf.* X.30.41.
78. Breyfogle, "Memory," 216.
79. *Conf.* VII.7.11; XIII.21.31.
80. Park, "Imagining," 805.
81. Park, "Imagining," 814.
82. *Mus.* VI.11.32.
83. Augustine tends to discuss the differences between the two as opposed to discussing their substantial identity. Park, "Imagining," 805.
84. Park, "Imagining," 805.

sections elucidates the significance. Both occurrences are prior to Book X. *Phantasiae* first appears in *Conf.* III.6.10 where he writes:

> But you, my love, for whom I faint that I may receive strength, you are not the bodies which we see, though they be up in heaven, nor even any object up there lying beyond our sight. For you have made these bodies, and you do not even hold them to be among the greatest of your creatures. How far removed you are from those fantasies (*phantasmatis*) of mine, fantasies (*phantasmatis*) of physical entities which have no existence! We have more reliable knowledge in our images (***phantasiae***) of bodies which really exist, and the bodies are more certain than the images. But you are no body.

There is a clear distinction between the use of *phantasmata* and *phantasiae*. Here, *phantasiae* are true and reliable images held in memory[85] that the soul uses to become aware of itself and the Divine. However, according to Park, *phantasiae* "can be beneficial for the human soul only if the soul is fully aware of the true Creator . . . by divine illumination."[86] *Phantasmata*, on the other hand, are fantasies created from *phantasiae* and are "physical entities which have no existence." In *Confessiones* Augustine thinks of *phantasmata* as false images of God that deceive the mind and distract from God.[87] Park proposes that *phantasmata*, although viewed negatively by Augustine, can still play a role in turning the soul's attention back to God.[88] Augustine experienced constant vacillations between *phantasiae* and *phantasmata*. He frequently lamented the fact that he succumbed to the distractions of *phantasmata*.[89] However, he also knew the soul could recognize the falsity of these *phantasmata* thus helping him as he strove to overcome their distraction and return to a focus on the Divine.

The second occurrence of *phantasiae* is in *Conf.* IX.10.25 and refers to acquiring an image through sense perception. Augustine writes:

> If to anyone the tumult of the flesh has fallen silent, if the images (***phantasiae***) of earth, water, and air are quiescent, if the heavens themselves are shut out and the very soul itself is making no sound and is surpassing itself by no longer thinking (*cogitando*) about itself, if all dreams and visions in the imagination

---

85. *Mus.* VI.11.32.
86. Park, "Imagining," 806.
87. *Conf.* III.6.10; 7.12; IV.4.9; 7.12; VII.1.1; 17.23.
88. Park, "Imagining," 806.
89. *Conf.* IV.7.12; VII.1.1; XIII.6.7.

(*imaginariae*) are excluded, if all language and every sign and everything transitory is silent.

Augustine here describes how *phantasiae* are derived from sense perception. Later on in the chapter, he asserts it is through divine illumination that the mind knows the truth. Again, Augustine attributes reality or truth to *phantasiae* but not to *phantasmata*. According to Djuth, *phantasiae* for Augustine was of considerable worth to his understanding of the soul's inner life, because *phantasiae* indicated the existence of a higher empirical function of the mind.[90]

The significance of these two mentions is that *phantasiae* are clearly true images whereas *phantasmata* are not. I would suggest that the more numerous mentions in *Confessiones* of *phantasmata* arise from Augustine's desire to make intelligible the serious nature of false images, their implications, and effect on the soul. Further, he wanted to provide instruction on how to resist the distractions of *phantasmata*.

Augustine ascribes three distinct aspects or types of *phantasmata*. The first is *phantasmata* that are false images derived from *phantasiae* that distract from the Divine. Djuth writes regarding *phantasmata*:

> [*Phantasia*] is found in memory, the latter [*phantasma*] is the product of mental labor, more often than not perverse in nature and burdening the mind with the weight of its own vacuity. As second order memory images voluntarily induced in the mind, *phantasmata* can impair the proper functioning of the intellect and hamper its efforts to find truth.[91]

Phantasmata replace actual, experiential knowledge; such fantasies are unruly, disorganized, and distracting, causing *memoria* in the mind to become limited in its capacity to seek God.[92] Djuth also comments that the multiplicity of *phantasmata* obscure the truth about both Augustine and God; they also inhibit reason from judging the merits of Augustine's opinion.[93] The ramification of *phantasmata* causing distraction from God is a struggle between succumbing to temptations and trying to live a life that is not distracted from truth, a struggle clearly evident in *Confessiones*. In *Mus.* VI.11.32, Augustine writes that those who live via *phantasmata* as the final truth live "the life of opinion" and emphasizes that to consider

---

90. Djuth, "Veiled," 80.
91. *Mus.* VI.11.32; Djuth, "Veiled," 80.
92. Hochschild, *Memory*, 127.
93. Djuth, "Veiled," 82; *V. Rel.* XXXIX.72–73.

phantasmata knowledge is the worst kind of error.[94] *De Vera Religione* also elaborates on this turmoil causing a hindrance to the truth.[95] The struggle that arose because of the unruly nature of *phantasmata* had a negative impact on Augustine who even became disillusioned with *phantasiae*. This was because *phantasiae* collaborated with *phantasmata* since both were formed from sense perceptions; but without *phantasiae*, *phantasmata* could not occur. As such, both engaged in a turbulent struggle between soul and body. Augustine warned that such imaginations should be shunned with great precaution.[96]

The second type of *phantasmata* is false images and fantasies such as those adopted by cults. Augustine attributed the use of *phantasmata* to designate false images and fantasies that were concocted together to explain a cult's religious belief. For example, Augustine used it with reference to the Manichaeans whose "fanciful notion of a race of darkness" was simply imagination distorting reality by organizing fantasies originating from true images.[97] Augustine considered Manichaean beliefs to be heretical since they were nothing but thoughtless *phantasmata* and/or rash and easy opinions concerning the nature of God and the soul.[98] The Manichaeans were not the only group who were at the receiving end of Augustine's view on heresy based on *phantasmata*. Other people or groups included the polemicists such as Petilian, Jovinian, Julian of Eclanum, and the Arians.[99] None of these individuals or cults could discern the true nature of God and the soul on account of their idolatrous lifestyle and their "rash and easy opinions" based on *phantasmata*. It was *phantasmata* that lead to idolatrous religion and idolatrous living; in fact, they are the root of idolatry.[100] When those enslaved by *phantasmata* worship new gods, they delude themselves. In this context, Augustine defines a new god as:

> An object that temporarily captivates the human imagination.[101]

---

94. "*Mus.* VI.11.32. "But some follow their phantasms [*phantasmata*] so headlong the only ground for all false opinion is to hold phantasias [*phantasiae*] or phantasms [*phantasmata*] for things known, known by the senses." Hochschild, *Memory*, 128.

95. *V. Rel.* III.3; X.18.

96. *Ep.* VII.2.4–5.

97. *Conf.* IV.4.9; Djuth, "Veiled," 85.

98. Djuth, "Veiled," 84–85.

99. *C. Litteras Petiliani* 3.27.32; *C. Iulianum* 1.2.4; *C. Iulianum Opus Imperfectum* 3.117. Taken from Djuth, "Veiled," 85.

100. Djuth, "Veiled," 86.

101. Djuth, "Veiled," 86.

Surely it is not an old god, or an eternal one, as the God of Christianity is. A new god, then, is either one or the other of two things: a stone or a *phantasma*.[102]

Such idolators are tricked by *phantasmata* into believing that God can be seen as a corporeal god. They do not "see" the true incorporeal God.

The third concept is where Augustine connects *phantasmata* with reference to God and Christ. Referring to his prior Manichaean beliefs, Augustine questions how the cross of Christ could save him if it were just a "phantom," as he had previously believed.[103] Here, Chadwick translates *phantasma* as phantom.[104] *Phantasmata* create false images of God and Christ and, like the Manichaeans, people do not see the true nature of Christ. In *Trin*. VIII.4.7, Augustine provides the example of those who read the Scriptures and imagine what Christ's physical body and face looked like; those images are really *phantasmata*. As Djuth says, the only ones who knew what his physical appearance was like were those who lived with and saw him in the first century.[105] She observes from this that Augustine differentiates two types of belief, faith and opinion, while at the same time distinguishing between belief and empirical knowledge; she writes:

> For it is one thing to believe that Christ is the Son of God born of the Virgin Mary and another to surmise that in his incarnate life he had a beard, long hair, and brown eyes. The former pertains to the stability of faith, the latter to the instability of opinion.[106]

Individuals who surrender to these *phantasmata* are incapable of recognizing truth; they are so imprisoned by them that they are incapable of lifting up their mind to a higher level of rational insight. Thus, the incarnation of Christ became a point in faith where the image of Christ could become distorted leading to distraction from God.

Temporal Dimension of *Memoria*

The temporality of memory in Book X implicitly underlies most of the discussion; however, there are only two distinct mentions of memory in relation to time. The first reference in X.8.13 is Augustine's comment that

---

102. *En. Ps.* 80.13–14; *V. Rel.* II.2; Djuth, "Veiled," 86.
103. *Conf.* V.9.16.
104. Chadwick, *Saint*, 58.
105. Djuth, "Veiled," 81.
106. Djuth, "Veiled," 81.

images stored within can be immediately present in that moment of time. Then in X.8.14 Augustine expands on this connecting of past, present, and future saying:

> Out of the same abundance in store, I combine these past events images of various things, whether experienced directly or believed on the basis of what I have experienced; and on this basis I reason about future actions and events and hopes, and again think of all these things in the present.

Manning, a neuropsychologist, makes the interesting point that Augustine likely was the first philosopher to put forward the idea that past and future were equivalent entities that exist as long as they were present in the consciousness.[107] Augustine does develop the concept of time and memory further than his predecessors; for him, memory exists in time past, present, and future at any given moment. The present recollects images from the past and those images are present in anticipation of the future. Time and memory are not just a linear, sequential occurrence. The second occurrence regarding the temporality of memory in Book X is at X.10.17 where Augustine mentions how learnt memories are stored in *memoria* and recalled in the present. The "realities" of images are also hidden in memory where they were formulated even before they were learnt. These memories are buried so deep in the recesses of *memoria* that they must be "dug out" (recollected) into the present, suggesting a "movement in time." Here too, the concept of a past, present, and future aspect of memory is evident. The significance of *memoria* and how time worked was such an intriguing enigma to Augustine that his mind was on fire to solve the intricate enigma of time.[108]

The *Beata Vita*

Augustine knew that his journey to find God and acquire the *beata vita* would not be straightforward; it would be convoluted, complicated, and enigmatic. His knowledge and understanding of God would grow but living the *beata vita* was not simply intellectual knowledge or understanding. It was a way of life infused with divine illumination. As Menn asserts, desiring the *beata vita* is not merely analogous to desiring God; the possession of the *beata vita* is only possible once one possesses God, and then desiring the *beata vita* becomes desiring God.[109] Much as he tried to live this life,

---

107. Manning et al., "St. Augustine's Reflections," 239.
108. *Conf.* XI.22.28.
109. Menn, "Desire," 88.

Augustine still fought the inner demons that made him succumb to worldly distractions resulting in digressions from the *beata vita*.

The focus in Book X now becomes how *memoria* is central to the search for God and the *beata vita*. Devoted to this discussion are twenty-four chapters, which is striking. This is twice as many chapters compared to his previous section on *memoria*. Augustine's dedication of twice as many chapters illustrates the importance and significance he attributes to the *beata vita*, and this sets the tone for establishing Augustine's priorities. The discussion of the *beata vita* in Book X has three distinct sections. They are:

1. Seeking the *beata vita* (X.20.29–27.38).
2. Struggles in acquiring the *beata vita* (X.28.39–39.64).
3. Transformation towards acquiring the *beata vita* (X.40.65–43.70).

All three are important components in the discussion of *memoria* and the *beata vita*.

Augustine recognized that he could not successfully acquire the *beata vita* on his own merits. The *beata vita* was not just some illusionary state of joy but rather a state of joy that came from knowing and possessing God and was to be found in *memoria*.[110] His incredible desire to know God was so that "my soul may live, for my body derives life from my soul and my soul derives life from you."[111] He asks God, "How then shall I seek the happy life? . . . [M]y question is whether the happy life is in the memory."[112] The remarkable conclusion is that there is knowledge and memory of the *beata vita* in *memoria*, otherwise it would be impossible to know, understand, or experience it.[113] The authentic *beata vita* is to set one's joy on God, to be grounded in him, and to acknowledge that the *beata vita* emanates from God and not any one person.[114] There is no possibility of true happiness and a life of *beatitude* apart from God. It is evident in X.21–22 that Augustine identifies God with both joy and the *beata vita*.[115]

Why is it that some desire the *beata vita* based on truth but not others? Augustine wondered if all people genuinely wanted to be happy since some did not appear to want to find their source of joy. He recognized that the pull between the flesh and the spirit is too much for many. These individuals

---

110. *Conf.* X.20.29, 22.32–23.33.
111. *Conf.* X.20.29.
112. *Conf.* X.20.29.
113. *Conf.* X.20.29–33.
114. *Conf.* X.22.32.
115. Bourke, *Augustine's*, 179.

acquiesce to the flesh. They are not happy because they cannot break from past experiences and memories (X.23.20–22); they cannot reconcile the past with the present and so, this leads to a divided self, one desiring the flesh, the other the happy life.[116] Augustine would argue that while the pull of the flesh was strong and often irresistible, people still preferred "to find joy in true rather than false things."[117]

In X.24.35–27.38, Augustine recapitulates that he is certain God is in *memoria*; however, he knew God was not contained in memory because God was not a physical object or image. Rather, God was the "Lord God of the mind." God "deigned" to dwell in his *memoria* and there is where Augustine finds God when he thinks of him.[118] Augustine is profoundly impacted by this reality and exclaims, "Late have I loved you, beauty so old and so new: late have I loved you."[119] This was important for Augustine to acknowledge before he embarked on the next section regarding the *beata vita*, the hurdles that made it difficult to attain the *beata vita*.

The next section in the search for the *beata vita*, X.28.39–39.64, elaborates on the struggle between flesh and spirit. Augustine struggled between the regrets of the wrongdoings of his past and the memories of good joys (X.28.39). X.28.39–39.64 is punctuated with Augustine's hope in God's mercy and grace as he attempts to resist the temptations of the flesh. It is interesting to note that Augustine experiences many struggles with temptations that arise from each of the five senses. First, he discusses the temptations of the flesh (touch) in X.30.41–42. Augustine was troubled by the "live images" of his past sexual acts. During the day Augustine was able to push them aside, however, at night he says, "In sleep they not only arouse pleasure, but they even elicited consent, and were very much like the actual act."[120] He appealed to God to heal the "sickness of my soul . . . by a more abundant outflow of your grace, to extinguish the lascivious impulses of my sleep."[121] Second, the next vice causing temptations were those that arose from the enjoyment of good food and drinking; the sense of taste presented in X.31.43–47. This enjoyment distressed Augustine as he tried to find the balance between the "necessity of food" and its "sweetness." He writes, "and often there is uncertainty whether the motive is necessary care of the body seeking sustenance or the deceptive desire for pleasure

---

116. Stock, *Augustine*, 225.
117. *Conf.* X.23.34.
118. *Conf.* X.25.36.
119. *Conf.* X.27.38.
120. *Conf.* X.30.41.
121. *Conf.* X.30.42.

demanding service."¹²² Augustine invoked God's help and received grace from God as he attempted to follow Luke 21:34, "your hearts shall not be weighed down in gluttony and drunkenness."¹²³ His struggle was constant, "every day against uncontrolled desire in eating and drinking,"¹²⁴ and yet throughout this Augustine confessed his weakness and magnified God's name. Third is the vice of smell and alluring perfumes in X.32.48. This did not bother Augustine much as he did not care whether the smell was present or not. Again, he reiterates the mercy of God as the one reliable promise and ground of confidence. Fourth, X.33.49–50 elaborates on the pleasures of the ears when listening to beautiful melodies and chanted sacred words. Augustine admitted this pleasure "had a more tenacious hold on me, and had subjugated me," but also God had set him free and liberated him from this hold.[125] There was an important moving and soothing of the soul that occurred when he heard sacred words being chanted. Even in these circumstances, Augustine erred on the side of severity by not listening to these chants until he finally conceded the utility of music in worship.[126] Augustine drew a line in the sand at this point. If the music moved him more than the subject of the song then he drew the line, that was when he pleaded to God for his mercy and healing. The fifth vice involves the eyes (X.24.51–35.54). The sight that came through the use of the eyes was noteworthy since it could be the contributor to temptation of the sensible and it could be the metaphysical sight for the soul. The wrestling was between the sights that pleased the body and those that pleased the soul. Arts and sensible things pleased the body but they could form images that "go far beyond necessary and moderate requirements and pious symbols. . . . [T]hey [men] abandon God by whom they were made, destroying what they were created to be."[127] Augustine warns of the danger of these bodily senses within the soul having a "vain inquisitiveness dignified with the title of knowledge and science."[128] This "appetite for knowing" arises from the "lust of the eyes" since the eyes play an important role in acquiring knowledge.[129] Sight is key as it applies to the other senses, e.g., see what you eat, see how that sounds, see what

---

122. *Conf.* X.31.44.
123. Augustine's translation of Luke 21:34 in *Conf.* X.31.45.
124. *Conf.* X.31.47.
125. *Conf.* X.33.49.
126. *Conf.* X.33.50.
127. *Conf.* X.34.53.
128. *Conf.* X.35.55.
129. *Conf.* X.35.55.

smells.¹³⁰ Augustine seems to echo Aristotle, who said that sight is the principle way in which knowledge is acquired (*Metaphysics* I.I). Augustine writes that from this observation, it is easier to distinguish the activities of the five senses in relation to pleasure verses their relation to curiosity. He writes:

> Pleasure pursues beautiful objects—what is agreeable to look at, to hear, to smell, to taste, to touch. But curiosity pursues the contraries of these delights with the motive of seeing what experiences are like, not with a wish to undergo discomfort, but out of a lust for experimenting and knowing.¹³¹

In X.35.56 Augustine exemplifies his struggles between desires of the sensible, temporal world, and the things that are good for his soul. Memories of images created by the senses plague him. However, it is with God's assistance that he manages to resist temptations; "In this immense jungle full of traps and dangers, see how many I have cut out and expelled from my heart, as you have granted me to do."¹³² At the same time, Augustine is not so arrogant as to think that he has expelled all temptations, and his acquiescence to them, merely because God has enabled him to do so. "How often we slip, who can count? . . . [M]y life is full of such lapses."¹³³ Yet again, Augustine declares that his one hope in managing this tumultuous struggle is God's great mercy.¹³⁴

Deep within Augustine is still the desire to seek praise and be loved by others because of the joy derived from such power.¹³⁵ He likes praise (based on vanity), even telling God that he cannot pretend that he does not like it! This is a temptation that has not ceased to trouble Augustine, and he suspects it will continue to trouble him his whole life. He writes, "it is a wretched life, and vanity is repulsive. This is the main cause why I fail to love and fear you in purity" (X.36.59). So strong is this predilection that Augustine writes four chapters on his battle with resisting this temptation of self-aggrandizement and growth in vanity (X.36.59-39.64). Augustine reaches the conclusion that being admired can actually be a good thing if accompanied by a good life and actions. Further, he believes he has managed to succeed in "restraining his mind from carnal pleasures and from

---

130. *Conf.* X.35.54.
131. *Conf.* X.35.55.
132. *Conf.* X.35.56.
133. *Conf.* X.35.57.
134. *Conf.* X.35.57-36.58.
135. *Conf.* X.36.59-39.64.

curious quests for superfluous knowledge."¹³⁶ He concludes in X.38.63 by asking God for his mercy "until my defect is repaired, and I am perfectly restored to that peace which is unknown to the arrogant observer."

The third main section regarding the *beata vita*, X.40.65–43.70, concerns the transformation or restoration required towards acquiring the *beata vita*. The role of *memoria* in this section is brought out as Augustine discusses the movement of his soul as he listens to, and learns from, God, whom he declares as the "abiding light."¹³⁷ Augustine struggled with the back and forth of temptation and obedience to God; all he could do was confess and pray to the incarnate Christ as the only mediator who could reconcile him to God as truth.¹³⁸ God, through the true Mediator, showed to humanity his mercy. In turn, Christ showed Augustine that he could be reconciled to the truth and be healed from his "sins and the pile of misery."¹³⁹ Through Christ Augustine was able to look steadily on the truth and strive towards fulfillment of the *beata vita*. He experienced momentary flashes of the *beata vita*, but in the end Augustine never really achieved complete fulfillment of the *beata vita* in temporality.¹⁴⁰ The desire for spiritual happiness had, in the present, a capacity for a past memory of the *beata vita*, and a future expectation. Stock writes that this desire is both a rediscovery of something forgotten before incorporation and of something to come afterwards.¹⁴¹ Gilson writes, memory of the happy life is not memory of past but present, in which God and the soul stand in a positive relation to one another along the vertical axis of experience.¹⁴² Hochschild asserts that memory is the locus of union and communication between the body and soul.¹⁴³ True happiness and the *beata vita* are equated solely with God who alone is unchangeable and eternal.¹⁴⁴

---

136. *Conf.* X.37.60.
137. *Conf.* X.40.65.
138. Menn, "Desire," 107.
139. *Conf.* X.42.67–43.70.
140. *Conf.* X.42.67–43.70.
141. Stock, *Augustine*, 225.
142. Gilson, *Christian*, 82.
143. Hochschild, *Memory*, 229–30.
144. Mourant, *Saint*, 42.

Memoria in Augustine's Writings Post *Confessiones*

De Trinitate and *De Genesi ad Litteram* are two key works of Augustine that have additional impactful contributions to his theology of *memoria*.

De Trinitate

Augustine started writing *De Trinitate* c. 400 AD and finished c. 416 AD.[145] The focus of *De Trinitate* is, of course, the Trinity; it was written to strengthen the faith of his fellow Christians.[146] The discussion on *memoria* is found in Books X–XIV, although the greatest focus is found in Book XI. In *De Trinitate* the fundamental insight is that memory is irreducibly trinitarian.[147]

Two authors, Hochschild and Grove, have written eloquent, thoughtful, and insightful books that include discussions of *De Trinitate*, Augustinian memory, and the Trinity.[148] Interestingly, Grove sees Augustine's argument regarding the Trinity as structural whereby the structure of *De Trinitate* reveals itself as an intellectual product of Augustine's work of memory.[149] He, however, argues that the structure and function of the Trinity is effectively lost when relegated to Augustine's inner self.[150] The inner triad of memory, understanding, and will in the mind fail because the self and mind are radically different to the Trinity.[151] According to Grove, the work of memory in the whole Christ bridges this failure of the inner self; he writes that it is Christ the Mediator, who

> provides the link between the failed interior triad of the human person and the remembering-understanding-loving God that renews the broken and tarnished image of God. Thus, the work of memory shows how the body of Christ is not secondary to

---

145. This is debated. Most scholars generally agree that *De Trinitate* was started in 400 AD and finished in 416 AD. McKenna, *Saint*, vii.

146. McKenna, *Saint*, ix.

147. Tell, "Beyond," 236.

148. Hochschild, *Memory*; Grove, *Augustine*.

149. Grove, *Augustine*, 199.

150. Grove, *Augustine*, 198–99. Grove's discussion on the "structure and function" of the Trinity is reminiscent of an architectonic analysis. Although he does not describe his discussion in this manner, he definitely brings out elements underlying an architectonic structure.

151. Grove, *Augustine*, 198.

Augustine's Trinitarian theology but the necessary precondition for it.¹⁵²

Hochschild recognizes the same Christology in Augustine; however, her work does not have a negative connotation to Augustine's interiority in the same way that Grove's does. She summarizes the role of *memoria* in *De Trinitate* as follows:

> Accordingly, memory is not simply a key in the argument about the unity of man's nature, but instead becomes a necessary element for a spiritual theodicy of participation in the body of Christ, and therefore in the life of the triune God.... According to the manner in which humanity is taken up into the life of the Trinity through Christ.¹⁵³

Both authors concur that within the work of memory, the incarnate Christ is a prerequisite to life in the Trinity, although they reach their conclusions via oppositional interpretations.

Trinitarian Motifs

Augustine in *De Trinitate* clearly documents how memory for him is irreducibly trinitarian. Augustine's fondness of, indeed propensity for, creating a tripartite composition or trinitarian motif to his descriptions of different concepts including *memoria* is exemplified in *De Trinitate*. For example:

- *velle* (willing), *meminisse* (remembering), *intelligere* (understanding)¹⁵⁴
- *memoria* (memory), *intellegentia* (intelligence), and *voluntas* (will)¹⁵⁵
- *memoria* (memory), *intellegentia* (understanding), and *amor* (love)¹⁵⁶
- *ingenium* (ability), *doctrina* (knowledge), *usus* (use)¹⁵⁷

---

152. Grove, *Augustine*, 211–12.
153. Hochschild, *Memory*, 195.
154. *Trin.* X.10.13; Ayres, *Augustine*, 303.
155. *Trin.* X.11.17. This triad finds its origin in Cicero. Ayres, *Augustine*, 304.
156. Augustine uses a variety of words for love, e.g., *caritas, cupiditas, dilectio, appetites*, but abandons them for *amor* and then *voluntas* in *De Trinitate*. Hill suggests that Augustine eventually settles on *voluntas* in order to emphasize the activeness of *amor*. Tell, "Beyond," 239; Hill, "Forward," 267.
157. *Trin.* X.11.17; Hochschild, *Memory*, 199–200.

In the first triad, the highest activity of the mind (i.e., intelligence) consists of the three distinct activities listed.[158] The second and third triads pertain to memory and both are of the same substance (i.e., consubstantial).[159] The second triad refers specifically to man, to his memory of himself, his understanding of himself, and to the will by which he loves himself.[160] It pertains to the three things the mind is certain of: *memoria*, *intellegentia*, and *voluntas*; all are co-equal and inseparable in the mind.[161] The third triad is an earlier version of the second triad adopted by Augustine. Here, this triad refers to man's memory of God, to his understanding of God and his love of God.[162] *Amor* is the active member of the triad whose function is to join and hold the together the other two members.[163] The fourth triad is mutually related to the previous two triads and concerns three aspects of learning; *ingenium* and *doctrina* are the province of all three but *usus* is in a special manner associated with *voluntas* whereby to use is to put something at the will's disposal.[164] According to Hochschild, the final two chapters of *Trin.* X affirm Augustine's preference for the triadic structure of *memoria*, *intellegentia*, and *voluntas*.[165] Augustine writes of this triadic structure:

> These three then, memory, understanding, and will, are not three lives but one life, not three minds but one mind. It follows of course that they are not three substances but one substance[;] . . . these three are one in that they are one life, one mind, one being, . . . but they are three in that they have reference to each other. And if they were not equal . . . they would not of course contain each other.[166]

This trinitarian description of this triad of *memoria*, *intellegentia*, and *voluntas* is reminiscent of the Trinity of God the Father, God the Son, and God the Holy Spirit. Matthews explains that this triad, according to Augustine, is the mind as remembering something, understanding something, and willing something.[167] Each of these are distinct but they are one substance,

---

158. Ayres, *Augustine*, 303.
159. Mourant, *Saint*, 47.
160. Mourant, *Saint*, 47.
161. *Trin.* X.11.18; Ayres, *Augustine*, 304; Mourant, *Saint*, 47.
162. Mourant, *Saint*, 48.
163. Tell, "Beyond," 237.
164. Hochschild, *Memory*, 199–200.
165. Hochschild, *Memory*, 199.
166. *Trin.* X.4.18.
167. Matthews, *Augustine*, 53.

namely the mind. Milbank mentions that the schema of trinitarian motifs could also "fit" to the "scheme by which Augustine locates the Trinity in the Father's creative act, the Son's beginning of creation in his wisdom, and the Spirit's completion of creation by linking heaven and earth through intellectual ordering."[168]

Augustine declares, "there is the Trinity, my God—Father and Son and Holy Spirit, Creator of the entire creation" (XIII.5.6). Without doubt, creation is inextricably connected to the Trinity and trinitarian motifs. Augustine's propensity for tripartite motifs is suggestive of a Trinitarian theology. In *Confessiones*, Augustine's Trinitarian beliefs are often more implicit in the text.

Incarnation

The incarnation was the pivotal moment in history for Augustine.[169] Memory was crucial to remember the significance and meaning of the incarnation. In *De Trinitate*, Augustine elaborates further on the incarnation within the understanding of the Trinity and also the spiritual disciplines required to have union with the Divine. Hochschild puts it this way: "Memory reveals the possibility of the creature with union with the eternal. The incarnation as a pedagogical principle unifies the temporal and eternal and is not merely a means to surpass one in exclusion of the other."[170] Hochschild contends that the theological unity of the last books of *Confessiones* and *De Trinitate* "lies in the emergence of the central role of the incarnation, epistemologically, spiritually, and argumentatively." The incarnation is a principle of unification of the temporal and the eternal.[171] Put somewhat differently, Grove writes that to Augustine memory is configured to life and existence mediated by Christ; the work of remembering and forgetting ends in becoming Christ together (communal life).[172] To both, Christ the Mediator is the key to participation in the Trinity, and the incarnate Christ is the temporal manifestation of union of the temporal and eternal.

---

168. Milbank, "Confession," 26–27.
169. Elaborated further in chapter 8.
170. Hochschild, *Memory*, 191.
171. Hochschild, *Memory*, 191.
172. Grove, *Augustine*, 226.

Vestigium Memoriae

The opening sentences in *Trin*. XI.1.1. says, "Let us endeavour, therefore, to discover, if we can, any trace at all of the Trinity even in this outer man, not that he himself is also in the same way the image of God." These opening words reveal several facts. Of note is the Augustinian concept of the inner and outer man and their roles in understanding and participating in the discovery of trace memories within the inner man; this is part of the examination of self and soul (interiority). Further, the concept of a "trace" of the Trinity references the memory traces within *memoria* in Augustine's earlier writings. Finally, the connection between the inner and outer man and their roles in discovering a trace of the Trinity is clear. Hochschild comments:

> The exercise of looking for traces of a trinitarian image in acts of sense perception is required by the fact that these are "more familiar" resulting in Augustine defending the unity of the body of the person; if the body is also "called man," then the external reality must reflect the internal ordering principles of the soul.[173]

Augustine asserts that it is the highest part of man that receives the divine imprint directly, without any intervening "nature" or mediator; "for the image is only then an expression of God in the full sense, when no other nature lies between it and God."[174] The ensuing discussion is much like that of *Confessiones* and even earlier writings where the "sickness of the soul" and a life of good is a balancing act.

An interesting perspective on a trace memory of God comes from Lyotard who assumes that for Augustine God is in *memoria* as a memory-from-within but this memory can only be remembered rhetorically.[175] Such memory-from-within is a result of the "scar" that the divine presence leaves behind upon entry into the human mind. Lyotard writes, "A wound, an ecchymosis, a scar attests to the fact that a blow has been received, they are its mechanical effect."[176] Lyotard understands memory-from-within as a "scar" that results from an extra-symbolic memorial practice that he calls "memory via mechanics."[177] However, Lyotard in saying this reduces trace memory (scar) in *memoria* to a purely mechanical practice where even a confessional act of Augustine cannot reveal this trace of memory. Augustine, on the

---

173. *Trin*. XI.1.1; Hochschild, *Memory*, 202.
174. *Trin*. XI.5.8.
175. Tell, "Beyond," 248.
176. Quote taken from Tell, "Beyond," 248; Lyotard, *Confessions*, 6–7.
177. Tell, "Beyond," 248.

other hand, believes in divine illumination as revelatory in understanding memory and revealing the *memoria Dei* within and divine truth.[178] Divine illumination is not simply a mechanical process. There is the metaphysical dimension of the soul, the location of the *memoria Dei* within, and God's divine agency in revelation to Augustine of this trace of God within. Even early on in his tumultuous battle to conversion, Augustine knew that within him there remained a memory of God (*Conf.* VII.17.23).

Scientia and *Sapientia*[179]

In *Trin.* XIII, Augustine discusses *scientia* and *sapientia* and the differences between the two; yet despite these differences, he finds a link between them in memory.[180] Augustine states that the "focal point of the union of *scientia* and *sapientia* is 'that most important temporal event'—namely, the joining of God with humanity in time" (XIII.19.24).[181] For Augustine, faith in the incarnate Christ both unifies *scientia* and *sapientia* and gives access to *sapientia* by a participation of union.[182]

De Genesi ad Litteram Libri Duodecim

This book was started between the years 399–404 AD.[183] Chapter XII discusses images, how they operate in realizing the spiritual vision in the form of a memory, and the role that the bodily senses play in conveying images to *memoria* where images of those bodies are formed and stored.[184] There are three kinds of vision: bodily, spiritual, and intellectual. The spiritual sense of *visio* (i.e., eyes) of the mind is the mediator between the mind and the body.[185] Corporeal and spiritual *visio* (eye and sight) are two different aspects of the same act of looking; after the object has disappeared and

---

178. From *Sol.* I.8.15. Throughout his later writings, Augustine defines divine illumination as God's revelation of truth, Truth, and memory

179. *Scientia* and *Sapientia* are discussed in chapter 5.

180. *Scientia* is knowledge of temporal matters while *sapientia* is knowledge of the eternal.

181. Hochschild, *Memory*, 212–13.

182. Hochschild, *Memory*, 213.

183. There is debate amongst scholars as to the original start date. It was completed in 416 with a pause in 410 where the first nine books were revised returning in 412 to complete the volume. Hill, *On Genesis*, 164n45.

184. *Gn. Litt.* XII.4.9; XII.11.22; XII.24.51; Knotts, *On Creation*, 56.

185. *Gn. Litt.* XII.24.51.

its vestigial memory remains, spiritual *visio* comes from that memory.[186] Spiritual *visio* is the soul's vision of images that have been impressed on it from the corporeal senses.[187] Thus, the body cooperates with the soul in providing both earthly sight and spiritual insight. Augustine writes that true knowledge and understanding attained by intellectual vision are only made possible through divine illumination (XII.31.59). The human intellect, without the divine light, is not able to "see" or understand any truth; the active mind is the "illumined" mind.

In XII.12.25–15.31, Augustine launches into the details of the function and distinct aspects of *memoria*. Bodily vision is distinguished from a spiritual vision.[188] The soul faces temptations as it navigates bodily images and spiritual attention to the Divine. Augustine links together sense perception, imagination, and memory, where perception involves the serial formation of mental images that are retained in the memory directly as the perception takes place.[189] Imagination is described as either the reproductive recollection of retained images or their creative manipulation.[190]

Retractationes

Retractiones was finished in 427 AD towards the end of Augustine's life. It was a systematic review of his written works with the purpose of correcting any errors or comments that might offend him or others.[191] Of interest is the fact that *Confessiones* and *Retractiones* are the two books of all his writings that are a recollection of his memory; recollection and reminiscences in terms of what he had experienced in his life, his theological expositions, and his written works. Noteworthy too, is the fact that both books reviewed and recollected, among other things, wrongdoings or errors in his life or his writings.[192] *Retractiones* actually has very little to say about *Confessiones*; Augustine wrote that he praised "the just and living God for my evil and good acts." He is pleased with the book as he knows that it has "given

---

186. *Gn. Litt.* XII.11.22; XII.24.51; Knotts, *On Creation*, 56.
187. *Gn. Litt.* XII.9.20.
188. *Gn. Litt.* XII.12.25.
189. *Gn. Litt.* XI.16.33; II.11.22; cf. *Mus.* VI.8.21; Daly, *Platonism*, 33.
190. O'Daly, *Platonism*, 33.
191. Augustine, *Retractions*, xiii.
192. By wrongdoings and errors, I mean Augustine's failures in succumbing to worldly desires in his life or unintentional errors in his writings that upon review Augustine believed to be wrong, a "failure" to transmit verbally in a clear manner to his audience; consequently, what he wrote could be misconstrued.

pleasure to many of my brethren."[193] There is not much mention of *memoria* in *Retractationes*. In his comments regarding *De Quantitate Animae*, he clarifies that he did not mean that the soul brought all the arts it had learnt from a previous life; learning is just remembering and recalling. The soul is made and ordered such that it learns when "it moves toward those things to which it is joined or toward itself."[194] It can only speak about arts with regard to the senses of the body.

Concluding Remarks

There is no doubt that Augustine's theology of *memoria* is ingenious and profound, yet it is complex, at times convoluted and paradoxical. The manner in which Augustine presents *memoria* is well thought out, deliberate, and is telling of his mode of hermeneutics, exposition, and pedagogy. The architectonic structure of memory is revelatory because it involves a far more in-depth examination than simply structure and function; it discloses the inner workings of Augustine's mind and the interplay between different facets and layers of memory. Significantly, it reveals the depths of Augustine's desire for knowledge and the profound and awe-inspiring complexities of memory. It shows a brilliant mind at work in sometimes torturous moments of struggle between his earthly desires and his desire for the *beata vita*.

This chapter has revealed several interesting observations. The architectonic structure of *memoria* observed in his early writings continues into his later works and sets the tone for the interrogation of *memoria* in *Conf*. X. The same symphonic forms of *memoria* and their fundamental affordances exist in both earlier and later writings and occur in the same sequence (*ordo*). This architectonic motif in *Conf*. X, built upon the symphonic forms of memory revealed in his earlier works, is to the best of my knowledge a novel perspective of Augustine's theology of *memoria*.

---

193. *Retr.* 32.1.
194. *Retr.* 7.2.

5

Memoria Through the Lens of Augustinian *Scientia* and *Sapientia*

"But I had already been taught by you, my God, through wonderful and hidden ways. . . . [N]one other than you is teacher of the truth, wherever and from whatever source it is manifest."[1]

AUGUSTINE SAW IN GOD's creative act a beautiful human body that was a manifestation of God's goodness; it was a purposefully created "physical structure" designed for the service of a rational soul.[2] God created the human body and soul together to make a living being: "he alone, coupling and connecting in some wonderful fashion the spiritual and corporeal natures, the one to command, the other to obey, makes a living being."[3] God gave the soul, a mind "in which reason and understanding lie."[4] It was abundantly clear to Augustine that God created, *ex nihilo*, a living being where the physical nature of the human body was interrelated to the metaphysical dimension, and they were dependent on each other.

---

1. *Conf.* V.6.10. Augustine makes this statement while discussing the Manichaean influence on his beliefs. He clarifies that truth is truth whatever way God shows him truth because it comes from God, and this includes truth that comes from the natural world.

2. *Civ. Dei.* 22.24; Retief and Cilliers, "St. Augustine," 96.

3. *Civ. Dei.* 22.24. Augustine has multiple references regarding the body and soul. Cf. *Quant. An.* 33.70; *Orig. An.* 2.4; *Imm. An.* 16.25; *Serm.* 243.7, to mention a few.

4. *Civ. Dei.* 22.24; Retief and Cilliers, "St. Augustine," 96.

Consequently, the metaphysical dimension and operation of *memoria* were intricately related to the physical structure and functioning of memory. Memory was the "connector" or "intermediary" between the physical and metaphysical, a fact that Augustine recognized as he delved deeper into every aspect of his knowledge and that of the temporal word to interrogate *memoria*.

Augustine was a man whose knowledge spanned many disciplines. This chapter explores how Augustine used his scientific and medical knowledge as he probed the magnitude and multiplicity of memory in support of his developing theology, and understanding, of *memoria*. He did so unapologetically, and in doing so, he was able to connect the physical with the metaphysical, the body with the soul, and *memoria* with the Divine.[5] What emerges is the picture of a man well-versed in many "-ologies" but who had one two-part goal in mind, to understand God's creation, and his own journey to know and understand the Creator God.

Augustine's Medical and Scientific Background

Augustine was an educated, highly intellectual man who was familiar with, and understood, the natural sciences, medicine, and the sciences of mathematics and logic.[6] What is astounding and impressive about Augustine is how much further advanced he was compared to his contemporaries and the modern science of his times, including his understanding of memory and the processes behind its operation. His sophisticated and technical knowledge of medicine and science is observed in the terminology he used.[7] His publications, both his writings and his sermons, included many references to medical concepts and scientific facts as he sought to strengthen

---

5. Augustine's use of medicine and science often go unnoticed in his writings on memory.

6. Mathematics is defined as the science of structure, order, and relation that has evolved from elemental practices of counting, measuring, and describing the shapes of objects. It deals with logical reasoning and quantitative calculation. Logic is the science and art of reasoning well. Logic as a science seeks to discover rules of reasoning; logic as an art seeks to apply those rules to rational discourse. Mathematics, for example, is a process of deductive logic. Fraser et al., "Mathematics"; *Logic Blog*, "Logic."

7. The sophistication of Augustine's language and knowledge of memory is recognized considering that in a historical context it was Hermann Ebbinghaus, a German psychologist, who in 1879 pioneered the experimental study of memory to examine acquisition (learning), forgetting of memory, and memory and time. This was fourteen centuries after Augustine. In 1970s and 1980s, Tulving developed a taxonomical model for memory virtually similar to Augustine's model (fifteen centuries after Augustine). Tulving, "Multiple," 67–80; *Encyclopedia Britannica*, "Hermann Ebbinghaus."

his theological arguments.[8] Augustine's use of mathematics is best seen in *De Musica*, where he uses numbers and rhythm to explain memory, and where he uses logical methodology to seek the rules behind the workings of memory. He also used mathematics and logic to explain the indispensable role of memory in the awareness of sensation.[9]

The medical sciences, natural history, physical sciences, astronomy, and physics would not have been included in the classical arts that Augustine learnt in the classroom as part of his formal academic education.[10] His knowledge of these contemporary medical theories and scientific practices was autodidactic, most likely through the reading of various medical books, public lectures, patient observation, and discussion with learned colleagues in those fields.[11] Augustine writes about teaching himself "the dimensions of figures and music and numbers.... My agile mind found no difficulty with these subjects, and without assistance from a human teacher I could elucidate extremely complicated books."[12]

Augustine would have had knowledge of the works of famous philosophers and physicians like Hippocrates, Aretaeus, Rufus, Soranus, and Galen, but these were written in Greek, so he was more likely to have read the Latin works of Vindicianus,[13] a famous physician of the fourth century and personally known to, and greatly admired by, Augustine.[14] He considered Gennadius a good physician, a believer, and his friend.[15] In a letter to the bishop of Carthage (*Ep.* 41.2), Augustine warmly recommended the physician Hilarinus, *archiater* (head city physician) and *principalis* (head of

---

8. Retief and Cilliers, "St. Augustine," 94.
9. O'Daly, *Augustine's Philosophy*, 88.
10. Reid, "First," 123.
11. Reid, "First," 122.
12. *Conf.* IV.16.31.

13. Augustine in *Ep.* 138.1.3 describes Vindicianus as the eminent figure in the medical profession of day. Scholars frequently conclude that he obtained most of his medical knowledge directly from Vindicianus. According to Reid, there is no firm evidence that Augustine read the medical treatises of any of his contemporary North African medical writers, even those of Vindicianus. Reid states that Courcelle is one example of a scholar who presumes that Augustine first heard about Hippocrates from Vindicianus, but this assertion seems extremely unlikely. Hippocrates' name and reputation would have been part of common culture, at least among the educated classes, and Augustine himself states that Hippocrates was mentioned in works of Cicero (Augustine's citation of Cicero's *De fato* in which Hippocrates is mentioned in *Civ. Dei* 5.2). Vindicianus does have a distinguished place in Augustine's work, appearing on three occasions, two of which are in *Confessiones*. Reid, "First," 123–24.

14. Retief and Cilliers, "St. Augustine," 95.
15. Retief and Cilliers, "St. Augustine," 97.

the city senate).¹⁶ According to Retief and Cilliers, Augustine maintained a practical bond between his understanding of medicine and his theological convictions and teaching.¹⁷ Further, Keenan writes, "Augustine . . . turns to medical art in defending certain doctrines such as the existence of the soul, the resurrection of the body, and design in nature."¹⁸ Augustine, was not opposed to using every available means as he examined *memoria* in his exhaustive search for God and the *beata vita*.

Augustine notes that anatomy is an essential aspect of medical training; he further adds that while knowledge of anatomy is known to few men, any man might acquire it if he wished, a statement that seems to imply the accessibility of anatomical demonstrations or lectures.¹⁹ One may speculate that the importance of anatomy to Augustine is surmised from his characterization of the ontological formation of the human body. According to Djuth, Augustine characterized this ontology in three ways: a unity of parts that exist in space, a temporal being that has a beginning and an end, and a body that is lower and less dignified than the soul which is the higher in their hierarchy of being.²⁰ Since the body is a living body, its unity consists in the participation of matter; harmony exists between the body that is visible matter and the soul as the unseen principle of life animating the matter of the body.²¹ Augustine writes, "It [the soul] pervades the whole body which it animates, not by a local distribution of parts, but by a certain vital influence."²² In his ontological characterization of the human body, Augustine saw the connection between body, soul, and medical science. *Orig. An.* is a work dedicated to Jerome in which Augustine is pertinacious in making sure that his views on the nature of the soul are both doctrinally and "scientifically" sound.²³ It is interesting that in *Enchiridion*, Augustine places knowledge of medicine and the body on a higher plane than knowledge of other aspects of the physical world.²⁴ Augustine argues that no Christian

---

16. Retief and Cilliers, "St. Augustine," 96.
17. Retief and Cilliers, "St. Augustine," 99.
18. Keenan, "Augustine," 169.
19. *An. et Or.* 4.6.7. "Because they have learnt the art of anatomy or experiment, which are both comprised in the physician's education, which few obtain, while others have refused to acquire the information, although they might, of course, if they had liked." Reid, "First," 150.
20. Djuth, "Body," 68.
21. *Quant. An.* 33.70; Djuth, "Body," 68.
22. *Orig. An.* 2.4; *Imm. An.* 16.25.
23. Reid, "First," 155.
24. *Ench.* 9.16; Reid, "First," 156.

should be ashamed of being ignorant of the natural world, such as astronomy or geography, since even philosophers are limited in their knowledge.[25] He writes regarding convulsions that the more important knowledge is that associated with a person and not convulsions associated with earthquakes; the concern should be for convulsions that affect a person's health, thereby forcing a consultation of physicians.[26]

Medical sciences were so important to Augustine that he elevated them to the same level as the arts of navigation and agriculture because all three arts provided services through which God worked.[27] All these arts were included in the larger category of arts, which comprised crafts, such as pottery and housebuilding, and physical pursuits, such as dancing, running, and wrestling.[28] Augustine reasons that what binds these disparate activities together is their relationship with time, "In all these arts knowledge gained from past experiences causes future ones to be inferred. None of these craftsman moves a muscle at his work except to link his experience of the past with his plans for the future."[29]

It is evident from the Augustinian corpus that Augustine views medicine as an art that is valuable in understanding the inner workings of the human body and soul. He justifies his use of the medical sciences by including them in the list of secular activities that he approves of.[30] Knowledge obtained from medical sciences, he believes, had to be knowledge that was helpful in transcending from the temporal to the eternal, and understanding the physical and metaphysical dimensions of that process. He mentions that in anatomy and scientific experimentation, there is the danger of moving beyond the accepted bounds of human knowledge.[31] This is illustrated in one of his sermons where he discusses the beauty of the human body, noting how perfectly its parts function and what harmony there is in its proportions.[32] Reid writes, "near the end of the sermon he adds that the body's beauty excites not just lust, but research by the studious or curious."[33] This statement is notable for two reasons. First, the implication that research driven by curiosity can be exhilaratingly lascivious just like lustfulness

---

25. Reid, "First," 156.
26. Reid, "First," 156.
27. *Doc. Chr.* 2.30.47; Reid, "First," 160.
28. Reid, "First," 160.
29. *Doc. Chr.* 2.30.47.
30. Reid, "First," 160.
31. Reid, "First," 161.
32. *Serm.* 243.7; Reid, "First," 161.
33. Reid, "First," 161.

generated by a beautiful body. Second, Augustine believed *curiositas* was dangerous as it could connote an inappropriate desire for knowledge.[34] Knowledge obtained to just fulfill a curiosity or just to gain knowledge was to Augustine wrong. Science based on reliable evidence when used wisely leading to sapiential knowledge is not contrary to the Scriptures and eternal matters.[35]

Augustine would have been tricked into thinking the soul was corporeal in nature had he not been "well versed" in his knowledge of the nature of the body, the form that is in the body, place, time, and motion (*Quant. An.* 31.63).[36] Twenty years on, Vincentius Victor would not accept Augustine's claim to the incorporeality of the soul and saw this as a sign of Augustine's own ignorance about the physical nature of the human body.[37] Augustine's indignant response regarding his supposed lack of education on such matters was to state, "For my own part, indeed, if I wished to display how far it was in my power to treat scientifically and intelligently the entire field of man's nature, I should have to fill many volumes."[38] Augustine was not wrong regarding his knowledge.

Augustine's Vocabulary

Augustine's specific medical and scientific vocabulary was extensive, highly sophisticated, and extremely technical. This was confirmed by Jean-Paul Rassinier, a French physician, who in 1991 undertook a quantitative and qualitative analysis of the medical vocabulary used by Augustine.[39] His database search of the Augustinian corpus identified over a hundred medical terms, with more than fourteen thousand textual occurrences; an extensive use of medical vocabulary by Augustine.[40] Rassinier, Reid, and O'Donnell all comment that there are many times when his use of medical terms was

---

34. *Mor. Eccl.* 1.21.38. Augustine warns against inquisitiveness which leads to pride. *Conf.* X.35.54–57: *curiositas* is characterized as a disease (*morbus cupiditatis*). Reid, "First," 161.

35. *Gn. Litt.* I.21.41.

36. Reid, "First," 164.

37. Reid, "First," 164.

38. *An. et Or.* 4.3.2.

39. Rassinier provides a quantitative indication to the extent of Augustine's use of medical terms. Reid's dissertation has an excellent and in-depth research into Augustine's use of medical terminology. Rassinier, "Vocabulaire," 379–35; Reid, "First," 166.

40. Rassinier, "Vocabulaire," 379–95; Reid, "First," 166n9.

metaphorical.[41] O'Donnell suggests that this use of medical metaphor in some of Augustine's writings might be due to his personal experience with physical suffering.[42]

Augustine used and correlated medical terminology, descriptions of diseases, and medicinal treatments in his sermons and in his written works in order to help his audience understand spiritual doctrines. His metaphorical use of highly sophisticated scientific/medical language established the connection and interrelatedness between the physical (science, medicine) and the spiritual (metaphysical). For example, Wright argues that Augustine uses the technical medical term *phrenitis* (acute delirium with acute fever) as a reiterative rhetorical strategy to strengthen and expand the conceptual system implied by the conventional metaphor "sin in sickness of the soul."[43] In late antiquity, *phrenitis* was understood to affect the brain and its cognitive functions.[44] To the ancient physicians, *phrenitis* was a dangerous illness because it was thought to be caused by inflammation in the part of the body where the ruling part of the soul was thought to be located, the brain; it was thus considered a condition of the brain.[45] Augustine would often invoke *phrenitis* as the cause of rejecting Christ's saving grace.[46] This metaphorical use of *phrenitis* also illustrates the connection between the physical body and the metaphysical soul.[47]

Reid offers three conclusions as to Augustine's use of highly technical and even, at times, obscure medical terminology.[48] First, it demonstrates that Augustine took great interest in medical issues, to the extent of picking up and retaining highly technical vocabulary which he then appropriated for his own purposes. Second, it affirms that there existed sufficient opportunities in the textual or oral culture for becoming familiar with this

---

41. For more on the metaphors used by Augustine, see Marciniak, "Medical," 373; Reid, "First," 250; O'Donnell, *Augustine*, I:xli–li; Rassinier, "Vocabulaire," 379–95.

42. O'Donnell, *Augustine*, I:xli–li.

43. Wright, "Preaching," 526.

44. Ahonen, *Mental*, 24n41.

45. It should be noted that some physicians thought the region was the heart and not the brain. McDonald, "Concepts," 78–79; Thumiger, *History*, 46–47; Wright, "Preaching," 527.

46. Augustine used *phrenitis* over forty times in his writings. Wright, "Preaching," 527, 538.

47. This connection is such that healing from *phrenitis* or sickness of the soul had to be a healing of *both* body *and* soul and not just one or the other; it was a caring of both body and soul, the totality of a human person. See Wright, "Preaching," 552; Marx-Wolf, "Good," 80.

48. Reid, "First," 168–69.

technical language. Third, it suggests that he has an audience that he could generally expect to understand his medical terms and allusions. Reid goes on to write that a closer examination of Augustine's employment of this vocabulary reveals that when he does use such technical medical language, in most cases it is to provide his audience, whether they be the congregation listening to his sermons or the readers of his treatises, with some sort of direct or indirect explanatory comment.[49] Keenan proposes that Augustine's purpose in incorporating material of a biological, medical, and scientific nature in his works is didactic.[50]

Augustine's Methodology

In *De Genesi ad Litteram*, Augustine describes a two-step methodology for incorporating scientific knowledge into the process of understanding the temporal and the eternal.[51] His discussion is focused on the "shape and form of the sky"[52] described in Genesis rather than the descriptions given by the physical sciences.[53] The first step is to evaluate whether the observed scientific principle or claim has any validity. This must be done by using the methods of science, empirical observation, and theoretical reasoning. Augustine considers it insufficient to quote the Bible against a scientific theory without evidence, again supporting the use of scientific principles in deciphering and supporting the truth. He believed that if there was any uncertainty regarding the proposed scientific conclusion, then it could be considered false, "This [truth] . . . is true which has divine authority behind it, rather than that which is the guesswork of human weakness."[54] The second step in the validation of scientific truth is that said truth must stand with the truth of Scripture and not be inconsistent with it. In Augustine's eyes, two truths cannot contradict one another. The reality is that all truth comes from God, and scientific fact and Scripture are but two different manifestations of God's revelation of truth.

---

49. Reid, "First," 169.

50. *Doc. Chr.* 2.24; *Ep.* 55.13; *Serm.* 2.11.16; Keenan, "St. Augustine," 588.

51. Howell briefly writes about an Augustinian two-step methodology for incorporating science and Scripture. I have developed his comments regarding methodology. Howell, "How Augustine," 3–4.

52. *Gn. Litt.* II.9.20.

53. *Gn. Litt.* II.9.20–22; cf. Gen 1:6–8, 14.

54. *Gn. Litt.* II.9.21.

Memoria and Sense Perception

Augustine recognized that transmitted stimuli from the sense perception of external objects, which resulted in memory formation, caused changes within the human body. In this way, the operation of *memoria* was inextricably linked to sense perceptions. A multitude of memory-impressions stored in *memoria* as sense perceptions which had traveled from the five senses to the brain; the senses are the messengers of the body (*quinque notissimis nuntiis corporis*) which report to and are directed by the soul.[55] The senses provided knowledge for the soul which then uses the bodily senses as the corporeal instruments of perception.[56] Augustine writes, "it is still not the body that is the subject of sensation, but the soul through the body."[57] This view of Augustine's of the active role of the soul in sense perception was similar to that of Plotinus.[58] Miethe argues that both the images associated with particular sensations and the ideas relating to them are brought into being by the activity of the soul.[59] Augustine understood the importance of sense perception in this capacity. He wanted to have a satisfactory explanation of the means by which sense-organs received impressions, and where and how these were correlated and coordinated, and then received by the soul.[60]

It is not surprising that Augustine is fascinated by human physiology and anatomy in understanding how sense perception works.[61] From a physiological perspective, Augustine held to the theory of humors as espoused by Hippocrates and the Dogmatists.[62] He recalls in *De Quantitate Animae* what he learnt about the body from physicians who observed the effects that the humors have on the body.[63] From a medical perspective, Augustine conceived of the body in terms of the four elements and the corresponding

---

55. *Gn. Litt.* XII.24.51; *Util. Cred.* 1.1; *Lib. Arb.* II.3.8; *En. Ps.* 145.4.
56. *Ord.* II.2.6; *Sol.* II.3.3; Djuth, "Body," 76.
57. *Gn. Litt.* III.5.7.
58. Miethe, "Augustine's," 259.
59. Miethe, "Augustine's," 259; *Gn. Litt.* XII.16.33.
60. Augustine in *Gn. Litt.* XII.24.51 elaborates even further the active role of the soul in this process. O'Daly, *Augustine's Philosophy*, 80.
61. Augustine's clearest exposition on the mechanics of sense perception can be found in *De Genesi ad Litteram*. Vision is one of the most important senses: *Mor.* I.20.37; *Lib. Arb.* II.18.48. On the physiology of the brain: *Gn. Litt*, I.16.31; IV.34.54; XII.16.32; 17.23–19.25.
62. Reid, "First," 173.
63. Djuth, "Body," 71.

humors associated with them.[64] He was cognizant of the relationship posited between the four elements with their accompanying oppositional qualities of hot/cold and wet/dry and the corporeal humors.[65] The alliances were:

1. hot air with wet blood.
2. hot, dry fire with bile and cold.
3. dry earth with black bile.
4. cold, wet water with phlegm.

He connects these four elements to the five senses of the human body in *De Genesi ad Litteram* where he cites the pre-Socratic philosopher Anaxagoras' maxim that "all the elements are in everything" (*elementa omnia in omnibus esse*); he notes that fire, the highest of the elements in the cosmic sphere, and therefore the element closest to the Divine, penetrates everything to give the human body motion.[66]

Augustine used both physiology and anatomy to further define the transmission of sense perception from the five senses to form memories and their storage in the *memoria* of the soul. His physiological understanding of the nervous system showed him that the sensory nerves attached to, and originating from, the brain transmit stimuli to and from the brain.[67] O'Daly provides a nice explanation of this process as understood by Augustine,[68] a process described in *De Genesi ad Litteram*.[69] There are thin tubes like passages called *tenues fistulae* that lead from the central part of the brain to the outer surface of the body and the various senses, sight, smell, taste, touch, and sound. Augustine highlights the sense of touch; it spreads out to the whole body and is governed by the same part of the central brain. The sense of touch was directed by the brain through the *medulla cervicis et columnae* (marrow of the neck and spinal column) throughout the body via *tenuissimi quidem rivuli* (very fine streams). The sense of touch is thus activated

---

64. References to the four humors and/or the four qualities, and the need for an internal balance of the humors and qualities, appear on numerous occasions, right from early works, such as *De Quantitate Animae*, through to later works, e.g., *Contra Julianum* (421. AD). *Lib. Arb.* III.5.13; *Quant. An.* 1.2; Reid, "First," 174; Djuth, "Body," 71.

65. Reid, "First," 176.

66. *Gn. Litt.* III.4.6–7; 5.7; Reid, "First," 176.

67. O'Daly, *Augustine's Philosophy*, 80.

68. O'Daly, *Augustine's Philosophy*, 80–105. O'Daly's chapter 3 has an excellent discussion on sense perception.

69. *Gn. Litt.* VII.13.20; 18.24; XII.20.42.

returning stimuli to the brain.[70] According to Augustine, physicians were actually able to demonstrate this transmission of stimuli.[71]

From an anatomical perspective, Augustine is very clear that the physiological seat of memory is the central ventricle of the cerebrum,[72] and that memory images are formed from sense-impressions.[73] He is precise regarding the source and terminus of sensation, and what controls sensation, the front ventricle. The third ventricle behind the neck is the source of the motor nerves.[74] This is the ventricle from which all movement comes. Augustine believed that the three ventricles were connected but the central ventricle, associated with memory, was the link between the first and third ventricle. It confirmed memory was active "otherwise, since movement follows upon sensation, you may fail to link to your perception what has to be done, if you have forgotten what you have done on previous occasions."[75] Further, bodily movement could not be performed over intervals in time were it not for memory located in the middle ventricle. Therefore, physiologically, memory is directly linked with sensation and the initiation of bodily actions (voluntary movements—*spontaneous motus*).[76] However, Augustine also writes that sensation, memory, or movement could become non-functional if the ventricles were damaged or defective.[77] For example, a defect could occur in an individual's sense-organ, e.g., a defective eye resulting in blindness.[78] This "defect" could also be used to explain Alzheimer Disease where past experiences and memories are forgotten due to defects in the brain caused by abnormal build-up of proteins in and around brain cells. With regard to the cerebral ventricle of the brain, it should be noted that Augustine is careful to stress that the cerebral ventricle is the servant (*ministerium*) of memory rather than memory itself.[79]

---

70. *Gn. Litt.* VII.13.20; Teske, *To Know*, 208–9.
71. O'Daly, *Augustine's Philosophy*, 81; *Gn. Litt.* VII.13.20; 18.24.
72. *Gn. Litt.* VII.18.24; O'Daly, *Augustine's Philosophy*, 133.
73. *Conf.* X; *Gn. Litt.* VII.12, 18–20.
74. O'Daly, *Augustine's Philosophy*, 81; *Gn. Litt.* VII.17.23–18.24.
75. *Gn. Litt.* VII.17.18.24.
76. *Gn. Litt.* VII.17.18.24.
77. O'Daly, *Augustine's Philosophy*, 81; *Gen. Litt.* XII.20.42.
78. *Gn. Litt.* XII.20.42.
79. O'Daly, *Augustine's Philosophy*, 133; *Gn. Litt.* VII.19.25.

Memoria and the Mind's Eye

Eyes, to Augustine, had an important role in the sense perception of perceived images and, therefore, memory. To him, the eyes were also the mind's eyes to the soul[80] and therefore significant in understanding *memoria*. Physics and biology have important roles in understanding eyes. Augustine uses the theory of rays (a physics theory)[81] to describe how this is the case. O'Daly summarizes this nicely as follows:

> Rays (*radii*) emanating from the pupil of the eye to impinge upon objects,[82] so that seeing becomes a kind of visual touching. A ray travels at great speed allowing for instantaneous perceptions of distant objects.[83] It then "bursts out" (*erumpit*) of the eyes and ranges abroad in vision:[84] "to have opened the eye is to have arrived"[85] at the seen object, no matter how far distant the latter is. In fact, seeing presupposes a space, not too great but none the less existent, between eye and object.[86]

The eyes cannot see themselves (*Trin*. IX.3.3), neither can they see a body directly superimposed upon their surface. O'Daly writes that this seems at first to create a difficulty, as it appears to run counter to the principle that bodies are physically contiguous with that which they feel (*Quant. An.* 43).[87] However, Augustine's use of the ray theory precisely counters this difficulty. It is not the eyes but their sight (*visus*) that senses something when we see; sight is where it sees, and at the same time the eye can only sense something where it is not.[88] The eyes through sight allow the soul to use them so that the soul can look and see. Healthy eyes are required for the soul to turn to the light of the Divine.[89]

There is a spatiotemporal dynamic associated with the sense of sight and the other senses. Time passes from when a ray from the eyes sees the object and the eye receives the image of the object. There is space because of the distance the ray travels between the eye and the perceived object, and

---

80. *Sol.* I.6.12.
81. The laws of reflection and refraction.
82. *Trin.* IX.3.3. *Serm.* 277.10.
83. *Ep.* 137.8.
84. *Quant. An.* 43.
85. *Serm.* 277.10.
86. *Serm.* 277.14. O'Daly, *Augustine's Philosophy*, 82–83.
87. O'Daly, *Augustine's Philosophy*, 82.
88. O'Daly, *Augustine's Philosophy*, 83.
89. *Sol.* I.6.13.

there is the space within the infrastructure of the *tenues fistulae, tenuissimi quidem rivuli*, and the brain. Sense perception which transmits the sensory stimuli to the soul is thus also a form of motion or change. Augustine describes sensory motion as one that runs counter to the motion set up in the body by the sensory stimulus where sentience is the product of the interaction of two movements.[90] Augustine says that this motion is caused by the soul (*Mus.* 6.10). It is "the something" which in each of the senses, corresponds to one of the elements of the material world.[91]

Memoria and Spatiotemporal Dynamics

Closely related to *memoria* and the formation of memories is time. Most of Augustine's interrogations of memory and time center on the continuum of time (past, present, and future), the spatiotemporal dynamics, and measurement of time. Memory, functioning in a temporal setting, is subject to spatiotemporal dynamics. Nordlund comments that even though physics as a formal discipline began in the tenth century AD, Augustine's apparent tendency to think in terms of physical quantities and their measurement, including his scientific capabilities and fixation on time, eternity, creation, and the nature of God and his relation to man, should qualify him as at least an honorary physicist![92] Augustine did not know the field of physics but he certainly used the known scientific principles of his time to understand *memoria* and time, another illustration of how significant the "art" of *scientia*[93] was to Augustine in deciphering eternal matters. And as is characteristic of Augustine, he also makes sure to inform his audience that he is "investigating . . . not making assertions."[94]

Confessiones XI is devoted to Augustine's interrogations of time in relation to *memoria* and is where he takes a deep dive into the many spatiotemporal conundrums of time. Augustine writes of memory, the senses, and time:

> When a true narrative of the past is related, the memory produces not the actual events which have passed away but words conceived from images of them, which they fixed in the mind

---

90. O'Daly, *Augustine's Philosophy*, 83.

91. O'Daly, *Augustine's Philosophy*, 84.

92. Nordlund, "Physics," 222.

93. Augustine uses *scientia* to describe knowledge that is obtained from physical and temporal processes.

94. *Conf.* XI.17.22.

> like imprints as they passed through the senses, ... but when I am recollecting and telling my story, I am looking on its image in present time, since it is still in my memory.[95]

Augustine recognizes three measurements of time in its continuum: past, present, and future.[96] He talks of time and memory in terms of the duration of time: "a long past is a long memory of the past."[97] However, Augustine wonders how it is possible to measure time when it comes from the future and passes into the past via the present.[98] The connection between time, memory, and eternity intrigues Augustine. O'Neill writes regarding Augustine's association of memory and eternity with time:

> Memory is a kind of wellspring from which the past, present, and future can be drawn. Prior to calling forth memories to attention, they somehow exist within the memory, existing in potency in the present despite their temporally past character. The power of the memory is a limited human mode of approximating God's being outside of time—His eternity. This approximation between divine eternity and the human soul is possible because in the soul's powers we have something akin to eternity: the memory, which prior to its activity contains all time in potential.[99]

The impressions that things make on a person as they pass by are the impressions created in the mind by temporal change that also create a measurable spatial extension, the space of memory.[100] Further, Augustine argues that there is such a thing as the "space of time."[101] One of the challenges in understanding the spatial and temporal dimensions pertains to how reality is affected if an additional space or time dimension is added. *De Musica* is a good example of a text that attempts to explain this, in this case in terms of the dynamics of sound.[102]

Baker writes that Augustine believes that a particular concept of time, "deictic" time, metaphysically depends on the mind; deictic time for

---

95. *Conf.* XI.18.23.
96. *Conf.* XI.20.26.
97. *Conf.* XI.28.37.
98. *Conf.* XI.21.27.
99. O'Neill, "Augustine," 8.
100. Baker, "Augustine," 2.
101. Augustine discusses this in relation to a person deciding how long they wished to utter a sound and planning that space of time in silence. *Conf.* XI.27.36.
102. See *Mus.* VI for the exposition of this concept.

Augustine is "flowing time."[103] Craig Callender, a philosopher of science, physics, and metaphysics writes about the importance of studying deictic time in terms of physics:

> One of manifest time's most important properties is temporal deictic structure. In our conceptualization of time, we can characterize temporal relationships either by reference to the present moment, or Now, or simply to another moment in the time series. The former conceptualization leads to a classification of events in terms of past, present, and future, whereas the latter leads to one in terms of the earlier than relation.[104]

Physics claims that space-time has no objective "flow of time"[105] or privileged "now."[106] Augustine's point regarding the "flow of time" requires a person to "measure" against the continuum of their minds. According to Callender, a person conceptualizes themselves as a moving self because of their immediate experience and memories, from which they develop agential expectations.[107] Baker asserts that Callender's argument that "flow" is primarily an experience of a change in us as an "updating ego" is similar to Augustine's claim that the change metaphysically underwriting time involves properties "passing away" in the substance of our minds.[108]

Augustine's interrogation of time and space and their link with memory is, suggests Nordlund, an attempt to formulate some of the quantitative laws of physics to describe the processes of memory with relation to time while explicitly demanding that faith in an unchanging and all-powerful God simultaneously fit with these formulations.[109]

---

103. Deictic structure and deictic time are spatial and temporal. The concept of deictic time is controversial among physicists and centers on the debate explaining whether manifest temporal deictic structure is possible while assuming that it is not fundamentally in the world. Callender states that there tends to be confusion surrounding temporal deictic structure with sequence time, i.e., conflating the "Now" with simultaneity; the critical point time is the Now (present) verses sequential time (flow of time). Callender, "Time," 27; Baker, "Augustine," 2.

104. Callender, "Time," 27.

105. "Flow" of time is the tripartite structure of past, present, and future. Callender, "Time," 29.

106. Baker, "Augustine," 5.

107. Baker, "Augustine," 5.

108. Baker, "Augustine," 8.

109. Nordlund, "Physics," 223.

Memoria, Scientia, and *Sapientia*

Augustine never thought of *scientia* and his theological beliefs as two separate entities or disciplines. His distinction pertained to how *scientia* was used. Was it used for acquiring knowledge just for the sake of knowledge thereby leading to "puffed up" men or was it used as "good" knowledge to inform divine wisdom (*sapientia*)[110] and move towards eternal truths? Augustine writes:

> For science, too, has its good measure if that which in it puffs up, or is wont to puff up, is overcome by love for eternal things which does not puff up but, as we know, edifies. For without science we cannot even possess the very virtues by which we live rightly and by which this miserable life is so regulated that it may arrive at that eternal life which is truly blessed.[111]

Augustine writes that "a transitory thought is committed to the memory by means of sciences in which the mind is instructed."[112] Augustine is careful to distinguish between *sapientia*, which belongs to the "intellectual cognition of eternal things," and *scientia*, which is "the reasonable cognition of temporal things."[113] He is careful to note the rightful place and use of *scientia* in acquiring favorable knowledge to understand the sources of wisdom and truth.[114]

The importance of *scientia* in attaining *sapientia* in the role of memory is illustrated in Augustine's inquiry into, and description of, sense perception. As mentioned earlier, sense perceptions convey information from the senses to form memories that are stored in *memoria* and that speak to the soul. When reliable information is conveyed in this way *memoria* gains knowledge.[115] This knowledge is ascribed to *scientia* gained from the senses and from temporal phenomena.[116] This is evidenced by the numerous passages in Augustine's corpus. This is what fascinated Augustine and impelled

---

110. Augustine defined *sapientia* in *C. Acad.* III.20 as situated *apud Deum* and in 3.31 as remaining itself (*in semetipso*). To him, *sapientia* in its deepest sense was God's own Wisdom, the Son of God. The soul clings to *sapientia* once it has found her. O'Connell, *Images*, 264–65.

111. *Trin.* XII.14.21; cf. *Conf.* V.3.6–6.11: Augustine warns of the dangers of bad science in his discussion with Faustus.

112. *Trin.* XII.14.23.

113. *Trin.* XII.14.25.

114. *Conf.* V.6.10; *Trin.* XIV.1.3.

115. O'Daly, *Augustine's Philosophy*, 92–102.

116. Miethe, "Augustine's," 259.

him to investigate sense perception using *scientia*. Augustine writes, "the human mind, therefore, knows all these things which it has acquired through itself, through the senses of its body, and through the testimonies of others, and keeps them in the treasure-house of memory."[117] The truth of what has been learnt by the bodily senses and the things in them that are known to us cannot be doubted.[118] The soul, while superior to the physical body, is involved in these processes and relates to both *scientia* and *sapientia*. In this capacity, the senses are considered messengers from which the soul is cognizant of the temporal and corporeal.[119] Here, *scientia* evolves towards *sapientia* because there is revelation that comes with increased knowledge, even temporal, and it participates in the informing of the soul.

Augustine used his knowledge of the medical sciences (i.e., *scientia*) in his role as a bishop to help his flock to understand sapiential matters. His *Epistolae* illustrate that Augustine is both a man who is familiar with medical phenomena and procedures and a bishop who cares about the purity of faith and the discipline of the church.[120] He describes the condition and problems of the church through a variety of medical metaphors.[121] His metaphorical use of *scientia* in doctrinal exegesis can be noted in his exposition of the biblical doctrine on the body of Christ[122] and his development of the idea of the healer (*medicus*),[123] Christ himself. Christ is the prime example of how *scientia* and *sapientia* meet, Christ's incarnation and death in temporal time and in human form (matter) and Christ's resurrection into the eternal. For Augustine, the unity and integrity of Christ's *scientia* and *sapientia* turns the mind ultimately towards God.[124] The incarnation and the resurrection, where eternity is inserted into temporality and temporality into eternity, are the points in temporal time where, for human beings, *scientia* and *sapientia* meet. Augustine does make certain that his audience knows that human knowledge (*scientia*) and human wisdom (*sapientia*) are distinct but related and inseparable, as it was with Christ. Augustine writes that "faith in the temporal things, which the Eternal One died and suffered for us in the man whom He bore in time and led to eternal things," reflects

---

117. *Trin.* XV.12.22.
118. Nash, *Light*, 42.
119. *Gn. Litt.* VII.13.20.
120. Marciniak, "Medical," 373–88.
121. Marciniak, "Medical," 385; Keenan, "St. Augustine," 589.
122. *Ep.* 140.18; cf. Col 1:18.
123. *Ep.* 266.3.
124. Carreker, "Integrity," 269.

the temporal/eternal nature of Christ.[125] It is a precondition of the temporal virtue needed for eternal life and it is where human wisdom will participate perfectly in divine wisdom.[126] Faith in the person and the reconciling work of Christ is, to Augustine, the way that leads from temporal knowledge (*scientia*) to eternal knowledge (*sapientia*).

Concluding Remarks

It is evident that Augustine's medical and scientific knowledge was remarkable considering he was neither a physician nor scientist. Augustine's utilization of *scientia* was a motivating factor in investigating memory via the discipline of genetics and Arc in an attempt to further elucidate some of Augustinian memory.

---

125. *Trin.* XIV.1.3.
126. *Trin.* XIV.1.3.

6

Re-Collecting Memory: Old Wine, New Skins

"The important thing in science is not so much to obtain new facts as to discover new ways of thinking about them."

—SIR WILLIAM LAWRENCE BRAGG[1]

MAX DELBRÜCK, ONE OF the founding fathers of molecular biology,[2] argues that the historical basis for a genetic involvement in biological processes was first proposed by Aristotle who, he says, was the first to discover "the principle implied" in DNA.[3] Aristotle did not believe, unlike Plato, that the generation of human beings resulted from semen with extracts from the human body, the semen thereby containing homunculi; he believed that the male contributed in semen a form principle that could

---

1. William Lawrence Bragg, physicist and crystallographer, won the Nobel prize in physics in 1915 for demonstrating the use of X-rays in revealing the structure of crystals. Despite his many discoveries in science, he still believed they were just a new way of thinking and discussing observed facts. Gray et al., *Braving*, 17; Lonsdale, "Sir Lawrence Bragg."

2. Max Delbrück, Alfred Hershey, and Salvador Luria won the 1969 Nobel Prize in Physiology or Medicine "for their discoveries concerning the replication mechanism and the genetic structure of viruses." *Noble Prize*, "All Nobel Prizes in Physiology or Medicine."

3. Aristotle, per Delbrück, could be classified as a biologist, as ascertained from the five books he wrote on biological and scientific principles. Delbrück, "How," 129–37.

determine both male and female form.⁴ In other words, the male contributed to the plan of development but not to the material body of the embryo; the female contributed the substrate since the form principle was missing as she did not produce offspring by herself.⁵ Zwart endorses Delbrück's view of Aristotle; he writes:

> Aristotle's hylemorphic conception of life can be regarded as a remarkably lucid anticipation of genomics. From an Aristotelean perspective, the genome can be considered as the formula, the programme or plan (λόγος) which guides the development of living beings from their embryonic state up to their full realisation (ἐγτελεχεια) as flourishing, self-sustaining, reproducing adults who have fully actualised their potential form (εἶδος). So, yes, from an Aristotelian viewpoint, the genome can meaningfully be regarded as the text of life, producing living beings from the chemical mayhem of their abiotic surroundings (i.e., inorganic matter).⁶

Augustine also made some indirect observations that are very pertinent to "the principle implied" in genetics.⁷ He believed that Hippocrates was correct in his assessment regarding the health of twins who fell ill and recovered at the same time.⁸ Augustine explained that the fetuses of twins are of the same constitution as the mother because they were contemporaneously part of the same body as the mother and were receiving the same nourishments from the mother. They, therefore, would respond similarly to the same illnesses and external environmental factors. Furthermore, he notes that this may continue to be true as the twins grow if they are exposed to the same foods, quality of air and water, and same exercise. However, what Augustine also notes regarding twins is how environmental variations can in different ways influence the behavior and the constitution of twins, even identical twins.⁹ This is, in fact, an observation that conforms to "the

---

4. Aristotle's conclusion is not based on genetics; however, of note is that sperm in semen contains either an X (female) or Y (male) chromosome. An embryo's sex is determined by whether they inherit an X or Y chromosome from sperm forming XX or XY embryos (ova will always have an X chromosome since they come from the mother). Aristotle's form principle of development of human beings is discussed in Delbrück, "How," 234.

5. Delbrück, "How," 135.

6. Zwart, "In the Beginning," 35.

7. "Genetics" refers to the study of genes and their function; "genomics" refers to the study of the function and structure of genes and DNA at the base pair level.

8. *Civ. Dei* 5.2.

9. Augustine may have written *Civ. Dei* 5.2 as a refutation to astrologers who

principle implied" in genetics given the similar response of the twins as a result of having the same constitution as the mother and exposure to the same external factors. The field of the genetics of inheritance was not known at the time, but there was some understanding of inheritance from the mother and consequent conferring of similar responses to external factors.

It can be concluded that "genetic principles" were known in Aristotelian and Augustinian times, well before the nineteenth to twenty-first centuries when theologians and scientists started taking these genetic principles to the next level. Indeed, as Bragg would say, they were not so much obtaining new facts but discovering new ways of thinking about them. The twenty-first century has brought forth a new way of thinking, as we shall see, regarding memory processes that can assist in expanding our knowledge and augmenting Augustine's theology of *memoria*.

A Novel Communication System Involved in Memory

Following in the footsteps of Augustine, who unapologetically used highly technical scientific and medical terminology, this discussion regarding the brain, memory, and the Arc gene[10] will include technical terminology in order to fully understand the importance of the role of this gene in memory.

The human brain is an organ of enormous complexity. A healthy human brain has approximately a thousand trillion synapses with two hundred billion neurons.[11] Each neuron is connected to as many as ten thousand other neurons which all pass stimuli to each other via as many as a thousand trillion synaptic connections, equivalent by some estimates to a computer with a one trillion bit per second processor; estimates of the human brain's memory capacity is approximately 2.5 petabytes (the nineteen million volumes in the US Library of Congress represents about ten terabytes of data).[12] In the cerebral cortex where implicit basic associative learning and memory occurs, there are more than 125 trillion synapses roughly equal to the number of stars in fifteen hundred Milky Way galaxies.[13]

It is in the mind within the brain where memory is formed, consolidated and available for recollection. Central to memory is a mass neuronal

---

believed that the constitution of twins was based on which constellation they were born under. Augustine calls this nonsense, declaring that "the medical hypothesis is far more acceptable and obviously more credible."

10. For information on genes, see Rolston III, "What," 471–97.
11. Zhang, "Basic," 2; Smith, "Stunning," 1.
12. Zhang, "Basic," 2; Smith, "Stunning," 1.
13. Smith, "Stunning," 1.

communication system facilitated by genetic and genomic processes that regulate synaptic activity between neurons. In fact, the adaptive capacity of the brain with regard to memory depends on synaptic plasticity, i.e., the ability of a synapse to change in strength in response to use or disuse.[14] This dynamic synaptic network through the mass neuronal communication system has the ability to receive, transmit, and store information resulting in the formation of a memory, its storage, and retrieval.[15]

Scientifically and psychologically, memories are experience-dependent internal representations, in other words, acquired models of the world encoded in the spatiotemporal activity of brain circuits.[16] Neurons and synapses are, therefore, involved in the very foundation, structure, and experience of one's life. This experience-dependent neuronal activity regulates, via molecular genetic and genomic processes, synaptic plasticity.[17] According to Kukushin and Carew, synaptic plasticity is generally accepted as the principal implementation of information storage in neural systems.[18] The connections between neurons are not static but dynamic, changing over time. When more signals are sent between two neurons, the amplitude of the post-synaptic neuron's response increases, becoming stronger; with each new experience and each remembered event or fact, the brain slightly re-wires its physical structure.[19]

Remembering past memories is an integral part of human existence; Augustine believed it important to recollect creation. Foster explains this in basic terms, if one did not have a good memory, one would not be able to drive to work, hold a meaningful conversation with one's children, read a book, or even prepare a meal.[20] Augustine may not have known the "finer" details of the brain and nervous system; however, he did understand the complexities involved with memory.[21] This is also emphasized by Mau, who writes that it is far too simplistic to say that memory processes involved in updating memory and the fluidity of memories are neural patterns that guide behavior.[22] He goes on to say that encountered environments are dynamic and probabilistic; therefore, the brain has the difficult task of shaping

---

14. Nikolaienko et al., "Arc," 34.
15. Beagen et al., "Three-Dimensional," 707–17.
16. Dudai, "Molecular," 211.
17. Flavell and Greenberg, "Signaling," 563–90; Shepherd and Bear, "New," 279.
18. Kukushkin and Carew, "Memory," 259.
19. Zhang, "Basic," 3.
20. Foster, "Memory," 1.
21. *Conf.* X.17.26.
22. Mau et al., "Brain," 1.

memory representations to address this challenge. The functioning of memory is not as simple as acquiring a memory and then recalling that memory.

In 2018/19, some immensely important breakthroughs in the discovery of a novel neuronal communication process shed new insights into how memories were formed, stored, and remembered. Pastuzyn and Shepherd demonstrated how a novel neuronal gene called Arc was important in regulating synaptic communication.[23] They proposed a new mechanism[24] of synaptic communication between neurons regulated via expression of the Arc gene. So important was this finding that it was reported by a number of news outlets.[25] Since January 2018, there has been further evidence supporting Arc as a master regulator and molecular mediator of synaptic plasticity. This evidence demonstrates that Arc plays an important role in controlling large signaling networks implicated in learning, memory formation and consolidation, and behavior.[26] The knowledge uncovered around Arc allows for the proposal of a genomic memory[27] process that could provide evidence of a physical system that assists in the metaphysical recollection of memory.

---

23. Pastuzyn et al., "Neuronal," 275–88.

24. The term "mechanism" is most commonly perceived, in today's culture, to mean "a system of parts working together in a machine"; however, it is also correctly defined as "a natural or established process by which something takes place, or the fundamental processes involved in or responsible for an action, reaction, or other natural phenomenon." Mechanism is used in terms of "natural and fundamental process" here and throughout this book. *Merriam Webster Dictionary*, s.v. "Mechanism," https://www.merriam-webster.com/dictionary/mechanism; NLST, s.v. "Mechanism," https://csrc.nist.gov/glossary/term/mechanism.

25. Kiefer, "Surprise"; Arnold, "Cells"; National Institutes of Health, "Memory." The BBC in 2013 had already reported a study by Steve Finkbeiner revealing the importance of Arc protein in memory loss. BBC, "Arc."

26. Key articles: Fila et al., "mRNA," 1–12; Hallin et al., "Structure," 323–40; Ashley et al., "Retrovirus-Like," 262–74; Shepherd, "Arc" 73–78; Campioni and Finkbeiner "Going," 346.

27. "Genomic memory" is a term I use to describe the concept of memory regulated specifically by gene expression and genetic processes, i.e., it describes the *operation* of memory at the genome level. This is different to "genetic memory," which is a *theorized* phenomenon in which certain kinds of memories could be inherited, being present at birth in the absence of any associated sensory experience, and that such memories could be incorporated into the genome over long spans of time.

Arc and Synaptic Communication

Konopka designed a study that was the first to identify correlations between gene data and brain activity during memory processing, providing a new window into human memory.[28] The search for immediate-early genes (IEGs)[29] that responded to neuronal activity independently of protein synthesis led to the discovery of Arc.[30] Arc, implicated in both acquired and innate memory mechanisms, regulates the transcription of over nineteen hundred genes controlling memory, cognition, synaptic function, neuronal plasticity, intrinsic excitability,[31] and intra- and intercellular signaling.[32] Arc is an interesting candidate memory gene in understanding Augustinian memory due to its unusual molecular structure, mode of action, and role in synaptic communication between neurons specifically involved in memory. Arc is required for protein-synthesis-dependent synaptic plasticity related to learning and memory and it is one of the key molecular players in cognition.[33] The brain processes information regarding memory formation, consolidation, storage, retention, and recollection via this synaptic communication system, which is elegantly regulated by expression of Arc, which occurs within minutes of neuronal stimulation.[34] Arc protein induction highly correlates with ongoing cognitive activity in the hippocampus[35] and in the cortex.[36] Any dysregulation of Arc or genetic mutation can result in memory and neurological disorders.

The role of Arc in the intra- and intercellular movement of genomic memory information is closely associated with its exquisite molecular architecture.[37] The α-helical Arc gene, located on chromosome 8 band region q24.3,[38] is unusual in that it is a highly conserved single-copy gene that

---

28. Cognitive Neuroscience Society, "Identifying."

29. IEG are a class of genes that are rapidly and transiently induced by a large number of cellular stimuli.

30. Pérez-Cadahía, "Activation," 62.

31. Intrinsic excitability is the electrical excitability of a particular neuron.

32. Leung et al., "Arc," 1.

33. Shepherd and Bear, "New," 279–84.

34. Shepherd and Bear, "New," 282; Fowler et al., "Regulation," 348–60; Tyssowski et al., "Different," 530–46 e511.

35. Ramirez-Amaya et al., "Spatial," 1761, 1765–67.

36. Tse et al., "Schema-Dependent," 891–95.

37. Fila et al., "mRNA," 7.

38. Kremerskothen and Barnekow, "Human," 655.

encodes[39] a single protein consisting of 396 amino-acids.[40] Zhang was the first to provide an atomic structure for Arc.[41] He showed that Arc has two structural domains connected by a flexible linker region.[42] This structural configuration of Arc was found to be similar to the HIV Gag protein.[43] The Arc protein contains retroviral[44]/retrotransposon[45] viral Gag polyproteins that originated from the Ty3/gypsy retrotransposon family. The Ty3/gypsy retrotransposons are ancient forms of RNA-based self-replicating elements that are present in animal, plant, and fungal kingdoms and are considered ancestral to modern retroviruses.[46] Arc protein is the only synaptic protein of this class. Arc, as a gene that originates from these retrotransposon insertions, contains conserved domains similar to the Gag protein, which are required for the formation of retrovirus capsids.[47]

Arc is fascinating because it does not conform to the "traditional" or "expected" structure and function of a typical gene. Paradoxically, it is a simple yet complex gene and is highly dynamic with unusual attributes. Arc functions like a virus and produces viral structures called capsids (they house mRNA) that infect other neurons. In these neurons Arc mRNA[48] transcripts[49] are translated into more capsid-like protein structures which

---

39. A gene's DNA has information encoded in a specific sequence of base pairs that is needed to make a protein. Proteins are composed of amino acids. They are required for the structure, function, and regulation of cells, tissues, and organs.

40. Bramham et al., "Arc," 131; Boldridge et al., "Characterization," 1–12.

41. Zhang et al., "Structural," 496.

42. Boldridge et al., "Characterization," 2.

43. Gag protein is part of the basic infrastructure of retroviruses. Zhang et al., "Structural," 497–98.

44. Retrovirus: a virus that uses RNA as its genetic material. When a retrovirus infects a cell, it makes a DNA copy of its genome that is inserted into the DNA of the host cell. Retroviruses behave differently from the typical genetic process of DNA making RNA, and RNA making protein. Bodine, NHGRI "Retrovirus."

45. Retrotransposons duplicate through RNA intermediates that are reverse transcribed and inserted at new genomic locations. One of the main differences between retroviruses and retrotransposons is whether they are infectious. Retroviruses are capable of moving between cells, whereas retrotransposons can only insert new copies into the genome present within the same cell and rely mostly on vertical transmission through generations. Cordaux and Batzer, "Impact," 691; Naville et al., "Not," 312.

46. Shepherd, "Arc," 74.

47. Freed, "HIV-1," 484–96.

48. Messenger RNA (mRNA): single-stranded RNA that is complementary to DNA strands of a gene.

49. Transcription and translation are genetic processes used by a cell to make all proteins needed for cellular and bodily functions. These genetic processes are initiated

are required for neuronal function.[50] The recipient neurons can then translate the Arc mRNA transcripts into even more capsid-like structures where they are released and inserted into other neurons just like a virus infecting host cell, and the cycle repeats itself over and over (Arc cycle).[51] Neurons thus communicate with each other by "trafficking" Arc mRNA between each other. This trafficking across synapses is critical for synaptic plasticity, which is important in memory processes. The Arc capsid cycle exemplifies Arc mediation. It is the arc-hitectonic structural versatility of Arc that facilitates its operation as a gene involved in memory. The Arc capsid is essential to the effectiveness of Arc in the mechanics of memory processes. Capsids form a closed shell that encapsulates and protects genetic material allowing for the intercellular transfer of newly synthesized Arc mRNA from one neuron to another.[52] The capsid's individual components have chemical features that allow them to fit together and to assemble to form the capsid. The Arc capsids are perfect icosahedral structures with a high degree of similarity to mature retroviral capsids from viruses like HIV.[53] Campioni describes how the capsids including Arc's also have spikes protruding from their surfaces, reminiscent of the spikes used by viruses to bind target cells,[54] actually very similar to the RNA SARS-CoV-2 (COVID-19) virus' protein spikes.[55] The Arc capsid contains amphiphatic[56] regions that extend from the capsid surface through the spikes which are reminiscent of viral-amphiphatic membrane-penetrating proteins.[57] This facilitates the capsid

---

by information stored in the sequence of bases in DNA (gene). During transcription, a piece of DNA that codes for a specific gene is copied into mRNA in the nucleus of the cell. The mRNA (transcripts) then carries the genetic information from the DNA to the cytoplasm, where translation occurs. During translation, proteins are made using the information stored in the mRNA sequence. National Cancer Institute, "Transcription."

50. Svetlana et al., "Structure," 10055.

51. Hallin et al., "Structure," 324.

52. Dodonova et al., "Structure," 10055; Kelly and Deadwyler, "Experience-Dependent," 6443–51; Ashley et al., "Retrovirus-Like," 262–74.

53. Campioni and Finkbeiner, "Going," 347; Budnik and Thomson, "Structure," 153.

54. Campioni and Finkbeiner, "Going," 347.

55. For a detailed description of the SARS-CoV-2 protein spike and similarities with Arc see Zhang et al., "Structure," 173–82.

56. A molecule is amphiphatic if it has both hydrophobic (lipophilic or fat-loving) and hydrophilic (water-loving) properties. In the case of the Arc capsid and its spikes, the hydrophilic and hydrophobic properties are thought to be involved in the penetration of, and release from, the neuron membrane. Hantak et al., "Intercellular," 254.

57. Erlendsson et al., "Structures," 172–5; Hantak et al., "Intracellular," 254.

penetrating through the membrane of a neuron in order to enter or exit the neuron. Arc capsid formation is influenced by the amount of Arc protein in neuronal synapses and interactions with other host proteins.[58] Extracellular vesicles (EVs), which contain the capsids, play a critical role in the neuronal memory communication process both in normal and diseased brains.[59] The role of EVs was elucidated in a key study by Ashley et al. while investigating the role of Arc1 in *Drosophila*.[60] They discovered how the Arc1 protein formed capsids and were loaded into EVs which then facilitated transfer from one neuron to another; the mechanism involved was similar to that of retroviruses and retrotransposons and was necessary for synaptic plasticity. At the same time as Ashley, Pastuzyn showed in another ground-breaking paper the involvement of mammalian Arc in inter-neuron Arc mRNA trafficking,[61] confirming the results obtained by Ashley. In another study, Popov noted that as a neuron became more active, there was an increase in the number of EVs produced that contained the Arc capsids.[62]

Spatio-Temporal Dynamics of Arc

Arc exhibits both spatial and temporal dynamics. The cyclic nature of the Arc neuronal memory communication pathway demonstrates its spatial dynamics. First, the formation of the capsid requires an understanding of spatial orientation as it occupies a given space, operates in that space, and moves through space to another target location; this confirms the spatio-temporal dynamic of the capsid. Second, the coordination of intra- and intercellular Arc mRNA trafficking requires the precise spatial and temporal expression of Arc at the protein level.[63] The cascade sequence of intra- and intercellular Arc mRNA trafficking results in synaptic activity at a target location; this not only demonstrates the spatial orientation of the capsid and Arc mRNA in different locations but also the time span of these steps, hence, the temporal dynamics of the transfer of mRNA from one location (i.e., one neuron) to another. According to Pastuzyn, this cascade sequence can be initiated from a behavioral experience resulting in the formation of

---

58. Shepherd and Bear, "New," 270–84; Hantak et al., "Intercellular," 252; Nielsen, "Capsid," 1071–81.

59. Paolicelli et al., "Cell-to-Cell," 148–57.

60. Ashley et al., "Retrovirus-Like," 262–74, e11.

61. Pastuzyn et al., "Neuronal," e18.

62. Popov et al., "Generation," 9.

63. Pastuzyn et al., "Neuronal," e18; Vazdarjanova et al., "Spatial," 317–29.

a memory.[64] Third, the Arc cycle and Arc expression initiate the spatial exploration of a novel temporal environment.[65] Arc is thus essential for spatial memory acquisition and consolidation. Vazdarjanova was the first to demonstrate that exploring a novel environment induces Arc in the principal neurons of the hippocampus, neocortex, and dorsal striatum.[66]

The temporal dynamics of the Arc gene itself can be observed in two ways. The Arc protein eventually degrades, as does its function and longevity over time. Wall was able to demonstrate the functional consequences of modifying the temporal profile of Arc expression and degradation.[67] He showed that disruption in the degradation of the Arc protein resulted in deficits in reversal learning strategy. Secondly, the temporal dynamic of Arc exists in the initial recognition of a signal within a spatial orientation in a given moment in time to the time a memory is formed and consolidated. Studies have shown that the time between a presynaptic and postsynaptic neuron firing in order to produce a change in synaptic strength is generally less than forty milliseconds because after forty to sixty milliseconds no plasticity occurs.[68] Short- and long-term memories can take anywhere from a few seconds to weeks to be consolidated into longer term memories to be recalled at a later time in the future.[69] There is a timescale that is involved, one that has an initial present that moves into the past akin to the Augustinian theory of time past, present, and future.

Summary of the Arc Gene

Arc has unique properties regarding its structure and function, which are summarized in Table 6.1.

---

64. Pastuzyn et al., "Neuronal," e18.
65. Vazdarjanova et al., "Spatial," 323.
66. Vazdarjanova et al., "Spatial," 328.
67. Wall et al., "Temporal," 1124–32.
68. Gershman, "Molecular," 3; Bi and Poo, "Synaptic," 10464–72.
69. For a good review, see Mau et al., "Brain," 1–24.

Table 6.1: Summary of the Arc Gene

Arc Gene	
Features	**Properties/Role**
Single copy gene	Arc regulates memory consolidation and reconsolidation processes
Highly conserved	Master regulator of synaptic plasticity
Expression induced in divergent behavioral pathways	Diverse in function Associated with and interacts with >1,900 genes Highly dynamic
Arc gene transcripts are trafficked into the synapse, activates neuron	Tightly regulated by neuronal activity and experience Local transportation of Arc proteins at synapses (critical for synaptic plasticity)
Arc mRNA finds its way to synapses that are recently active (local synaptic support and strengthening)	Arc protein expression observed in the nucleus of neurons Involved in regulating expression Activating neurons mobilizes Arc, triggering release of capsids
Viral-like features	Viral-like functions Involved in learning
Uptake/transfer of RNA by Arc protein occurs in absence of envelope (lipid layer)	Alpha-helical, Arc capsid with quaternary arrangement N- and C-terminals Flexible linker region Formation and consolidation of memory
Arc gene selectively expressed when neuron has high level of activity	Capable of oligomerization Storage of memory
Similar to HIV in structure and function	Retrieval of memory

Old Wine, New Skins

With due understatement, memory is a complex process. This becomes even more evident in this section as the homogeny between Augustine's theology of *memoria* and the molecular memory processes regulated by Arc are discussed. Following Augustine, this section will elaborate on the same eight symphonic forms of memory and their sequence identified in *Conf.* X: location of memory, power of memory, sense perception, teaching and learning, recollection and forgetfulness, images, *phantasia*, and *phantasmata*, the temporal dimension of *memoria*, and the *beata vita*.

The Location of Memory

Memory's huge cavern, with its mysterious, secret, and indescribable nooks and crannies...[70]

The brain is shown to have three ventricles ... the third in between the two, in which they demonstrate that memory is active.[71]

The exact location of memory in the mind has been debated for centuries. Identifying the location of memory was important for Augustine because memory was the place where God dwelt.[72] Metaphorically, Augustine visualized the location of memory as "the fields and vast palaces of memory"[73] located in *memoria* within the *mens* of the rational soul and where the numerous memories and images were stored in the "mysterious, secret, and indescribable nooks and crannies."[74] However, Augustine, from his understanding of anatomy, had surmised a specific physical location in the brain where memories were located. In *Gn. Litt.* VII.18.24 Augustine writes:

> The brain is shown to have three ventricles, one in the front, at the face, from which all sensation is controlled; a second behind at the neck, from which all movement comes; the third in between the two, in which they demonstrate that memory is active; otherwise, since movement follows upon sensation, you may fail to link to your perceptions what has to be done, if you have forgotten what you have done on previous occasions.

---

70. *Conf.* X.8.13.
71. *Gn. Litt.* VII.18.24.
72. *Conf.* X.25.36.
73. *Conf.* X.8.12.
74. *Conf.* X.8.13.

In the same section, Augustine reiterates that his understanding of the ventricular theory of the brain was confirmed by medical knowledge:

> These medical men say there are sure and certain indications to prove all this, as when these parts, affected by some disease or defect, have each made clear enough what they are for by failure in the functions of sense perception, or of movement of limbs, or of remembering how to move the body.

It is thought Augustine obtained this information from Vindicianus who was likely to be familiar with, and influenced by, Galen, a Greek physician and philosopher.[75] Galen, in the second century AD, held a ventricular theory of the brain, and wrote about the location of memory in the *hêgemonikon*, the ruling center of the soul located in the brain.[76] Galen's model of the nervous system including the ventricular theory of the brain had considerable support, especially in Britain until the 1830s.[77] Modern science has mapped the location of memory in the brain and has demonstrated that Galen and Augustine had informed insight into the location of memory. When memories are initially formed, they are thought to be stored in the hippocampal-entorhinal cortex (HPC-EC) network.[78] Augustine believed the hippocampus was central to memory storage since it was located in the "second ventricle" now known as the temporal lobe. Episodic[79] memories initially require rapid synaptic plasticity within the hippocampus for their formation after which they gradually consolidated in neocortical networks for permanent storage.[80] It is known that both short-term and long-term memories are formed simultaneously in the hippocampus and prefrontal cortex where the memory cells become more silent or active over time based on the type of memory.[81] Arc regulates Arc protein induction in the hippocampus and in the cortex which correlates with ongoing cognitive

---

75. Green, "Where?," 140; Rocca, "Galen," 227–39.

76. Rocca, "Galen," 227–39; Graßhoff and Meyer, "Mapping," 681; deLacy, *On the Doctrines*, VIII 1.3–5.

77. Rocca, "Galen," 227n2.

78. HPC-EC network plays an essential role for episodic memory. It preserves spatial and temporal information regarding the occurrence of past events. Kitamura et al., "Engrams," 73.

79. Episodic memory involves the ability to learn, store, and retrieve information about unique individual experiences that occur in daily life. These memories typically include information about the time, the place of an event, and detailed information about the event itself. Dickerson and Eichenbaum, "Episodic," 87.

80. Kitamura et al., "Engrams," 73.

81. Kitamura et al., "Engrams," 73.

activity and both short-term-memory (STM) and long-term-memory (LTM) consolidation. Its absence causes severe memory disorders.[82] Further, prolonged inhibition of the hippocampal or neocortical networks during the consolidation period produces deficits in remote memory formation.[83] Augustine was aware of how damage to the brain and disruption of memory processes created either temporary or permanent forgetfulness; he wrote of this in *Conf.* X.

Specific locations in the brain are associated with memory storage. Augustine's description of the "fields and vast palaces of memory . . . indescribable nooks and crannies" was metaphorical but a great descriptor of the different locations of memory.[84] His anatomical description of the ventricular system of the brain with regards to memory aligns closer to modern science than one would think. It should be noted that in Latin, *ventriculum*, from which ventricle is derived, means "little belly"; this is the same term used by Augustine in *Gn. Litt.* VII.18.24 when he says, "the brain is shown to have, as it were, three ventricles (little bellies)." In *Conf.* X.14.21, Augustine uses this term for his metaphorical use of "belly" or "stomach" as in "memory is the stomach of the mind" (*ergo memoria quasi* **venter** *est animi*).[85]

The prefrontal cortex, located in the frontal lobe, is responsible for memory-related tasks that originate from perception, semantic activities, and encoding of task relevant information in working memory.[86] The frontal lobe was, according to Augustine, associated with the control of sense perception.[87] The cerebellum, identified by Augustine as the second ventricle, is important in procedural memories, motor learning, and classical conditioning. According to current neurobiology, the cerebellum plays a role in processing procedural memories, such as how to play the piano. Augustine would likely relate memory in the cerebellum to a musician learning how to play an instrument; music was influential in Augustine's development of his theory of memory. The total number of neurons in the cerebellum is approximately 105 billion, all of which require Arc expression to regulate synaptic communication regarding memory.[88] The third ventricle correlates to

---

82. Ramirez-Amaya et al., "Spatial," 497; Tse et al., "Schema-Dependent," 891–95.

83. Zelikowsky et al., "Contextual," 3393–97; Kitamura et al., "Engrams," 73.

84. *Conf.* X.8.12–13.

85. Hill, *Works*, 334n17.

86. Kathryn Dumper et al., "Parts"; Kapur et al., "Neuroanatomical," 2009–10; Baddeley, "Working," 829–39.

87. *Gn. Litt.* VII.18.24.

88. Andersen et al., "Quantitative," 549; Pastuzyn et al., "Neuronal," e18.

the temporal lobe within which are the medial temporal lobe, hippocampus, and amygdala. It is the third ventricle where Augustine claimed memory to be located and actively operational.[89] The amygdala is involved in emotive memories (e.g., fear) while the hippocampus is associated with declarative and episodic memory and recognition of memory. The hippocampus is a critical and active hub in the mechanics of memory, particularly crucial to the encoding of memory; it has the ability to integrate and interpret contextual clues to drive recall, but it is also important in the discrimination and association of memory data.[90] The vital role of the hippocampus in memory is demonstrated in patients who have partial brain resections. In 1953, Henry Molaison underwent a bilateral medial temporal lobe resection which included his hippocampus, amygdala, and partial loss of the adjacent parahippocampal gyrus to cure his profound epileptic seizures, which had seriously incapacitated him, despite high doses of anticonvulsant medication.[91] The surgery controlled his epilepsy but resulted in severe memory impairments. The results obtained from examining Molaison from the surgery until his death in 2008 established the fundamental principle that memory is a distinct cerebral function, separable from other perceptual and cognitive abilities; the medial aspect of the temporal lobe was identified as the important region for memory.[92] According to Squire, the implication was that the brain, to some extent, has to separate its perceptual and intellectual functions from its capacity to lay down in memory the records that ordinarily result from engaging in perceptual and intellectual work.[93] Molaison was unable to convert STM into LTM post his surgery. Consequently, he was forced to live entirely in the present; each day brought no recollection of the previous day due to his implicit memory deficits. However, Molaison retained his capacity to remember information that he had acquired before his surgery; this led to the key insight about the organization of memory, where it was stored, and medial temporal lobe function.

Memories from early life appear to be intact unless the damage extends well into the lateral temporal lobe or the frontal lobe, in which case memory loss can sometimes extend back for decades.[94] The structures damaged in Molaison are important for the formation of LTM and its maintenance and memory consolidation. The consequences of the bilateral medial temporal

---

89. *Gn. Litt.* VII.18.24.
90. Matin et al., "Contextual," 417–28; Goode et al., "Integrated," 807.
91. Squire, "Legacy," 6–9.
92. Squire, "Legacy," 7,
93. Squire, "Legacy," 7.
94. Squire, "Legacy," 10.

lobe resection illustrate that memory becomes impaired with the loss of these structures. This suggests that memory consolidation and storage are also located in the hippocampus. This is attested to by the fact that the hippocampus is one of the brain regions most affected by Alzheimer's disease, which is characterized by severe memory loss. Alzheimer's disease involves neurodegeneration, or the deterioration and death of neurons. While this neurodegeneration is widespread, neurons in the hippocampus are particularly susceptible.

The Power of Memory

"The power of memory is great, very great, my God."[95]

Memory is undeniably powerful. Whether it be in its storage capacity, or where memory itself is located and managed, or the different types of memory and their roles, or the intricate and elegant molecular regulation by Arc, memory is fascinating, mysterious, and astoundingly powerful. Arc could be likened to a control center managing and interconnecting neuronal activity and memory operations. Arc is immensely powerful in its functionality and beautiful in its elegance. It is no wonder that Augustine first wanted his readers and audience to grasp the enormity of the power of memory before he taught and wrote about the finer details; they would be able to get an even greater appreciation and perspective on the operation of memory and recognize its very specific role in their journey to God.

Memory and Sense Perception

"Memory preserves in distinct particulars and general categories all the perceptions which have penetrated, each by its own route of entry."[96]

Augustine had described in *Gn. Litt.* VII.18.24 the anatomical structure for the transmission of "messengers" from the five senses to the brain where memories of these sense perceptions were made and stored. He wrote of the sense of touch being directed by the brain throughout the body via the *"tenuissimi quidem rivuli"* (very fine streams) that ran through the *"tenues fistulae"* (fine tubes) that led from central part of the brain to the outer

---

95. *Conf.* X.8.15.
96. *Conf.* X.8.13.

surface of the body.⁹⁷ These sense perceptions led to the formation of sensory memories, which were created in an immediate fashion as soon as the information reached the brain. Sensory information remains in the brain for one to two seconds. During this period, the information of the object is processed, thus allowing the brain to recall previous memories of said object; this process of recalling enables the brain to identify and name the object.⁹⁸ Arc and the Arc cycle ensure that STM and LTM are encoded and consolidated. As the five senses operate, the brain is continuously assembling and sorting perceptions of the outside world, including acquisition of spatial surroundings. Augustine's description of messengers of sense perception transmitted to the brain via *"tenuissimi quidem rivuli"* in *"tenues fistulae"* from the external senses is surprisingly analogous to peripheral nervous system and the role of Arc within. The nervous system comprising of the peripheral central nervous systems compares to the Augustinian *tenues fistulae* and the *medulla cervicis et columnae et mens*, respectively, which correlate to the peripheral nerves, spinal cord, and brain. The transmission of neurotransmitters between synapses (Arc capsids trafficking Arc mRNA) correlate to Augustine's *tenuissimi quidem rivuli* carrying messengers. With the anatomical homology between Augustine's theory and current neurobiology, it is not surprising that there are also similarities between the functional operation of sensory memory. The formation of memories via sense perception is important because memories are crucial to survival. Martins in her work demonstrated that vision not only involves the formation of an optically perfect image but also perception.⁹⁹ Augustine understood how vision was a function of sense perception and could be explained by what is currently known as "physics."¹⁰⁰ The role of vision in retina–brain interactions is significant given the importance Augustine gave to vision as the mind's eye of the soul.¹⁰¹ In this capacity, the eyes (vision, *visio*) provided temporal information that informed the soul and allowed it to know how to adapt in order to turn towards the Divine. When processing a visual scene, there are mechanisms for selecting relevant information, which include perceptual learning and long-term adaptation and filtering out of irrelevant information.¹⁰² This is the precise mechanism that the rational soul adapts when filtering relevant information through the "mind's eye."

---

97. *Gn. Litt.* VII.13.20; VII.18.24; XII.20.42.
98. *Human Memory*, "Memory Processes."
99. Martins et al., "Plasticity," 1, 9.
100. O'Daly, *Augustine's Philosophy*, 82–83.
101. *Sol.* I.6.12.
102. Schneider et al., "On the Time Course," 1492.

This mechanism is regulated by Arc; however, Arc expression is activated by visual stimulation, but only occurs after opening of the eyes.[103] In fact, loss of Arc triggers an abnormal ocular dominance response thereby reducing visual acuity.[104] Arc, therefore, is required to establish and modify synaptic connections in the visual cortex.[105] McCurry concluded that Arc is a critical component of the molecular machinery that leads to lasting modifications in the quality of sensory experience.[106]

Memory's Role in Teaching and Learning

"All these ideas I hold in my memory, and the way I hold them in my memory is the way that I learnt them."[107]

Augustine recognized the interdependency between learning and teaching. Each had the necessity of acquiring new memories, coordinating these memories, and converting them into longer-term memories. Memory was important with regard to learning. A teacher was obligated to continually learn in order to teach and impart sound wisdom. According to Mau, "Memories do not simply conserve veridical representations of the past but must continually integrate new information to ensure survival in dynamic environments."[108] While this statement is written in the context of episodic memory, it does apply to teaching. Augustine uses "memory" with regard to both the student and teacher; but does it have the same implication for both since it is the teacher who must manage the "dynamic environment of learning and teaching?" Yes, and no. For the student, memory is used in acquiring and storing new information. For the teacher, memory is used in two ways. First, the student, in the context of learning, procures new information, both to solidify current memory and also to acquire new memories that support and augment their knowledge. The second is memory in the context of teaching, where the teacher imparts knowledge to the student in order that the student may learn. The updating of old memories must occur without corrupting original memories and must have the ability to add

---

103. McCurry et al., "Loss," 450–57; Plath, "Arc/Arg3.1," 441.

104. McCurry et al., "Loss," 450–57.

105. Visual cortex: primary cortical region of the brain that receives, integrates, and processes visual information from the retinas.

106. McCurry et al., "Loss," 456.

107. *Conf.* X.13.20.

108. Mau et al., "Brain," 1–24.

new memories to augment prior memories or create new ones. Augustine describes a very tight correlation between memory, learning, and teaching. The interdependency of molecular genomic processes, which include Arc, also demonstrate a tight synergistic relationship with regard to their role in memory, learning, and teaching. The fundamental cellular and molecular mechanisms underlying memory in learning and teaching have been studied extensively.[109] Immediately after learning, newly formed memories are stabilized through the induction of synaptic plasticity,[110] where Arc controls long-term changes in the strength of synapses.[111] Arc also has an important role in the late phases of learning and memory.[112]

Chen proposes that neuron excitability plays a vital role in memory formation regulating three fundamental phases of memory: allocation, consolidation, and updating.[113] First, allocation of memory is to a specific ensemble of neurons. Second, learning induces an increase in the excitability of ensemble neurons and works synergistically with synaptic plasticity mechanisms to facilitate memory consolidation resulting in successful learning. Third, neuron excitability may also contribute to multiple dynamic memory updating processes. Interestingly, the time course of excitability after learning can vary across distinct behavioral tasks, different brain regions, cell types, and the diverse experimental methods used to measure it.[114] Neuron excitability promotes both the stability and flexibility of memories, helping to shape, update, and organize memories accumulated across a lifetime.[115] Neuron excitability exerts lasting effects on memory from the initial formation to consolidation. Its transient nature makes neuron excitability an ideal cellular property governing the dynamic process of integration during memory updating. Arc, as we have seen, is intricately involved in the regulation of neuron excitability, and therefore, the formation, consolidation, and regulation of memory in teaching and learning.

---

109. Reviews offering good summaries: Mau et al., "Brain"; Richards and Frankland, "Persistence," 1071–84; Dunn and Kaczorowski, "Regulation," 107069; Jeong et al., "Synaptic," 3915–28.

110. Chen et al., "Role," 107266.

111. Leung at al., "Arc," 8.

112. Korb and Finkbeiner, "Arc," 595.

113. Chen et al., "Role," 5, 12.

114. Chen et al., "Role," 7.

115. Chen et al., "Role," 9.

Types of Learning

Learning involves different types of memory. One type is fast-learning.[116] According to Piette, fast-learning mechanisms are best characterized by single-trial learning paradigms which lead to memory formation after a single and brief (few hundred milliseconds to few minutes) exposure to relevant stimuli.[117] Physical memory traces (engrams)[118] are rapidly formed without requiring repetition of the learning experience.[119] A fast-learning task is sufficient to activate Arc and invoke long-term synaptic plasticity changes.[120] In mice, long-term structural and synaptic plasticity changes have been reported after a fast-learning experience such as fear conditioning.[121] Hippocampal neurons activated by a single fear-conditioning protocol become more excitable during several days, thereby potentially facilitating subsequent learning.[122] Emotive episodes are fast-learning experiences. Augustine refers to emotions and memories in *Conf.* X.14.21–22. He can call to mind from memory the four emotions of "cupidity, gladness, fear, and sadness" even when he is not physically experiencing the emotion, e.g., fear and/or sadness that once was or even happiness. Augustine questions whether this means that memory is independent of the mind. However, he concludes, "When they are entrusted to the memory [*memoriae*], they are as if transferred to the stomach [*ventrum*] and can there be stored; but they cannot be tasted." Essentially, Augustine believes that there can be long-term storage of memory traces related to emotionally charged unique experiences.

Learning also occurs via the integration of new memories into existing ones for the purpose of either updating old memories or creating new memories. This process of integrating new memories into existing ones is known as "rule and schema" learning and is critical for survival.[123] The brain can utilize the established rule or schema when similar information is encountered to achieve more efficient learning. Chen describes rat

---

116. Lechner et al., "100 Years," 77–87.

117. Piette et al., "Engrams," 1.

118. Richard Semon theorized that learning induces persistent changes in specific brain cells that retain information and that are subsequently reactivated upon appropriate retrieval. He called this hypothetical material basis of learnt information "the memory engram." Asok et al., "Molecular," 15.

119. Piette et al., "Engrams," 2.

120. Piette et al., "Engrams," 2.

121. Clarke et al., "Plastic," 2652–57.

122. Piette et al., "Engrams," 2.

123. Chen et al., "Role," 7.

experiments where a rule or schema is created through repeated training of an odor discrimination task during which water-deprived rats learned to distinguish between pairs of odors to obtain a water reward.[124] These findings indicate that prior learning of an associative schema may facilitate faster encoding and memory consolidation when learning new associations. The dynamic nature of memory makes it possible to integrate new information during memory updating while reducing the influence of outdated knowledge; this is crucial for memory-guided decision making, and up-to-date teaching.[125] In a dynamic environment, whatever is learned from a single memory may also need to be updated over time, as the initial memory may not hold true for future experiences.[126] The brain has the ability to cross-reference and store information and memories while maintaining stability and fidelity.[127] Both the anatomical structure of the brain and the regulation of memories via Arc are central to these processes.

Innate Memory

Much like Augustine, who believed in innate memory and *a priori* knowledge, some modern-day scientists do argue for the existence of innate memory that leads to an *a priori* knowledge.[128] Mau asserts that spontaneous remodeling of the synaptic connectivity space uses *a priori* knowledge when permitting memory-updating.[129] Continual remodeling and synaptic plasticity modulation must occur for the memory neural network to adapt once dynamic conditions are imposed; this requires an *a priori* knowledge or memory. Mau writes regarding this:

> This suggests that slow synaptic turnover may facilitate the ability to draw from a prior knowledge base (by storing connectivity patterns that are slow to decay) while still flexibly exploring related options through stochastic probing of new potential connectivity patterns, built atop existing ones. Such an implementation may underlie flexible behaviors that are based on memories for past outcomes.[130]

---

124. Chen et al., "Role," 10.
125. Chen et al., "Role," 10.
126. Mau et al., "Brain," 1.
127. Richards and Frankland, "Persistence," 1071–84.
128. Articles discussing innate memory: Mau et al., "Brain," 1–24; Perin et al., "Synaptic," 5419–24; Treffert, "Genetic"; Netea et al., "Innate," 13–26.
129. Mau et al., "Brain," 7.
130. Mau et al., "Brain," 7.

Perhaps the most understood and studied example of innate memory in humans is found in the immune response system where there are extremely specific innate immune cells that play a critical role in immunity. Host immunity is divided into innate and adaptive immune responses where memory is a characteristic recognized within both arms of the immune system.[131] The innate memory cells react rapidly and non-specifically to pathogens, whereas the adaptive memory cells respond in a slower but specific manner, with the generation of long-lived immunological memory.[132] During an infection, innate immunity is the first to be triggered (the inflammatory reaction), taking several minutes up to hours to be fully activated; innate immunity is crucial for the host's defense in the first phase of infection.[133] Adaptive immunity comes into play after this initial first phase. What is interesting is that innate memory immune responses can adapt allowing for sustained defense.[134] Innate immune memory is thought to exist in newborns and is not a property that is learnt as one grows; it is a built-in memory that resides in the genome.[135]

Researchers at Blue Brain Project[136] discovered that a neuron network of about fifty neurons formed the "building blocks" or ensembles of more complex knowledge but they contained basic innate knowledge.[137] This is much like the innate immune memory cells developing adaptive responses. BBP's scientists ran tests on the neuronal circuits of several rats and ascertained that if the neuronal circuits had only been formed based on an individual rat's experience, the tests would bring about very different characteristics for each rat.[138] However, the rats all displayed similar characteristics, which suggests that their neuronal circuits must have been established prior to their experiences, it must be inborn. This BBP research supports an innate genetic structure of some of the fundamental representations of

---

131. Sadeghalvad et al., "Structure," 24–38; Netea et al., "Innate," 13.

132. Netea et al., "Innate," 13.

133. Netea et al., "Innate," 13.

134. Netea et al., "Trained," 355–61; Netea et al., "Innate," 14.

135. Simon et al., "Evolution," 20143085.

136. Blue Brain Project (BBP): a Swiss brain research initiative that aims to create a digital reconstruction of the mouse brain. The project was founded in May 2005 by the Brain and Mind Institute of École Polytechnique Fédérale de Lausanne (EPFL) in Switzerland. Its mission is to use biologically detailed digital reconstructions and simulations of the mammalian brain to identify the fundamental principles of brain structure and function.

137. Pousaz, "New," 1.

138. Pousaz, "New," 1.

basic knowledge.¹³⁹ This knowledge is inscribed in our genes and present at birth.

It is possible to acquire knowledge via innate knowledge that is genetically inherited. For example, when a horse is born, it can immediately walk. The foal did not learn this behavior; it simply knew how to do it.¹⁴⁰ Another example of a built-in innate knowledge is discussed by Treffert with regard to innate or genetic memory in savants.¹⁴¹ He argues that savants have what he calls "factory-installed software" and that they are convincing examples of "genetic inheritance of actual instruction and knowledge that precedes learning."¹⁴² He, agrees with Carpenter,¹⁴³ who believes that savants have a congenital aptitude for certain mental activity "which showed itself at so early a period as to exclude the notion that it could have been acquired by the experience of the individual."¹⁴⁴ Savants are an exceptional example of innate knowledge, but at least, comparatively speaking, a basic innate knowledge or memory still exists in all persons. Augustine presents many examples, but one is the learning of liberal arts where, as in the case of music, there is an innate knowledge of music that comes forth from a musician when they compose.¹⁴⁵ There is also a learnt or acquired knowledge in music where the musician learns from another musician.¹⁴⁶ Another Augustinian example would be actual numbers that are kept in memory and not their images, and which are present before the person knows how to speak that number.¹⁴⁷ For Augustine, mathematics played an entrenched role in deciphering memory and in the search for truth. A. S. Fokas, in his Harvard presentation on "Mathematics, Innate Knowledge, and Neuroscience," argues that mathematics has a crucial role in the search for truth.¹⁴⁸ Additionally, Arc is believed to have an innate memory as it too carries *a priori* directives regarding its expression, operation, and role in memory.

---

139. Pousaz, "New," 1.
140. Sipe, "What Is?"
141. Treffert, "Genetic," 1.
142. Treffert, "Genetic," 4.
143. William Carpenter, a nineteenth-century British physician and neurologist, is one of the founders of the modern theory of the adaptive unconsciousness. He believed in the existence of an innate knowledge. Wikipedia, s.v. "William Benjamin Carpenter," https://en.wikipedia.org/wiki/William_Benjamin_Carpenter.
144. Treffert, "Genetic," 4.
145. *Mus.* I.5.10.
146. *Mus.* I.5.10.
147. *Conf.* X.15.23.
148. Fokas, "Mathematics."

Consolidation of Memory

Memory consolidation[149]—the process by which memory traces of encoded information (e.g., images) are strengthened, stabilized, and stored—operates within an architectonic structure. Consolidation is the next step in the formation of a memory; it works most effectively when the images that are stored can be linked to an existing neuronal network. New memories are consolidated after learning and memory allocation; the newly acquired memories are then transformed into long-term memory.[150] Both long-term-memory and short-term-memory formation is facilitated by Arc, which stabilizes synaptic plasticity.[151] Long-term-memory consolidation involves both the formation of new synapses and the elimination of pre-existing synapses."[152] Synaptic consolidation is assumed to last minutes to hours after encoding within the local circuit and synapses.[153] Systems consolidation, on the other hand, is considered to take days to months or even longer and involves the reorganization and distribution of the memory representations across different brain regions.[154] These two levels of consolidation (synaptic and systems) are closely related.[155] Leung writes that Arc plays a critical role in memory consolidation, which is demonstrated by the fact that knockdown[156] of Arc expression interferes with stabilization of memory.[157] The data presented by Leung shows that Arc regulates the expression of a large number of synaptic proteins with functions in both the

---

149. Müller and Pilzecker were the first to adopt the term "consolidation" to describe post-experience processes of memory stabilization. Müller and Pilzecker, *Experimentelle*, 1–300.

150. Dudai, "Molecular," 211.

151. Korb and Finkbeiner, "Arc," 1.

152. Holtmaat and Caroni, "Functional," 1553–62.

153. Asok describes three types of consolidation. Storage consolidation which is the conversion of short-term memory into long-term memory within a defined neuronal ensemble in the time frame of hours. Synaptic consolidation is the molecular mechanism associated with increase synaptic activity linked to a long-term memory. Systems consolidation is the maturation of long-term memory to recruit more heavily cortical/neocortical brain regions. Asok et al., "Molecular," 15; Dudai, "Neurobiology," 51–86; Chen et al., "Role," 4.

154. Dudai, "Neurobiology," 52.

155. Neurobiologists distinguish between slow and fast memory consolidation. Their different kinetic properties reflect qualitatively distinct underlying processes. Dudai, "Restless," 227–47.

156. "Knockdown" is the inhibition of gene expression using molecular techniques.

157. Leung et al., "Arc," 6.

pre- and post-synaptic compartment.[158] Leung describes a new mechanism by which Arc can control long-lasting changes in synaptic structure and function required for memory consolidation.

Cellular Consolidation

The phrase "cellular consolidation" refers to the initial stabilization of a memory trace in the hours following learning at the molecular level. Cellular consolidation is essential for memory retention; it is the cascade of molecular processes that occur immediately after learning and that stabilize the cellular and synaptic changes produced by learning. It is dependent on *de novo* protein synthesis, which ultimately leads to long-term structural and functional neuronal changes and the stabilization of a memory trace.[159] Arc expression constitutes the cell's earliest genomic response to stimulation, and the Arc protein can either directly modify the structure and function of a cell to stabilize a memory or activate late-response genes to facilitate cellular consolidation.[160]

Memory Traces

The allocation of particular neurons to a memory trace is controlled by molecular mechanisms and structural changes within the neuronal network. This is important to understand as it demonstrates how information is preserved during consolidation. Research has uncovered fundamental rules about neuronal allocation within a long-term memory trace;[161] yet, according to Asok, the molecular mechanisms which drive this neuronal allocation remain elusive.[162] However, some progress has been made. Similar, but nonidentical, aversive memories (i.e., fear conditioning using different tones or contexts) that are acquired closely in time recruit an overlapping ensemble of neurons in the amygdala and CA1 neurons.[163] These ensembles can represent each memory in a synapse-specific manner, although the likelihood of overlap diminishes when the acquisition of similar long-term

---

158. Leung et al., "Arc," 8.
159. Yonelinas et al., "Contextual," 364; Jeong et al., "Synaptic," 8.
160. Barry and Commins, "Temporal," 44.
161. Abdou et al., "Synapse-specific," 1227–31.
162. Asok et al., "Molecular," 19.
163. CA1-3 neurons form a neural circuit operational in memory and located in the hippocampus. Asok et al., "Molecular," 20–21.

memories has greater temporal separation. Once a memory trace has been consolidated, the memory trace can be stored for later retrieval indefinitely. The storage consolidation phase of memory traces requires *de novo* Arc protein synthesis, which is tightly regulated by the Arc gene.[164] Arc also enables consolidation of weak memories and plays a role in behavioral tagging in the hippocampus. A role of Arc in cognitive flexibility was suggested based on results showing a strong positive correlation between Arc mRNA levels in the rat hippocampus and behavioral performance during spatial reversal tasks.[165] Altogether, these results suggest a feedback-like relationship; Arc expression may be regulated by large networks linked with learning and memory on the one hand, but on the other, Arc expression may form new and/or modify existing networks.[166]

Degradation of Memory

Memories need to survive the degradation that time brings and continue to exist. The theory that explains the dynamic interaction of preservation and degradation is known as the "persistence of memory."[167] A fluidity must exist between old and new memories; they should not collide and become distorted. It is the dynamic memory ensembles that encapsulate how memories can be both persistent and fluid. Reversal learning, reconsolidation, schema learning, and systems consolidation all describe how previously learnt behaviors can be modified to accommodate new learning.[168] The hippocampus is often thought of as the flexible learner that trains neocortical networks to store memories long term; however, neocortical networks still undergo continual modifications as a person learns over a lifetime.[169] The brain has the capacity to store memory long term with persistence of that memory over time. However, it is not the active state of the LTM that persists; rather, what persists is the capacity to reactivate or reconstruct the original or a similar representation by the process of retrieval.[170] This again, is reminiscent of Augustine's teacher who needs to learn and retain the memory of the learnt material over time and then reactivate it as he teaches, or when one

---

164. Yap and Greenberg, "Activity-Regulated," 330–48.
165. Guzowski et al., "Experience-dependent," 5089–98.
166. Fila et al., "mRNA," 4.
167. Mau et al., "Brain," 2.
168. Mau et al., "Brain," 2.
169. Mau et al., "Brain," 2.
170. Dudai, "Molecular," 211.

"reactivates" the words of a song when it is sung. Long-term memories are thought to be supported by a "backbone" of stable neurons that store gross features of memory while some other neurons constantly undergo plasticity to encode more detailed representations. Thus, a significant portion of the neural network is dynamic,[171] supported by an architectonic structure that allows for a fluidity between the formation and degradation of memories.

Retrieval of Memory

The last step in forming memories is retrieval,[172] which is the conscious recollection of information that was encoded and stored. Retrieving information from memory depends upon contextual information or cues and how effectively the information was encoded and stored into memory.[173] If the information was not properly encoded because of a distraction, a person may be less likely to retrieve details of the event or information. Consolidated memories may thus become generalized or lacking in detail, including the extent to which they elicit visceral or physiological reactions.[174] Emotional, semantic knowledge, olfactory, auditory, and visual factors can function as cues for contextual information to help in the retrieval of episodic memory. For example, when recalling where you parked your car, you may use the color of a sign you parked near as a reminder.[175] Research also states that episodic retrieval can be associated with a sense of re-experiencing (i.e., "re-collecting") the event; to remember where you parked or did not park your car, you must mentally travel back to the moment or time you parked.[176] The neuronal network activity during this re-collection and retrieval process is observed to be highly dynamic, with Arc protein increasing and rapidly decreasing.[177]

---

171. Mau et al., "Brain," 4.

172. There is a distinction between retrieval and recall or recollection/remembrance of memory. Memory retrieval requires revisiting the nerve pathways formed during the encoding and storage of the memory. Memory recollection is not just pulling things from the storage of memories, rather it is a process of creativity in which the relevant information is gathered from the scattered, puzzle-like information in the brain. *Human Memory*, "Memory Recall."

173. Straube, "Overview," 5.

174. Yonelinas et al., "Contextual," 364–75.

175. UCSF Weill Institute for Neuroscience, "Memory."

176. UCSF Weill Institute for Neuroscience, "Memory."

177. Ramirez-Amaya et al., "Spatial," 1761–68.

The recollection of experiences is contingent on three steps of memory processing: encoding, consolidation/storage, and retrieval.[178] When retrieving a memory, a person can revisit the state that memory was in. This was demonstrated by Polyn, who used multi-voxel pattern analysis (MVPA)[179] to analyze human memory activity patterns during learning and recollection.[180] Polyn provided direct evidence that when people retrieve a specific memory, their brain revisits the state it was in when it encoded that information. More recently Chen found that brain activity across fifty scenes of the opening episode of a Sherlock Holmes movie could be clearly distinguished from one another.[181] These patterns were remarkably specific, at times telling apart scenes that did or did not include Sherlock, and those that occurred indoors or outdoors. Near the hippocampus and several high-level processing centers, such as the posterior medial cortex, the researchers saw the same scene-viewing patterns unfold as each person later recounted the episode, even if people described the specific scenes differently. They even observed similar brain activity in people who had never seen the show but had heard others' accounts of it.[182] Augustine discussed this aspect of memory, "the ocean (which I believed on the reports of others) I could see inwardly with dimensions just as great as if I were actually looking at them outside of my mind" (*Conf.* X.8.15). To quote Chen, "It was a surprise that we see that same fingerprint when different people are remembering the same scene, describing it in their own words, remembering it in whatever way they want to remember."[183] These results suggest that brains, even in higher-order regions that process memory, concepts, and complex cognition, may be organized more similarly across people than expected.

Memories can become destabilized or fractured during the retrieval process leaving them vulnerable to interference upon reactivation. In order to stabilize the retrieved memory it must be reconsolidated, a process that induces Arc expression.[184] Reconsolidating memory is a complex process occurring within distributed networks of neurons throughout the brain. According to Chen, memories can be linked not only during initial

---

178. Straube, "Overview," 1–10.

179. MVPA is an analytical technique that identifies neural patterns involved in task conditions including spatial patterns of activity.

180. Polyn et al., "Category-Specific," 1963–66.

181. Chen et al., "Shared," 115–25.

182. Chen et al., "Shared," 115–25; Zadbood et al., "How," 4988–5000.

183. Chen et al., "Shared," 148.

184. Lee et al., "Update," 531; Nakyam et al., "Long-Delayed," 819–30.

memory encoding but also during retrieval.[185] Chen states that memory integration during retrieval is a further demonstration of the dynamic nature of memory, and retrieval-induced intrinsic excitability increases may play an important role in mediating this process. Augustine discusses this process of associative memories and temporal linking of memories in *Conf.* X.11.18. He writes:

> By thinking we, as it were, gather together ideas which the memory contains in a dispersed and disordered way, and by concentrating our attention we arrange them in order as if ready to hand, stored in the very memory where they lay hidden, scattered, and neglected.

Recollection/Remembering and Forgetfulness in Memory

"Memories are islands in an ocean of forgetting."[186]

Augustine knew from his deliberations on memory that there was a very strong link between recollection or remembrance and forgetting; one could not exist without the other. He found this paradoxical and, I suspect, even frustrating, since despite his extensive interrogations of memory, he was unable to find all the answers regarding this inter-relatedness between the two. This is clear in *Conf.* X.16.25 when he writes, "Yet in some way, though incomprehensible and inexplicable, I am certain that I can remember forgetfulness itself, and yet forgetfulness destroys what we remember." Augustine continuing with the phenomenon of forgetfulness (*Conf.* X.18.27–19.28) writes about the seriousness of the loss of memory just before his discussion on the *beata vita*.

Recollection (*re*-collection, *re*-call) or remembering a memory and forgetfulness are of paramount importance to Augustine's theology of *memoria*. Augustine asserts that all the images held in his memory can be recovered through recollection (*Conf.* X.9.16). According to O'Daly, the "mind's vision is formed by the memory-image and can recall previously perceived objects"; he comments that recollecting is primarily concerned with actualizing memory-traces.[187] He bases this on Augustine's remarks in

---

185. Chen et al., "Role," 6.

186. Jorge Luis Borges from *Funes el Memorioso*, which first appeared in the Argentinian daily newspaper *La Nación* in June 1942. The story is about a man who after a riding accident could remember everything.

187. O'Daly, *Augustine's Philosophy*, 133; *Trin.* XI.3.6.

Mag. 39 that it is not the objects of past-perceptions themselves but rather the images derived from them that we speak of when we talk about past perceptions.

Most neuroscientists now believe that recollection occurs when the neurons involved in memory fire again and replay the activity patterns associated with past images and experience.[188] This clearly aligns with Augustine's concept, as O'Daly puts it, of actualizing memory-traces. The molecular dynamics behind this Augustinian active will of recollection includes the involvement of Arc in actualizing memory recollection. The Arc gene initiates and regulates the synthesis of *de novo* Arc protein whenever active recollection occurs and neurons "fire again." This is true every time a familiarization memory is reactivated, no matter how consolidated it is.[189] According to Morin, the original memory becomes labile, requiring a restabilization process, i.e., reconsolidation managed by *de novo* Arc protein synthesis.

The process of memory retrieval alters the composition of neuronal subpopulations that activate Arc transcription in the amygdala located in the middle ventricle where Augustine understood memory to be operationally active.[190] This activity in the amygdala is also necessary for the stabilization of emotional memory, e.g., reactivated fear memory.[191] Yamasaki states that subpopulations in the lateral amygdala appear to be involved in individual fear memory throughout the processes of its acquisition, consolidation, retrieval, and reconsolidation.[192] Further, Arc, as a master regulator of synaptic plasticity, is essential for consolidation of synaptic plasticity and spatial memory, object-recognition memory, contextual and auditory fear memory, and taste aversion memory. It is Arc transcription that engages in the reactivation of retrieval-relevant neural activity and. therefore, both the recollection and retrieval of memory.[193] Of note, post-retrieval inhibition of neural activity and Arc protein synthesis causes impaired retention of reactivated fear memory.[194] Any malfunction or alterations of Arc expression could result in forgetfulness.[195]

---

188. Shen, "Portrait," 147.
189. Morin et al., "New," 8.
190. *Gn. Litt.* VII.18.24; Yamasaki, "Off-line," 3454–55.
191. Yamasaki, "Off-line," 3451.
192. Yamasaki, "Off-line," 3456.
193. Yamasaki, "Off-line," 3455.
194. Yamasaki, "Off-line," 3455.
195. Straube, "Overview," 1–10.

The brain, each and every day, recognizes many details and information as unnecessary and inconsequential and thus does not retain them in memory. In one sense, this could be considered an immediate forgetting. Forgetting can be a spontaneous or gradual process in which old memories are unable to be recalled from memory storage.[196] It can be a temporary or permanent inability to retrieve a previously acquired memory.[197] Gravitz quotes Oliver Hardt regarding the importance of forgetting; forgetting is not a "glitch" of memory, rather to have proper memory function you have to have forgetting.[198] Augustine saw this connection between the functions of forgetting and remembering. He writes that both memory and forgetfulness are present in the mind, and "unless we could recall forgetfulness, we could never hear the word and recognize the thing the word signifies. Therefore, memory retained forgetfulness" (*Conf.* X.16.24). Forgetfulness also involves the actions of remembrance and recollection; Augustine sees this as an active process and necessary in the functioning of memory. Gravtiz makes the point that to understand how we remember, we must also understand how, and why, we forget.[199] This was precisely the point that perplexed Augustine as he explored the paradox of remembering forgetfulness.[200] Augustine realized that forgetfulness played a role in memory function, but he was perplexed as to how memory recognized forgetfulness.[201] What has become evident from the many studies in this area is that forgetting, or dis-remembering, is an active process, as Augustine deduced, and it works in collaboration with consolidation, remembrance/recollection, and retrieval of memory. Forgetting seeks to eliminate memories from the brain via apparent loss or modification of information already encoded and stored in short-term memory and long-term memory.[202] Forgetfulness is an adaptive process that endows a person with knowledge about the world while continuously updating that knowledge. Forgetting is, therefore, a critical process for selecting and maintaining those memories that will drive advantageous behavior.[203] Forgetting is also critical for memory generalization, the process that allows memories of specific situations to

---

196. Wikipedia, s.v. "Forgetting," https://en.wikipedia.org/wiki/Forgetting.
197. Shen, "Portrait," 147.
198. Gravitz, "Importance," S12.
199. Gravitz, "Importance," S14.
200. *Conf.* X.16.25.
201. *Conf.* X.16.24–25.
202. Gravitz, "Importance," S12–S14; Shen, "Portrait," 147–48.
203. Noyes et al., "Memory," 3218.

be used to make predictions about similar, but non-identical situations.[204] In this process, forgetting causes the loss of memory details and allows the memory to be retrieved using broad similarities rather than details present during acquisition. Augustine posited that a memory could be retrieved through the prompting of others, e.g., the recollection of a name could perhaps be recalled via promptings that were unlike the original memory.[205] However, memory can also be totally forgotten and not just a temporary or partial forgetfulness; it is "wholly effaced from the mind" as Augustine said in *Conf.* X.19.28.

Shen writes that there have been several proposed pathways responsible for the inability to recall memories.[206] These include natural time-dependent decay of memory traces, change of context between acquisition and retrieval, and interference. Khan observed that there is a critical balance between excitation and inhibition of neuronal function.[207] This is a delicate balance as any alterations of Arc's regulation or expression can cause deficits in memory resulting in neurological disorders and severe memory loss, as in Alzheimer's disease.[208] Partial forgetting must be differentiated from amnesia; both have memory loss, but while forgetting is a natural process, amnesia is a pathological one.[209] Augustine discusses forgetting that is partial loss or recoverable memory loss where a memory may return upon prompting (*Conf.* X.15.23–X.19.28).[210] Here too, Augustine is puzzled as he tries to understand the nature of what is being recalled since forgetting (*oblivio*)[211] is the absence of memory (*privatio memoriae*); how can it be present to memory?[212] Augustine's explication was that the memory of an

---

204. Noyes et al., "Memory," 3218.
205. *Conf.* X.19.28.
206. Shen, "Portrait," 147.
207. Khan, "Master."
208. Leung et al., "Arc," 1; Palop et al., "Vulnerability," 9686–93.
209. Medina et al., "Neural," 103.

210. This brings to mind an interesting perspective on forgetting and remembering posited by Locke. He states that forgetting can be temporary and remembered years later. However, the man who forgets the performance of an action for twenty years is not the same person as the one whose action it was. Only when he remembers does the action become his again. Locke regards this kind of forgetting as happening in the real world. Locke, *Essay*, II.xxvii.23. Also see Stuart, *Locke's*, 363.

211. O'Daly, *Augustine's Philosophy*, 147. I agree with O'Daly's translation of *oblivio*. He translates *oblivio* as "forgetting" rather than "forgetfulness," since Augustine's argument deals with instances of loss of memory rather than a stable mental condition or tendency, such as is implied by "forgetfulness."

212. O'Daly, *Augustine's Philosophy*, 146–47.

object may be lost to sight, yet the memory itself was still held in memory.[213] He had to accept that recognizing by means of forgetting is as good as remembering it.[214] According to O'Daly, Augustine attempts to solve the problem of remembering what we have forgotten. He writes:

> But there can be no doubt that in positing an instance of forgetting that is less than total, and so implies the latent presence of what is forgotten to the mind, Augustine attempts to solve the problem posed by this tenet that, if we recognize the meaning of the term "forgetting," we remember forgetting.[215]

Fading of Memory Over Time

Forgetting is a temporal process during which there is a time-dependent decline of a memory. Ebbinghaus discovered that there is a very rapid loss of recall within the first hour after learning, up to a 60 percent loss after nine hours, and thereafter, information retention decreases by approximately 50 percent each day when there is no attempt to retain information.[216] However, there is an improvement in retention with repetition, which increases further with multiple repetitions. Behavioral studies on human subjects and animal models suggest several factors contribute to forgetting.[217] These include natural decay, where neuronal correlates of memory dissipate over time, and interference, whereby previously formed memories are displaced by information acquired after learning. Psychophysics studies also suggest that forgetting could result from failed retrieval of the memories; they suggest the possibility that forgetting does not erase the memory but renders it less accessible, as Augustine suspected.[218]

Disorders of Memory Forgetting

Interference of Arc regulation could occur at the formation and consolidation of, or even at the moment of retrieving, a memory resulting in memory disorders.[219] Wixted suggests that the amnesic effect of a new learning on

---

213. *Conf.* X.18.27.
214. *Conf.* X.16.24; O'Daly, *Augustine's Philosophy*, 146.
215. O'Daly, "Augustine's" 148.
216. Ebbinghaus, *Memory*.
217. Liu et al., "Forgetting," 1.
218. Liu et al., "Forgetting," 1.
219. Leung et al., "Arc," 1; Palop et al., "Vulnerability," 9686–93; Wixted, "Psychology," 235–69.

previously encoded material could be related to limitations in the brain structure, the number of synaptic connections, and/or the amount of plasticity-related proteins, including Arc protein.[220] Additionally, Martinez discusses how limited Arc protein synthesis impacts memory interference.[221] Further, Arc availability in memory competition can deeply influence the stabilization of the engrams; any deficits would also impact memory forgetfulness.[222] Genetic alterations, mutations, and variants can also alter Arc expression and effect Arc protein synthesis and are implicated in different diseases such as schizophrenia, autism, intellectual disabilities, and Alzheimer's disease.[223] Moreover Arc dysregulation contributes to various mental disorders, such as fragile X syndrome (elevated Arc protein levels) and Angelman's syndrome.[224] It is also known that traumatic neuronal injury causes an increase in Arc expression.[225]

Interestingly, Augustine had described how errors or malfunctions of memory resulted in the concept of "forgetfulness of memory" or permanent loss of memory.[226] Alzheimer's disease involves a permanent loss of memory and would thus be a condition that conforms to Augustine's definition. Alzheimer's disease is a devastating neurodegenerative disorder characterized by the progressive loss of synaptic function and long-term-memory formation. A landmark study published in 2011 showed that Arc is involved in permanent memory loss and the formation of amyloid (Aβ) plaques.[227] Arc-dependent mechanisms control activity dependent generation of Aβ plaques that characterize brain pathology and are relevant in the pathogenesis of Alzheimer's disease.[228] Arc controls the expression of susceptibility genes for Alzheimer's disease, as well as that of many other genes associated with the pathophysiology of Alzheimer's disease.[229] Leung demonstrated that the prevention of Arc induction altered the expression profile for over nineteen hundred genes, including genes associated with

---

220. Wixted, "Psychology," 235–69.

221. Martinez et al., "Memory," 166.

222. Martinez et al., "Memory," 165.

223. Plath et al., "Arc/Arg3.1," 437–44; Leung et al., "Arc," 1; Chuang et al., "Rare," 105–6; Zhang et al., "Structural," 490.

224. Chuang et al., "Rare," 106; Park et al., "Elongation," 70–83; Zhang et al., "Structural," 490.

225. Chen et al., "Arc," 7.

226. *Conf.* X.19.28.

227. Wu et al., "Arc/Arg3.1," 615–28.

228. Wu et al., "Arc/Arg3.1," 617; Hashimoto et al., "Collagenous," 1.

229. Leung et al., "Arc," 1.

synaptic function, neuronal plasticity, intrinsic excitability, and signaling pathways. Interestingly, about one hundred Arc-dependent genes are associated specifically with the pathophysiology of Alzheimer's disease. Of note, there is a specific polymorphism in the Arc gene that is involved in Alzheimer's disease susceptibility, which actually reduces the risk for developing Alzheimer's disease.[230] There is a precision regulation required of Arc in memory processes; a fine balance that exists between normal and aberrant expression.

Forgetting and the Future

The temporal dimension of memory is such that it involves the future, but so does the forgetting of memories. The rigors of forgetting and remembering becomes the ongoing and active work of Christian existence, something that Augustine was acutely aware of.[231] According to Grove, forgetting is just like remembering; it is a bidirectional activity.[232] It is forgetting that enables forward movement in life and in pilgrimage with Christ.[233] Forgetting the past is a forgetting into Christ; this results in a deeper union with Christ.[234] Throughout this pilgrimage Augustine the *peregrinus* remembers Christ, and thus the reality of eternity. Through Christ, memories merge into the finitude of eternity and the present becomes a remembrance of the beginnings, i.e., past and creation; present and the memory of the incarnation, death, and resurrection; the future and memory of eschatological expectation. The memory of the eschaton in the future requires the letting go of past memories that hinder progression towards the *beata vita*.

Arc's Role Regarding Images, *Phantasiae*, and *Phantasmata*

"*Imagination is the eye of the soul.*"[235]

"*Imagination is the beginning of creation.*"[236]

---

230. Landgren et al., "Novel," 838.
231. Grove, *Augustine*, 157.
232. Grove, *Augustine*, 156.
233. Grove, *Augustine*, 157.
234. Grove, *Augustine*, 156–57.
235. Joseph Joubert (1754–1824 AD), French moralist and essayist.
236. An oft-cited quotation attributed to George Bernard Shaw.

Augustine was well aware that memory did not only consist of true images but also false iterations of existing stored memories or even completely new false images. Corruption in the updating process of memories or formation of new images that are unlike the original or complete fabrications are a result of Arc dysregulation. Dysregulation occurs via mutation or inhibition of Arc expression. Molecular mechanisms and Arc regulation of memory processes are thus involved in the formation of *phantasiae* and *phantasmata*.

Imagination can conjure up creative, frightening, and false images; it can elaborate on complex, false dreams, and can also occur while awake and throughout the day. According to Burge, the process of imagining differs from memory, not necessarily in its content but in its representational function.[237] Imagining is non-committal, unlike memory or perception. There is no need for imagination to produce accurate images because such images, whether accurate or inaccurate, do not constitute a representational failure.[238] Imagination produces images that do not need to remember how to do something, i.e., the action of speaking, feeling, or touching. Lui and Ramirez suggest that the formation of some *phantasmata* may occur by internally driven retrieval of previous experiences and their association with external pleasant or unpleasant emotive stimuli.[239]

The brain regions associated with true memory and false memory are very similar.[240] Both true and false memories produce activity in the core regions in the brain associated with long-term-memory retrieval, e.g., the hippocampus and sensory processing regions.[241] Augustine in *Mus.* VI.2 suggests that the production of *phantasmata* is analogous to the formation of images of perceived objects.[242] He seems to imply that *phantasmata* and true memories are formed in the same region of the brain. However, differences in brain activity do occur between true and false memories; there is greater activity for true memory compared to false memory in the more posterior early visual processing regions.[243] Mnemonic errors that occur with the correlation of memory and predictions based on false images change the role of the hippocampus; these errors cause a reversal of the

---

237. Burge, *Perception*, 641.
238. Burge, *Perception*, 641.
239. Liu et al., "Inception," 20130142; Ramirez et al., "Creating," 390.
240. Burge, *Perception*, 642.
241. Liu et al., "Inception," 20130142; Ramirez et al., "Creating," 387–91.
242. O'Daly, *Augustine's Philosophy*, 108.
243. Liu et al., "Inception," 20130142; Ramirez et al., "Creating," 387–91.

relationship between hippocampal activation and memory outcomes.[244] Sinclair examined the mechanisms of this shift in neural processing and showed that such errors disrupted the temporal continuity of hippocampal patterns and allow memories to be modified, consistent with an adaptive updating mechanism.[245] They were able to demonstrate that hippocampal activation was associated with memory preservation and protection against false memories that destabilized the original memories.

Arc operates in a flexible, multifunctional, and interactive hub directing Arc expression and Arc protein synthesis; this is required in the modification and re-stabilization of a memory trace.[246] Here Arc expression and structural synaptic stability (plasticity) works in conjunction with the hippocampus.[247] The functional versatility of Arc recognizes Arc as a highly specialized master organizer of long-term synaptic plasticity, critical for the reconsolidation of images.[248]

Arc and the Temporal Dimension of Memory

Augustine proposed that memory not only exists in the past or future but also in the present.[249] Time and memory do not, and cannot, exist without each other. This concept has broad ranging and specific implications. Augustine found this topic was so complex, so difficult to explain, yet so important that he devoted a whole book (*Conf.* XI) to try to understand and explain the association between memory and time. Likewise, in his footsteps, I devote a full chapter (chapter 7) to this topic as it is too important to mention briefly in a few paragraphs.

Memory, Arc, and the *Beata Vita*

The denouement of Augustine's strategic approach into understanding memory was a result of his search for God and the discovery of *memoria* in his mind. Consequently, he knew that memory was crucial in this journey towards fulfillment of the *beata vita*, and as such, he devoted twice as many chapters in *Conf.* X. to the *beata vita* compared to the operation and

---

244. Sinclair et al., "Prediction," 1.
245. Sinclair et al., "Prediction," 8.
246. Castello-Waldow et al., "Hippocampal," 1; Nikolaienko et al., "Arc," 33.
247. Castello-Waldow et al., "Hippocampal," 1.
248. Castello-Waldow et al., "Hippocampal," 1.
249. *Conf.* X.8.13–14.

function of memory. It is well worth giving this topic of memory and the *beata vita* a lengthier discussion since it held such a prominent place in Augustine's theology of *memoria*. The role of memory in the *beata vita* and the associated physical molecular dynamics including Arc are discussed in chapters 7 and 8.

Molecular Architectonics

The architectonics of memory also applies to the domain of human molecular genetics. Within molecular genetics there is the field of DNA architectonics, which exists as a sub-specialism.[250] The genomic DNA sequence is not only composed of base-pair building blocks, but it has a 3D spatial setting analogous to Augustine's memory palace, with many nooks and crannies. The specific structure of Arc defines and drives its operational and functional roles. Additionally, Arc functions within the confines of time and its 3D structure confers a spatial dynamic. This architectonic structure also bestows upon Arc the ability to have a multi-functional role impacting over nineteen hundred genes and different aspects of memory, including those outlined by Augustine.

Theological Implications of Arc

Arc does not singularly operate within the constrictions of the genome or within the physical realm but it plays an important role in the metaphysical recollection of the *memoria Dei* in the soul and, significantly, in participating in directing the soul's attention towards the Divine. Augustine writes that memory is the mind's way to God (*Conf.* X.17.26); it is also the mind's mode of apprehending wisdom and truth. The *memoria Dei* was therefore, for the rational soul, an aperture to the Divine and a knowledge and understanding of God. While the soul did have a *memoria Dei* within as an innate memory, it still had to recollect the *memoria Dei* within. It was through this recollection that the soul rediscovered the pathway to return to its origins and the Divine. The soul, however, while superior to the body, still needed the body's help in this recollection of *memoria Dei*. Arc, with the novel neuronal synaptic communication and memory process that it regulates, is centrally involved in the recollection of memories and therefore helps to facilitate the recollection of the *memoria Dei* within the rational soul.

---

250. Key articles: Stulz, "DNA," 4456–69; Ghosh et al., "Molecular," 124–40; Wang et al., "Beauty," 359–82.

Recollection of the *memoria Dei* requires both the action of Arc and the action of the soul, and the soul has to be cognizant of the temporal and corporeal. The involvement of Arc in the recollection of the *memoria Dei* is necessary to the soul, and so Arc, as part of the genomic structure in the body, is the body participating in the life of the soul. The physicality of the body, in this case signified by Arc, is integral in pointing to its spiritual nature. Arc becomes a pointer to the Divine and recollection of the *memoria Dei* in the soul becomes the aperture to the Divine. In this manner, Arc unifies its physical and metaphysical dynamics and thus plays its role in the unity of body and soul. Arc is an exemplar of a genomic process that demonstrates the inter-relatedness between body and soul. This inter-relatedness is Augustinian in its theology.

Further, to Augustine's creation *ex nihilo* theology, the world and all that exists contains vestiges or traces of divine creation. Such vestiges are traces of God found in the physical and sensible order and even in the realm of self-knowledge.[251] The human body has a *vestigium*, or trace, of God within (*memoria Dei*). Augustine is convinced that he remembers God and that God is within him; he declares, "you conferred this honour on my memory that you should dwell in it."[252] Chandler writes that Augustine commits himself to "charting the mind's landscape," which allows him to arrive in the spiritual world, the realm of God.[253] This journey is possible due to the nature of memory. Arc elaborates on some of the specific functions of the human body in relation to its signatory value as a pointer to the Divine in Augustine's spiritual journey. Arc as such was, and is, a *vestigium* of the divine creation, a *vestigium* integral to memory processes that include innate and genomic memory. Arc assists the mind in creating memories, storing them, retaining them, and enabling a recollection of that which is buried deep in the caverns of *memoria*, including the *memoria Dei*, the *vestigium* of the Divine. Arc, a physical creation, holds the memory of the promise of God as it is able to provide the soul with the ability to remember the *memoria Dei*.[254] Arc's role is a physical, corporeal act that results in an incorporeal, metaphysical recollection of the Divine that ultimately is the aperture to union with, and participation in, the Divine. This concept

---

251. Portalié, *Guide*, 134–35.

252. *Conf.* X.25.36.

253. Chandler, "Present," 394.

254. A scriptural correlative here would be the ark of the covenant where ark of the covenant is a material object that holds the memory of the promise of God (Exod 25:10–22; Rev 11:19). The Arc gene holds the memory of the promise of God, and it provides the soul with the ability to recollect the *memoria Dei*.

stands true to Augustine's theology of the body and soul. Augustine identified himself with his soul for the purpose of ascending towards God but he continued to believe himself to be a composite of a soul and a body that God had created.[255] In *Confessiones*, it is clear that Augustine maintained a body–soul duality but with a non-dualistic integrated relationship between body and soul. The body with its Arc gene participates in the life of the soul; this reflects the soul's inter-relation with the body to be able to remember God while still maintaining its superiority over the body. For Augustine, the soul was always active and remembering was a process that never rested. Memory was where Augustine meets himself and finds God. Recollecting God was crucial in his quest to discover more of God and to journey towards fulfillment of the *beata vita*. Hence, the importance of Arc's role in assisting the soul in recollecting God is centrally significant.

Memory as a context in which we can attempt to find God is both finite and infinite at the same time; and in this respect, it reflects the finite-infinite structure of the soul as it journeys toward God. The actual memory itself is a finite memory but it approaches the infinite in its permanence, in its capacities, and in its powers.[256] Arc and its structure can also be said to be both finite and infinite. The finitude of Arc is its physical structure, which in each individual memory does exist only in the temporal world. Yet, Arc does have a reality that progresses towards infinitude. Arc is transmitted from generation to generation, resulting in the transmission of the ability to remember innate memory and the continued ability to be expressed and function in a genomic memory system. The progression towards infinitude is that journey towards eternity, in a sense, the same journey that the soul makes; the soul has a memory of its origin and kinship in heaven to which it desires to return. This movement of Arc through physical time is also a movement of memory through time. Bergson defines memory as "not a thing; it is a process; it is a movement."[257] The structure of memory, both in a physical and metaphysical dimension, becomes the condition that makes that journey toward God possible. Without memory, Augustine would cease to be since memory is where Augustine meets himself and God, and where his journey towards God starts. Memory is a representation of each moment in life, including his spiritual life. Asok eloquently write, "Memory is the canvas upon which we paint the portrait of our lives."[258] Thus, no memory, no portrait. Should Arc not function or become dysregulated,

---

255. Vaught, *Access*, 40.
256. Mourant, *Saint*, 37.
257. Perri, "Bergson's Philosophy," 844.
258. Asok et al., "Molecular," 14.

memory processes are disrupted and loss of memory can occur including permanent loss of memory. The genomic architecture of Arc is foundational to the cellular architecture of the memory trace.[259] It allows for persistence of the vestigial memory trace of the Divine and recollection of the *memoria Dei* by the soul.

The genomic memory mechanism involving Arc in the recollection of memory functions in a dynamic state where temporal scientific knowledge contributes to eternal wisdom and truth. Augustine connects knowledge and wisdom (*scientia/sapientia*) in terms of memory.[260] According to Grove, it is at this point where Augustine's view of memory became christological.[261] Grove continues to say concerning knowledge that there are eternal, intelligible, nonbodily, and nonspatial ideas that an acute mind can indeed contemplate (*Trin.* XII.14.22). Biological wisdom arises from sciential knowledge. It is the information/knowledge that genes impart in their expression; it is the type of wisdom that results in more than just spatiotemporal implications. The biological wisdom obtained from knowledge and expression of Arc is pivotal in pointing to that ontological memory and reality of the Divine. It should be noted that Arc's involvement in the creation of memories is a function that is also true when the *memoria Dei* reveals the presence and knowledge of God.[262] Augustine encountered God through this memory of God, but he knew he could not abide in this encounter nor could he experience a permanent union with eternity. He knew it was a momentary transition but he could through memory recollect that momentary encounter with eternal reality and union with God. Consequently, memory has an ongoing role to play in human knowledge and "is capable in rather profound ways of transitory brushes with eternal wisdom."[263] True memory (*phantasia*) draws one towards God and eternal wisdom and fulfillment of the *beata vita*. *Memoria*, as Javelet wrote, "is an existential rapport of the soul with God."[264] And so the biological wisdom resulting from Arc's regulation of memory not only informs of the physical structure of genes or the mechanisms they regulate but also provides information that sheds light on the *memoria Dei* and facilitates the soul's existential rapport with God. Biological wisdom is part of the soul, albeit the lower sensitive soul, but it still functions in collaboration with the higher rational

---

259. Asok et al., "Molecular," 14.
260. Grove, *Augustine*, 205.
261. Grove, *Augustine*, 205.
262. Hallin et al., "Structure," 324.
263. Grove, *Augustine*, 206.
264. Javelet, *Image*, 60.

soul in the soul's journey in its ascent to God through divine illumination and participation. Biological wisdom, therefore, is not dualistic resulting in data that suggests a distinct separation of the body and soul. Any apparent materialistic reductionism diminishes once the genome, and Arc, becomes a source of biological wisdom. The Arc gene supports a genomic model that illustrates the inter-relatedness between the body and the soul while maintaining the distinct roles of each. Genomic memory mechanisms are both physical and metaphysical as they point both to that ontological memory and the reality of the Divine. The genome, including Arc, provides information and a memory process of recollection that contributes to understanding how the rational soul remembers the *memoria Dei*.

Augustine maintained a practical bond between his understanding of science and medicine and his theological convictions. The pathway to truth became clearer through the knowledge he gained via the scientific and medical processes of his time that resulted in biological wisdom. The biological wisdom revealed by Arc would have informed the sapiential wisdom of Augustine's theological beliefs and unraveled further the mysteries of memory, in particular how it was that he remembered God.

Concluding Remarks

The biological wisdom of Arc has been shown to inform sapiential wisdom. This biological wisdom emerges from Arc's architectonic uniqueness as a single-copy gene with virus-like behavior that has ancient genomic elements. Arc is perfectly situated to participate in a novel neuronal communication system involved in memory, juxtaposing the physical and metaphysical. Definitive characteristics and features of Arc and its role in memory have been revealed. Memory, Arc expression and regulation, and brain function all follow an architectonic sequence in their operation. Arc is recruited by the rational soul much in the same way that the soul uses the body's eye as the "mind's eye to the soul."[265] Arc's primary role in this capacity would be to provide the rational soul the "ability to remember," an ability which it does via a physical function of the human body. This unity of the body (physical) and the soul (metaphysical) is compatible with Augustine's understanding of body-and-soul unity where the soul remains superior to the body with which it collaborates.

The investigation of Augustine's theology of *memoria* via a specific genomic memory process involving Arc is a novel methodology in

---

265. *Sol.* I.6.12.

Augustinian studies and has allowed for the role of memory in *memoria* to be further elucidated. This chapter illustrates the complexities behind *memoria* and memory. Notwithstanding, there is, as Augustine's acknowledged, much that still is unknown.

7

Enigmatic Arc-hitectonics of Time and Memory

> *"Time past and time future*
> *What might have been and what has been*
> *Point to one end, which is always present."*
> —T. S. ELIOT, "BURNT NORTON," *FOUR QUARTETS*[1]

> *"A moving image of eternity . . . we have been calling time."*
> —PLATO, *TIMAEUS*, 37D5–7.

ANY CONVERSATION ABOUT AUGUSTINIAN memory would not be complete without consideration of time's role in memory. The importance of time was so intricately intertwined with memory that Augustine devoted a whole book (*Conf.* XI) to the subject. A much clearer understanding of Augustine's philosophy of time[2] is only apparent when one includes Books XII and XIII. Book XI–XIII are often determined to lack

---

1. Eliot, "Burnt Norton," 14.

2. I use the term "philosophy of time" to denote Augustinian thought on time. There is debate regarding whether Augustine had a philosophy of time. Scholars debate the Platonic and/or Plotinian origins of his philosophy of time, including similarities to the Stoics, but this discourse shall focus on interrogations of time in Books XI–XIII. O'Daly, *Augustine's Philosphy*; Teske, *Paradoxes*; Milbank, "Confession," 5–13.

unity with the first ten books; this really is not the case. What is different in these three books is that, according to O'Donnell, Augustine's "speaking voice, and that of which it speaks . . . is now unequivocally in the present."[3] Understanding the "grammatical present" in the context of time is key to gaining an insight into Augustine's philosophy of time and how he views the connection between past, present, and future. Augustine recognized memory as associated with time, not just the past but also the present and future. Memory and time were interconnected. To Augustine, this was the enigma of time: on the one hand, there is no memory without time and there is no time without memory, and on the other, the past, present, and future all exist simultaneously.

Books XI–XIII are a testament to Augustine's extraordinary theology, and the depth and extent of his thoughts. In typical fashion, Augustine does present his theory of time in a meandering and circuitous manner.[4] Yet, these books produce an Augustinian theology of time that is unparalleled but still with gaps and unanswered questions.[5] They illustrate how Augustine's theology of time was firmly rooted in his theology of creation, incarnation, eternity, time, and memory. In XI, Augustine attempts to understand the nature of time in the context of creation and memory, and as an entity distinct from, and at the same time seamlessly intertwined with, eternity. Intrinsic to Augustine's philosophy of time was his theology of time, consisting of three cardinal divine moments and memories[6]—creation, in-

---

3. O'Donnell, *Augustine*, III:250.

4. Helm refers to this meandering style of Augustine's writings regarding his ideas of time. However, there are many other scholars who have identified this writing style in Augustine. Helm, "Thinking," 137.

5. Augustine did have some gaps, but his work on time set the stage for later work involving the A- and B-series of time, including the work of McTaggert, Mellor and Perry, and Helm. McTaggart conceived time in two distinct ways, called A- and B-series. The former establishes that every moment is either past or present or future, while the latter determines that every moment is earlier or later than each other moment. Of these authors, Helm is one who is aware of how similar the A- and B-series are to Augustinian thought. Matthews suggests that for Augustine, the A-series would relate to minds that experience the present, remember the past, and anticipate the future. The B-series would relate to measured time by creating things that move and change. McTaggart, "Unreality," 456–74; Mellor, *Real*, 4; Perry, "Problem," 3–21; Helm, "Thinking," 135–54; Manning, "St. Augustine," 236; Matthews, *Augustine*, 84.

6. The definition of creation, incarnation, eternity as three cardinal moments and memories of time is artifactual in the sense that they are temporal divisions as understood by humankind within temporal time. In reality, creation, incarnation, and eternity are not isolated events within "eternal time." See Cunningham, *Darwin's*, 383–84, for more details on simultaneity of creation, incarnation, and redemption.

carnation, and eternity—as revealed by the physical manifestation of the Divine at the insertion of eternity into temporality. These cardinal manifestations of God's divine action exist in eternity and are pivotal moments in temporal time. Temporal time is the bi-directional flow of memories from past-to-present-to-future and from future-to-present-to-past. Included in Augustine's theory of time is physical time, i.e., time that progresses forwards via the functional mechanisms of the physical human body involved in memory processes. Physical bodily structures, in this case Arc, provide functional knowledge (*scientia*) that evolves as biological wisdom towards sapiential knowledge as it physically moves towards eternity. Physical time, therefore, references time with physical structures and created order. Attempting to understand all these aspects of time is difficult. (An understatement, to say the least, as even Augustine could not explain all these dimensions to the degree he would have liked. As he discovered, time was simply paradoxical, aporetic, and enigmatic.)

Architectonics of Time and Memory

Time is a construct. So too is memory. Without one, the other could not exist, and both exist within the larger schema of creation and participate within eternity alongside their temporal manifestations. This was the truth that Augustine appreciated as he interrogated *memoria*. Time and memory are integral and intertwined components of Augustinian memory. Augustine discerned three main categories within the architectonic structure of time: eternity, temporal time, and physical time. An attempt to blend all three dimensions of time—eternity, temporal time, and physical time—while explaining their seamless interrelatedness is presented in a visual diagrammatic illustration in Figure 7.1. The three cardinal moments of creation, the incarnation, and eternity, along with memory, appear as fixed temporal points in created time, the past, present, and future. They exist also outside of created time in eternity and yet paradoxically moving in a bidirectional flow of time between each temporal memory in the past, present, and future. Temporal time is noted as the bi-directional flow of time from and between the past, present, and future, all of which include memory, the driver of time. Physical time, represented by Arc, is described in more detail in Figure 7.2. Arc is an exemplifier of the relationship between the physical manifestation of time and memory in the human body, temporal time, and eternity as it relates to the rational soul and its journey towards eternity. Eternity is intertwined with temporal time and physical time.

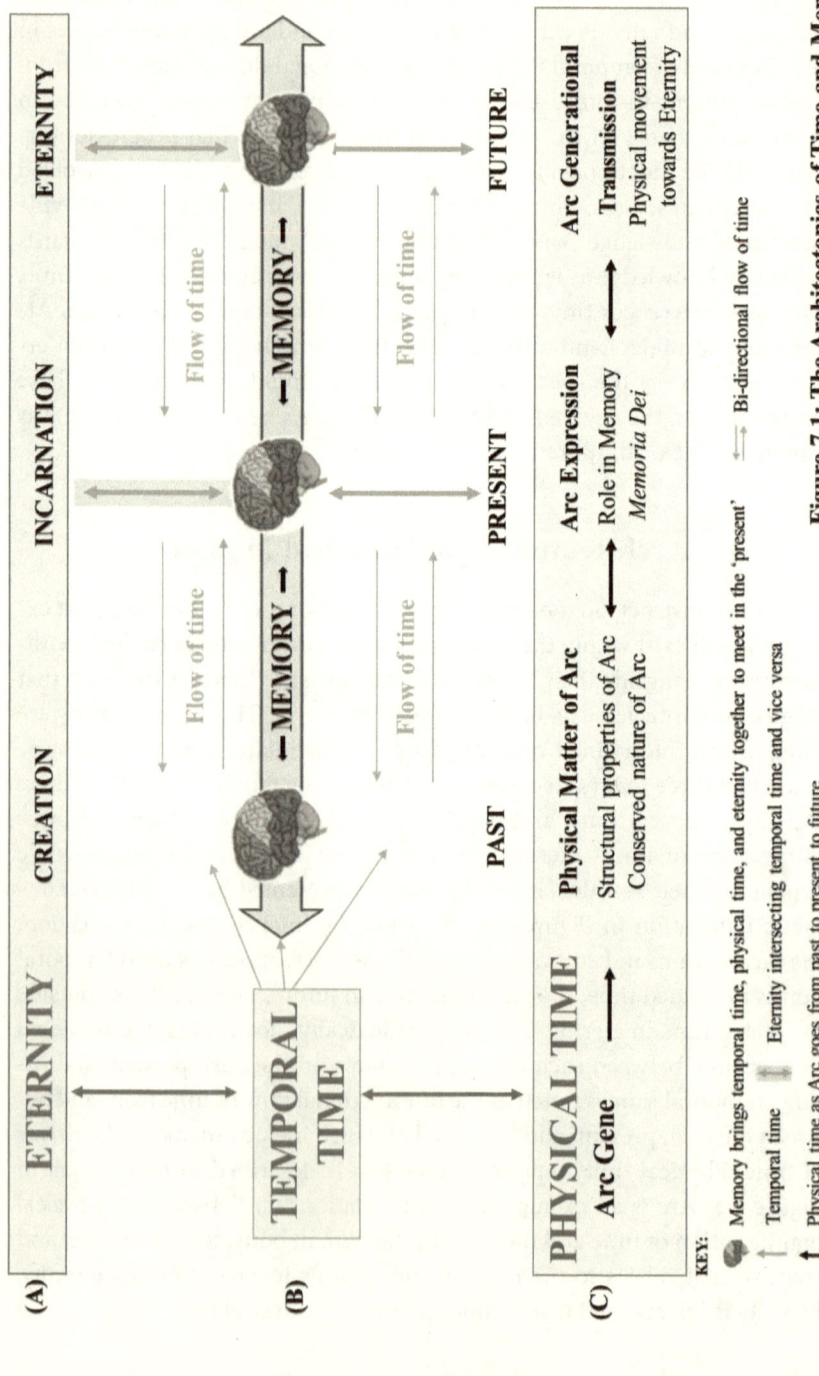

Figure 7.1: The Architectonics of Time and Memory

Eternity

Augustine's insights into eternity came from his understanding of the *historia* of time particularly in relation to the *historia sacra* of Christ.[7] As Augustine grew in faith and understanding of God, he came to expand his cognition and comprehension of the magnitude of *historia sacra* in time and memory.[8] The three categories of time presented in Figure 7.1 are best understood through *historia sacra* and the lens of creation, the incarnation, and eternity.

Historia Sacra

". . . from the beginning in which you made heaven and earth until the perpetual reign with you in your heavenly city."[9]

The *historia* of temporal time required Augustine to not only conceptualize but experience eternity and temporal time meeting in the same space and present time. According to Carr, Augustine's "temporal configuration" as he lived in the temporal present was a result of his past, and it would lead up to something else in the future.[10] In this movement of time, Augustine came to understand the importance of the temporal dispensation of God's action in time, specifically the *historia sacra* of Christ.[11] It is through the *historia sacra* that Augustine expanded the notion of the present and provided a long-lasting significance to time. Clemmons argues that through *historia sacra*, present time or the "present now" always includes the *memoria* of God's activity, its continued presence, and the expectation of its culmination.[12]

Augustine was thoroughly convinced that God created time "in the beginning" at creation.[13] This was true to the scriptural account in Gen 1 where Augustine believed that there were deeper truths than just mere

---

7. Helm, "Thinking," 1; Clemmons, "Time," 16.

8. *Historia sacra* for Augustine started at the incarnation and was encapsulated on one side by creation and on the other side by eternity. It went beyond the documentation of these events. Augustine was far more interested in the meaning of these events and how they influenced his own personal *historia*. Secular history to Augustine was "profane history." Van Oort, "End," 1.

9. *Conf.* XI.2.3.

10. Carr, "Phenomenology," 150.

11. Clemmons, "Time," 16.

12. Clemmons, "Time," 16.

13. *Conf.* XI.13.15–16; XI.14.17.

historia. This was similar to Origen, who said that the Genesis account of creation "enshrines certain deeper truths than mere historical narrative ... and contains a spiritual meaning almost throughout, using 'the letter' as a kind of veil to profound and mystical doctrines."[14] This temporal timeline, which travelled through life from creation towards eternity, was interrupted by the incarnation, at least as viewed from a human perspective. As such, the incarnation is that space and time where the eternal and temporal time meet in the present; it was God's intention from the beginning.[15] As Augustine wrote in *V. Rel.* XXXXIII.81, "everlasting Truth, who orders all things, both enters into time and stands motionless in eternity above all times."

Augustine's theory of time included a future time of expectation (temporal anticipation) which was as important as the past time of remembrance; both were instrumental to living in the present. Past time was driven backwards by the future and future time was the consequence of the past and also driven by what occurs in the present (XI.11.13). Augustine believed time and eternity were together without confusion or separation. This allowed for a spatial-relational dynamic whereby his soul was not disconnected from God but rather drawn towards God. Marion asserts that the question of time arises within the specific theological ambit of relationship with God.[16] The description of how time past, present, and future are intertwined and existing together while at the same time existing as their own separate ordinal moments at given or fixed points in "human" historical time is known as the *historia*[17] of time. The convergence of temporal *historia* and *historia sacra* reveals God's action in time, and the recollection and revelation of God to human beings within *memoria*-time where earthy time and eternity unite.[18] In other words, temporal *historia* is a gradual unfolding of salvific history (*historia sacra*).

---

14. Origen, *On First Principles*, 3.5.1, translated by Bouteneff, 102.

15. Per Cunningham, creation should not be isolated from incarnation because if "incarnation and redemption are no less part of God's purpose than creation, then the created order has an eschatological dimension from the very beginning." Incarnation was always God's intention. Cunningham, *Darwin's*, 384. See also Le Blond, *Conversions*, 19.

16. Marion believed that time exists in relation to God's eternity since time and the world are created. Gschwandtner, *Marion*, 97–117. Marion, *In the Self's*, chapters 5 and 6.

17. Augustinian *historia* of time describes the events of the historical time of humankind as described in the "timeline" within the Scriptures. The *historia* of temporal events and the *historia sacra* of Christ both meet in temporal time.

18. *Memoria*-time is a term coined by Ratzinger to describe the temporal nature of the human consciousness and temporality closely bound up in relationality. *Memoria*-time establishes the continuity between earthly time and God's eternity. Ratzinger, *Eschatology*, 184.

Importantly, central to creation and eternity was the incarnation. Ratzinger alludes to this when he writes that there is an indestructible relation between human life and history.[19] He comments that this is shown to us on the deepest level with Christ's incarnation where "in the man Jesus God has bound himself permanently to human history." The profundity of the incarnation was not lost on Augustine. He declared that he was called by God to understand the Word (John 1:1), for God created heaven and earth "in your Word and in your Son."[20] He recognized Christ as the mediator between God and humanity.[21] Christ was the one who would redeem him and save him through mercy and compassion. He knew that the presentness of time foreshadowed eternity and therefore, for fallen creation, this "present-ness" could only be found by reaching into the "future" and eternity.[22] The incarnation was the point in the *historia sacra* where eternity became "reachable" for Augustine. Hence, it was through the incarnation *in time* that Augustine hoped he would escape the temporal implications of the "beginning" of Gen 1:1, and consequently, come to know, and look forward to, eternity.[23]

In the *historia sacra* of Christ, time, however, is just a *vestigium* or copy (*imitatio*) of eternity.[24] The term *vestigium* is one Augustine had already appropriated to describe the *vestigium* (image), or memory, of God within the rational soul.[25] Thus, eternity was played out in temporal time via memory. Kaethler suggests that Ratzinger establishes continuity between earthly time and God's eternity as *memoria*-time as the perfect present.[26] Along this timeline was also physical time, which facilitated the remembrance of these cardinal moments of *historia sacra* and ordinal moments in time. This would suggest that Augustine recognized both memory and time were vehicles to knowing the Divine and eternity, even though he could only see them as *vestigia*.

The *historia sacra* precisely encapsulates why Augustine had a circuitous and vacillatory thinking regarding time, as he found the nature of time too complex to find or understand all the answers. At times, he had to settle

---

19. Ratzinger, *Eschatology*, 187.
20. *Conf.* XI.7.9; XI.9.11.
21. *Conf.* XI.7.9; X.43.68.
22. O'Donnell, *Augustine*, III:250.
23. Chadwick, *Saint*, 227n14; Clemmons, "Time," 9.
24. *Gn. Litt. Imp.* XIII.38; *Ps.* 9.17; *Mus.* VI.29; O'Daly, *Augustine's Philosophy*, 152.
25. *Gn. Litt.* XII.24.51; Sweeney, *God*, 686.
26. Kaethler, "(Un) Bound," 384n33.

with the knowledge that the best he knew was enough. He writes, "if I have not the strength to discover the answer, at least I know that wherever they are, they are not there as future or past, but as present."[27] Importantly to Augustine, in the present, he could live in remembrance of the incarnation and in anticipation of the fulfillment of the *beata vita* in eternity. Connecting time with the memory of God brought together creation and eternity to a place of meeting in the temporal. In understanding this, Augustine would gain more insight into his journey towards the Divine. Augustine understood that, in a complicated manner, time and memory worked together to connect creation, the incarnation, and eternity.

Creation of Time

Time was precious to Augustine; indeed, he believed that too much of his time was consumed by his duties as a bishop.[28] He wished that he had more time to spend meditating in God's law; he said, "The drops of time are too precious to me." He accepted that the "moments [of time] fly by."[29] He developed a desire to understand the nature of time and its context in terms of creation *ex nihilo* for he believed time began with the creative act "in the beginning," as expounded in Books XI–XIII. Time existed because God made time; God did so prior to the creation of human beings.[30] Time had a beginning, which was the point when God began to create the universe. Augustine writes:

> We should, therefore, say that time began with creation rather than that creation began with time. But both are from God. . . . The statement "time began with creation," should not be taken to mean that time is not a creature.[31]

Augustine viewed time as a "creature." This has, in a manner, Platonic overtones. Plato in *Timeaus* viewed time as a creature, although his reasoning is somewhat different from Augustine's. Plato described the universe as a "Living Creature," however, its nature was not a totality of the One who created the universe and therefore, he made it a "moveable image of Eternity (αἰώνιον) . . . moving according to number, even that which we have named

---

27. *Conf.* XI.18.23.
28. *Conf.* XI.2.2.
29. *Conf.* XI.2.3.
30. *Conf.* XI.13.15.
31. *Gn. Litt.* V.5.12.

Time."³² In doing so, Plato associated time with the nature of a "creature" if not the creature itself. The term *image*, in relation to time, recalls Genesis 1:26–27 where man is created in the image and likeness of God. Plato's interpretation of time, and Augustine's based on Genesis 1, acknowledges time to be a "creature."³³ Hernandez describes how Augustine viewed time as a creature of God.³⁴ He breakdowns Augustine's argument in XI in the following logical manner:

1. God created time.
2. Time is not eternal.
3. Time began when God created the universe *ex nihilo*.
4. When God created the universe, humans were still not created; humans were created some "days" after the universe was created.
5. Therefore, time is a creature of God that existed prior to human consciousness.
6. Thus, time is independent of human consciousness. Time, seen as a creature, began when the universe began.

Time is a precedent of human creation but it is distinctly a creature of creation who receive its existence from the Creator. Therefore, since time is a creature it must have a link to the Creator and must give access to God's eternity.³⁵ With the creation and motion of creatures, Augustine states that "time began to run its course."³⁶ He continues, "if there was no motion of either a spiritual or corporeal creature by which the future moving through the present would succeed the past, there would be no time at all." Gross posits that time is the ontological consequence of creation *ex nihilo*, and it is the distinguishing feature of finite creation.³⁷ She contends that Augustine frequently turned to the physical account of time to distinguish between stable eternity (*semper stans*) and ever-changing temporality (*numquam stans*); he did this to deny the possibility of temporality being antecedent to creation.³⁸ There is a distinct foundational creation theology to Augustine's

---

32. Plato, *Timaeus*, 37d.
33. Plato, *Timaeus*, 37d3, 37d7.
34. Hernandez, "St. Augustine," 38.
35. Tóth, "Eternity," 385.
36. *Gn. Litt.* V.5.12.
37. Gross, "Augustine's Ambivalence," 136.
38. Gross, "Augustine's Ambivalence," 131, 136.

theory of time. In Figure 7.1, this can be seen in the alignment of both temporal and physical time with creation.

Röck argues for an ontological understanding of time as temporality where temporality is associated with the process of change involving human beings as they "become, change, and perish."[39] Gross and Röck both lend support to Augustine's view of ever-changing temporality in which actual time is the process of change. Amongst the ancient philosophers, Aristotle held that the reality of time depended on the occurrence of change(s) in the physical world and, additionally, on the capacity to discern various stages in any change that is observed.[40] Further, he related time and change to the past and future and defined time as "the number of changes in respect of the before and after."[41] Temporal time was ever-changing in finitude as it progressed from past-to-present-to-future towards infinity.

The WORD and Words in Time

Augustine saw in Gen 1:1 that God through his Word and the Words (eternal words: speech) created (*ex nihilo*) the universe and all living things. Augustine wrote regarding the relationship between time and speech, that speech functioned as a mediator between unity and multitude.[42] Karfíková argues that through speech, in which time is present, human beings connect things of the past (memory) into a whole, and they transform past or expected things into present ones, thus performing their task of unifying the passing plurality.[43] The syllables of a word, which are pronounced one by one, try to capture a whole that can be grasped simultaneously, and do so in an ordered methodology. Aristotle in *The Categories* defines speech as a quantity since it is measured in short and long syllables, and he associates the syllables with time.[44] He writes, "there is no common boundary at which the syllables join, but each is separate and distinct from the rest." None of its parts has an abiding existence: "When once a syllable is pronounced, it is not possible to retain it."[45] Syllables are associated with time, both for Aristotle and Augustine.

39. Aristotle, *Physics* 11:218b20–219a1; Röck, "Time," 33.
40. Popa, "On the (In)consistency," 379.
41. Aristotle, *Physics* 11:219bl–2.
42. Karfíková, "Memory," 189.
43. Karfíková, "Memory," 189.
44. Aristotle, *Categories*, 35–47.
45. Aristotle relates time with syllables that form words which join to form sentences; cf. *Conf.* XI.27.35–28.38. Augustine links syllables into words as he gives the

Augustine wrote in *Conf.* IV.11.17 that the whole of individual syllables pronounced together created a unity that delights; this exemplified the *ordo* that arises from the cardinal moment of creation and the delight God experienced in his creation.[46] According to Karfíková, Augustine required memory as a source for narration, and in the same manner, he had to have human speech in order to deal with time.[47] It is Karfíková's contention that both memory and speech attempt to concentrate time into a kind of unity, which is enabled by the unity of temporal sequences in eternity. They can only imitate this latter unity very remotely. She argues:

> Even this fragment, though, will make it possible to put together a story from Augustine's memories and his narration, a story in which he as the narrator finds not only himself but also his God. Both these achievements, however, are only preliminary and both will continue to escape him, for it cannot be otherwise during our temporal life.[48]

However, while the Word is the initiator of creation and thus time, Karfíková's claim that Augustine can only deal with time through human speech is not only limiting but is a diminution of Augustine's theology of time. Augustine's thought regarding the nature of time was far more complex. God's creative Word starts creation and time, but it is not a passing word as would be identified with words in a speech, words that sound and pass away.[49] On a temporal perspective, Augustine articulated through speech the grammar of eternity and temporality from the standpoint of the creature, and while important, Augustine's speech does not determine time.[50] God alone creates time: "Time would not elapse before you made time."[51] In this sense, time becomes a more complex concept, since now moments, movements and measurement of time, consideration of the present now, and the relationship between creation and eternity all come into play. Temporality exhibits a multiplicity of layers.

The Words of God at creation saw the formation of memory, necessary to recollect creation, the incarnation, and eternity as Augustine, the

---

examples of the *Deus Creator Omnium* and reciting a psalm. Aristotle, *Categories*, 35–47.

46. This is consistent with the architectonic principle of parts making up a whole creating a unity.

47. Karfíková, "Memory," 190.

48. Karfíková, "Memory," 190.

49. *Conf.* XI.6.8.

50. Helm, "Thinking," 147.

51. *Conf.* XI.8.15.

peregrinus,⁵² wandered through life. The same Words created time, past, present, and future, all of which are ontologically equal. When God revealed his Name to Moses in Exod 3:14, "I AM WHO I AM" (אֶהְיֶה אֲשֶׁר אֶהְיֶה), God said, "This shall be my name forever. This my appellation for all eternity."⁵³ God's spoken Word to Moses establishes that he is the everlastingly God, the I AM of eternity. In terms of temporality, God's spoken Word has now connected creation with eternity and is a reminder of Divine continuity. To Augustine, "I AM WHO I AM" was a revelation of God in temporal time. God the I AM is a reassurance that God is "leading us from temporal realities to eternal life."⁵⁴ Glowasky asserts that Augustine would view Exod 3:14 as a temporal revelation of God's eternity and writes, "God's temporal name is God's eternal name, and God's eternal name is God's temporal name."⁵⁵ In *En. Ps.* 130.13, Augustine said to his audience that God's temporal revelation was the means to knowledge of God in eternity, which comes from embracing God's descent into human history.⁵⁶ The incarnation was a continuation of God's spoken Word as a temporal revelation. In Matt 3:17, at the baptism of Jesus, a voice from heaven said, "This is my Son, the Beloved, with whom I am well pleased." Later, post his death, Jesus returned and spoke to the disciples, again divine revelation in temporality. The incarnation thus allowed time to travel backwards to creation and forwards to eternity. God affirms the continuity of the Word from creation to incarnation to eternity through both eternity and temporality. That is why Augustine saw the incarnation as that pivotal cardinal moment in time.

In addition to the WORD and eternal Words, Augustine wrote about temporal words (i.e., human words and speech) in many of his works. The difference between the articulation of eternal Words and temporal words in time was, for Augustine, a striking and stark difference, as it emphasized the difference between the immutability, incorporeality, and eternity of God and the mutability, corporeality, and finitude of temporal humankind. Augustine was fond of music and used its syllables, words, and meter as an exemplar to understand time, eternity, memory, duration, and the measurement of time.⁵⁷ Augustine chose Ambrose's evening hymn, the *Deus Creator Omnium*,⁵⁸ as an example to clarify time's relation to Eternity (God). Time's

---

52. Claussen, "'Peregrinatio,'" 33–75.
53. Hebrew text from Biblia Hebraica Stuttgartensia.
54. Glowasky, "Naming," 182.
55. Glowasky, "Naming," 182.
56. Glowasky, "Naming," 186.
57. E.g., *Mus.* VI; *Conf.* X, XI.
58. *Conf.* XI.27.35; Chadwick, *Saint*, 241n28.

relation to eternity actually resides in the meaning of this verse: "God, creator of all."[59] Here, Augustine relates God to creation, the Word, and eternal Words illustrating the significance of creation theology to Augustine. He used the words of this song to investigate time and memory because, as a song, the words are kept in memory, are known in the present, and are to be sung in the future, although they are not yet sung in the future; since the words are known they are present in memory as something to be produced.[60] While singing, the soul is attentive simultaneously to three times.[61] Syllables also allow Augustine to investigate the meter and duration of speaking words in time.[62]

Augustine clarifies time's relation to eternity; this clarification is embedded in the meaning of its words and its performative power.[63] *Deus Creator Omnium* declares the incomparable power of God who created all and that only God is the creator of all. Augustine correlates singing with human life. Ayoub writes:

> What happens in singing also happens in human life, either in each part (seconds, minutes, hours, days, event) or in its totality (the life of each human being), and even in the totality of human lives (and here there is the absolute universalisation of the consideration of time the human being). Singing, like life, is thought of in terms of durations or times.[64]

Further, Augustine asserts that the parts of a psalm that join to make a whole are "valid in the entire life of a human person, where all actions are parts of a whole, and of the total history of 'the sons of men' (Ps. 30:20) where all human lives are but parts."[65]

Augustine's Inner Word

In his examination of human temporal words, Augustine realizes the impact such words have on his inner self and his inner word (*verbum interius*).

---

59. Ayoub, "Time," 81.
60. Ayoub, "Time," 81.
61. Ayoub, "Time," 81.
62. Ayoub, "Time," 82; *Conf.* XI.27.35: it is not necessarily the syllables themselves that are measured but rather something in Augustine's memory.
63. Ayoub, "Time," 83.
64. Ayoub, "Time," 84.
65. *Conf.* XI.28.38. This is consistent with the architectonic principle of parts making up a whole creating a unity.

His *verbum interius* in his soul is separate from any natural human language and repetition of linguistic utterances within the silence of his mind.[66] Oliva argues, "Augustine distinguishes between the spoken outer word, the word recited in the soul in a way that imitates outer speech, and then the inner word itself, which he identifies with the image of God within the soul."[67] Gadamer thinks otherwise. The inner word is not distinct from thought but is the very expression of thought itself: "the inner mental word is just as consubstantial with thought as is God the Son with God the Father."[68] To Gadamer, the inner word is not any novel product of thought but the logical result of thought consciously realized by a thinking subject.[69] Gadamer's concept of the *verbum interius* as thought and expression diminishes the concept of time duration associated with expression of speech from inner words to language in the mind to speech. However, as Oliva states, a consequence of *verbum interius* is the capacity to produce speech, which implies a temporal "processual" character.[70] Augustine also viewed his *verbus interius* as having a temporal processual character. He related the movement of his *verbus interius* from the incarnation of the eternal Word to the "incarnation" of human thought in outer speech.[71] The *verbum interius* provides the possibility of continuous communication via outer speech between individuals. The inner word never leaves the individual even if the outer words return to the original speaker.[72] The cyclical nature of temporal words can be observed here: *verbum interius, verbum mentis, verbum dictum, verbum interius*. This infers a passage of time and thus duration where Augustine sees the inner word in the soul as atemporal and related to the temporal word of external utterance; this is also true of the incarnation of the eternal Word in time and space.[73]

Creation, Temporal and Physical Time

Figure 7.1 illustrates how at creation both temporal time and physical time start and move forward yet at the same time exist in the simultaneity of eternity. Augustine discusses this fact in *De Genesi ad Litteram*: "When God

---

66. Knotts, "Inner Word," 93–94.
67. Oliva, *Innere*, 26.
68. Gadamer, *Truth*, 438.
69. Gadamer, *Truth*, 441.
70. Oliva, *Innere*, 27.
71. Knotts, "Space-Time," 4.
72. Knotts, "Inner," 98.
73. Knotts, "Inner," 99.

created all things simultaneously, man was made in order to come into being in the future—there was the idea or formula of one to be created."[74] He mentions the Word of God whereby there are differences between those things all created simultaneously to come into the future and those things created in their own time in accordance with its simultaneously created causes.[75] Augustine compares the work of God in creating grass from the earth, and seed from grass, and man made into a living soul, a work that continues over time, "In all these cases things already made received the characteristic activities of their own proper time."[76] All these things carry a repetition of their selves in the hidden power of reproduction derived from their primordial causes in which they were inserted into the world that was created.[77] This is a description of physical time and in the power of reproduction exists exemplifiers of physical time involved in reproductive processes and thus the transmission of physical matter, e.g., genes such as Arc (Figure 7.2). Reproduction and repetition are signifiers of temporal time as both move between past and present, present and future, and future back to past. The repetition of these processes is indicative of the cyclical nature of time and change whereby eternity and creation are both the start and end. Memory participates in this repetitive nature of time and is, in fact, the driver of these bidirectional flows of time (Figure 7.1). Grove writes that "memory becomes the locus where the past, present, and future are simultaneously coherent."[78] In the beginning there is an end, and in the end there is a beginning, all meet at the incarnation, which remembers the beginning and the end; Christ is the re-enactment of creation. God's divine action of creation is fulfilled in the simultaneity of eternity. Thus, Augustine connects creation with temporal time, physical time, and eternity, all of which occur simultaneously yet in the continuum of time (Figure 7.1).

Incarnation

"L'Incarnation, insertion de l'éternel dans le temps."[79]

The incarnation of the Word revealed God's absolute supernatural and definitive redemption of the human race, not by removing evil and sin

---

74. *Gn. Litt.* VI.9.16.
75. *Gn. Litt.* VI.10.17.
76. *Gn. Litt.* VI.10.17.
77. *Gn. Litt.* VI.10.17.
78. Grove, *Augustine*, 29.
79. Le Blond, *Conversions*, 19.

through power but by transforming evil into good through the life, death, and resurrection of Jesus.[80] In the incarnation of the Word, the eternal is incarnate in the temporal and witnessed as present in time. Hence, everlasting Truth, who orders all things, both enters into time and stands motionless in eternity above all times.[81] This is an important insight for Augustine. Eternity was not competitive with time. Eternity seemed to function in a different modality than time; eternal life, according to Augustine, surpasses temporal life by its vivacity.[82] The reality of the "insertion of the eternal into temporality" is God descending from eternity and entering temporal time in a physical, corporeal form. Christ the incarnate is the temporal manifestation of divinity. However, the incarnate act of the Divine did not start in the "present now" but rather in "time past" at creation. This was the point in the *historia sacra* of Christ where Augustine also envisioned creation (past memories) meeting in the mystery of the simultaneity of eternity and the present time of temporality.

T. S. Eliot's poem "Burnt Norton" has the line "only through time time is conquered."[83] Latta reads this line to mean that time is where the eternal can be met.[84] He writes that this line is an extension of the underlying theology in the poem that privileges the incarnate act.[85] For Eliot, at the incarnation, the temporal was breached, inhabited, and forever changed by the eternal; in other words, temporal time was conquered by "time" eternal. Latta, regarding Eliot's "Burnt Norton," discusses the conquering of temporality by eternity via the incarnation and the conscious act of remembering the past. He writes:

> Temporal time can be conquered by eternal time because memory is the conscious act of bringing past time into the present, because the timeless eternality of the present defines the temporality of the present, and because experiencing the present is the way to the Incarnate. The conquering of temporality by eternality is the very nature of the Incarnation.[86]

Time is the conduit for the incarnation.

---

80. Lamb, "Eternity," 129.
81. *V. Rel.* XXXXIII.81.
82. *V. Rel.* XXXXIX.97; Clemmons, "Time," 14.
83. Eliot, "Burnt Norton," 16.
84. Latta, *When*, 130.
85. Latta, *When*, 148.
86. Latta, *When*, 130.

Both time (temporal and physical) and the incarnation are inherent marks of creation (Figure 7.1). Incarnation is the second cardinal moment in the *historia sacra*, where memory resides in the present and physical time is active in its expression in the present. The expression of physical time occurs in an orderly fashion in temporal time in the present. Arc, the exemplifier of physical time, enables remembrance of the incarnation in the present and works in conjunction with time to recollect the past (creation) and the future (eternity). It does so in a pre-ordained and particular manner.

Eternity

"Lord, eternity is yours, so you cannot be ignorant of what I tell you."[87]

This declaration is the very first sentence of Book XI. Augustine very rightly declares that eternity is the Lord's. He wishes to make this declaration as he sees eternity with God as the end of his temporal journey and his search for the *beata vita*. However, this statement of Augustine's regarding ignorance can also be considered as somewhat shocking if just taken at face value; one might consider that Augustine is making this statement in a less than humble demeanor that some accuse him of having. However, this is not the case. The deeper meaning to this statement, and a more accurate interpretation, is that Augustine is inferring that although God resides in eternity and in unchangeable eternity *(inconmutabiliter aeternus)*[88] he is still knowledgeable of Augustine's words in the present time. Augustine finds this paradox hard to explain. Karfíková also finds this paradoxical connection of eternity and temporality in created things very difficult to conceive.[89] She argues that Augustine addresses the concept of eternity first in his writings because he is confronting a Manichaean issue. He does this by employing the Platonic notion of eternity, which "stands forever," unlike time, which will "never stand still."[90] Clemmons goes further and asserts that in Augustine's early writings one can see the link between Plotinus' conception of eternity

---

87. *Conf.* XI.1.1.

88. *Conf.* XI.31.41.

89. Karfíková, "Memory," 182.

90. Taken from Karfíková, "Memory," 182, "While referring to the question of what God did "before [*antequam*]" creating the world (*Conf.* XI.10.12), Augustine probably has Manichaean questioners in mind. However, the same question also appears in the Epicurean polemic against the Stoics; see Cicero, *Nat. Deor.* I.9.21; Lucretius, *Rer. Nat.* 5.168–69.

and the link between *rationes* in the soul and *Ratio* itself.[91] This link permits the ascent of the *soul* to *Ratio*, perhaps even in this lifetime. Hence, the soul can share in eternity amid the flux of time.

According to Karfíková, Augustine wants to know what makes time different from eternity because eternity gives time its unity.[92] Augustine's analysis of this is found in *Conf.* XI; however, it leaves the framework of Neoplatonic metaphysics behind and focuses on how time is known to human beings.[93] Augustine writes that "in the eternal, nothing is transient, but the whole is present, but no time is wholly present" (*Conf.* XI.11.13). Everything is present "simultaneously," while time is never present all at once. Helm writes that eternal simultaneity is not a temporal simultaneity but the simultaneity of God's ineffable, immediate knowledge of all times of creation (*Conf.* XI.31.41), whereas the temporal order is one that is consistent with God's "now" or God's "today" (*Conf.* I.1.10).[94] Here, Augustine invokes his foundational creation theology. "Before" God created heaven and earth there was no time in which God could be "creating." God does not precede time in a temporal way, but he includes all future and past things into his eternity and thus precedes time in the sense of being elevated above it.[95] What is eternity *is* present eternity *is* incarnation *is* creation and true in the reverse also, resulting in the cyclical nature that defines temporality. Eternity aligns creation, incarnation, and eternity into God's "now." Kaethler writes that eternity is not the exact opposite of human time but its fulfillment.[96]

Bergson's theory of time explains that "past, present, and future shrink into a single moment, which is eternity."[97] Similarly, according to Latta, God's duration collapses past, present, and future into an existential singularity; the conflation of past and present points to one end, which is "always present."[98] To experience a "single moment" is to experience the eternal, and the place where and when the eternal can be met in the temporal. Eternity brings that moment in time where the clash between the

---

91. Clemmons, "Time," 5.

92. Karfíková, "Memory," 183.

93. This is the reason Augustine's analysis of time is often accused of "subjectivism." However, this might be a misunderstanding that neglects the argument in the *Confessions* as a whole. Karfíková, "Memory," 184.

94. Helm, "Thinking," 152.

95. *Conf.* XI.13.15–16. Karfíková, "Memory," 182.

96. Kaethler, "(Un)Bounded," 94.

97. Bergson, *Creative*, 160.

98. Latta, *When*, 144.

immutable, unchanging, and incorporeal God and the human being who is mutable, changing, and corporeal occurs, and the difference is striking. At this juncture of eternal and temporal homogenization (i.e., the incarnation), Augustine remembers and recalls; so as he sits at the Eucharistic table where, in the sacrament of memory[99] and time, he recalls Christ's command to "do this in remembrance of me" (Luke 22:19). Through the Eucharistic sacrament, he momentarily experiences the meeting of the "presence" and the present in what he only knows as temporal time. Clemmons interestingly contrasts eternity and temporal time by presenting the difference between "presence" and the "present."[100] He writes that eternity is only perceived through understanding because it does not change or possess intervals of time such as past or present future movements. The past ceases, the future is not yet; eternity simply is eternity and consists of a kind of presence. To be more precise, eternity *is* presence. Clemmons believes Augustine's concept of eternity as "presence" is derived from his understanding of the "full present" which provides an image of eternity, at least in *De Vera Religione*.[101] This also explains why Augustine can both argue for the resurrection of the body into eternal life, which suggests "time," and at the same time explain how the resurrected "dwell" unendingly in God's eternity. Augustine also describes how *memoria* holds the past, present, and future together in unity, and as such, God is in an eminent sense "pure memory," i.e., the ultimate source of temporality and identity realized in eternity.[102] His existence through time has an eschatological expectation and realization of eternal life.

The Eucharistic sacrament also brings together physical time, temporal time, and eternity. The communion wafer and the wine consist of physical matter; however, they are metaphysically the body and blood of Jesus. In Communion there is an experiential conjoining of past, present, and future (i.e., creation and the incarnation, death, and resurrection of Jesus) and eternity. Through the incarnation and the Eucharistic sacrament, Augustine can see a glimpse of the eternal. Just as God can enter time, human beings, although temporal beings, can be drawn by God to share in eternity. This is an extremely crucial point to understand because this truth is the metaphysical reality and understanding that union of the created being with the Creator God is possible. This union is what Augustine so sought after. In the

---

99. Chapter 8 discusses the significance of memory as a sacrament as understood by Augustine.

100. Clemmons, "Time," 15.

101. Clemmons, "Time," 16.

102. Tóth, "Eternity," 383.

Eucharistic moment of remembrance, as God drew Augustine to himself, Augustine attained union with God, albeit momentarily. Through the sacrament of memory, Augustine moved towards eternity in temporal time.

In *Conf.* XI, Augustine discusses time in terms of Scripture, which points to the incarnate Christ as the mediator of time and eternity.[103] Memory in this regard is expectation, and the mediator of a person's experience of time and eternity. Augustine longs for eternity because he comprehends eternity to be that place where he escapes the constraints of temporality and achieves the fulfillment of the *vita*. Eternity creates and redeems time.[104]

Physical time also aligns with both temporal time and eternity. It moves forward towards eternity in the generational (reproductive) transmission of physical matter, including genes like Arc. The *ordo* of generational transmission is such that, from creation, physical matter is transmitted through temporal time and makes its way towards eternity by following specific encoded directions and sequences of events. Further, time brings creation and eternity together in temporality, and it is the anchor of the incarnation that enables humanity to move forward in time in the present towards eternity.

Temporal Time

"It is perfectly true, as the philosophers say, that life must be understood backwards. But they forget the other proposition, that it must be lived forwards."

—SØREN KIERKEGAARD, *JOURNALS* IV A 164 (1843)

Straus writes, "time springs from eternity to which it returns."[105] Figure 7.1 illustrates this; as time progresses bi-directionally in whichever direction, it originates in eternity and returns to it. Kierkegaard remembered this when he recognized that life must also be lived forward. The continuum of time is related to motion and, for Augustine, memory and this movement of time could not be separated. He asserts in XI.28.37, "for the mind expects and attends and remembers, so that what it expects passes through what has its attention to what it remembers." For example, Augustine states that when reciting Psalms, the words pass into memory.[106] Kukushkin and

---

103. Grove, *Augustine*, 54.
104. Lamb, "Eternity," 133.
105. Straus, "Temporal," 85.
106. *Conf.* XI.28.38.

Carew maintain that they "place time and temporal patterning at the center of the concept of memory."[107] They also state, "the nervous system's extraordinary ability to represent time at multiple timescales is a prerequisite for its unmatched capacity for information storage [memory]."[108] Again, time and memory cannot be separated. It becomes evident to Augustine as he interrogated memory that he could not do so without an analysis of time; neither time nor memory could be understood without an examination of the interplay and connectivity between the two. Indeed, as Kukushkin and Carew argue, the "structure of memory lies in the temporal domain."[109] Ratzinger's term *"memoria-*time" describes how memory is the unifying activity of holding together past, present, and future in a meaningful manner associated with human existence.[110] Figure 7.1 illustrates this interplay and demonstrates how the temporal timeline is connected via memory as it slips forwards and backwards through past, present, and future. The three-dimensionality of the mind (i.e., its orientation to the present, the past, and the future, united in the present) provides the basis for speech, which, although it unites passing things, is of a temporal nature.[111]

Time and Memory

Confessiones XI associates the creation of memory in context with the creation of time where each cannot exist without the other. This is exceedingly clear to Augustine. In XI.17.22, Augustine writes:

> Or do they [past, present, future] exist in the sense that, when the present emerges from the future, time comes out of some secret store, and then recedes into some secret place when the past comes out of the present? Where did those who sang prophecies see these events if they do not yet exist? To see what has no existence is impossible. And those who narrate past history would surely not be telling a true story if they did not discern events by their soul's insight. If the past were non-existent, it could not be discerned at all. Therefore both future and past events exist.

This clearly alludes to the storehouse of memory described in *Conf*. X., the descriptions of memories of times past and future, such as past events

---

107. Kukushkin and Carew, "Memory," 260.
108. Kukushkin and Carew, "Memory," 260.
109. Kukushkin and Carew, "Memory," 261.
110. Ratzinger, *Eschatology*, 184; Tóth, "Eternity," 382–82.
111. Karfíková, "Memory," 189.

(e.g., past history) and future events (e.g., sung prophecies of the future).[112] Augustine explains this by comparing the speaking of the narrative of past history to how the actual events have passed away. Past historical narrative becomes images that are recalled in present time which then allow a narrative to be spoken in the present (XI.18.23). Memory recalls into the present what has vanished into the past. Augustine correlates the recitation of a psalm and the passage of its words through time to the passage of time in his life: "it is also valid of the entire life of an individual person, where all actions are parts of a whole, and of the total history of 'the sons of men' where all human lives are but parts."[113] He also believes his life is a distension of time pulled in several directions.[114] Augustine's struggle with the temporal movement of time is summarized succinctly in XI.29.39:

> You are my eternal Father, but I am scattered in times whose order I do not understand. The storms of incoherent events tear to pieces my thoughts, the inmost entrails of my soul, until that day when purified and molten by the fire of your love, I flow together[115] to merge into you.

Despite this discombobulated sense of time, Augustine still found stability and solidity in God's truth.[116] The flowing together that Augustine mentions in XI.29.39 implies movement of time. Milbank writes: "The past survives in finite memory despite its ontological vanishing because it persists always in God. Memory of the vanished past can occur because memory, also, participates in the divine eternal presence."[117] As Tóth comments, "God is in an eminent sense 'pure memory': the ultimate source of temporality and identity realized in eternity."[118] According to Chadwick, the ascent to divine eternity is a recovery from the disintegrative experience of temporal successiveness.[119]

Augustine finds this movement of time to be an extraordinarily complex quandary beyond his ability to reconcile without divine illumination. He believes that God's Word helps him in this endeavor. He writes:

---

112. Cf. *Conf.* X.8.12–14.

113. *Conf.* XI.28.38.

114. *Conf.* XI.29.39.

115. Chadwick comments: Augustine's image of the historical process is that of a flowing river or rivers with many stormy cataracts. Chadwick, *Saint*, 244n31.

116. *Conf.* XI.30.40.

117. Milbank, "Confession," 44.

118. Tóth, "Eternity," 383.

119. Chadwick, *Saint*, 244n31.

> Everything which begins to be and ceases to be begins and ends its existence at that moment when, in the eternal reason where nothing begins or ends, it is known that it is right for it to begin and end. This reason is your Word, which is also the Beginning in that it also speaks to us. Thus, in the gospel the Word speaks through the flesh, and this sounded externally in human ears, so that it could be believed and sought inwardly found in the eternal truth where the Master who alone is good teaches all disciples.[120]

In these few sentences, Augustine connects "the beginning" (creation) with the Word speaking through flesh (incarnation) and eternal reason/truth (eternity). He recognized Christ was the connector between creation and eternity: "And in this way he is the Beginning because, unless he were constant, there would be no fixed point to which we could return."[121] Temporality was more than just the mere passage of time to Augustine. He saw time as a re-creation of his own earthly creation as a physical human being (birth to death) and as a spiritual being moving from creation to eternity where he would eventually achieve his eschatological hope and the *beata vita*. Temporal death did not negate the concept of *memoria* nor the holding together of the past, present, and future. In fact, God's eternal present is life without a beginning or end, not confined to a temporal timeline.[122] Therefore, while Augustine saw himself as a temporal self, he knew he was not constrained by a temporal timeline. Time, however, in a metaphysical sense, helped him understand creation, the incarnation, and eternity in a much deeper, and even personal manner. Nevertheless, the *modus operandi* of time still seemed complicated to Augustine.

A Paradox of Time: Three Times, One Present

> *"The distinction between past, present,*
> *and future is only a stubbornly persistent illusion."*
>
> —ALBERT EINSTEIN[123]

---

120. *Conf.* XI.8.10.

121. *Conf.* XI.8.10.

122. Tóth, "Eternity," 383.

123. Einstein wrote this in 1955 in a letter to the family of Michele Besso who had recently died. Venning, "Time's Arrow."

Augustine's inquisitive mind drove him to delve deep into the significance of time, but there he encountered a paradox of time, the three times of the past, present, and future. It was paradoxical because the very existence of time itself was questioned. If the present time faded into the past then it no longer was. If future time came into the present then it also no longer was. In his own way, Augustine was saying the same thing as Einstein: time was an illusion if it did not exist in the present or co-exist with the past and the future.[124] Or could it be that the illusion is that human beings see themselves as a fixed point in time rather than participants in the flux-like character and temporal directions of time? How are these illusions compatible with the reality of the existence of God created temporal time?

It would be fair to say that, with respect to time existing in the past, present, and future, Augustine did not believe that time existed *except* momentarily in the present, since what took place in the past no longer existed and the future did not yet exist. Augustine maintains:

> If then, in order to be time at all, the present is made that it passes into the past, how can we say this present also "is"? The cause of its being is that it will cease to be. So indeed we cannot truly say that time exists except in the sense that it tends towards non-existence.[125]

This is Augustine's "illusion." He knows time has to exist in the present, yet he also knows that it passes into the past and thus becomes non-existent. This Augustine attempted to understand, but it remained, in part, a paradox.

Augustine uses three grammatical tenses to describe time: past, present, and future.[126] However, it is important to consider that there is an ambiguity that exists in Augustine's use of *tempora*.[127] In the Augustinian corpus, *tempora* can mean both "times" and "tenses."[128] Augustine does, however, argue that strictly speaking there are only three present times when he

---

124. *Conf.* XI.14.17–22.28. Here, Augustine talks about the non-existence of time in the present and the connectors between past, present, and future. Time as non-existence could be likened to Einstein's illusionary concept of past, present, and future.

125. "Non-existence" can also be translated "non-being" (*tendit non esse*). *Conf.* XI.14.17.

126. Augustine's architectonic structure of time as past, present, and future was not entirely original to him, although he developed it much further than his predecessors. The concept of time as past, present, and future is found in Aristotle, especially in *The Categories* where these aspects of time form a continuous whole. In *Physics* time is movement associated with change and motion with a before and after and events embedded in the flow of time. Aristotle, *Categories* I.6; *Physics*, IV.10–14.

127. O'Daly, *Augustine's Philosophy*, 157.

128. *Conf.* XI.17.22; cf. XI.20.26.

refers to the past, present, and future of time. In XI.20.26 he says, "It is an inexact (*non proprie*) language to speak of three times—past, present, and future. Perhaps it would be exact to say: there are three times, a *present* of things past, a *present* of things present, a *present* of things to come."[129] Augustine's emphasis here is on the "one tense of the present."[130] Despite the ambiguity conferred by Augustine's use of *tempora*, his use of "one tense of the present" does help one understand the direction of Augustine's thinking regarding the unfolding role of time in his theology of *memoria*.

Augustine constantly reminded himself in his deliberations of memory and time that central to his life was his journey (*in via*) in seeking the *beata vita* and ascending to God. This propelled his forward movement in time. Yet he lived in the "present now" of time, within its constraints. Augustine was not, however, ignorant of the fact that time moved bi-directionally between the three ordinal moments of temporal time (past, present, future). Time would not exist otherwise. He writes regarding the passage of time from future to present to past:

> But I confidently affirm myself to know that if nothing passed away there would be no past time; and if nothing arrives, there is no future time, and if nothing existed there would be no present time (*non esset praesens tempus*).[131]

The nature of the present is such that it is constantly transformed into the past; if it did not, it would not be time, but eternity.[132] Karfíková says regarding this paradox of time, "Time, in fact, is the time of things that are about to reach the end of their being: without these things and their passing there would be no time at all."[133] While this is the case, Augustine recognizes that past, present, and future are present in memory and expectation; as such, one may have access to past or future events as they are objects of intellectual perception and therefore, exist in some way.[134] Time therefore also moves in the opposite direction from past into present via memory. Time and memory are recalled and appear from "some secret store" into the present whereupon they both can then recede back into that secret place to be stored as memory.[135] This movement of memory and time from past into

---

129. Italics mine.
130. O'Daly, *Augustine's Philosophy*, 155.
131. *Conf.* XI.14.17 cf. IV.8.13.
132. Karfíková, "Memory," 184.
133. Karfíková, "Memory," 184.
134. O'Daly, *Augustine's Philosophy*, 156.
135. *Conf.* XI.17.22.

present and future and then back into the past illustrates the biderectionality of time as Augustine understood it.

Augustine considers recollection of the past and past memories important in his life journey as he thinks of his own creation and that of the Creator God, and yet, in order to live in the present, he has to leave the past, while not forgetting to live in anticipation of the future. Leaving the past means leaving the memory of living the past to live in the present. Augustine was trying to leave the "scars" of his past behind him in order to lead a virtuous life. However, memory is not abandoned by Augustine in his attempt to live in present time. Memory is the center of his thoughts, his theology, and his life in searching for God (on his own he could not live a virtuous life). Figure 7.1 depicts this as memory progressing along the temporal timeline. Memory is pivotal in the remembrance of what the Creator God has, and is doing, and in the sacrament, especially the Eucharist where Christ is remembered (Figure 7.1, the incarnation and eternity). And, in this sense, time and memory become blended into one truth; eternity and temporal time existing in the same space at the same moment of the present but in remembrance of the past and in anticipation of the future.

Bergsonian time incorporates elements of Augustine's theory of time when it presents the concept of past, present, and future time flowing seamlessly into one another as one durative state (i.e., the present).[136] This seamless flow of time can also be observed in Figure 7.1 where it is presented as the bidirectional flow of time moving seamlessly between and through past, present, and future time. They conflate into one existential singularity where the past through memory brings moments outside of present time (i.e., past time) and places them in the present where they are experienced and where they empower the present thereby becoming the future.[137] Perri describes this ongoing continuity of past memories being placed in the present in Bergsonian terms; Bergson associates past time with parts consisting of individual memories which are then synthesized into the totality of all the parts to make a whole in the continuous present.[138] In other words, multiple memories are joined together to form a memory in the present. This concept has an architectonic structure where a multiplicity of parts become

---

136. Latta writes that Bergsonian time does not go as far as espousing a Christian view of time, even though he did believe in an eternity of life that transcended both time and temporal experience. Rather, his theories tend to be the middle ground between non-Christian philosophies (i.e., positivism, scientific mechanism) and Christian theology. He supports a metaphysical understanding of time working in synthesis with an intuitive view of mental states. Latta, *When*, 47–48, 62.

137. Bergson, *Matter*, 166; Latta, *When*, 147.

138. Perri, "Bergson's Philosophy," 840.

a whole. Unlike Bergson, Augustine places a much stronger emphasis on the present influencing the future, and "touching eternity" through remembrance of the past in the present via the incarnation and the Eucharist. This can be observed in *Conf.* X.53.68–70, which has such an intense Eucharistic exposition; O'Donnell states that it is "a passage of such dense Eucharistic imagery that it may be best thought of as perhaps the only place in our literature where a Christian receives the eucharist in the literary text itself."[139]

The Scientia of Time

Time is an enigma, says Augustine.[140] In attempting to answer how time is measured and to understand the movement of time in terms of past, present, and future, Augustine pleads with God:

> My mind is on fire to solve this very intricate enigma. Do not shut the door, Lord my God. Good Father, through Christ I beg you, do not shut the door on my longing to understand these things which are both familiar and obscure. Do not prevent me, Lord, from penetrating them and seeing them illuminated by the light of your mercy.[141]

Augustine's sense of urgency in trying to understand the enigma of time was in part driven by his eagerness to gain knowledge (*scientia*), but more importantly to gain sapiential knowledge illuminated by the Father through Christ. He also knew that memory could not entirely overcome the conditions of the temporal.[142] This created a spiritual dilemma. As Hochschild writes:

> By memory, the temporal becomes intelligible, and the foundation for a *scientia*. But it also signifies what is for Augustine the tragedy of the temporal: the sense of loss, the frustration of distance, the dramatic unlikeness of the human and the divine perspectives of creation.[143]

Despite these enigmas of the temporal and time, Augustine was determined to resolve these paradoxes.

---

139. O'Donnell, *Augustine*, I:xxxvii.
140. *Conf.* XI.22.28.
141. *Conf.* XI.22.28.
142. Hochschild, *Memory*, 166.
143. Hochschild, *Memory*, 166.

Duration of Time

Augustine desired to solve the paradox of how the duration of the flow of time could be measured, since the past no longer existed except in memory and the future did not yet exist, only as expectation.[144] Hochschild writes, "Augustine tells us that time is the measurement of a past thing, or else he is not actually measuring the passage of time at all."[145] When the present slips into the past, there duration can be measured.

Augustine's fondness for music led him to draw his explanations of the duration and measurement of time from the syllables of songs and psalms. He is conscious of intervals of time and wonders whether "short" and "long" intervals of time can be measured, especially since "perception is the basis of measurement."[146] By comparing the syllables and words of a song, Augustine was able to investigate the meter and duration of time, since their correct duration was defined by their interrelation.[147] Long syllables should be twice as long as short ones.[148] According to Ayoub, this correlation requires some stabilization of the duration of their sounds in one's memory.[149] Memory is also intricate to this process because it requires that the syllables themselves be held in memory waiting to be recollected. Further, Ayoub asserts that the chanting of the song requires internalization of the reality of time, which would not be possible if time were just an exterior fleeting reality.[150]

Bergson presents his concept of duration from an interesting metaphysical perspective.[151] Bergson argues that duration is not measurable in terms of time since there is no separation between past and present conscious states.[152] Remembering past states "does not set them alongside its actual state as one point alongside another but forms both the past and present states into an organic whole, as happens when we recall the notes of a tune, melting, so to speak, into one another."[153] Bergson also writes

---

144. *Conf.* XI.14.17; 18.23–24; 20.26–22.28; 27.36–29.39.

145. Hochschild, *Memory*, 164.

146. *Conf.* XI.15.18–16.21.

147. Ayoub, "Time," 82.

148. *Conf.* XI.26.33.

149. Ayoub, "Time," 82.

150. Ayoub, "Time," 82.

151. Bergson presents his metaphysical perspectives on duration in his essay, *Time and Free Will*.

152. To Augustine conscious state is the same as the mind. *Conf.* XI.27.36.

153. Bergson, *Time*, 100; Martin, "Memory," 183–85.

that duration "has some kind of trajectory, and . . . present and future are conditioned by the past such that the past is conserved but, because of all the intervening moments, cannot be repeated identically."[154] Bergsonian time is not Augustinian time; however, it does have some overlap regarding the aforementioned aspects of time and duration that are worth considering.

Temporality encompasses not just the physical movement of time but physical matter as it experiences the movement of time (e.g., in terms of *scientia*, biological systems moving from beginning to end and thereby towards eternity, human being from birth to death).[155]

Physical Time

"What is time? Who can explain this easily and briefly? Who can comprehend this even in thought so as to articulate the answer in words"?[156]

Augustine assumed the challenge to understand the physical aspect of time when he asks the question "what is time?" Ayoub is correct when she asserts that Augustine asked this question for the very same reasons that he wanted to know exactly what memory was. She writes that the underlying reason for Augustine's inquiry into the nature of time is "in the context of what time means in a life directed toward the fulfilment of the imperative desire for happiness."[157] Discovering what time *is* brings it from a metaphysical dimension to a physical reality thus providing some understanding of temporal time and its interconnectedness to the relationship with God within the confines of temporality. Ayoub contends:

> Augustine's text [*Conf.* XI] is attentive to the humanization of time, which cannot be mechanized or dictated by parameters of happiness that do not bring stability. Rather it is a time that operates to bring one into a closer relationship with the Divine. . . . [O]nly virtuous delight, operating in the terms of another temporality, brings us closer to the experience of eternity-truth-happiness.[158]

---

154. Martin, "Memory," 185.

155. Biological systems would include the generational transmission of genomic data, cellular proliferation, and the life (birth and death) of a human being, to mention a few. See *Conf.* XI.18.24.

156. *Conf.* XI.14.17.

157. Ayoub, "Time," 84.

158. Ayoub, "Time," 85.

Confessiones XI does not resolve all the conundrums of the nature of time, memory, and creation.[159] However, it does pay attention to the bodily senses, the external world, and the finer details of time, explicating on its structure, measurement, and function through ordinal moments in past, present, and future.

Arc-hitectonics

Arc via its Arc-hitectonic structure is well positioned to establish a timeline of its role and function from time past through to time future with its expression best illustrated in time present. Physical time, one of Augustine's three classifications of "time" (eternity, temporal time, physical time, Figure 7.1) is exemplified, in this case, by Arc (Figure 7.2). Physical time is cyclical in nature as it flows from creation to eternity, and then from eternity to creation (Figure 7.2).

In Figure 2, the life cycle of Arc (A) is the movement from gene to mRNA to capsid formation, translocation of mRNA in synapses to creation of Arc protein which, facilitated by its Arc-hitectonic structure, flows through time and space. (B) demonstrates Arc's role and function in past, present, and future time and (C) illustrates the bi-directional flow from creation to eternity and the bi-directional flow of Arc through time.

The Life Cycle of Arc and the Flow of Time

The life cycle of Arc operates within the confines of physical time and temporal time. Arc traverses through time from one neuron to the next. This flow through time is accompanied by structural alterations to Arc and changes that transpire as a result of the "instructions" provided by the Arc gene. As noted previously, memory formation takes time, including the involvement of short- and long-term plasticity and modification of protein synthesis; times can last from milliseconds to hours.[160] In other words, there are temporal intervals between associated events or stages in the life cycle of Arc. Augustine suspected that there were temporal intervals between events, or even knew it, but he did not know how to prove it. He did well in his discussion of the measurement of syllables and words where he was able to explain this concept yet continued to be befuddled by the backward and forward flow of time.[161] The involvement of Arc in memory formation and

---

159. Gross, "Augustine's Ambivalence," 140.
160. Kukushkin and Carew, "Memory," 259.
161. *Conf.* XI.22.28, 25.32–27.36.

ENIGMATIC ARC-HITECTONICS OF TIME AND MEMORY

its associated temporal intervals helps to provide an answer to this dilemma of Augustine.

Figure 7.2: Physical time as exemplified by the Arc gene.

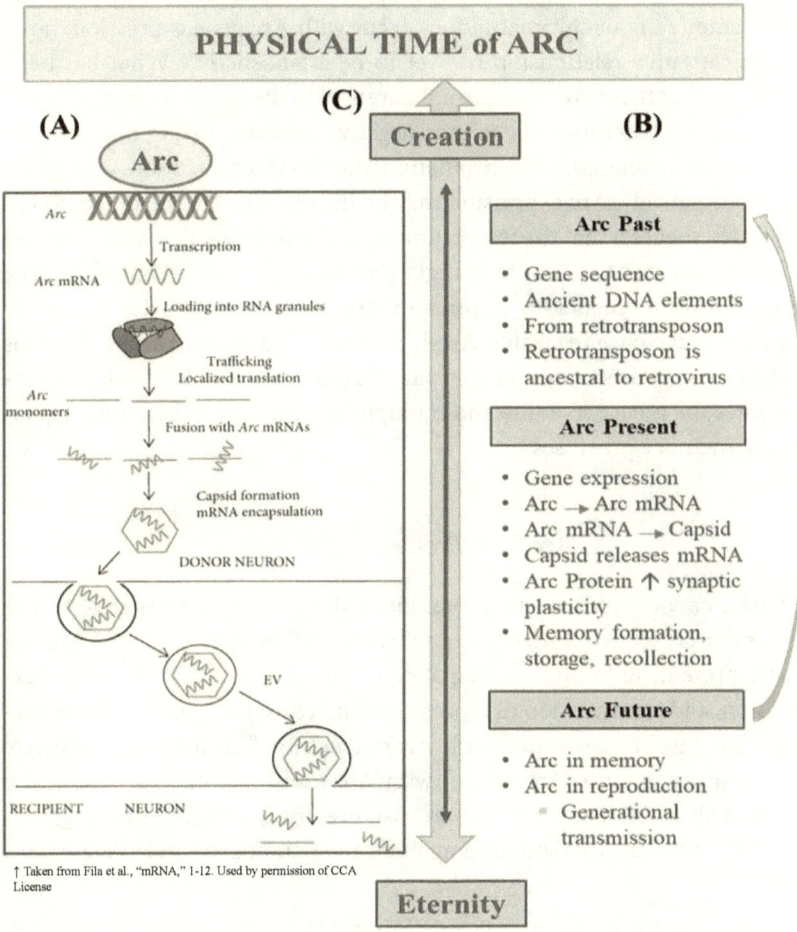

PHYSICAL TIME of ARC

(A) Arc

- Arc
- Transcription
- Arc mRNA
- Loading into RNA granules
- Trafficking / Localized translation
- Arc monomers
- Fusion with *Arc* mRNAs
- Capsid formation / mRNA encapsulation
- DONOR NEURON
- EV
- RECIPIENT NEURON

(C) Creation

(B)

Arc Past
- Gene sequence
- Ancient DNA elements
- From retrotransposon
- Retrotransposon is ancestral to retrovirus

Arc Present
- Gene expression
- Arc → Arc mRNA
- Arc mRNA → Capsid
- Capsid releases mRNA
- Arc Protein ↑ synaptic plasticity
- Memory formation, storage, recollection

Arc Future
- Arc in memory
- Arc in reproduction
  - Generational transmission

Eternity

↑ Taken from Fila et al., "mRNA," 1-12. Used by permission of CCA License

Impact of Changes in Arc Structure

Changes in Arc structure occur either as part of its expression in a positive manner (i.e., the neuronal communication system involving synaptic plasticity) or negatively due to alterations and/or mutations of Arc. The life cycle of Arc exemplifies the positive aspect of how Arc changes in its structure and function as it regulates memory processes. Negative alterations to Arc structure occur when Arc's expression is altered or mutated and causes neurodegenerative disease and memory disorders.

Leung in 2022 proposed a second mechanism that facilitates the functioning of Arc but occurs through changes in the chromatin[162] structure of Arc-positive neurons.[163] This is different than the changes specific to Arc itself, and the "new" structures (e.g., capsids) elucidated in the life cycle of Arc. Remodeling of chromatin does occur with Arc gene expression; however, a causative relationship has yet to be established.[164] What has been noticed is that there are significant differences in the structure of chromatin in Arc-positive neurons versus Arc-negative neurons. Leung posits that it may be that an alteration in chromatin structure is required for Arc expression, alternatively, Arc expression may be the cause of chromatin remodeling.[165] He suggests that the interaction of Arc and chromatin structure may provide a mechanism that seemingly confers epigenetic[166] control of gene transcription by regulating chromatin structure. Leung's article enhances the knowledge base regarding Arc-hitectonics. It does not negate previous findings (e.g., Arc's neuronal communication pathways) but instead demonstrates the great versatility and multiplicity of Arc in its genomic regulation of memory processes.

Arc Past, Present, and Future

Augustine's view of time as "a present of things past, a present of things present, a present of things to come" seems rather apt for Arc.[167] Arc has a past, present, and future participation in time in terms of its structure, expression, and transmission as represented in Figure 7.2.[168] Generally speaking, "Arc past" is associated with Arc's structure, "Arc present" with Arc gene expression, and "Arc future" with Arc transmission. True also is the fact that all of Arc's participation in past, present, and future time is manifest in the present. This sounds enigmatic and paradoxical, as in Augustine's

---

162. Chromatin consist of protein-DNA complexes that condense to form chromosomes found in cells. Chromatin participates in gene regulation. Widom, "Structure," 285–327.

163. Leung et al., "Arc," 1–51.

164. Leung et al., "Arc," 25.

165. Leung et al., "Arc," 25.

166. Epigenetics is the study of how behaviors and environment cause changes that affect the way a gene works. These changes do not alter DNA sequences and are reversible.

167. *Conf.* XI.20.26.

168. The terms "Arc past," "Arc present," "Arc future" are used to identify the aspects of Arc that are situated in times past, present, and future.

own deliberations of this aspect of time,[169] but it can be logically explained much in the same manner that Augustine did regarding syllables and words in *Conf.* XI.

"Arc past" pertains to its architectonic structure and specific elements within that promote the expression of Arc in memory and time. Arc operates within the continuum of time and space where both time and Arc interconnect. As creatures, both formally participate in eternity. However, it is the continuity provided by memory that is essential for making the temporal become intelligible.[170] Both time and Arc are connected by memory.

As described earlier, Arc is structurally designed so that it has operational functionality directing memory processes that occur in the past, present, and future. Figure 7.2 (B) lists the architectonic constituents of Arc past. The architectonic structure of Arc is unique and confers upon Arc an operational competency within its life cycle. Arc's genomic structure initiates and regulates Arc expression in the "Arc present" of time. Arc expression initiates the life cycle with its formation of mRNA and capsids which are transported via extracellular vesicles into recipient neurons where the cycle starts over.[171] Arc acts in the past utilizing its genomic structure that has withstood the evolution of time. Arc, as a gene, has a deep history of the past, which is why Arc can work in the present to recollect the *memoria Dei* embedded in the rational soul from the creation of humankind. In the present, Arc calls upon the temporality of its past and its genomic structure in its function as a neuronal communication system to initiate memory formation, retention, and recollection. This is a flow of time that results in change as memories are formed, recalled, and acted upon. In the "Arc future" of time, Arc moves towards the future and eternity as the cells that contain the genome, including Arc, proliferate and divide as new generations of human beings are born. Innate memory, perhaps even the *memoria Dei*, and certainly the ability to remember, is passed on from one generation to the next through the flow of time from past to present to future.[172] Future time is thus dynamically shaped by the humans' past and present in a physically manifested interaction that occurs between the genome, memory, and

---

169. *Conf.* XI.20.26–22.28.

170. Hochschild, *Memory*, 163.

171. Fila, "mRNA," 1–12.

172. Studies in *C. elegans* have demonstrated that they can maintain a gene expression memory for fourteen generations. This is hard to test in humans as the typical maximum number of generations at most is five; however, traumatic memories have been proven to be generationally transmitted in three generations in humans. Klosin et al., "Transgenerational," 320; Kizilhan et al., "Transgenerational," 81.

the environment.¹⁷³ Evolution has endowed Arc with the capacity to work within temporal time to perform its role in neuronal communications. The temporality of Arc, in this sense, becomes a function of the genome as Arc, memory, and time blend together in the past, present, and future of time. Arc thus brings to light a biological aspect to the physical time of temporality and memory. Further, Arc's metaphysical ability to remember time and memory persists through generational transmission towards eternity and yet, at the same time, touches eternity in temporal time when the rational soul remembers its God.

The flow of time from past-to-present-to-future is evident, and it also blends with the "flow of time" in eternity from creation to eternity. This movement in time in the physical body of the human being is pertinaciously associated with genes in the genome. The Arc gene was embedded in the genome at creation. Through temporal successiveness, Arc has survived throughout millennia, highly conserved, as has its role in the neuronal communications and operations involving memory, which, in itself, requires that re-collection occurs from the past to the present. Arc acts by not only deep diving into the past to recollect memory but acts also in the present to activate re-membrance and re-collection of memory. Arc's progression from present to future occurs when Arc is passed on from one generation to the next as it hurtles towards eternity. Creation recurs in the present at conception and in the birth of human beings who now have received the Arc gene transmitted from their parents. Per Röck, at the ontological level, a human being has a becoming, changing, and perishing, which reflects the dynamic aspect of temporality.¹⁷⁴ At this ontological level, Arc participates in a process of change, for it has a past, present, and future. Arc links human beings to the past via memory, shapes their present via memory, and allows for possibilities in the future via memory.¹⁷⁵ Temporal time thus moves (flows) from the emergence of life until temporal extinction where biological creatures move from the past into the present and onwards into a future constrained by both past and present.¹⁷⁶ Arc future also returns to the present via the past. Arc thus acts in time and temporal succession and does so within the context of memory which is the driver of time.¹⁷⁷

---

173. Love, "Re-Thinking," 55–56.

174. Röck, "Time," 33.

175. Love discusses how genes not only characterize and distinguish human beings but also contain information linking past, present, and future. Love, "Re-Thinking," 40.

176. Love, "Re-Thinking," 35.

177. Here, memory would be the innate memory embedded in Arc's genomic structure that is present at the creation of a human being and given by the Divine. In

The human body and memory are thus temporally timed phenomena since they experience the present time while stepping into both past and future. Arc represents the physical temporality of time and memory, and it blends seamlessly into the three cardinal moments of eternity: creation, incarnation, and eternity.

Spatio-temporal Dimensions of Time

Arc, in a sense, operates with time in causing a *distentio* of the mind. Memory recalled in temporal time, such as the memory of the death and resurrection of Christ ("do this in memory of me"), results in temporal time meeting eternity in that moment of union with Christ during the Eucharist. The memories formed and recalled in the rational soul facilitated by Arc also cause Arc's movement back in time where it recollects and retrieves memory and then forward as memories are remembered in the present and are anticipated in the future. Further, Arc's work occurs in space as synaptic plasticity increases, causing Arc capsid formation and transmission from neuron to neuron through space. Time and space are seen to be two aspects of the same corporeal reality.[178] They are both distinct in that time passes but space does not.[179]

Einchenbaum authored an article about the integration of time, memory, and space.[180] He connects the dots between time, memory, and space by demonstrating how time and space are integrated in the representation of memories. He presents data that hippocampal networks are able to map moments in temporally organized experiences.[181] These hippocampal

---

this context, memory within Arc would act as a driver of time as it initiates and sustains various cellular functions, physical responses, and the ability to recollect memories whether innate or formulated memories. This is not incongruent with Augustine's theology that time begins with creation. Although, time with regard to creation starts in the beginning of creation, with regard to human life, time, as experienced by the human, cannot start until their creation. Time is still associated with creation. Regarding Arc, time begins with the creation of Arc in the human and continues via the genomic actions of Arc.

178. In 1905 Einstein published his special theory of relativity. Minkowski (1908) commenting on this in a presentation put it this way three years later, "Henceforth space by itself, and time by itself, are doomed to fade away into mere shadows, and only a kind of union of the two will preserve an independent reality." Minkowski, "Raum und Zeit," 75–88; Mbagwu et al., "Review," 65–71.

179. Knotts, "Space-Time," 1.

180. Einchenbaum, "On the Integration," 1007–18.

181. Einchenbaum, "On the Integration," 1007.

networks map these moments via genomic mechanisms such as the one involving Arc. In summary, Einchenbaum describes how brain pathways for spatial and temporal cognition involve overlapping and interacting systems that converge on the hippocampal region. In his conclusion, Einchenbaum writes:

> The evidence presented here suggests that space and time are initially processed by overlapping brain networks and coded in different scales, then spatial and temporal signals are integrated within the hippocampal region to create a framework for the spatial-temporal organization of memory. Although movement through space and time are intrinsically coupled, spatial and temporal coding can be observed differentially in hippocampal regions under some behavioural demands or combined by individual neurons that code both dimensions into the overall population representation.[182]

Einchenbaum is discussing the neurological and anatomical aspect of spatio-temporal association. Arc and its operational mechanics is an exemplar of this association. Time, memory, Arc, and space all blend into one another as they participate in spatio-temporal memory formation and recollection.

Concluding Remarks

"Time is a companion that goes with us on a journey."[183]

Captain Jean-Luc Picard, although a fictional character, makes a very apt statement about time, one that Augustine would agree with. Whatever point a person is in their life, they are accompanied by time. Past memories invade their present time and present time invades their future time, and vice versa. Time lives side by side with a person. The significant moments and memories of time define the journey. In this chapter, there are three categories of "time"—eternity, temporal time, and physical time—which operate together in a blended and seamless manner. Each category provides insights into the nature of time and memory. In Augustinian terms, temporal time through Christ the Mediator takes a person to the cardinal moments in eternity of creation, the incarnation, and eternity. Physical time is explicated via Arc, which illustrates how physical matter in the form of its molecular architectonic structure operates within the human body in

---

182. Einchenbaum, "On the Integration," 1015.
183. Captain Jean Luc Picard, from *Star Trek: The Next Generation*.

conjunction with memory and time. Augustine understood that memory travels with time and was intricately connected with time. Hence, the necessity to interrogate memory.

8

The Archaeology of Memory by Recalling Creation

"Deus Creator Omnium."[1]

THE PREVIOUS SIX CHAPTERS have discussed the development of Augustine's theology of *memoria* by examining the manner in which he came to understand the function and organizational operation of memory. They demonstrated an architectonic structure to Augustine's logic regarding *memoria* and memory and have revealed how Augustine developed his theory and communicated it to his readers. This architectonic structure has unearthed new concepts regarding Augustinian memory providing further understanding of *memoria* and laying the foundation for this chapter.

Augustine's commentary on *Confessiones* in *Retractationes* starts by emphasizing "the thirteen books of my confessions."[2] Augustine clearly thought both at the time of writing *Confessiones* and later, towards the end of his life, that the thirteen books were one volume, and each book was connected in the larger schema of the whole volume. It is fair to say that the debate regarding the unity of these thirteen books has been extensive, centuries old, and quite varied in its conclusions. Most theologians and scholars have a tendency to hinge on only one aspect of Augustine's philosophy, theology, metanarrative, metaphysics, literary, temporal/eternal, etc. They exclude many other facets found in *Confessiones*. Consequently,

---

1. *Conf.* XI.27.35.

2. Augustine's original title for *Confessiones* was *Confessiones Libri Tredecim*, alluding to the unity of its thirteen books. *Retr.* 2.6.1; Hammond, "Title," 17.

the unity comes from a cohesiveness pertinent to a particular motif and, therefore, reconciliation of Books I–XIII[3] often becomes tenuous due to this reductionist approach and lack of a more holistic, multi-dimensional investigation. It is my contention that the unity of I–XIII is found in the fact that XIII is a recapitulation of I–XII. XIII addresses the multi-dimensionality of the previous twelve books and the many motifs within. The allegorical exegesis of Gen 1 is clearly intercalated with these motifs, thus cementing the holistic cohesiveness of *Confessiones*. This cohesiveness includes the thematic presence of memory, time, and creation throughout all of *Confessiones*. The ingenuity of XIII is the fact that Augustine chose to recapitulate I–XII through his exposition of creation in Gen 1. This is not surprising considering that creation and the Creator God were foundational and fundamental to Augustine in his interrogation of, and approach to, theological, philosophical, and scientific concepts.

Books I–XIII are clearly thoughtfully written with a common purpose of documenting Augustine's journey from his creation to his desire for achievement and fulfillment of the *beata vita*; it is a trajectory that sees the soul's yearning to return to its origins and which supports the unity of *Confessiones*. The many themes including memory within I–XIII all participate in defining this trajectory. *Confessiones* is about memory since temporal memory starts at creation and continues to and within eternity. While the architectonic structure of the symphonic forms of memory is not as clearly delineated in XIII, the principles of memory and its constituent symphonic forms and fundamental affordances are present, whether explicitly or implicitly, in the text of XIII. The architectonic structure of XIII is a buttress to the findings and conclusions of Augustine's intense searching of himself, his soul, his journey (as a viator), and God, but it is also the apotheotic culmination of Augustine's writings in *Confessiones*.

The Theory of Recapitulation:[4] XIII Is a Recapitulation of I–XII

The recapitulation motif in *Confessiones* has not been considered a theory in its own right by scholars. Some do touch upon motifs that are recapitulatory,

---

3. Going forward, the Books of *Confessiones* will be written just by the Roman numerals without "Book" in front of them i.e., Book XIII will be written as XIII. The exception will be Book I since I could be mistaken for the pronoun "I."

4. The phrase "theory of recapitulation" from here on refers specifically to the theory of recapitulation that I am proposing, where Book XIII is a recapitulation of Books I–XII.

but not in a cohesive fashion that formulates a theory.[5] McMahon's work is the closest to a recapitulation theory when he describes the cyclical nature of *Confessiones*. However, he views this "recapitulation" via a prayer format and a meditative structure anchored to an *exidus-reditus* motif.[6] This recapitulative viewpoint appears weak as it hangs on to a single thread as the unifying factor. The premise of the theory of recapitulation in Book XIII of *Confessiones* is a bringing together, via Augustine's strong foundational creation theology, of the multiple motifs that Augustine has written about in I–XII. Augustine, by writing XIII as a recapitulation of I–XII, confirms the cohesive unity of all thirteen books of *Confessiones* and reiterates the importance of God's creative act and memory in his journey towards the Divine and the *beata vita*.

The architectonic structure of XIII delineates the integrants that form the recapitulation theory. They are:

1. The Consummation and the Prolegomenon
2. The Architectonic Structure of Creation
3. *A* Memory and *The* Memories
4. The *Beata Vita*
5. Temporality and Time
6. The *Confessio* of *Confessiones*

Each integrant is presented in tabulated form so that the correlation between texts in I–XII can be compared to texts from XIII. The texts presented are not exclusive to the pertinent topic; they are a selection to illustrate the theory of recapitulation. Further, some texts are equivalent/implicit in wording while others are based on the thematic interpretation of the text which thus allows correlation.

The Consummation and the Prolegomenon

The unity and structure of I–XIII is evident from the very first words of XIII, for they start in the same manner as Book I. Augustine calls upon God (*invocare*) to come into him. His desire at the consummation and the prolegomenon is the same: Augustine desires to seek and know God. In Table 8.1 the consummation of XIII and the prolegomenon of Book I illustrates that in *Confessiones* the end and starting points begin at the same place.

---

5. Kotzé, "Structure," 28–45; Le Blond, *Conversions*, 17; Landsberg, "Conversion," 31–56; Solignac, "Introduction," 23–24.

6. McMahon, *Understanding*, 69.

Table 8.1: Side-by-side comparison of the texts in Books XIII and I.

THE CONSUMMATION AND THE PROLEGOMENON	
Book XIII (1.1; 38.53)	**Book I (1.1; 2.2)**
XIII.1.1 I call* upon you, my God, my mercy ... I call you unto my soul which you are preparing to receive you through the longing which you have inspired in it * *invocare:* invoke, petition, plead[7]	**I.1.1** I would seek you, calling upon you **II.2.2** How shall I call upon my God? Surely when I call on him, I am calling on him to come into me
XIII.1.1 Before I called you, you were there before me ... Before I existed you were, and I had no being to which you could grant existence	**I.2.2** I would have no being, I would not have any existence, unless you were in me
XIII.1.1 Here I am as a result of your goodness, which goes before all that you have made me to be, and all out of which you made me **XIII.38.53** As for ourselves, we see the things you have made	**I.1.1** Man, a little piece of your creation ... you have made us for yourself **I.2.2** Heaven and earth which you have made and in which you have made me
XIII.38.53 Only on your door can we knock. Yes indeed, that is how it is received, how it is found, how the door is opened (*fulfillment of I.1.1–2.2*)	**I.1.1–2.2** Grant me to know ... I would seek you calling upon you ... surely when I call upon him ... so why do I request you to come to me (*action of petitioning analogous to "knocking"*)

The first thing to note is the ending of XIII which circles back to the start of Book I. Augustine is reminding his readers through his own example of calling out to God. The calling out to God does not change; in other words, it is a continual calling out throughout one's life in order to stay connected to the Divine. This is a persistent theme in *Confessiones* and critical to Augustine in his own desire to know God. The Latin word for

---

7. *Merriam-Webster Dictionary*, s.v. "Invoke," https://www.meriam-webster.com/dictionary/invoke.

"call" in both XIII and Book I is *invocare*. This translates better as "invoke," which has a stronger sense and emphasis of "to petition for help" or "make an earnest request for help." XIII.1.1 uses this verb throughout as Augustine pleads with God, "Do not forsake the one who is pleading (calling) with you now" (*nunc invocantem te ne deseras*).[8] *Invocare* suggests that there is an urgency to this request for help as Augustine recognizes that on his own he is unable to do anything, he needs God's help.

The cyclical nature from XIII–I–XIII reinforces the importance and necessity of calling out to God in the search for the *beata vita*. From the few chapters in Table 8.1, the importance of creation theology in Augustine's understanding of both the nature of man and God and the relational desires of humankind is clearly illustrated. Without God, humans would not exist, a poignant point to Augustine in understanding the goodness of God and how God has prepared Augustine's soul to receive God and facilitate a relationship. Augustine elaborates further in XIII and in I–XII. Throughout *Confessiones* Augustine describes his longing for God but also his fallenness from God. He sees the gulf that exists between him (created being) and the Creator. He recognizes his innate orientation towards God, his longing for God, and his sense of lack or incompleteness without God.[9] Augustine knew that this was not because he had fallen away from God but because he was not Being but a created being who was defined by temporality, mutability, and corruptibility.[10] However, Harrison writes, "creation is of grace; its continued existence is of grace; the goodness, form, and unity it possesses is of grace."[11] As such, Augustine saw God in creation, and divine grace both through creation and the continuation of creation in Christ. This led Augustine to seek and attain truth, and in that search, discovered a longing and yearning for God. He experienced a restlessness in his longing and desire for truth. This restlessness is observed at the very beginning of *Confessiones* when he writes, "our heart is restless until it rests in you" (*Conf.* I.1.1). Augustine's pertinacious quest for truth has this sense of urgency as he longs to experience the Divine. At the end of XIII, restlessness abates when he enters the door that is opened once knocked upon (*Conf.* XIII.38.53). Nevertheless, he remains fully cognizant that his heart will not be at complete peace until he achieves fulfillment of the *beata vita*. In *Confessiones*, Augustine discovers the meaning of his life; God's presence is the origin and end of his restless heart.

---

8. My translation.
9. Harrison, *Rethinking*, 91–92.
10. Harrison, *Rethinking*, 91–92.
11. Harrison, *Rethinking*, 92.

Augustine wanted his readers to arouse their minds and emotions towards God,[12] and he encourages this from the beginning to the end, and vice versa. Further, both sections of I–IX and X–XIII require memory to remember creation, God, and the nature of a human's existence. McMahon's view of the cyclical nature of I–XIII based on a meditative and prayer structure fits within this architectonic structure of the consummation and the prolegomenon. Yet, this is but one trope unifying *Confessiones*. Kotzé also sees a circular connection between XIII and I.1.1–2.2; she focuses on XIII.38.53 with Matt 7:7 as the unify factor of *Confessiones* where it becomes "a vehicle for expressing Augustine's search to understand God."[13] XIII.38.53 can therefore, be understood as the answer to Augustine's petitions in I.1.1–2.2. Both McMahon and Kotzé identify a cyclical component to I–XIII, but they do so by recognizing a singular "strand."

Table 8.1 demonstrates how in the texts listed multiple themes are present. First, the theme of petitioning (calling on) God and Augustine's desire for God to come into him. Second, creation theology whereby Augustine acknowledges that he would not have existed or have a being were it not for God's creative act. Third, the goodness of God in creating human beings for himself. Fourth, it is only by knocking on God's door that human beings can know God. XIII.38.53 becomes the fulfillment of I.1.1–2.2. This recapitulation in XIII functions to demonstrate the cycle from end to beginning to end.

The Architectonic Structure of Creation

It is evident from the beginning of XIII that Augustine considers the creation events to be good, in the same way that God considered his creation to be good. Further, Augustine believed in the goodness of God as Creator. His first exclamation was "You [God] made me . . . here I am as a result of your goodness."[14] Important to this understanding of creation is the fact that Augustine viewed his conversion as a continuation of God's creative work on himself.[15] From that perspective, *Confessiones* is an allegory of creation. Vaught argues that the metanarrative of *Confessiones* begins with creation, moves towards the fall, points to salvation, and culminates with fulfillment.[16] He goes on to say that Augustine's interpretation of Gen 1 correlates with

---

12. Clark, *Augustine*, 84.
13. Kotzé, "Structure," 38.
14. *Conf.* XIII.1.1.
15. Fischer, "What's?," 76–77.
16. Vaught, *Access*, 151.

the "metanarrative that makes Augustine's journey toward God possible and reflects the structure of his experience."

Augustine's exegetical, allegorical, metanarrative, and metaphysical study of Gen 1 in XIII illustrates how the architectonic structure of his analysis is already present in I–XII and tenaciously joins I–XIII as one cohesive volume. Table 8.2 illustrates how XIII recapitulates the creation statements in I–XII.

Table 8.2: Creation in XIII recapitulates creation from I–XII

CREATION	
Book XIII	**Books I–XII**
XIII.1.1 Here I am as a result of your goodness XIII.2.2 Your creation has its being from the fullness of your goodness	I.1.1 Man, a little piece of your creation VII.5.7 Here is God and see what God has created. God is good . . . and being God, he created good creatures
XIII.2.2 Heaven and earth, which you made in the beginning XIII.3.4 Among the first acts of creation you said, "let there be light" XIII.8.9 From the beginning you had said "let there be light" XIII.24.36 In the beginning God made heaven and earth	VII.9.13 In the beginning was the Word and the Word was with God and the Word was God . . . all things were made by him XI.2.3, 3.5, 9.11 From the beginning in which you made heaven and earth XII.12.15, 13.16, 17.24–25, 19.28, 20.29, 22.31, 28.38, 29.40 In the beginning you made heaven and earth XII.15.18 He made the creation

CREATION	
Book XIII	**Books I–XII**
XIII.2.3 Physical matter... would not exist unless you had made it... we are a spiritual creation in our souls XIII.3.4, 18.22 Let there be light (first act of creation)... I do not think it out of harmony with the sense if we take this to mean the spiritual creation XIII.18.22 Let there be "lights in the firmament"... it is also your spiritual people established in the same solid firmament... by an eternal design at the appropriate times you gave heavenly blessings to the earth	I.7.12 You, Lord my God, are the giver of life III.6.10 For priority goes to your spiritual creation V.3.6 Recall many true observations... about creation itself. I particularly noted the rational, mathematical order of things, the order of seasons, the visible evidence of stars V.10.19 Lord of heaven and earth, maker of all things visible and invisible VII.3.4 God who made not only our souls but also our bodies XII.5.5 It is matter out of which bodies are made
XIII.5.6 My God—Father, Son, Holy Spirit, Creator of the entire creation XIII.12.13 In his Christ God has made a heaven and earth XIII.27.32 Lord our God, our Creator	I.2.2, 10.16 God made heaven and earth. Creator of all things III.8.15 God, the governor of all his creation III.8.16 The one true Creator... of the entire universe IV.10.15 Creator of all V.1.1, 3.5 Your entire creation V.5.9 Creator of all things V.10.19 Lord of heaven and earth, maker of all things visible and invisible

CREATION	
Book XIII	**Books I–XII**
	VII.9.13 All things were made by him, and without him nothing was made ... out of nothing you made heaven and earth **IX.6.14; 7.32** Creator of all **X.25.57** Marvelous Creator of all things **XI.2.4** You made all things **XI.27.35** God, Creator of all things **XII.19.28** It is also true that everything mutable implies for us the notion of a kind of formlessness, which allows it to receive its form **XII.20.29–22.31** [several interpretations offered by Augustine of formless matter, given form, physical creation]
XIII.5.6 Earth invisible and unorganized ... the dark abyss ... flux of spiritual formlessness **XIII.21.29** Land separated out from bitter waters which produced ... a living soul ... the earth which you have established **XIII.33.48** You gave form to its formlessness with no interval of time between	**XI.7.7** He imposes form **XII.4.4** Formlessness of matter ... out of which you made so lovely a world **XII.19.28** It is also true that everything mutable implies for us the notion of a kind of formlessness, which allows it to receive its form
XIII.8.9 How great a thing is the rational creature you have made **XIII.15.17** There is a testimony to you, "giving wisdom to infants"	**VII.3.4** the true God who made ... all rational beings **I.9.15** Not, Lord, that there was a deficiency in memory or intelligence. It was your will to endow us sufficiently with the level appropriate to our age.

CREATION	
Book XIII	**Books I–XII**
XIII.22.32; 26.40 Lord our God, Creator . . . let us make man according to our image and likeness XIII.24.35 Our God, who created us in your image XIII.26.40 You are a man renewed in the knowledge of God after the image of him who created you . . . a living soul	I.1.1 Man, a little piece of your creation VI.3.4 You made humanity in your image VII.3.4 God who made not only our souls but also our bodies IX.8.18 You have created us IX.9.21 You created me X.31.45 You have made man XI.2.4 You made all things including myself XI.12.14 You our God, are the Creator of every created being
XIII.20.28 All things are beautiful because you made them XIII.33.48 Creation *ex nihilo* . . . they [your works] were made out of nothing by you . . . you made the matter from absolutely nothing, but the beauty of the world from formless matter	XI.4.6 You, Lord, who are beautiful, made them for they are beautiful XII.2.2 For this physical totality . . . has received a beautiful form in its very lowest things
XIII.28.43 You God saw all that you had made . . . it was very good . . . in each category of your works, when you said they should be made and they were made, you saw every particular instance is good. Seven times I have counted scripture saying you saw that what you had made is good . . . but on the eight occasion . . . not merely good but very good.	VII.12.18 It was made clear to me that you made all things good . . . for our God has made "all things very good" X.31.46 All your creation is good XII.7.7 Since you, both omnipotent and good, make all things good

CREATION	
Book XIII	**Books I–XII**
XIII.28.43 A body composed of its constituent parts, all of which are beautiful, is far more beautiful as a whole than those parts taken separately	**X.6.9** I see in myself a body and a soul, one external and the other internal **XI.5.7** By your creation the craftsman has a body, a mind by which he commands its members ... from your creation come the bodily senses

The architectonic structure observed in XIII correlates to, and recapitulates, the structure within I–XII. The sequence of the structure within I–XII is as follows:

1. Creation of Augustine, result of God's goodness
2. Creation has its being from the fullness of God's goodness
3. Creation "in the beginning"
4. Creation of physical matter and spiritual creation
5. Creator of the entire creation
6. Form given to formlessness
7. Creation of rational creature
8. Human beings made according to image and likeness of God
9. All things of creation beautiful
10. God's creation is good, very good
11. Body composed of constituent parts, more beautiful as a whole
12. Matter made out of nothing, beauty of world from formless matter

As Augustine studies the creation account he first acknowledges that he is a creation, a result of God's goodness. One can see as he works through the creation account in Gen 1 that there are parallels with God the Creator, creation, and human beings in I–XII. There are two distinct patterns regarding the architectonic structure that is observed in these twelve statements. The first pattern consisting of all twelve statements can be divided into two distinct sections. The first section, points 1–8, pertains to creation and who is created. Point 8 illustrates the goodness of creation, including human beings created in God's image and likeness. The second section concerns the beauty of the result of creation, points 9–12. What God the Creator creates, is both good and beautiful. This is the beauty that Augustine sees as he examines creation in Gen 1. The second pattern revealed in the architectonic structure is the cyclical pattern of creation present in XIII. Points 1–6 describes creation, which starts with Augustine culminating with God creating the entire universe and giving form to the formless. Points 7–12 start at the creation of rational creatures and human beings, describes the beauty of God's creation, and ends with the beauty of the world that was created from formless matter. This attests to the complex, multi-layered structure to XIII, and again, how complex Augustine's thought process must have been.

The beginning of creation as presented in Gen 1 from the first day to the seventh is recounted in XIII. The seventh day of creation, which has no evening and no ending is a day of rest. This Augustine interprets to be the final achievement of eternal rest:

> After your "very good" works . . . you rested the seventh day (Gen 2:2–3). This utterance in your book foretells for us that after our works which, because they are your gift to us, are very good, we also may rest in you for the sabbath of eternal life.[17]

This is the culmination of Augustine's search and journey from a restless heart to rest (I–XIII). Creation exemplifies Augustine's life and journey from his creation to his eventual return to the Divine in eternity; it is the story of Augustine's theological anthropology and specifically, of the return of the soul to its origin. Chadwick too, concludes that the story of the entire created order is also the story of the soul wandering away from God and then finding its way home through conversion; he says this is particularly illustrated in X–XIII.[18]

The creation of form from formlessness is mentioned several times in XIII and often in relation to spiritual creation. According to Harrison, "form" is an ontological category as it does not just refer to outward shape or appearance, but to existence and being.[19] Accordingly, form is received from God, who is eternal and immutable Form. Form is significant for Augustine because, as he describes it, formless matter is "far off" from God because it is "unlike" God.[20] Formless matter comes from God without being from God's substance.[21] Created form can be deformed (*de-formed*) when human beings fall away from God; but form is regained (*re-gained*) when

---

17. *Conf.* XIII.26.51.
18. Chadwick, *Augustine*, xxiv.
19. Harrison, *Rethinking*, 101.
20. *Conf.* XII.7.7; Hochschild, *Memory*, 173.
21. Anderson and Bockmuehl, *Creation*, 164.

human beings convert to God (*re-member*) and are reformed (*re-formed*).[22] Form belongs ultimately and supremely to God, who is Divine Form,[23] and therefore, God is able to re-form the original form itself. This point is made by Augustine, particularly in XI and XII. Human beings as "form" are, consequently, able to point beyond themselves towards the Divine Source moving from creation towards eternity. Hochschild writes that the account of creation is:

> Not merely a metaphor for the soul's journey from the darkness of sin to the light of heavenly presence, it is actually the conversion of the soul as a coming-into-being, a realization of its nature, of its intended species. Between the darkness of formless matter, and the *ratio* of the Word in creation, there is a unity forged.[24]

Harrison posits that "created reality has form, unity, and order 'bestowed' upon it, and in so far as it 'participates' in God."[25] Augustine's discussion of the creation of form from formless matter also alludes to creation as created order from chaos and the order of the human soul as it climbs out of the chaos of the dark abyss of sin towards God. Thus, formless matter is a contributory motif in the unity of *Confessiones*.

Augustine emphasizes that human beings, human souls, and indeed creation itself, were created out of nothing (i.e., *ex nihilo*) by an immortal God (XIII.2.3).[26] In XIII.33.48 Augustine states that matter was formed out of nothing and the beauty of the world created out of formless matter. Nunziato argues that Augustine treats matter as the "mystery by which God articulates divine form as something other than God."[27] Further, he asserts that God in order to create, creates matter, and Augustine attributes matter even to spiritual substances.[28] Augustine distinguished two kinds of spiritual matter: the matter of angelic beings and that of the human soul. Angels are conceived as pure spirits limited by the fact that they are composed of essence and existence whereas the human soul is essentially spiritual while

---

22. De-formed and re-formed are my wording and italicization. Form is *re-formed* because it is the original form that is restored after it had been de-formed. Form cannot be lost or destroyed; it remains since it is created by God who will not allow its destruction. See Harrison, *Rethinking*, 102, for her phraseology of "deform" and "reform."

23. Harrison, *Rethinking*, 104.

24. Hochschild, *Memory*, 174.

25. Harrison, *Rethinking*, 104–5.

26. *Imm. An.* 8.14; 11.18; Harrison, *Rethinking*, 50.

27. Nunziato, "Created," 362.

28. Nunziato, "Created," 364.

at the same time animating matter.²⁹ Armstrong asserts that matter is the key to creation.³⁰ He accords matter the "architectonic centrality" that it actually possesses; he maintains that it is "one of the great recurring themes in Augustine's thought." Both Nunziato's and Armstrong's work support the concepts of matter and form as a thread that weaves throughout *Confessiones*. This lends support to XIII as a recapitulation of I–XII with regard to creation, matter, and form.

Augustine writes, "all things are beautiful because you made them" (XIII.20.28). Augustine wrote of human beings created to the image and likeness of God and how the body is composed of constituent parts that are more beautiful when observed as a whole. In I.7.12 Augustine writes that God gives life and a body to a baby, has endowed the baby with its senses, and has coordinated his limbs. He goes on to write, "You have adorned it [the baby] with a beautiful form, and for the coherence and preservation of the *whole* you have implanted all the instincts of a living being." The body and soul are united as a whole. This is what God saw as good in his creation. Augustine regarded the creation of human beings to the image and likeness of God as literally true as written in Gen 1.³¹ Augustine also believed the soul was the place where the image and remembrance of God resided.³² This must have encouraged Augustine that God remembered him and left a vestigium of himself, a *memoria Dei* within his soul, which drew Augustine to the Divine and thus allowed Augustine to live his story from creation to redemption towards fulfillment of the *beata vita*. Moreover, he was seen by God as good and beautiful because he was created by God. Augustine saw that it was not just human beings who were deemed beautiful but the world as well.³³ His appreciation for the Creator grew as he marveled at creation, as he read Gen 1, and as he remembered the *historia* of his own life as it played out. God created new life in him much like the way the world was created anew.

In sum, creation is fundamental to Augustine's thought and understanding of the Divine and even his own beginnings in creation. The architectonic structure of XIII emerges as Augustine examines the creation account in Gen 1. Augustine works through the six days of creation and the

---

29. O'Toole, *Philosophy*, 103–4.
30. Armstrong, "St. Augustine," 6.
31. Chaffey, "Examination," 95.
32. Oliva, "Innere," 26.
33. Beauty of body: *Conf.* XI.4.6; 5.7; XII.2.2; XIII.20.28; 28.43. Beauty of God's creation and world: *Conf.* XI.4.6; XIII.20.28.

seventh day: I–XII mirrors these six days and also the seventh day of the sabbath. Hence, XIII recapitulates I–XII.

"*A*" Memory and "*The*" Memories

Confessiones XIII is a book about *a* memory (the creative act of God) whereas I–XII are books about *the* memories that arise in Augustine's life.[34] The idea of *a* memory versus *the* memories can be difficult to understand or visualized unless XIII is adjudged to be a recapitulation of memories in I–XII. Book XIII is Augustinian memory as viewed through creation *ex nihilo*. Thus, XIII describes the memory of God's creative act in creation; this is the "*a* memory" of all God did in his creation. This memory leads to *the* memories of Augustine's life, his journey towards God and towards fulfillment of the *beata vita*. Everything, whether it be creation, the incarnation, or Augustine's search for God, is remembered via memory, which results from *a* memory that emanates from eternity. As a consequence, the intricate details of Augustine's theology becomes known. The creative act of God at the beginning is also the creative act at the incarnation and the creative act of eternal rest. Hence, God's creative act is *a* memory of creation that moves forward in time yet leads back to the beginning, a movement that occurs in time. Augustine remembers *the* memories of his life as he writes *Confessiones* and sees the same forward and backwards movements to his beginnings, his origin, and to the *beata vita* and eternal rest. Within this recapitulative movement, Augustine provides an account of his own being in terms of all Being.[35] While this is observed throughout I–XII, it is in XIII where the theological implications of this is noted. Augustine progresses spiritually by his return to his origins and his understanding of his creation as a being who is diametrically opposed to the Creator who is immutable, unchanging, infinite, and incorporeal. Memory becomes the *principium* of Augustine's beginnings from creation (*a* memory) and his *historia* (*the* memories). His memories and his life parallel the memories and origin of all history and is divinely inspired. The memories of history also include the memory of the incarnate Christ who is also the recapitulation of creation itself. Augustine's memories are transcended by the humility of the

---

34. Burke relates I–IX and X–XIII as turning from a "narrative of memories" to the "principles of Memory." However, his definition of memory is different from my definition of "*a* memory." Burke defines memory as the storehouse of images. Burke, *Rhetoric*, 124.

35. McMahon, *Augustine's Prayerful Ascent*, 152.

incarnation.[36] Augustine recognizes and accepts the incarnate Christ as *a* memory since it is the Creator, God the Father, who recapitulates creation through God the Son. Augustine, through *the* memories journeys towards the incarnate Christ and moves forward to redemption and momentary union at the Eucharistic remembrance of the death and resurrection of Christ. At the Eucharist Augustine remembers the broken body of Christ upon the cross but also the Christ who was still the *totus Christus* and the Christ who brought Augustine wholeness through grace. In the Eucharistic moment, Augustine can experience union with God. The memories of momentary union and participation in God propel Augustine towards fulfillment of the *beata vita* where creation is also to be found. *The* memories of Augustine's life (I–XII) is a recapitulation of *a* memory (XIII), which in turn is a recapitulation of I–XII; in a sense, Augustine's mind is ordering *the* (his) memories so he can "see" clearly. *The* memories of his life are stored in *memoria* in his mind but they are indelibly undergirded by *a* memory of God's creative act.

The memories identified in *Confessiones* XIII essentially arise from four of the symphonic forms of memory: (i) teaching and learning, (ii) recollection and forgetfulness, (iii) images, *phantasiae*, and *phantasmata*, and (iv) sense and sense perception. Table 8.3 compares memory and its symphonic forms in XIII, X, and I–XII. It is subdivided into four smaller tables: Tables 8.3a, 8.3b, 8.3c, 8.3d.

Teaching and Learning

Teaching and learning are important constituents of memory. This is noted in XIII. While the term memory is not mentioned with regard to teaching and learning, memory is implicit in the context of the chapters. Teaching or learning cannot occur without memory, as seen in I–XII. Table 8.3a parallels statements in XIII with I–XII.

---

36. "Humility of the incarnation" is a term used by Rowan Williams. Williams, *On Augustine*, 14.

Table 8.3a: Memory/memories regarding teaching and learning as documented in XIII, X, and I–IX, XI–XII.

A Memory and *The* Memories		
Book XIII	**Book X**	**Books I–IX, XI–XII**
Teaching and Learning		
XIII.6.7 Light that teaches truth **XIII.7.8** Teaching us concerning the things of the Spirit **XIII.14.15** His word is a light to your feet **XIII.24.36** Truth my light **XIII.26.41** From you, my God, I have learnt	**X.6.10** Truth says to me **X.10.17** So they* were there even before I had learnt them . . . the answer must be they were already in memory * things learnt **X.40.65** I listened to you teaching me and giving instruction. **X.41.66** You are the truth presiding over all things	**III.6.10** Truth, truth; how in my inmost being the very marrow of my mind sighed for you **IV.12.18** Look where he is—wherever there is a taste of truth **IV.15.25** For I did not know that the soul needs to be enlightened by light from outside itself, so that it can participate in truth **V.6.10** But I had already been taught by you, my God, through wonderful and hidden ways, and I believe you have taught me because it is true, and none other than you is the teacher of the truth **XI.8.10** Lord I hear your voice speaking to me, for one who teaches us speaks to us . . . who is our teacher except reliable truth

THE ARCHAEOLOGY OF MEMORY BY RECALLING CREATION

A Memory and *The* Memories		
Book XIII	**Book X**	**Books I–IX, XI–XII**
Teaching and Learning		
XIII.6.7 Let not my heart tell me vain fantasies (I think Chadwick has mistranslated this ... *tibi admoveo cor meum, ne me vana doceat*—I lift up my heart to you, so that it does not teach me in vain—my translation) **XIII.18.22** You teach us to distinguish between intelligible and sensible things as between day and night, or between souls dedicated to the intelligible realm and souls dedicated to the material world of the senses	**X.40.65** Truth, when did you ever fail to walk with me, teaching me what to avoid and what to seek after	**III.6.10** The dishes placed before me contained splendid hallucinations (*phantasmata splendida*) ... but those fantasies (*similia*—like) had not the least resemblance to you as you now have told me, because they were physical images (*corporalia phantasmata*)

Six distinct points are evident in XIII:

1. Light teaches truth
2. Teaching things concerning the Spirit
3. Truth is my light
4. Learn from God, taught by God
5. Calling on God so heart does not teach in vain
6. God teaches so that the intelligible can be distinguished from the sensible

These six truths from XIII recapitulate texts from I–XII. In XIII, Augustine acknowledges truth is taught by the Divine. The teaching of truth includes the "things of the Spirit," "His word," and the ability to "distinguish between the intelligible and sensible things." There is a play on words too that reflect Scripture and teaching, e.g., "light teaches truth" and "truth is my light." Jesus is the Light of the World and the Truth; Jesus in John 8:12 and 9:5, "I am the light," and in John 14:6, "I am the way, and the truth, and the life." The psalmist in Psalm 119:105 says, "Your word is a lamp to my feet and a light to my path." The light that teaches truth reminds Augustine of God creating light in Gen 1. Thus light and truth reflect a cyclical pattern within this aspect of memory. Table 8.3a summarizes what is said in X and in the other books of *Confessiones*. The importance of learning and teaching in discovering truth is exemplified by Augustine when he exclaims in XIII.30.45, "I listened, Lord, my God; I sucked a drop of sweetness from your truth and I understood." Finding truth and the Truth means a further understanding and knowledge of God that leads eventually from restlessness to rest.

Recollection and Forgetfulness

Both recollection and forgetfulness are central to the architectonics of memory. Memory is present at the beginning of Augustine's life (i.e., at creation) then continues to be formed, remembered, or forgotten, and recollected throughout his life. This recollection includes the remembrance of the incarnation, which in itself enacts creation, the promise of eternity through the sacrament of the Eucharist, and finally culminates in the reality of eternal rest in eternity, allegorically, the seventh day of creation. The references to memory with regard to recollection and forgetfulness are documented in Table 8.3b.

Table 8.3b: Memory/memories regarding recollection and forgetfulness as documented in XIII, X, and I–IX, XI–XII.

A Memory and *The* Memories		
Book XIII	**Book X**	**Books I–IX, XI–XII**
Recollection and Forgetfulness		
XIII.1.1 I forgot you (mis-remembered), you did not forget me (re-membered)	X.4.5 You never abandon what you have begun	V.7.13 My God, did not forget my soul IX.4.8 When I called* upon you, you heard me *invocarem* (I would invoke) XII.10.10 I remembered you. I heard your voice behind me calling me to return

A Memory and *The* Memories		
Book XIII	**Book X**	**Books I–IX, XI–XII**
Recollection and Forgetfulness		
XIII.7.8 To whom can I expound, and what words can I express, the weight of cupidity pulling us downwards into the precipitous abyss and the lifting up of love given by your Spirit ... How can I speak about it ... for it is not about literal places ... this symbolic language contains a resemblance ... it means our feelings and our love **X.14.15** Yet still my soul is sad	**X.14.22** Not also that I am drawing on my memory when I say there are four perturbations of the mind—cupidity, gladness, fear, sadness and from memory I produce whatever I say in discussing them ... I find in my memory what I have to say and produce it from that source. Yet none of these perturbations disturb me when by act of recollection I remember them	
XIII.11.12 For I am and I know and I will ... let him consider himself and reflect and tell me what is there **XIII.22.32** The person ... who contemplates and understands your truth	**X.5.7** For what I know of myself I know because you grant me light **X.8.14** There also I meet myself and recall what I am, what I have done, and when and where and how I was affected when I did it	**VII.10.16** I was admonished to return to myself ... I entered into my innermost citadel ... I entered and with my soul's eye, such as it was, saw above that same eye of my soul the immutable light higher than my mind ... eternal truth and true love **IX 1.1** Who am I and what am I? **IX.10.24** We ascended further by internal reflection ... we entered into our own minds ... where you feed Israel eternally with truth for food

A Memory and *The* Memories		
Book XIII	**Book X**	**Books I–IX, XI–XII**
Recollection and Forgetfulness		
XIII.12.13 Because our soul was "disturbed" within ourselves, "we remembered you Lord from the land of Jordan"... he forgets the things behind	X.8.14 There [in the vast hall of my memory] also I meet myself and recall (*recolo*) what I am, what I have done, and when and where and how I was affected when I did it. There is everything I remember X.16.24 It is I who remember, I who am mind	II.1.1 I make the act of recollection (*recordari*). The recalling (*recolens*) of my wicked way is bitter in my memory... you gathered me together from the state of disintegration IV.6.11 Look into my heart, my God, look within. See this, as I remember it, my hope; for you cleanse me from these flawed emotions XII.10.10 I remembered (*recordatus*) you. I heard your voice behind me calling me to return
XIII.12.13 Forgets the things behind and stretches out to those things which lie ahead		IX.10.23 Forgetting the past and reaching forward to what lies ahead

A Memory and *The* Memories		
Book XIII	Book X	Books I–IX, XI–XII
Recollection and Forgetfulness		
XIII.12.13 in your name we are baptized, Father, Son, and Holy Spirit; in your name we baptize, Father, Son, and Holy Spirit **XIII.20.26** God, your mysteries have crept through the midst of the water of the world's temptations to imbue the nations with your name through your baptism **XIII.20.27** What is one thing for our understanding can be symbolized and expressed in many physical movements . . . these physical things have been produced to meet the needs of peoples estranged from your eternal truth . . . through your word, those signs emerged **XIII.20.28** Subjection to corporeal sacraments do not make further progress unless in the spiritual realm their soul comes to live on another level and, subsequent to the word of initiation, looks towards their perfection **XIII.24.36** At the bodily level it is expressed by many sacraments **XIII.24.37** Signs given in corporeal expression are the creatures generated from the waters, necessary because of our deep involvement in the flesh	**X.3.4** Transform my soul by faith and your sacrament **X.43.68** The true Mediator you showed to humanity in your secret mercy . . . he is the Mediator between God and men, the man Christ Jesus	**III.4.8** This name of my Saviour your Son . . . and at a deep level I retain the memory **V.8.15** When I was full of abominable filth, so as to bring me to the water of your grace [baptism]. This water was to wash me clean **VII.9.14** But the word was made flesh and dwelt among us **VII.17.23** But with me there remained a memory of you . . . I carried with me only a loving memory **IX.6.14** When the time came for me to give my name for baptism . . . we were baptized

A Memory and *The* Memories		
Book XIII	**Book X**	**Books I–IX, XI–XII**
Recollection and Forgetfulness		
(cont.) **XIII.34.49** We have seen in your Word, in your unique Son, "heaven and earth," the head and body of the church . . . you produced from physical matter sacraments . . . all these things we see, and they are very good, because you see them in us		
XIII.14.15 In the morning I will stand up and will contemplate you . . . in the morning I will stand and I will see the salvation of my face, my God		**VII.14.20** I woke up in you and saw you to be infinite in another sense, and this way of seeing you did not come from the flesh
XIII.34.49 So as to reveal hidden secrets and bring order to our disordered chaos	**X.11.18** Ideas which the memory contains in dispersed and disordered way, and by concentrating our attention we arrange them in order as if ready to hand, stored in the very memory where previously lay hidden, scattered, and neglected . . . were ordered ready to hand—things we are said to have learnt and to know	

Augustine remained unsettled by the concept of forgetfulness, where a memory could be forgotten. It was aporetic to Augustine. Remembering that he had forgotten was a reality that continued to be paradoxically perplexing to Augustine for he never found the answers. He remembers that he forgot God, and yet in XIII, Augustine appears less unsettled regarding this paradox; he has come to a better place of peace, acceptance, and understanding that he does not need to provide or know all the answers, and this comes through in the text. Important to Augustine was to recognize before God that when he forgot (mis-remembered) God, he knew God had not forgotten him. He understood the significance of God's act of remembering. The divine act of remembering was the unembodied, incorporeal God-given form (embodied) in the person of Christ who is both Truth and Mediator. Eternity is thus reflected in Christ and fulfilled through Christ.

The architectonic structure in XIII regarding recollection and forgetfulness starting from XIII.1.1 is as follows:

1. I forgot you, you did not forget me
2. Symbolic language of the allegory of the deep abyss, the lifting up of love, and the resemblance of the language, perturbation of the mind
3. Person who contemplates understands truth
4. Disturbances within the soul caused Augustine to remember God
5. Forgetting past, stretching out to what lies ahead
6. Remembrance through the sacraments of baptism and the Eucharist
7. Contemplating God first thing in the morning and "seeing" God
8. Recollection of hidden secrets, bringing order to chaos

The above architectonic structure is the summation and sequence of events that occur in recollection and forgetfulness. This sequence may not have been intentionally planned by Augustine in XIII. However, truth naturally unfolds the order and sequence of the events.

Sacramental Nature of Memory

The texts pertaining to sacraments in Table 8.3b illustrate how significant memory was with regard to sacraments. Memory itself, for Augustine, was sacramental in nature because it allowed the soul to transcend the body and unite with the Divine. Memory emanated from eternity; it pointed towards God and eternal rest. O'Gorman defines the function of a sacrament as something that points beyond to something else and further, engages the reality to which it points.[37] Memory allowed truth to be known; memory was, therefore, sapiential and it provided the gateway to the Divine and eternal truth. The revelation of temporal knowledge (*scientia*) assisted memory as it recollected truth (sacramental remembering); *scientia*

---

37. O'Gorman, "Imagination," 435.

accordingly evolved into *sapientia*, the reality of eternal truth. This is borne out in XIII, which portrays a motif of *scientia* approaching *sapientia*.[38]

The magnitude of the sacramental nature of memory for Augustine was asseverated in the Eucharist when the memory of the death and resurrection of Jesus resulted in a momentary union with the Divine (see XIII, Table 8.3b starting at XIII.20.28). Grove writes how the remembering has a location in the body of Christ; it is Christ who "prompts individuals to remember that they are forgetful.... [I]n response to their own forgetfulness ... [they] can cry out, remembering to eat."[39] The sacramental connection with the mysterious becomes apparent in matter; the bread and wine taken in the memory of Jesus, and through which one can glimpse the soul.[40] The Eucharistic bread is Christ and the memory of Christ; thus it became for Augustine the intersection between memory and hope. Cavadini states, "the person bound to the Eucharist in faith is bound to a memorial of God's mercy that configures or even defines all of one's own memory ... and impels it into hope."[41] Cavadini interestingly writes that X emerges out of IX's ascent to the Eucharistic altar and out of Eucharistic remembering; X continues in this vein and deepens this Eucharistic remembering.[42] Cavadini continues, "Those who seek the Lord by a Eucharistic act of remembering, of memory, praise the Lord because they find him, in memory." The Eucharist was for Augustine a memory of the salvific act and participation in the Divine, and therefore, a sacrament. Understanding the nature of memory and how it functioned helped Augustine profoundly deepen his understanding of the Eucharist, his participation in the Divine, and his eschatological hope. In fact, this act of remembering helped fight off forgetfulness. Grove asserts that the mystery of the memory and the act of remembering means, according to Augustine, becoming Christ in the process.[43] Augustine encountered memories in the Eucharistic sacrament but not simply a collection of memories and images but rather an *ordo* of the symphonic forms that facilitated recollection, forgetfulness, and understanding of the profundity of that Eucharistic moment where memory and hope intersected.

Cavadini views the exegesis of Gen 1:1—2:3 in XI–XIII as a "Eucharistic exegesis" where XI is the Book of the Father, XII the Book of the Son, XIII the Book of the Holy Spirit.[44] Augustine believed that the memory of

---

38. Yam and Dupont, "Mind-Centered," 30.
39. Grove, *Augustine*, 123.
40. O'Gorman, "Imagination," 435.
41. Cavadini, *Visioning*, 186.
42. Cavadini, *Visioning*, 191–92.
43. Grove, *Augustine*, 126–27.
44. Cavadini, *Visioning*, 196–97.

THE ARCHAEOLOGY OF MEMORY BY RECALLING CREATION

creation itself was sacramental because the redemptive act was intricately linked to the act of creation; when the *Logos* became flesh (John 1:4) in the beginning, creation *ex nihilo* (first creation) became new creation.[45] As such, the incarnation and resurrection of Christ could be viewed as occurring as one action.[46] Augustine understood the sacramental nature of memory and creation to exist from creation's very beginnings (origin) and its completion in Christ and eternity. Cavadini posits that "Eucharistic exegesis of the creation narrative enables one to see the economy of redemption as, in a way, not merely the restoration, but the completion of creation."[47] To Augustine the completion of creation was the hope of perfection and attainment of the *beata vita* to be found in the rest of the eternal Sabbath. Milbank writes, "Creation saves finite reality from nothingness and eternal form from material chaos preceding time, while redemption recreates finite reality."[48] Thus, the memory of creation was memory of the sacred because it was a remembrance of when God in a sacred act created in creation and when the incarnate Christ created new life in Augustine. Milbank describes memory as "the miracle of the continuous resurrection and recuperation of what has vanished, which alone salvages loss as redemptive harmony."[49]

The language of "beginning" in Gen 1 is contextualized "in the gratuitous, merciful remembering of God and in our Eucharistic remembering of God's remembering"; further, creation is also a "Eucharistic awareness of God's mercy." Cavadini describes how it is only from the perspective of the Spirit-filled person, whose mind is formed in Eucharistic remembering by the God's love, "that one can truly ascend to 'see' creation."[50] This recapitulative sequential nature of Eucharistic memory, creation, incarnation, death and resurrection of Jesus, and eternity, presented a temporal timeline through which Augustine could glimpse God's timeless eternity. Christ in the flesh (VII.9.14) is a living memory both on earth and in eternity; in the same manner, when Augustine finally reached the eschatologically promised vision, he became a living memory of his death and the mercy of God.[51] On earth, Augustine was a living memory of God's creation.

Christ the living memory juxtaposed both temporal and eternal memory since the descent of the Divine into temporality was a recapitulation

---

45. Chambers, *Reconsidering*, 130.
46. Milbank, "Confession," 15.
47. Cavadini, "Eucharistic," 107–8.
48. Milbank, "Confession," 15.
49. Milbank, "Confession," 25.
50. Cavadini, *Visioning*, 198.
51. Cavadini, *Visioning*, 206n70.

of creation. Hopkins poetically describes this as "God's infinity dwindled into infancy" where infancy metaphorically also speaks to "the Beginning" at creation.[52] Thus, remembrance of the incarnation is sacramental to Augustine. Sacramental too, is the beginning of life in Christ, which starts at creation realized at the resurrection and in eternal life in Christ. According to Ratzinger, in so much that we are united in Christ "we have today passed from death to life" and are already living eternal life in communion with Christ.[53] The resurrection of Christ is not merely the memory of a past event. It is a continual experience of new life (the new creation, a beginning) and eternity. The remembrance of Christ via the sacraments was the manner in which, through memory and his soul, he could envision with expectation complete union and participation with the Divine in eternity. Augustine writes in XIII.20.28, "subjection to corporeal sacraments do not make further progress unless in the spiritual realm their soul comes to live on another level and, subsequent to the word of initiation, looks towards their perfection." Thus, a sacrament expresses the connection of the embodied finite human to the un-embodied infinite God; it is a communication between the human being and God.[54] It is a communication initiated by the Divine and which calls and moves Augustine into a deeper consciousness where he becomes aware of his connection to the Divine and the merging of God embodied and God un-embodied.[55] Further, the physicality of the sacraments centers the awareness of God's will in the body where it can be enacted in community.[56] O'Gorman describes the sacraments as both an encounter with, and a transformation in, Jesus and an energizing contact with the presence of God.[57] Memory in Eucharistic remembering is sacramental in nature.

Baptism, the sacrament of entrance into the Christian life, is another sacrament present in *Confessiones*. According to McMahon, baptism proves a *"figura"* to be fulfilled by entrance into God's eternal life, and which prepares the soul by cleansing it of sin.[58] Baptism is symbolic with participation in Christ's death and resurrection, and hence, with the resurrection on the last day. Baptism is recurrently and emphatically linked with eternal rest in God and with release from anxiety (*sollicitudo*): "We were baptized and

---

52. Hopkins, "Blessed," 173.

53. This is the homily given by Ratzinger at the mass of the Easter Vigil at the altar of the *Confessio* in St. Peter's Basilica on March 26, 2005. Ratzinger, "Awake," 1.

54. O'Gorman, "Imagination," 433.

55. O'Gorman, "Imagination," 433.

56. *Conf.* XIII.20.27; Hogue, *Remembering*.

57. O'Gorman, "Imagination," 436, art. 4.

58. McMahon, *Augustine's Prayerful Ascent*, 113.

disquiet about our past life vanished from us."⁵⁹ McMahon argues that this emphasis in IX on baptism, eternal rest, and release from anxiety links IX to Augustine's allegory on God's ninth act in Genesis in XIII.⁶⁰ He goes on to say that this is one of the principal ways in which the allegory of XIII proves the paradigm for I–IX; however, McMahon neither includes nor explains how X–XII fits into this paradigm.

The millstones of past life do not hinder the ability to experience the sacraments in life going forward. The sacramental nature of baptism, for Augustine, was found in the freeing from the torments of past life and being able to move forward in his Christian life. The sacrament of baptism, therefore, was a ritual event that permitted the "touching" of the temporal with the eternal, i.e., the corporeal, embodied, finite human with the incorporeal, unembodied, infinite God. The baptism of Jesus was a holy exemplar of the temporal touching eternity. Upon his baptism, the heavens were opened and a voice said, "This is my Son, the Beloved, with whom I am well pleased" (Matt 3:16–17). Baptism freed memory to remember the Mediator in creation, the incarnation, and the Eucharist, and pointed to the future memory of eternal rest. Aquinas described baptism as the door to other sacraments.⁶¹

In the sacraments, Clark aptly proposes that what Augustine deemed important was not *what* he remembered from his past, but *how* he remembers the past.⁶² Augustine believed that the past was not the direction to move in, rather he needed to "reach/stretch" out to the things that lay ahead (IX.10.23, XIII.12.13). It was the mental activity of remembering that paved the way to reflect on his existence in relation to God; such contemplations led to knowing God.⁶³ This allowed Augustine to reach forward in expectation of union with the Divine and eternal rest; this solidified the sacramental nature of memory for Augustine. Memory underpins Augustine's understanding and experience of the sacraments, including the importance of remembrance and thus memory.

Images, Phantasiae, and Phantasmata

Images, *Phantasiae,* and *Phantasmata* are all memories, whether they contain true or false images. XIII mentions specific instances and type of

---

59. *Conf.* IX.6.14; McMahon, *Augustine's Prayerful Ascent,* 113.
60. McMahon, *Augustine's Prayerful Ascent,* 113.
61. *Summa Theologiae* IIIa q. 68, art. 6.
62. Clark, *Augustine,* 46.
63. Cessario, *Godly,* 16.

memories that are also analogous specifically to texts in III–IV, VI–X, and XII. Table 8.3c compares these texts.

Table 8.3c: Images, *Phantasiae*, and *Phantasmata* as documented in XIII, X, and III, IV, VI, VII, VIII, IX, and XII

A Memory and *The* Memories		
Book XIII	**Book X**	**Books I–IX, XI–XII**
Images, *Phantasiae*, *Phantasmata*		
XIII.5.6 Here is an enigmatic image (1 Cor 13:12) ... I discern the Trinity, which you are, my God ... there is the Trinity—Father and Son and Holy Spirit, Creator of the entire creation [*ecce apparet mihi in* **aenigmate** *trinitas quod es, deus meus* ... behold, it appears to me in the **enigma (riddle)** of the Trinity that you are, my God ... (my translation)] **XIII.15.18** Your word appears to us in the **enigmatic** obscurity of clouds and through the "mirror" of heaven (1 Cor 13:12) not as it really is [*verbum autem tuum manet in aeternum quod nunc in* **aenigmate** *nubium et per speculum Caeli, non sicuti est*—but your word remains for ever, which now appears in the **enigma (riddle)** of the clouds and through the mirror of heaven, not as it is (my translation)]	**X.5.7** We see now through a mirror in an enigma (*aenigmate*), not yet face to face (1 Cor 13:12)	**VIII.1.1** Of your eternal life I was certain, though I saw it in an enigma (*aenigmate*) and if in a mirror (1 Cor 13:12) **IX.10.25** Nor through the sound of thunder, nor through the obscurity of a symbolic utterance [*nec per sonitum nubis nec per* **aenigma** *similitudinis*—not by the sound of thunder, nor by the **enigma (riddle)** of similitude][64] **XII.7.7** God one in three in one **XII.13.16** The intellectual non-physical heaven where the intellingence's knowing is a matter of simultaneity—not in part, not in an **enigma**, not through a mirror, but complete, in total openness, "face to face" (1 Cor 13:12)

---

64. Chadwick translates *nec per sonitum nubis nec per aenigma similitudinis* as "nor through the sound of thunder, nor through the obscurity of a symbolic utterance," while Watts translates this as "nor by the sound of thunder, nor in the dark riddle of a resemblance." Watts is closer to the original text and also close to my translation of "nor by the sound of thunder, nor by the enigma (riddle) of a similitude."

THE ARCHAEOLOGY OF MEMORY BY RECALLING CREATION

A Memory and *The* Memories		
Book XIII	**Book X**	**Books I–IX, XI–XII**
Images, *Phantasiae, Phantasmata*		
(cont.)		[*caelum intellectual, ubi est intellectus nosse simul, non ex parte, non in* **aenigmate**, *non per speculum, sed ex toto, in maifestione, facie ad faciem*—intellectual heave, where the intellect is understood to know at the same time, not in part, not in an **enigma (riddle)**, not through a mirror, but entirely, in manifestation, face to face (my translation)]
XIII.6.7 Let not my heart tell me vain fantasies* * I think Chadwick has mistranslated this . . . *tibi admoveo cor meum, ne me vana doceat*—I lift up my heart to you, so that it does not teach me in vain [my translation]		**III.6.10** The dishes placed before me contained splendid hallucinations (*phantasmata splendida*) . . . but those fantasies (*similia*) had not the least resemblance to you as you now have told me, because they were physical images (*corporalia phantasmata*) **III.7.12** How could I see this when for me "to see" meant a physical act of looking and of forming an image (*phantasma*) in the mind **IV.7.12** When I thought of you, my mental image was not of anything solid and firm; it was not of you but a vain phantom (*phantasmata*) **VII.1.1** My heart vehemently protested against all the physical images (*phantasmata*) in my mind

A Memory and *The* Memories		
Book XIII	Book X	Books I–IX, XI–XII
Images, *Phantasiae, Phantasmata*		
		IX.4.9 For in the fantasies (*phantasmatis*) which I had taken for truth, there was vanity and deceit* * (*mendacium*) a lie **XII.11.14** Only a person whose empty heart makes his mind roll and reel with private fantasies (*phantasmatis*)
XIII.32.47 We see the beauty of . . . the sun sufficing for the day, the moon and stars to cheer the night, and all of these provide an indication and sign of passing time	**X.15.23** Images of them [sun, stone] are available to me in memory . . . I mention the numbers by which we count things . . . in my memory are present not their images but the numbers themselves	

The discussion of images, *phantasiae*, and *phantasmata* in XIII is presented sequentially as follows:

1. Enigmatic image
2. Trinity: Father, Son, Holy Spirit
3. Vain fantasies
4. Beauty of sun, moon, and stars

Enigma is defined as "something that is mysterious and seems impossible to understand completely."[65] Augustine seems to have this understanding in mind. This, and his reading of 1 Cor 13:12, reveal there is a sense of obscurity and mystery in fully understanding God's Word and the Trinity. There is, too, an inability to see clearly "face to face," for God, indeed, is unimaginable mystery.

---

65. *Cambridge Dictionary*, s.v. "Enigma," https://dictionary.cambridge.org/dictionary/english/enigma.

There are only two occurrences of the word *aenigmate* in XIII. They occur in reference to the enigma of God's Word and the Trinity, and in both cases, one can identify a dependence on memory. According to Djuth, Augustine's use of "enigmatic image" and the "enigmatic obscurity of the clouds" is because memory images are "opaque in terms of what they reveal about the nature of divine reality."[66] Enigma, and indeed, the enigmatic image is a memory that is mysterious and incomplete in that the Trinity and eternity are all discerned as through a "mirror," as if an image of the reality, but not reality itself. Augustine in *De Trinitate*, referring to 1 Cor 13:12, attempts to define what is meant by enigma and mirror.[67] Enigma, he says, is used in an obscure allegorical sense. He writes:

> By the word "mirror" he [Paul] wanted us to understand an image, and by the word "enigma" he was indicating that although it is a likeness, it is an obscure one and difficult to penetrate. Now we can indeed take it that by use of the words "mirror" and "enigma" the apostle meant any likenesses that are useful for understanding God with, as far as possible; but of such likenesses none is more suitable than the one which is not called God's image for nothing.[68]

Augustine uses this word *aenigmate* in the same allegorical context in XIII, and VIII, IX, X, and XII. On earth and in temporal time, Augustine cannot see the Divine clearly, only opaquely; however, in the incarnation and Eucharistic remembering, the mirror becomes less cloudy. Augustine understands that it is Christ the Mediator who points the way to see the Divine more clearly;[69] this provides Augustine with hope and an eschatological expectation. In XIII he recapitulates the previous books; in one chapter, indeed just two sentences, Augustine recapitulates the obscure enigma that he must contend with in temporality.

Augustine viewed fantasy as dangerous (XIII.6.7); "I lift up my heart to you, so that it does not teach me in vain." *Phantasmata* obscured God's truth, thereby creating turmoil between the body and soul.[70] They distract *memoria* in the mind by restricting *memoria's* capacity to seek God. Park argues that images, both *phantasiae* and *phantasmata*, have an important

---

66. Djuth, "Veiled," 89.
67. *Trin.* XV.3.15.
68. *Trin.* XV.3.16.
69. *Conf.* VII.19.25; VIII.12.29; IX.13.34–37; X.42.67–43.70.
70. *V. Rel.* III.3; X.18.

and necessary role in Augustine's conversion.[71] Even so, Augustine astutely recognizes the detrimental role of *phantasmata* (IV.7.12) when he poignantly expresses, multiple times, regret over his false *phantasmata*. Augustine knew he required Divine help and illumination to prevent these *phantasmata* teaching him vain fantasies. He also understood that sin was the cause of "dis-membering" God and his hope of eternity; the "icon" of eternity was forgotten or "dis-membered" and the enigmatic image became more obscure. Augustine, therefore, lifted his heart to God (XIII.6.7). As he grew in knowledge of the truth, and the renewal of the "image" (memory) of God within, his faith led him to understand that the obscurity of looking "through a mirror in an enigma" (X.5.7) was temporary. Augustine was also cognizant that there were many good memories residing in his mind of beautiful images, such as the sun and moon, which he could also physically observe during the day and night. These sights and true images, which were good and beautiful, provided proof of God's creative act and the passage of time (day and night).

Senses and Sense perception

Sense and sense perception are vital to memory-formation as most images in memory, both true and false, are a result of sense and sense perception. Table 8.3d documents how the power of the senses impacts the affections of the soul.

---

71. Park, "Imagining," 804.

Table 8.3d: Memory/memories regarding senses and sense perception as documented in XIII, X, and I–IX, XI–XII.

A Memory and *The* Memories		
Book XIII	Book X	Books I–IX, XI–XII
Senses and Sense perception		
XIII.23.34 He [the spiritual person] judges the "living soul" in its affections made gentle by chastity, by fasting, by devout reflection on things perceived by the bodily senses **XIII.38.53** We see the things that you have made ... we see outwardly that they are, and inwardly that they are good	**X.6.8** Yet there is a light I love ... a light, voice, odour, food, embrace of my inner man, where my soul is floodlit by light which space cannot contain, where there is a sound that time cannot seize, where there is a perfume which no breeze disperses, where there is a taste for food no amount of eating can lessen, and where there is a bond of union that no satiety can part **X.8.13** Memory preserves in distinct particulars and general categories all the perceptions which have penetrated, each by its own route of entry **X.14.22** The mind itself perceives them through the experience of its passions and entrusts them to memory **X.40.65** Starting from myself I gave attention to the life of my own body, and examined my own senses ... some things I observed in interrogating the reports of my senses	

A Memory and *The* Memories		
Book XIII	**Book X**	**Books I–IX, XI–XII**
Senses and Sense perception		
XIII.26.39 Those who enjoy these foods are fed by them; but those "whose God is their belly" derive no pleasure from them... Paul, served God, not his belly... the source of his joy was the source of his nourishment	**X.14.21** No doubt, then, memory is, as it were, the stomach of the mind	**IX.4.10** With starving minds they can only lick the images (*imagines*) of these things
XIII.30.45 I listened, Lord, my God; I sucked a drop of sweetness from your truth, and I understood	**X.3.4** The heart is aroused in the love of your mercy and the sweetness of your grace **X.40.65** And sometimes you cause me to enter into an extraordinary depth of feeling marked by a strange sweetness	**I.15.24** Bring to me a sweetness surpassing all the seductive delights which I pursued **VIII.4.9** Come Lord, stir us up and call* us back... be our fire and our sweetness *revoca (recall) **IX.4.7** My memory calls* me back to that period and it becomes sweet for me, Lord, to confess to you by what inward goads you tamed me *revocat (re-calls)

The sequential observations in XIII are:

1. The spiritual person judges the living soul in its affections
2. Reflection on things perceived by the senses
3. Outward sight versus inward
4. Prioritization of food: "whose God is their belly" versus food from serving God
5. Listening to God and "tasting" his truth

Augustine utilizes the senses in his allegorical exegesis in XIII to stress the importance of reflecting (remembering) on those things that are perceived by the senses; reflection implies that senses are stored in memory, otherwise reflection would not be possible. According to Karfíková, *imagines* of things perceived by the senses are stored in the "courts" of memory and are arranged according to the senses they belong to as follows:

- "visual perceptions of light, colors, and form,
- auditory perceptions of various sounds,
- olfactory perceptions of odors,
- gustatory and tactile perceptions."[72]

The sense of sight was considered by Augustine as the "superior" sense since it was through the use of temporal sight that the rational soul was able to "see" the vision of God.[73] Boersma writes that "seeing God is the theological cipher through which Augustine develops his theology of the incarnation and his valuation of the sacraments."[74] The door to eschatological remembrance had its door opened through "sight"; in this way, via the sacraments, the mind had access to eternity at the same time it was embedded within the temporal flow of the present.[75] Thus Augustine reminds his readers to recognize what is observed outwardly and to see the inward reality that they themselves are good, a result of God's creation, and to distinguish between temptations of the body versus that which feeds the soul. Seeing in this manner and the appropriate use of the senses and sense perceptions facilitate remembrance and allow forward movement. Further, not only is truth seen but Augustine's "listening" to God led to "tasting" the sweetness of truth (XIII.30.45).

The *Beata Vita*

Augustine sought fervently after the *beata vita* as this to him was the final achievement of the Christian life. The *beata vita* could be achieved in Augustine's earthly life only momentarily, but was fully achievable in eternal life. Thus, the *beata vita* in eternity is not in pure opposition to that achievable in temporality but rather it is a fulfillment thereof. The following

---

72. Karfíková, "Memory," 176.
73. Karfíková, "Memory," 176.
74. Boersma, "Augustine," 16.
75. Grove, *Augustine*, 29.

section examines the recapitulation of the *beata vita* in XIII. It is divided into two parts, (i) the *beata vita* and fallenness that inhibits its achievement, and (ii) experience of the *beata vita*.

Part 1: The Beata Vita

Augustine's yearning for the *beata vita* is as strong in XIII as in the rest of *Confessiones*; yet, in XIII it appears Augustine is providing his readers with supportive, encouraging, and affirmatory statements regarding the *beata vita*. Part 1 of the *beata vita* is presented in Table 8.4a.

Table 8.4a: Part 1: The *beata vita* in XIII and I–XII

The *Beata Vita*	
Book XIII	**Books I to XII**
XIII.3.4 Both the fact of its life and the fact of its living in a blessed state is owed only to your grace . . . to you it is not one thing to live, another to live in blessed happiness, because you are your own blessedness **XIII.8.9** Whatever is less than you can never be sufficient to provide itself with the rest of contentment to itself **XIII.9.10** In your gift we find our rest . . . there are you our joy. Our rest is our peace . . . by your gift we are set on fire . . . we grow red hot and ascend . . . we climb the ascent of our heart. **XIII.10.11** Happy is that created realm which has known nothing other than bliss **XIII.36.51** We may also rest in you for the sabbath of eternal life	**I.1.1** Our heart is restless until it rests in you **II.10.18** My desire is for you . . . the person who enters into you, enters into the joy of the Lord **III.4.8** How I burned, how I burned with longing to leave earthly things and fly back to you **IV.12.18** Rest in him and you will be at rest **IV.12.19** Come down so you can ascend, and make your ascent to God **VI.11.18** When I began to burn with a zeal for wisdom **VI.11.20** I longed for the happy life **VII.17.23** And so step by step I ascended from bodies to the soul which perceives through the body . . . I ascended to the power of reasoning

The *Beata Vita*	
Book XIII	**Books I to XII**
(*cont.*)	**VIII.3.8** You are eternal to yourself, you are your own joy **X.7.11** Through my soul I will ascend to him **X.8.12** I will therefore rise about that natural capacity in a step-by-step ascent to him who made me **X.287.38** You touched me, and I am on fire to attain the peace which is yours
XIII.4.5 To see light in his light and to become perfect, radiant with light and in complete happiness **XIII.12.13** His soul thirsts for the living God, like a hart for the spring waters ... when shall I come? He wishes to put on his habitation from heaven **XIII.12.13** What a beautiful light that will be when "we shall see him as he is" **XIII.17.21** But souls which "thirst after you and appear before you" ... you water with your hidden and sweet spring	**I.13.22** I confess to you the longing of my soul **X.20.29** How then am I to seek for you, Lord? When I seek for you, my God, my quest is for the happy life. I will seek you that "my soul may live" for my body derives life from my soul and my soul derives life from you ... my inquiry is whether this knowing is in the memory because, if it is there, we had happiness once ... my question is whether the happy life is in the memory **X.21.30** But the happy life we already have in our knowledge **X.21.31** The happy life is found in the memory
XIII.8.9 My love falls short of that which is enough to make my life run to your embraces, and not to turn away until it lies hidden "in the secret place of your presence"	**VI.1.1** I was seeking you outside myself, and I failed to find "the God of my heart" **X.34.53** However, you rescue me Lord, you rescue me ... I am pitifully captured by them [beautiful externals] and in your pity you rescue me

The *Beata Vita*	
Book XIII	**Books I to XII**
XIII.9.10 In your gift we find our rest … there are you our joy. **XIII.26.39** The source of his joy was the ground of his nourishment **XIII.26.40** What gives you nourishment … joy **XIII.27.42** The mind is fed by the source of joy	**II.10.18** My desire is for you … the person who enters into you, enters into the joy of the Lord **V.4.7** You alone are his source of happiness **VIII.3.8** You alone are the source of his happiness **X.22.32** This is the authentic happy life, to set one's joy on you, grounded in you, and caused by you **X.23.33** The happy life is joy based on the truth. This joy is grounded in you, O God, who are the truth, my illumination, the salvation of my face, my God.
XIII.21.29 You are the lifegiving pleasure of a pure heart	**II.10.18** The person who enters into you "enters into the joy of the Lord" **IV.9.14** Happy is the person who loves you **VIII.5.10** The new will, which was beginning to be within me a will to serve you freely and to enjoy you, God, the only source of my pleasure **X.2.2** You are radiant and give delight **X.40.65** I can find no safe place for my soul except in you

Reading from the beginning of XIII, one can see that there is an architectonic sequence to Augustine's presentation of the *beata vita* as evidenced in Table 8.4a. This sequence is listed below:

1. The blessed state is a result of God's own blessedness
2. What is less than God cannot result in happiness
3. Resting in God in the sabbath of eternal life
4. The soul thirsts for God
5. Becoming perfected in complete happiness
6. Running to God verses running from God
7. Joy is found in God, mind fed by source of joy
8. God is the life-giving pleasure of a pure heart

Augustine's yearning for the *beata vita* is seen yet again in XIII.12.13, "his soul thirsts for the living God, like a hart for the spring waters," and "he wishes to put on his habitation from heaven."[76] This is a common theme throughout *Confessiones* from I.1.1 to XIII.38.53. In XIII, Augustine wants to encourage his reader with his experience; while his yearning continues, it does result in comforting awareness, peace, joy, even happiness, and temporal experience of the Divine. In XIII.17.21, he writes that God waters his soul with his "hidden and sweet spring." In XIII.9.10, he writes, "In your gift [Holy Spirit] we find our rest. There are you our joy. Our rest is our peace." Finally, in XIII.21.29, Augustine writes, "you are the lifegiving pleasure of a pure heart." The turmoil of yearning is quietened by the knowledge of peace and joy found in the Divine.

Marion describes the desire for the *beata vita* as a theoretical first principle because it is a desire for the *beata vita* not knowledge or possession of it.[75] Marion continues, "the *mens* remains ignorant of the *vita beata* of which it is ignorant inasmuch as it thinks it, but it knows it insofar as it desires it." As such it is a principle of desire; a desire evident throughout *Confessiones*. Augustine acknowledges that desire for the *beata vita* is present, but he does not know how.[76] Augustine attributes this desire to *memoria*; "*quaero utrum in memoria sit beata vita.*"[77] If in *memoria*, then the *beata vita* is accessible to those who desire it, but all want it, concludes Augustine. He defines the *beata vita* as "joy based on the truth. This is the joy grounded in you, O God, who are the truth."[78] Here, Augustine defines a *beata vita* that can be enjoyed when acknowledging God is the truth. However, for Augustine the authentic *beata vita* goes even beyond his daily life. He lives

---

76. Ps 42:1–2; 2 Cor 5:2.
75. Marion, *In the Self's Place*, 89.
76. *Conf.* X.20.29.
77. *Conf.* X.20.29. "My question is whether the happy life is in the memory."
78. *Conf.* X.28.33. See also *Conf.* X.22.32; X.23.33.

in the struggles and vacillations of temporal life, at times acquiescing to his temptations which impede the attainment of the *beata vita*. He knew he was dependent on God for restoration, life, and the *beata vita*. Knowledge that the *beata vita* was actually and eventually attainable, encouraged Augustine; he knew fulfillment of the *beata vita* was possible because he knew the truth of God. The *beata vita* was achieved in the eternal rest of the sabbath.[79] Augustine knew his ability to achieve the *beata vita* was solely due to God's own blessedness and grace; it could not be obtained elsewhere from earthly attentions. The soul innately knows this and desires to return to its origin. Harrison writes, "It [the soul] is also the place where human beings remember God, are conscious of him, and seek to know him."[80] This fueled Augustine's compulsion to seek the *beata vita*.

Part 2: The Place of Rest and Fallenness

The restlessness of the soul is exemplified by a struggle between misremembering (fallenness) and remembering the Divine. Fallenness leads to enjoyment of earthly matters and results in a distraction from, or misremembering of, the Divine. Remembering the Divine results in movement of Augustine's soul towards God. The pulling back and forth between these two dimensions of life torments Augustine and causes a restlessness within. The journey to rest is mediated by Christ,[81] and the *beata vita* becomes the focal point of a transitory existence that moves towards the eternally divine and away from earthly things.[82] Augustine saw that the Creator God moved through creation in six days resting on the seventh. He realized that he, Augustine, moved through his creation towards eternal rest. XIII ends the journey towards finding rest in the sabbath of eternal life, but it also returns to I.1.1 where the restless heart seeks rest, "Lord, grant us peace" (XIII.35.50), and where Augustine hopes to find rest, "We hope to find rest in your great sanctification" (XIII.38.53).

FALLENNESS

According to Clark, the autobiographical aspect of *Confessiones* has a particular focus.[83] She argues that past life, present lifestyle, and future lifestyle

---

79. *Conf.* XIII.36.51; 38.53.
80. Harrison, *Rethinking*, 59.
81. *Conf.* VII.19.25; VIII.12.29; IX.13.34–37; X.43.69–70.
82. Guardini, *Conversion*, 61.
83. Clark, *Augustine*, 46.

are important only because they explain the spiritual state of the person who is attempting to live a life centered on God and displaying God's mercy. Human beings are made for happiness with God, but their capacity to achieve the *beata vita*, whether inchoatively on earth or consummately in eternal life, is limited by worldly, temporal struggles. God's intervention and help in this struggle is necessary. Augustine found this struggle to be such an obstacle that he committed a large section of X to this issue of fallenness followed by the way to restoration. XIII warns of the dangers of falling away from following God. XIII also emphasizes that human beings are spiritual creations in their souls and thus are drawn to God. Table 8.4b addresses the pitfalls encountered because of fallenness.

Table 8.4b: Part 2: Fallenness that hinders attainment of the *beata vita*

The *Beata Vita*	
Book XIII	**Books I to XII**
XIII.2.3 We are a spiritual creation in our souls and have turned away from you, our light **XIII.8.9** Whatever is less than you can never be sufficient to provide itself with the rest of contentment itself	**I.7.11** Alas for the sins of humanity **II.2.4** But I in my misery seethed and followed the driving force of my impulses, abandoning you **II.6.14** So the soul fornicates when it is turned away from you **III.7.12** In my ignorance ... while travelling away from the truth, I thought I was going towards it **IV.12.18** You seek the happy life in the region of death **VI.1.1** I was seeking for you outside myself, and I failed to find "the God of my heart" **VII.17.23** I was caught up to you by your beauty and quickly torn away from you by my weight

The *Beata Vita*	
Book XIII	**Books I to XII**
(*cont.*)	**VIII.1.1** But in my temporal life everything was in a state of uncertainty **X.37.60** Every day, Lord, we are beset by these temptations. We are tempted without respite
XIII.4.5 More and more to live by the fount of life, to see light in his light, and to become perfect, radiant with light, and in complete happiness **XIII.5.6** It is dark [the dark abyss] because of the disordered flux of spiritual formlessness; but it became converted to him from whom it derived the humble quality of life it had, and from that illumination became a life of beauty **XIII.14.15** Yet my soul is sad because it slips back and becomes "a deep," or rather feels itself to be a deep . . . why are you sad soul . . . we were "once darkness," . . . hope in the Lord . . . we have received assurance . . . we are saved by hope and are "sons of light" **XIII.16.19** My soul is "like waterless land before you." Just as it has no power to illuminate itself, so it cannot satisfy itself. For "with you is the fountain of life," and so also it is "in your light" that "we shall see light." **XIII.17.20** They pursue the same end of temporal and earthly felicity	**III.11.19** From this deep darkness you delivered my soul **VIII.4.9** Come Lord, stir us up and call us back, kindle and seize us, be our fire and our sweetness **XI.9.11** Wisdom, wisdom it is which shines right through me, cutting a path through the cloudiness which returns to cover me as I fall away under the darkness and the load of my punishments . . . by hope we are saved

THE ARCHAEOLOGY OF MEMORY BY RECALLING CREATION

The *Beata Vita*	
Book XIII	**Books I to XII**
XIII.8.9 the human soul fell . . . my God, give me yourself, restore yourself to me	**I.15.24** Deliver me from all temptation to the end **VI.11.20** I did not postpone the fact that every day I was dying within myself. I longed for the happy life, but was afraid of the place where it had its seat, and fled from it at the same time as I was seeking it **I.18.28** To be far from you face is to be in darkness of passion **II.2.2** The recalling of my wicked ways is bitter in my memory **II.6.14** The soul fornicates when it is turned away from you and seeks outside you the pure and clear intentions which are not to be found except by returning to you **VIII.4.9** Come Lord, stir us up and call us back, kindle and seize us, be our fire and our sweetness **X.42.67** Who could be found to reconcile me to you **XI.2.3** Listen to my soul and hear it crying from the depth **XII.16.23** I beg you, my God, not to stay away from me in silence. Speak truth to my heart

The *Beata Vita*	
Book XIII	**Books I to XII**
XIII.19.24 And come, says the Lord, let us reason together **XIII.19.24** But first, "wash, be clean, remove malice from your souls and from the sight of my eyes" that dry land might appear **XIII.21.30** Restrain yourself... by avoiding this world the soul lives, by seeking it the soul dies	**I.20.31** An inward instinct told me to take care of the integrity of my sense... I developed a good memory **II.1.1** It is from love of your love that I make the act of recollection. The recalling of my wicked ways is bitter in my memory, but I do it so that you may be sweet to me **IV.12.18** You seek the happy life in the region of death; it is not there. How can there be a happy life where there is not even life?
XIII.21.30 The haughtiness of pride, the pleasure of lust, and the poison of curiosity are the passions of a dead soul... its death comes about as it departs from the font of life, so that it is absorbed by the transitory world and conformed to it **XII.21.30** Restrain yourself from it. By avoiding this world the soul lives, by seeking it the soul dies. Restrain yourself from the savage cruelty of arrogance, from the indolent pleasure of self-indulgence, and from knowledge 'falsely so called' (1 Tim. 6:20)	**I.10.16, 19.30** In competitive games I loved the pride of winning... The same curiosity increased my appetite for public shows... I was overcome by a vain desire to win **II.6.13** Pride imitates what is lofty, but you alone are God most high above all things **IV.11.16** Do not be vain, my soul. Do not deafen your heart's ear with the tumult of your vanity **VII.20.26** Worse still, I was puffed up with knowledge **X.31.45** Every day I try to resist these temptations. I invoke the help of your right hand **X.34.51** There remains the pleasure of the eyes of my flesh which I include in confessions... so we may conclude the account of the temptations of the lust of the flesh which still assail me despite my groans and my "desire to be clothed with my habitation which is from heaven"

THE ARCHAEOLOGY OF MEMORY BY RECALLING CREATION

The *Beata Vita*	
Book XIII	**Books I to XII**
(*cont.*)	**X.35.54** Besides the lust of the flesh which inheres in the delight given by all pleasures of senses (those who are enslaved to it perish by putting themselves far from you), there exists in the soul, through the medium of the bodily senses, a cupidity which ... delights ... in perceptions acquired through the flesh **X.37.61** I cannot pretend that I am not pleased by praise ... but I have to admit not only that admiration increase my pleasure, but that adverse criticism diminishes it

The architectonic structure elucidates the pitfalls of fallenness and God's deliverance from said pitfalls. The structure is as follows:

1. We are a spiritual creation in our souls
2. God is the fountain of life even when the soul slips back
3. The insufficiency of that which is not of God
4. Plea for restoration
5. Let us reason together, says the Lord
6. Remove malice and restrain yourselves so that soul lives

Augustine in XIII, encourages his readers from the outset to remember that they are spiritual creations in their soul and that God will still be their deliverance when the soul slips back into the "dark abyss." Augustine's profound and torturous struggle between the dark abyss in the temporal and his endeavors to achieve the *beata vita* are recounted both in XIII and I–XII. In XIII.21.30, Augustine summarizes in one sentence and three words the dangers that poison the soul and impede its journey towards its origin—pride, lust, and curiosity. Augustine is striving to live a virtuous life, but the road to the *beata vita* requires Augustine to exhibit restraint towards his multifarious temptations for his rational soul to live and not fall into the deep abyss. Augustine warns his readers in XIII.21.30 to "restrain yourself ... by avoiding this world the soul lives, by seeking it the soul dies." XIII is a recapitulation of the things that tempt Augustine in I–XII and a caution to not let the soul die by continuing in erroneous habits.

Augustine's pleads with God not to be silent. He pleads for restoration and is rewarded by hearing God asking him to come and reason with him. In this, there is a movement from fallenness to restoration that requires God's intervention and grace. According to Lobel, many scholars see in Augustine's thought process a new move toward thinking about the necessity of grace, a movement guided by reason.[84] Augustine is providing his readers with definitive instruction and a reminder of his teachings through his own example.

Temporality and Time

Book XI is Augustine's precis of his interrogation of time and the paradoxes he encountered in that endeavor. As per usual, Augustine is quick to make a declaration about eternity and God (XI.1.1) forming a link between I.1.1 and XIII.36.51–37.52. XIII recapitulates key aspects of Augustine's conclusions about time. These are documented in Table 8.5.

Table 8.5: Temporality and time in XIII and its correlatives in I–XII

Temporality and Time	
Book XIII	**Books I to XII**
XIII.2.2 Heaven and earth, which you made in the beginning XIII.3.4 The first acts of creation . . . In the beginning . . . among the first acts of creation you said, "let there be light" XIII.8.9 From the beginning you had said "let there be light" XIII.24.36 In the beginning God made heaven and earth	I.6.9 You are before the beginning of ages, and prior to everything that can be said to be "before" VII.9.13 In the beginning was the Word and the Word was with God and the Word was God . . . all things were made by him XI.2.3; 3.5; 9.11 From the beginning in which you made heaven and earth XII.12.15; 13.16; 17.24–25; 19.28; 20.29; 22.31; 24.33; 28.38; 29.40 In the beginning you made heaven and earth

---

84. Lobel, "St. Augustine," 146, 151.

Temporality and Time	
Book XIII	**Books I to XII**
XIII.10.11 For in us there are distinct moments of time since at one stage we were darkness and then were made light. **XIII.18.22** By an eternal design at the appropriate times you give heavenly blessings to the earth	**I.6.10** But you are the same; and all tomorrow and hereafter, and indeed all yesterday and further back, you will make a Today, you have made a Today **VII.15.21** For all periods of time both past and future neither pass away nor come except because you bring that about, and you yourself permanently abide. **XI.14.17** There was therefore no time when you had not made something, because you made time itself **XI.20.26** Perhaps it would be exact to say: there are three times, a present of things past, a present of things present, a present of things to come. In the soul there are these three aspects of time
XIII.12.13 He forgets the things behind and stretches out to those things which lie ahead **XIII.18.22** Old things have passed away and new things are created	**IX.10.23** Forgetting the past and reaching forward to what lies ahead **XI.7.9** A thing dies and comes into being inasmuch as it is not what it was and becomes what it was not
XIII.14.15 In the morning I will stand up and will contemplate you . . . in the morning I will stand and I will see the salvation of my face, my God	**VII.14.20** I woke up in you and saw you to be infinite in another sense, and this way of seeing you did not come from the flesh

Temporality and Time	
Book XIII	**Books I to XII**
XIII.15.18 For "in heaven" Lord, is your mercy and your truth reaches the clouds. The clouds pass but the heaven remains. Preachers of your word pass from life to another life, but your scripture is "stretched out" over the peoples to the end of the age... heaven and earth will pass away but your words will not pass away **XIII.29.44** Yet scripture speaks in time-conditioned language, and time does not touch my Word, existing with me in an equal eternity... your vision of them is temporally determined, my seeing is not temporal, just as you speak of these things in temporal terms but I do not speak in the successiveness of time	**VII.7.11** That in Christ your Son our Lord, and by your scriptures... you have provided a way of salvation whereby humanity can come to the future life after death **XI.6.8** But that mind would compare these words, sounding in time, with your eternal word in silence and say: "it is very different, and the difference is enormous. The sounds are far inferior to me, and have no being, because they are fleeting and transient. But the word of my God is superior to me and abides forever"
XIII.17.22 But you are the same and in you "years which never cease" **XIII.36.51** The seventh day has no evening and has no ending **XIII.37.52** But you Lord are always working and always at rest. Your seeing is not in time, your movement is not in time, and your rest is not in time	**XI.1.1** Lord, eternity is yours **X.11.13** In the eternal, nothing is transient, but the whole is present **XII.15.18** But "our God is eternal"

Temporality and Time	
Book XIII	**Books I to XII**
XIII.19.24 So that we may discern everything by a wonderful contemplation, even though for the present only by signs and time and days and years **XIII.32.47** We see the beauty of . . . the sun sufficing for the day, the moon and stars to cheer the night, and all of these provide an indication and sign of passing time **XIII.33.48** Your works . . . they have a beginning and an end in time, a rise and a fall, a start and a finish **XIII.34.49** But then you began to carry out your predestined plan in time . . . to bring order to our disordered chaos **XIII.35.50** The entire most beautiful order of very good things will complete its course and then pass away; for in them by creation there is both morning and evening **XIII.36.51** The seventh day has no evening and has no ending	**XI.15.19** Human soul . . . to you the power is granted to be aware (*sentire*, to sense) of intervals of time, and to measure them **XI.23.29** There are stars and heavenly luminaries to be "for signs and for times. And for days and for years"
XIII.21.30 The haughtiness of pride, the pleasure of lust, the poison of curiosity are the passions of a dead soul . . . the soul's death does not end all movement. Its death comes about as it departs from the font of life, so that it is absorbed by the transitory world and conformed to it.	**I.10.16; 19.30** In competitive games I loved the pride of winning . . . The same curiosity increased my appetite for public shows **IV.11.16** Do not be vain, my soul. Do not deafen your heart's ear with the tumult of your vanity **X.31.45** Every day I try to resist these temptations. I invoke the help of your right hand

Temporality and Time	
Book XIII	**Books I to XII**
XIII.21.31 But the Word, O God, is the fount of eternal life and does not pass away... and exploring temporal nature only to the extent sufficient to contemplate eternity	**I.11.17** I had heard about eternal life promised to us through the humility of God **VII.7.11** That in Christ your Son our Lord, and by your scriptures... you have provided a way of salvation whereby humanity can come to the future life after death **VII.8.12** But you, Lord "abide for eternity and you will not be angry with us forever" **VII.15.21** You alone are eternal **VII.17.23** I found the unchangeable and authentic eternity of truth to transcend my mutable mind **XI.8.10** Your Word, which is also the Beginning in that it also speaks to us **IX.10.24** The pleasure of the bodily senses, however delightful in the radiant light of this physical world, is seen by comparison with the life of eternity to be not even worth considering. Our minds are lifted up by an ardent affection towards eternal being itself **XI.7.9** And so by the Word coeternal with yourself, you say all that you say in simultaneity and eternity **XII.15.18** But "our God is eternal"
XIII.37.52 Your seeing is not in time, your movement is not in time, and your rest is not in time. Yet your acting causes us to see things in time, time itself, and the repose which is outside time	**I.6.10** In you the present day has no ending, and yet in you it has its end

The linearity of Augustine's thought as he writes about time in XIII is evident as one studies its architectonic structure. His linear thought process is as follows:

Augustine

1. reiterates creation "in the beginning"
2. emphasizes distinct moments of time
3. talks about forgetting the past and expecting the future, new things created
4. contemplates (remembers) God in the mornings
5. finds (recollects) the words of Scripture to speak "in time conditioned language" and to stretched out to the "end of the age"
6. acknowledges God and eternity
7. encourages seeing the beauty that God has created, for even creation has a beginning and end in time
8. warns of the pitfalls of the five senses
9. declares that the Word is the fount of eternal life; exploring temporal nature should be in the context of contemplating eternity
10. sees "things in time" and the "repose which is outside time"

The above illustrates through I–XIII the pitfalls and struggles Augustine encounters throughout his life and his actions in counteracting these pitfalls. Augustine starts with the journey of his life from infancy to conversion, his struggle with earthly temptations, and his journey towards God. This is presented in a logical manner with a defined pedagogical directive as it proceeds from points 1 to 10. While XIII reiterates these aspects of Augustine's life, it also serves to provide a pathway to remembering significant aspects of one's journey to eternal rest and the return of the soul to its origin. Time for Augustine points away from the temporal towards the eternity in which it participates.[85] McMahon argues that Augustine sees time to be "a moving image of eternity"; this is a Platonic descriptor of time.[86] In present time, Augustine contemplates his God first of all at the beginning of the morning in order to remember his God. The start of the day is the beginning and

---

85. Milbank, "Confession," 35.
86. McMahon writes, "Eternity, to be sure, cannot be defined, but it can be understood by analogy, and the most important understanding in ancient philosophy is articulated in Plato's *Timaeus*: 'time is a moving image of eternity' (37d–e). Here the model is cosmological." McMahon, *Understanding*, 148.

alludes to creation "in the beginning," and as the day goes on, time moves forward to completion, the end of the day, towards eternity and eternal rest. Solignac describes this as "the cycle of time."[87] He writes, "Time is opened for us out of eternity by the fiat of the Creator and it is closed in the eternity of the heavenly rest, without ceasing to be governed by the transcendence of the divine eternity." Cessario discusses how Solignac's statement emphasizes the scope of Augustine's allegory: it is in the totality of creation, both physically and spiritually, and it also encompasses the sweep and direction of all time, which proceeds from God's eternity and returns to it.[88]

Augustine in XIII has laid out the pathway for his readers and himself to understand how to live in temporal time but with eyes are focused on the movement towards eternity.

The *Confessio* of Confessiones

Many scholars have argued that *Confessiones* is a volume about Augustine's confession (*confessio*) as he goes through his life.[89] Certainly, a survey of *Confessiones* does indicate some truth to this, and at the very least, it is one of the key themes that runs through *Confessiones*, contributing to its unity. *Confessio* is certainly very important to Augustine and one of the indispensable keys to understanding *Confessiones*. It is, therefore, understandable how many authors believe *Confessiones* to be purely a book about Augustine's confessions. *Confessio* is one of the motifs that constitutes my multifaceted theory of recapitulation. However, when considered on its own, it is reductionist and does not do justice to Augustine's *Confessiones*.

The theme of *confessio* throughout *Confessiones* is best studied by starting in the beginning, Book I. The confessional statements are remarkably similar throughout *Confessiones*. Augustine's desire to confess even to the point of exhaustion is observed in I–XIII with XIII recapitulating I–XII. Table 8.6 is a list of some of the comparative confessional statements found in each book.

---

87. Solignac, *Confessions*, 23–24.

88. Cessario, *Godly*, 16.

89. Some scholars argue that *confessio* is a central doctrine in *Confessiones*, e.g., David, "Towards," 45–76; Ratzinger, "Originalitat," 375–92; Solignac, *Confessions*, 25.

Table 8.6: A brief survey through *Confessiones* from I–XIII regarding the connecting theme of *Confessio*

CONFESSION	
Book I	**I.13.22** I confess to you the longing of my soul **I.15.24** That my soul . . . may not suffer exhaustion in confessing to you your mercies
Book II	**II.3.5** Nothing is nearer to your ears than a confessing heart **II.7.15** I will love you, Lord, and I will give thanks and confession to your name
Book III	**III.11.20** I confess to you Lord **III.12.21** I am hurrying on to those things which especially urge me to make confession to you
Book IV	**IV.6.11** Now is the time not to be putting questions but to be making confession to you **IV.12.19** To him my soul is making confession, and he is healing it
Book V	**V.1.1** Accept the sacrifice of my confessions . . . let my soul . . . confess to your mercies that it may praise you **V.2.2** In the name of those who make confession to you
Book VI	**VI.6.9** I recall this and confess to you **VI.7.12** Your mercies make confession to you from the marrow of my being
Book VII	**VII.4.6** So I confess that whatever you are, you are incorruptible **VII.6.8** May your mercies, my God, make grateful confession of that to you from the innermost parts of my soul

CONFESSION	
Book VIII	**VIII.1.1** In my thanksgiving I want to recall and confess your mercies over me **VIII.2.3** For the story gives occasion for me to confess to you in great praise for your grace
Book IX	**IX.4.7** my memory calls me back to that period and it becomes sweet for me, Lord, to confess to you by what inward goads you tamed me **IX.12.32** but I confess this to your mercy, father of orphans
Book X	**X.1.1** This I desire to do, in my heart before you in confession **X.2.2** My God, my confession before you is made both in silence and not in silence **X.3.4** I also, Lord, so make my confession to you . . . my Lord, every day my conscience makes confession **X.4.6** When I am confessing not what I was but what I am now **X.5.7** Let me confess what I know of myself. Let me confess what I do not know of myself **X.37.61** What then, Lord, have I to confess to you in this kind of temptation **X.37.62** I beseech you, my God, show me myself so that to my brothers who will pray for me I may confess what wound I am discovering in myself
Book XI	**XI.2.2** For a long time past I have been burning to meditate in your law and confess to you what I know of it **XI.2.3** Let me confess to you what I find in your books **XI.18.23** I confess, my God, I do not know **XI.25.32** I confess to you, Lord **XI.26.33** my confession to you is surely truthful

CONFESSION	
Book XII	**XII.2.2** My humble tongue makes confession to your transcendent majesty **XII.6.6** For myself, Lord, if I am to confess to you with my mouth and pen **XII.23.32** Which I confess to you, my God
Book XIII	**XIII.12.13** Proceed with your confession, my faith **XIII.15.17** Which so persuasively move me to confession **XIII.24.36** I confess myself to believe, Lord

In each book of *Confessiones*, Augustine's confessional statements are evident and multiple. Some attention should, therefore, be given to this motif. Barry David has authored a good article regarding the notion of *confessio* as the unifying factor in *Confessiones*.[90] David agrees with other authors that Augustine's presentation is essentially progressive, universal, and structured by an *exitus-reditus* pattern.[91] However, he argues that *Confessiones'* unity is found in Augustine's articulation and sharing of his profound notion of *confessio* as a human being's proper disposition towards God/Wisdom/divine goodness. David writes that *confessio* is "mutable man's teleological spiritual union with an immutable God (I.1.1–5.6) given through God's mediation in Christ (I.1.1, I.5.5)." David asserts that, according to Augustine, God's presence to mind is intimate, consisting of God himself united with the mind: "In this respect, we notice that, based on his account of divine presence in *Conf.* X, Augustine is now paralleling more of God in Himself with mind in itself."[92] Further, this relationship between God and Augustine constitutes *Confessiones'* fundamental ground or baseline, i.e., this relationship encapsulates *confessio's* coherence and gauges its development.[93] David describes *confessio* as an intrinsically dynamic reality centered in enjoying

---

90. Barry David's article is excellent, portraying an in-depth exposition of his work relating to *confessio* as the primary motif of *Confessiones*. See David, "Towards," for his exposition on *confessio*.

91. David, "Towards," 46.

92. David, "Towards," 55.

93. David, "Towards," 47.

and augmenting man's right relationship with God. David argues that *Confessiones* progressively recounts the stages whereby Augustine's heart (i.e., understanding and love) comes to embrace *confessio* and what that entails, first on the personal level, but ultimately on eschatological and theological levels.[94] David writes that *Confessiones*' structure follows Augustine's original account of *confessio* and, therefore, unites *Confessiones*' conclusion with its beginning.[95] This structure develops the theme of the ascent to God which leads ultimately to the Godhead.[96] David asserts that the practice of *confessio* is encouraged by Augustine by transitioning through Christ's mediation (I.1.1). The transition divides the books of *Confessiones* as follows:[97]

1. I–IV: transition from the realm of sense, first ascending and then descending to
2. V–VII: the realm of the mind to
3. VIII–X: God via the mind's principal powers, intellect and will, joined together in union with Christ to
4. XI–XIII: meditating on Scripture, divine creating, human selfhood, and God's church, in the context of considering the Godhead that is above all and in all.

David asserts that the symmetry between Augustine's introduction and conclusion demonstrates that the nature of *Confessiones*' progress is more circular than linear. In this regard, the text has an *exitus–reditus* or "return to origin" structure wherein linear progress is built into circular progress."[98] David's exposition of the *confessio* motif as the unifying aspect of *Confessiones* is detailed and is influential in the examination of the architectonic structure of *Confessiones*. This *exitus–reditus* structure as a unifying aspect of *Confessiones* is true of other authors who uphold this motif.[99]

Of note, Marion asserts that for Augustine *confessio* is twofold: confession of sins and confession of praise.[100] Marion attests to *confessio* constituting the first thought and, thus, the starting point in *Confessiones*; this is the *confessio* of praise, which launches the *Confessiones*.[101] However, Augustine

---

94. David, "Towards," 52.
95. David, "Towards," 62–63.
96. David, "Towards," 60.
97. David, "Towards," 60.
98. David, "Towards," 62.
99. Discussed later in this chapter.
100. Marion, *In the Self's Place*, 13.
101. *Conf.* I.1.1; Marion, *In the Self's Place*, 13.

when he praises God also includes *confessio* of his wretchedness, as written in Books II to IX. The architectonic structure of Augustine's *confessio* of his failings is observed throughout *Confessiones* (Table 8.6). Marion posits that *confessio* "unites the admission of sin (which I am) and the praise of glory (that God is) so well that it defines the permanent state of the Christian, confessing man, who thinks first by confessing."[102] In X.2.2 Augustine writes that he no longer does this (*confessio*) by mere physical words but by words from his soul and a cry from his mind. According to Marion, *confessio* is about turning towards God indirectly at first by directing upon oneself the very gaze of God, and then directly by directing upon God himself my finally free gaze.[103] Finally, in XIII.14.15, *confessio* is a unique work of the soul, as Augustine declares, "I pour out my soul upon myself in the voice of exultation and confession." *Confessio* thus encapsulates several images in the recollection of one's sin and in the praise of God. *Confessio* is one of the motifs that provides evidence for my theory of recapitulation.

Motifs Found in *Confessiones* That Contribute to Its Architectonic Structure, Unity, and the Theory of Recapitulation

"confessionum mearum libri tredecim"[104]

There are a few theories regarding the unity of *Confessiones* that stand out and that have been studied more extensively, offering insight into the architectonic structure and theory of recapitulation. Interestingly, Kotzé in 2020 wrote that the unity of *Confessiones* no longer preoccupies scholarship; she believes that the postmodern reader is more comfortable with the notion of complexity and with the absence of one solution generally accepted by all.[105] However, it would seem that academic scholarship is not entirely inattentive to this topic given that she herself wrote these comments in her 2020 chapter entitled "Structure and Genre of the Confessions"![106] The unity of *Confessiones* continues to be debated in the twenty-first century and continues to build upon the work of prior centuries resulting in new

---

102. Marion, *In the Self's Place*, 29–30.

103. Marion's description recalls to mind Augustinian interiority particularly *meditatio/ingressio* and *contemplatio*. Marion, *In the Self's Place*, 31.

104. *Retr.* 2.6.1.

105. Kotzé, "Structure," 30.

106. Kotzé, "Structure," 30.

insights.[107] These theories have evolved from consideration of individual themes, such as *confessio*, praise, *exidus-reditus*, the Trinity, language, narrative, autobiography, assortment of triads, Neoplatonic influenced structure, literary, and even the Prodigal Son. David is correct when he writes that *all* the varied interpretations provide insight into the unity of *Confessiones*.[108] However, some authors assert that *Confessiones* is not written as a planned structured piece of work designed to unite all its books.[109] O'Meara, for example, claims that *Confessiones* is "a badly composed book" and suggests that scholars who think otherwise "deny the evidence of their senses and forget that Augustine had no expectation of producing what has come to be regarded as a masterpiece."[110] Others, like Courcelle, have largely ignored XI–XIII.[111]

McMahon offers an extensive study on a theory of unity that examines XIII as paradigmatic for I–XII based on a meditative structure and an *exidus–reditus* interpretation.[112] McMahon describes XIII as Augustine's ponderings on Gen 1 and the incorporation of all his thoughts and comments on creation from I–XII but, as McMahon reiterates, from the perspective of a prayerful and meditative structure. This recapitulation in XIII has a cyclical nature because it is the beginning moving towards the end and vice versa. McMahon quotes, "This movement forward in time proves simultaneously a movement backward, towards origins [*exidus-reditus*]."[113] It should be noted that McMahon also unifies the *exidus-reditus* theme and Augustine's autobiography and perplexities in *Confessiones* by distinguishing between Augustine the speaker and Augustine the author; this would account for the differences in style.[114] However, distinguishing between Augustine the speaker and Augustine the author creates a dualist Augustine rather than a holistic, non-reductionist Augustine, thereby constricting the authentic

---

107. See the following for a more detailed overview of unity theories of *Confessiones*: McMahon, *Understanding*; Kotzé, "Structure"; O'Connell, *Images*, 5–12; Crossen, "Structure," 84–97; O'Donnell, "Introduction," xli–li; David, "Towards"; Rogers, "Beyond," 1–22.

108. David, "Towards," 46.

109. Verheijen, "*Confessions*."

110. O'Meara, *Young*, 13.

111. Courcelle, *Resherches*, 18.

112. McMahon, *Understanding*, 65.

113. McMahon, *Understanding*, 144.

114. McMahon, *Augustine's Prayerful Ascent*, 41. Augustine the author's approach is to show God's providential plan for Augustine while the speaker is unaware that there is a God-inspired understanding of Genesis and creation. I, like Ortiz, am not convinced of this argument. Ortiz, "Creation," 328–29.

Augustine. McMahon's work is considered to be a classic in the studies of the unity of *Confessiones*.[115] However, while comprehensive and containing important insights, his work is still focused on one central theme. Other authors who promote an *exitus–reditus* structure include Ortiz, Chadwick, and Harrison.[116] Ortiz believes the overall motif of *Confessiones* is a return to God whereby the structure of *Confessiones* "embodies the dynamic motion of all creation and the dynamic orientation back to the Creator given to human beings in creation and brought to completion in re-creation."[117] He believes that Augustine in writing *Confessiones* recapitulates and participates in God's redeeming action in creation. Ortiz writes, "In the *Confessions*, God works through Augustine to take up all of creation liturgically and offer it back to God in a kind of Eucharistic offering of praise in thanksgiving."[118] Ortiz argues that this is the deep meaning of the deliberate structure, unity, and purpose of Augustine's *Confessiones*. Ortiz suggests that there is a unity of *Confessiones* based on a Trinitarian motif that is more evident in XI–XII but also alluded to in I–X.[119] Ortiz states that "all of creation is created in a Trinitarian act of *creatio, conversio, formatio* in which all creatures bear a dynamic orientation toward God in their very being." The *Confessiones*, he argues also bears this Trinitarian stamp and dynamic orientation toward God. *Confessiones* is an "example of a larger pattern of redemption, and an act of the whole Trinity re-creating what it has created" and is marked by Trinitarian vestiges.[120] Starnes supports a Trinitarian approach as a unifying motif and assigns a person of the Trinity to each section of *Confessiones*.[121] He argues that I–IX pertains to the Father as Creator, X to the Son, who unites the Divine and the human, and XI–XIII to the Holy Spirit, who has inspired the Scriptures that Augustine is exegeting. O'Donnell and Crosson also believe there are Trinitarian patterns throughout *Confessiones*.[122] They do not, however, support the Trinity as a predominant motif in the structure of the *Confessiones*. O'Donnell believes the last three books have a

---

115. See McMahon, *Augustine's Prayerful Ascent*; McMahon, *Understanding*; McMahon, *Structure*.

116. Ortiz, "Creation," 328–29; Chadwick, *Augustine*, xxiv; Harrison, *Rethinking*, 59.

117. Ortiz, "Creation," 328–29.

118. Ortiz, "Creation," 329.

119. Ortiz, "Creation," 330–31.

120. Ortiz, "Creation," 327, 330–31.

121. Starnes, "Prolegomena," 95–103.

122. O'Donnell, *Augustine*, I:xl; *Augustine*, III:251–52, 300–301, 343–44; Crossen, "Structure," 31.

Trinitarian structure because they deal with creation and eternity, Scripture (God of the Word), and the church (God who acts through the church), the province of the Father, Son (Word), and Holy Spirit, respectively, although he does not see the Trinity as a predominate motif throughout *Confessiones*.[123] Crosson sees Trinitarian vestiges in Augustine's descent into sin in II, III, and IV, the sinful triad of lust, curiosity, and pride; then in VI–VIII sins are healed.[124]

Some scholars like Landsberg and Le Blond propose time as the principle unifying factor in *Confessiones*. Both link the principle of unity to time as past, present, and future. I–IX concerns the past and relies on memory, X the present, which requires management of the author's conduct, and XI–XIII the future, which requires *expectatio*.[125] Le Blond finds, within this context, memory as a unifying theme, claiming that the *Confessiones* are a work of Augustinian memory, which includes the evocation of the past, implies the memory of oneself in the present, and the tension towards the future.[126] Thus, I–IX concerns memory in Augustine's past, X memory in the present, and XI–XIII memory stretching out into the future. McMahon also sees a connection with time as a unifying factor, but in the context of *Confessiones* presenting itself as an ongoing prayer, again, the meditative and prayer motif.[127] His proposition is that the temporal progress of Augustine's life is recounted in I–IX, X is his present state of conscience, and XI–XIII pertains to Augustine performing his present and future duties in expounding Scripture. Since *Confessiones* is a prayer being made in an ongoing present, it is composed as originally occurring in that temporal order and acts as a return to the origin.

Interestingly, Heidegger believed Augustine's meditation on time in XI unified *Confessiones* I–XIII. According to Heidegger, XI is not merely or primarily a treatise on time, or separate from the other books of *Confessiones*, it is what provides the inner jointure (*Fügung*) of the *Confessiones* as a whole.[128] The meditation of time results in a *confessio*, at which point *Confessiones* reaches its most authentic depth,[129] whereby Heidegger even

---

123. O'Donnell, *Augustine*, III:251, 300, 343.
124. Crosson, "Structure," 31.
125. Le Blond, *Conversions*, 17; Landsberg, "Conversion," 31–56.
126. Le Blond, *Conversions*, 6.
127. McMahon, *Augustine*, 143–244.
128. Coyne, *Heidegger's*, 161.
129. Coyne, *Heidegger's*, 161, 266n11. Marion thinks similarly to Heidegger in this regard: "precisely because at first glance it does indeed concern time, its definition and its aporiae, it behooves us to keep this essay within the *confessio*, alone capable of

THE ARCHAEOLOGY OF MEMORY BY RECALLING CREATION

contends that meditation on time is the very ground of confession for Augustine.[130] Accordingly, in XI, *Confessions* reaches its true aim, its own metaphysical ground.[131] Heidegger also contends that in XI Augustine's meditation of time actually conveys Augustine back to the eternal Word as the source of created being, allowing him to attune his spiritual ear to the silence of the eternal Word.[132] This, according to Heidegger, is time; thus, *confessio* relates temporality to eternity.

Some other unifying themes presented by other authors warrant a mention. Nunziato and Armstrong see form and formless matter as a unifying and recurring theme.[133] Harrison and Hochschild argue that creation of form out of formless matter presents a unifying factor, since it is out of darkness into light that the soul traverses.[134] This also dovetails into the theme of time. Crouse posits a unity based on a recurring pattern of *exteriora-interior-superiora* throughout *Confessiones*.[135] I–IX is the *exteriora* of Augustine's biography, X the *interior* of the soul, and XII–XIII the *superiora* of eternal truth evidenced by the meditation upon the eternal Word as the principium of creation. Fischer believes that *Confessiones* is not a book about Augustine but a book about God the Creator within which runs the motif of praise as a unifying factor.[136] He claims that Augustine probes the meaning of his own existence by calling upon and praising the Creator God whose creative act had brought him into being. Durling proposes an interesting theory.[137] He views the "gathering of the scattered" as of central importance and believes Book VII to be the central book. He works outwards towards XIII and also towards Book I to establish his recapitulation premise. While Durling's view has its merits, it is still centered on one motif. Burke argues that I–IX and X–XIII involve the distinction between "rectilinear" and "circular" terminologies based on the first three chapters of Genesis.[138] In this transition, there is a turn from a "narrative of memory" to the "principles of Memory"; it is a logological equivalent of a turn from

---

securing for it a place, in the sense that Saint Augustine understands it." Marion, *In the Self's Place*, 191.

130. Coyne, *Heidegger's*, 161.
131. Coyne, *Heidegger's*, 161.
132. Coyne, *Heidegger's*, 162.
133. Nunziato, "Created," 364; Armstrong, "St. Augustine," 6.
134. Harrison, *Rethinking*, 104–5; Hochschild, *Memory*, 173–74.
135. Crouse, "Recurrens in te unum," 391.
136. Fischer, "What's?," 74–80.
137. Durling, "Platonism and Poetic Form."
138. Burke, *Rhetoric*, 124.

"time" to "eternity." Further, his definition of "Memory" is the storehouse of images, unlike mine.[139] Burke recognizes a circular pattern in X–XIII. Burke makes some valuable contributions in his discussion of memories versus Memory, yet his approach still lacks cohesiveness.

Other scholars rest on the literary structure of *Confessiones* as the unifying factor. Spengemann presents *Confessiones* as a narrative where Augustine is described as the "converted narrator" and the "wandering protagonist."[140] Harrison alludes to *Confessiones* being a literary work of art as do Courcelle and Ferrari.[141] However, both Courcelle and Ferrari believe that the account of Augustine's conversion is fictional.[142] They argue that this is the case because the central text of Augustine's confession account in *Conf.* VIII.12.29–30 is not found in his earlier writings. Therefore, if the account is fictional, *Confessiones* is a literary work that incorporates fiction to promote his views on conversion. These are but a few examples of authors who subscribe to a literary view of *Confessiones*. Care must be taken when reading *Confessiones* to not reduce it to purely a literary work. Augustine was not a literary figure; he used literary trope as a form of rhetoric as a vehicle for argument to persuade his readers. The danger of seeing Augustine as a literary figure is that we lose touch of who he was; we seek to control him (his narrative and works) rather than allowing Augustine to inform us.

All these motifs provide corroborative and important contributions to explicate XIII as a recapitulation of I–XII. However, such a recapitulation cannot be based on one motif alone, nor can the unity of *Confessiones* be substantiated by one motif alone. Individual motifs standing alone are simply reductionist and miss the overall impact of *Confessiones*. A multifaceted approach in which the multiple key motifs are considered together corroborates the unity of *Confessiones* and presents a theory of recapitulation that is far more holistic.

The Significance of the Architectonic Structure in the Theory of Recapitulation and Unity of *Confessiones*

Examination of the architectonic structure of XIII allowed for the principle motifs of Augustine's *Confessiones* to be viewed in a holistic, multi-faceted,

---

139. Burke, *Rhetoric*, 125.

140. Spengemann, *Forms*, 7, 1–33.

141. Harrison, *Rethinking*, 5; Courcelle, *Resherches*, 188–202; Ferrari, "Saint," 151–70.

142. Courcelle, *Resherches*, 188–202; Ferrari, "Saint," 151–70; Harrison, *Rethinking*, 5–6.

and unified manner. It allows for the identification of a recapitulative format recognized through Augustine's unfolding of his creation theology as he recapitulates the motifs within I–XII. The theological construct in XIII as a recapitulation of I–XII becomes evident through Augustine's journey towards God and an assertion of his yearning and coming to a place of greater understanding of memory and the *beata vita*.

My discovery of an architectonic structure that supports such a recapitulation in XIII of I–XII has provided several insights into Augustine and his writings. These insights fall into the following categories: Augustine's cerebration, Augustine's creation theology, Augustine's pedagogy, Augustine's unity of *Confessiones*, and Augustine's recapitulation.

Augustine's Cerebration

The architectonic structure of XIII and memory in X reveals much regarding the inner working of Augustine's mind. The seemingly, at times, jumbled and circuitous writing in his works betray the logic that is actually nestled in his mind; this is manifest in the architectonic structures found within *Confessiones*. Within this structure, Augustine becomes exposed as he navigates through the narrative of *Confessiones*. He is passionate with a dogged determination to solve intricate enigmas, and his "mind is on fire."[143] He pleads with God to resolve his perplexities.[144] Augustine seems to have a multiple thought-stream[145] ability; perhaps a good example of this process is revealed at Cassiciacum where he wrote his four books. Augustine had a habit of asking questions of himself as he sought to understand himself and God. In *Soliloquia* he debates with his own reason. In *Confessiones* he does this after the death of his friend in Thagaste. In the entire works of *Confessiones* he asks over seven hundred questions![146] These interior dialogues remained a lifelong feature of his writings.[147] Augustine's mind never stopped thinking. In XIII, the complexity of the inner workings of Augustine's mind and his constant desire for answers is evident.

---

143. *Conf.* XI.22.28.

144. *Conf.* I.1.1; XI.22.28.

145. Multiple thought streams are defined as a state of mind in which a person has more than one internal narrative or stream of consciousness simultaneously occurring within their head. *PsychonautWiki*, s.v. "Multiple Thought Streams," https://psychonautwiki.org/wiki/Multiple_thought_streams.

146. Ortiz, "Why," 3.

147. Fox, *Augustine*, 332.

Augustine was critical of his own thinking. This criticism, according to Chadwick, "marks an epoch in the history of human moral consciousness."[148] Further, as Augustine discovered more of his own mind, he realized that "thinking awareness" (i.e., memory) in his mind was actually related to the mind of God, and this was where he found the activity of his mind to be manifest.[149] Augustine's intellectual ability and cerebration was well beyond his time; as mentioned earlier, it took almost sixteen hundred years for a taxonomy of memory to be developed, only for it to be discovered that it was virtually identical to Augustine's taxonomic structure of memory.[150]

Augustine's mind had a vast capacity and ingenuity. Brown writes that through his education Augustine had developed "a phenomenal memory, a tenacious attention to detail, an art of opening the heart."[151] Augustine did not limit himself to one particular field of study. He studied and interrogated multiple motifs through the lens of philosophy, theology, medicine, science, and pedagogy, easily blending every discipline with every other and making no explanation or apology for doing so. The metaphysical dimension of Augustine's cerebration in which he understood God as Being and the principle cause of all other beings, was founded against the background and his understanding of Scripture[152] and creation. He was able to interrogate the metaphysical with the physical utilizing all the different disciplines. He understood, as he examined creation and his journey towards God, that all disciplines were inter-connected, and his mind was able to connect the dots. Augustine was in constant "dialogue with the wider world of the non-Christian thought of his time, accepting its excellences, quarrelling selectively with its errors, sharing a common ground of debate and discussion."[153] At the same time, the profundity of his mind encouraged him to go to enormous lengths to examine and try to understand all that he learnt of and about God, and the depth of his experience of God as his temporal journey moved towards achieving the *beata vita*. Augustine allows his mind to constantly examine new revelations, consequently, his ideas and thoughts evolved and matured over time. This is important in understanding Augustine's cerebrations.

Augustine was an eloquent speaker who used both literary and philosophical allusions and was an exquisite writer who used his mastery

---

148. Chadwick, *Augustine*, 93.
149. Hankey, "Mind," 564.
150. Cassel et al., "From," 21–41.
151. Brown, *Augustine*, 26.
152. Anderson, *St. Augustine*, 10.
153. O'Donnell, *Augustine*, I:xxii.

of language to teach truth. Such mastery meant Augustine could adapt his language according to his audience.[154] Kirwan writes about the "Augustinian picture of language" that philosophers speak about.[155] This "Augustinian picture of language" does not convey the whole context of Augustinian thinking, nevertheless, it does provide an insight to his use of language to enlighten and educate his readers.

It can be said without doubt that Augustine was a man of high intellect, in fact, quite simply, a genius.

Augustine's Creation Theology

XIII confirms how important creation theology was to Augustine.[156] The architectonic structure of XIII aligns creation with the events of Augustine's life, his thought process and awareness, his resolution and non-resolution of the various paradoxes that are the bane of his perplexities, his interrogation of *memoria*, time, the incarnation, and eternity. Williams asserts that in Augustine's theology of creation *ex nihilo* the created world is a self-communication of God; however, the world does not simply offer a bland reproduction of recognizable and timeless truths.[157] He goes on to say, "to be serious about creation's meaning and value is to weigh properly its integrity as a moving and changing image, as a limited and fluid whole that is not God, but is saturated with God." To Augustine, creation *ex nihilo* allowed for and established a relationship between the created and the Creator but not simply a relationship that coexisted within a metaphysical continuum.[158] This relationship also pertained to life lived on earth where God's ongoing creative activity was manifest through his creation and the power he endowed on his creatures.[159] This relationship was one where the creature gained everything and even power, from a benevolent, transcendent God

---

154. See *Conf.* V.6.10. People "refuse to accept the truth if it is presented in polished and rich language." He says in the same chapter regarding the acceptance of truth, "whether the words are ornate or not does not decide the issue." Chadwick, *Augustine*, 95.

155. "Augustinian picture" is a term that Wittgenstein used to describe Augustinian language. Kirwan, "Philosophy," 186.

156. Augustine's desire to understand creation as he exegetes Gen 1 is observed in the books he wrote regarding Genesis: *Gn. Con. Man.*; *Gn. Litt. Imper. Lib.*; *Gn. Litt. Lib. Duo.*; *Conf.* XI–XIII; *Civ. Dei.* 11–12.

157. Williams, *On Augustine*, 75.

158. Chambers, *Reconsidering*, 78.

159. McFarland, "God," 270.

who saw that his creation was very good (Gen 1:31). Moreover, in this relationship with creation, according to Williams, Augustine saw the grace of God.[160] Augustine's beginnings in creation draw him to the incarnate Christ, eternal reality, and joy in God.

Knuuttila asserts that there was nothing radically new about Augustine's conception of creation as it built upon late second- and early third-century theologians.[161] Perhaps, however, what is new is that Augustine, as he explicated in XIII, saw creation as integral to *his own* creation, *his* story, and *his* journey towards remembering, knowing, and understanding God, the *beata vita*, and eternity. He knew with certainty that God called him to participate in his own creation, and thus, truly be created.[162] Augustine's life was a continuation of his own creation and life orientated towards God was inseparable from creation *ex nihilo*. Augustine's understanding of the creation narrative in Gen 1 and in his own life reveals the architectonic structure of creation *ex nihilo* as it pertained to Augustine's theology and his own creation. Vannier describes life as a continuation of a human being's creation in three stages: *creatio*, the original creation from nothing; *conversio*, the turning of the created human being toward God in the Word and living a life of continuing configuration to the Word made flesh; and *formatio*, the end result provided by the eschatological repose in God through perfect configuration to Christ.[163] These three stages of a human being's creation also comprise the whole process of creation.

Created from nothing, creatures (Augustine included) are restless within themselves.[164] Augustine desires to know joy in God whose eternal life is joy and mutuality.[165] As such he only finds his *beata vita* in the Creator, not in himself. The indelible connection between creation and the Creator God was for Augustine, via the rational soul, the *memoria Dei*, and his creation in the image and likeness of God. Even more significant, Christ at the incarnation was a recapitulation of creation in temporal time where eternity intersected temporality, thereby further establishing the continuity of creation and the relationship between the Creator God and Augustine. The pivotal relationship between creation, the Creator God, Christ the Mediator, and Augustine, unfolds as the architectonic structure of XIII, and its recapitulation of I–XII is recognized and comprehended.

---

160. Williams, *On Augustine*, 75.
161. Knuuttila, "Time," 103.
162. Anderson and Bockmuehl, *Creation*, 169n11.
163. Vannier, *"Creatio,"* 106–9.
164. *Conf.* I.1.1.
165. Williams, *On Augustine*, 76.

Vaught writes the relationship between God and Augustine, both its unity and its separation, "expresses itself in creation *ex nihilo*, in the fateful transition from finitude to fallenness, and in the quest for fulfilment that attempts to re-establish peace with God."[166] He argues that all this requires a figurative discourse in order to be adequately expressed. A performative use of language is necessary to reflect the "dynamism of God, the discord of our fragmented spirits, and the vibrant interaction that can develop between the soul and the ground of its existence."[167] He goes on to say that performative discourse is the language of creation, the language of a restless heart, and the language that permits God and the soul to confront one another in the space that opens up between them. XIII exemplifies this performative discourse as it unravels creation's foundation and purpose in recapitulating I–XII. XIII reveals how Augustine saw that creation could not be fully explained or understood. God is mysterious, unknowable, and required Augustine to accept that paradoxes still existed in temporality.

The exegesis of Gen 1 in XIII is systematic and follows a temporal sequence. Its architectonic structure follows the six days of creation and the seventh day of rest. Moreover, the architectonic structure of creation reinforces that the "inanimate creation shares through its order and proportion."[168] Augustine, in his ingenuity, uses this exegesis of creation to demonstrate how foundational creation is to his thinking and theology and to recapitulate the most significant and important motifs in I–XII. Incredibly, XIII recounts in sequential order the motifs as they arise in I–XII in a structured pattern; it is difficult to imagine that Augustine had not thought this out. A possible alternative perspective is that Augustine could have intuitively established this structure as the truth unfolded in his writings through divine illumination. Perhaps, it was a combination of both; nevertheless, the architectonic structure is revealing in its parallels and sequences. Augustine uses his understanding, exegesis, and revelation of creation, to find an authentic voice in which to share his life and his knowledge with his reader.

Augustine's Pedagogy

Augustine's method and practice of teaching included various styles, as is evident in *Confessiones*. He used narrative, linguistic style, philosophic discourse, theological insights, scriptural exegesis, medical and scientific

---

166. Vaught, *Access*, 2.
167. Vaught, *Access*, 2.
168. Williams, *On Augustine*, 77.

knowledge, and historical events. This did not result in a confused and disordered piece of work but a beautiful and exquisite interpretation of his life, his thought, his interrogations and remembrance of God and eternity. Augustine's pedagogy drew his reader into his story and his intimacy with God and provided for them a pathway and invitation to journey towards the Divine. It promised the reader an eschatological hope and expectation upon conversion based on Augustine's own life story and the promise of Christ the Mediator. Growing into knowledge of the incarnate Christ meant the reconstruction of desire into hope for God and expectation.[169] Augustine's pedagogy provided a logical progression through Augustine's interrogations of memory, time, creation, and eternity. XIII's architectonic structure elaborates on this pedagogy and illustrates the logic in Augustine's methodology.

Augustine's Unity of *Confessiones*

Augustine's own words "the thirteen books of my Confessions"[170] imply a unified format. As observed in the previous chapter, the architectonic structure of XIII demonstrates the recapitulation of I–XII which fortifies the unity of *Confessiones*. The many motifs described all propose one common objective, the unification of *Confessiones*. If only considered individually, each motif does *Confessiones* a disservice, not because they are untrue but rather because they are reductionist. The architectonic structure of XIII, in recapitulating I–XII, demonstrates how the unity of *Confessiones* is substantiated by adopting a multi-faceted approach that incorporates holistically the main multiple motifs. The architectonic structure of XIII lays out in greater detail this unity through its exegesis of creation and recapitulative interdependence with I–XII. The profound connection between the temporal sequence of creation and the significance of each day in remembering Augustine's own creation and temporal passage through time is incontrovertible.

Augustine's Recapitulation

Confessiones reveals a recapitulative progression where Augustine moves from his creation to his redemption in Christ, and towards the *beata vita*. Augustine's exegesis of Gen 1 in XIII reflects this movement but reiterates that the consummation is also the prolegomenon, and vice versa, brought

---

169. Williams, *On Augustine*, 143.
170. *Retr.* 32.1.

to light by XIII's recapitulation of I–XII. There is a constant temporal movement in time, and a remembrance of the soul's origin, Augustine's journey, and eternity. As Augustine remembers *the* memories of his life, he recognizes his is a journey of understanding God's creative act (*a* memory). Memory is what motivates Augustine, for within his soul he re-members God. Without memory Augustine recognizes that nothing would exist; without memory there is no creation and therefore, by default, no eternity. XIII therefore, is not solely a recapitulation of Augustine's life, but also a recapitulation of creation and the allegory of Gen 1. As Augustine's reflects on the memories of his creation, he recognizes that moment of his conversion and the incarnation of Christ. He believes Christ to be the Mediator who recapitulates the beginning of creation thereby causing Augustine to remember the goodness of God the Creator in creation and in his life. Christ is also the fulfillment of the promise, the eschatological hope of eternal rest in eternity. Augustine's eschatological hope propels him forward in time towards consummation in eternity, which in turn leads back to the prolegomenon at creation. Augustine's temporal life is a constant recapitulation.

Concluding Remarks

The discovery of an architectonic structure within XIII, as presented in this chapter, is a novel theory not found in previous research, to the best of my knowledge.[171] Further, the theory of recapitulation, that XIII is a recapitulation of I–XII, has not been previously described as presented in the context of a holistic approach with a multiplicity of prominent motifs. This approach supports the unity of *Confessiones* and prevents a reductionist reading of *Confessiones*.

---

171. I have extensively researched this and cannot find any references to the theory that I am presenting of XIII recapitulating I–XII as described in this chapter. This also pertains to the theory regarding the architectonic structure contributing to the theory of recapitulation and the unity of *Confessiones*. This is not to say that there might be an obscure article or references to such.

9

Re-Thinking Augustine's Theology of *Memoria*

THE RESEARCH IN THIS book has brought to light some novel insights regarding Augustine's theology of *memoria* and has evoked a new way of thinking[1] about the same theories and ideas that Augustine developed as he interrogated *memoria*. Augustine never resolved all his questions regarding *memoria*. He came to the realization that there were aspects of it that would remain mysterious. Yet, amidst all the questions and paradoxes, Augustine managed to develop a theology of *memoria* that was complex, advanced for his times, and remarkably similar to theories of memory developed in the last 160 years.[2] Augustine cerebrations were simply quite brilliant.

Architectonic Structure of Memory: Four Novel Insights

Four main novel insights regarding Augustinian memory have been presented in this book, all of which allow for a re-thinking of Augustine's theology of *memoria*. First, the identification of a specific architectonic structure and sequence (*ordo*) to memory. This revealed eight symphonic forms and

---

1. Sir William Bragg would say it is really just a new way of thinking about, and presenting, the same facts that always existed. Gray, "Braving," 17.

2. Ribot was first to present a theory of memory in 1881, later published in his book, *Diseases of Memory*.

fundamental affordances of memory found in *Conf.* X which emerged from his earlier works prior to 396 AD. Both physical and metaphysical aspects of memory come together to provide further insight into Augustine's method of interrogating memory, its inner workings, and deciphering the role memory played in his journey to know God. Second, the arc-hitectonics of Arc, the memory gene that is presented as a master regulator involved in a genomic memory process that allows further understanding of Augustinian memory. Arc-hitectonics so intricately intertwines with and undergirds Augustine's own examination of memory. The arc-hitectonics of Arc both stimulates and expands one's thinking regarding the physical, and even metaphysical, dimensions of Augustinian memory. Third, the architectonics of time, where time is presented as cardinal time, temporal time, and physical time. These times exist in simultaneity, fluidically, physically, and metaphysically in continuity with memory. Fourth, the theory of recapitulation where the architectonic analysis of Augustinian memory reveals that the symphonic forms and fundamental affordances of Augustinian memory identified in *Conf.* X are also observed in *Conf.* XIII viewed through the lens of creation. The correlation of each day of creation in Gen 1 with specific symphonic forms of memory confirms that XIII is a recapitulation not merely of X but also of I–XII. This theory of recapitulation results from a novel strategy through the utilization of an architectonic methodology that provides a holistic, multi-faceted approach to understanding Augustinian memory and the unity of *Confessiones*.

Symphonic Forms and Fundamental Affordances of Memory

As I read *Confessiones*, especially X, a pattern emerged regarding the manner in which Augustine interrogated, described, and wrote about memory. It is my contention that there is an architectonic structure to memory that unfolds as Augustine's work progresses in his writings. It would seem reasonable that Augustine premeditated his writings regarding his interrogations of *memoria*. The presence of a definitive structure brings to light the eight symphonic forms of memory present in the same sequence in X, XIII, and Augustine's early works from 386–395 AD. As I studied this aspect of Augustinian memory, I began to wonder whether Augustine had deliberately and logically thought out this sequence of the different symphonic forms of memory or whether they naturally unfolded over time as he interrogated memory. The structure and sequence of the different aspects of memory unveil the following architectonic structure to memory in this particular sequence: location of *memoria*, power of memory, sense perception, teaching/

learning, recollection and forgetfulness, images, *phantasiae* and *phantasmata*, transiency of memory, and the *beata vita*. This is not to say that there are no overlaps; there are, but the main motifs of memory follow a specific pattern. This pattern has matured in *Conf.* X compared to his earlier writings. From this sequence, it can be deduced that Augustine was meticulous in his cerebration and process of questioning. He followed a logical pattern that might not immediately be evident due to his often-convoluted manner of writing, but it is there, present, behind the scenes. It seems dubious that his interrogation of memory was an unplanned pedagogical, epistemological, hermeneutical, ontological, or other "-ogical" investigation. Whether consciously aware of this structure or not, the reader is lured into the inner workings of memory to see the creative actions of God, while envisioning Augustine's journey towards the Divine by trying to understand the role of memory in that journey. The architectonic structure brings out the brokenness in Augustine's life and makes him whole as he journeys through creation, in time, to eternity, and back to creation in a cyclical pattern. This is also the structure and repetition of memory viewed through the lens of creation described in XIII and which recapitulates I–XII.

The architectonic structure of memory blends the physical with the metaphysical as observed in the physical manifestation of memory and the metaphysical and sacramental nature of memory. The symphonic forms of memory act metaphorically as the ladder to ascent. As Augustine works through his interrogation of *memoria* he discovers, as it were, each rung on the ladder that needed to be climbed in order to achieve fulfillment of the *beata vita*. It is the same ladder he wishes his readers to climb. The architectonic "ladder" ascribes a spiritual nature to the structure of *memoria* whereby *memoria* is identified as the gateway to the Divine. The symphonic forms reveal a dynamic and fluidic sequence from the discovery of the location of memory through to the fulfillment of the *beata vita*.

Why is it important to recognize and understand the architectonic structure of memory? When Augustine interrogated memory, he may have recognized a sequence to his own questioning and understanding of memory. Consequently, it is natural that the same pattern follows in his discussion of memory. This may be a presumption; however, I think there is some merit to this observation. This sequence is important since it unfolds how Augustine's thought process built a case for his theology of *memoria*. The logic behind the sequence of the symphonic forms in some manner reflects his training in rhetoric and his experience in rhetorical practice. It should be remembered that rhetorical practice was a method of training the mind to remember a series of memories such that an orator could move backwards and forwards through the series in either direction.³ Rhetorical practice was also the art of persuasion that Augustine used to motivate his audience to remember God through memory. For example, a rhetorical practice that Augustine taught was the art of confession, which he used to remember God, paradoxically, without locating (or confining, placing) God in memory while certain that God did dwell in his memory (X.25.36–26.37). The rhetorical practice of confession is a way of remembering that which cannot be placed in memory.⁴ While this is certainly true, Augustine went beyond rhetorical practice or training of memory (*ars memoria*) in his theology of *memoria*. He was the first to appreciate memory in its own terms rather than just treating memory as an available means of persuasion used by orators in the training and application of memory.⁵

How do the individual symphonic forms of memory relate individually and together? The metaphysical theory of mereology⁶ underpins the concept of parts and the whole and the relationship between the parts and the whole and the whole to the parts. Varzi writes that as a formal theory (in Husserl's sense of "formal," i.e., as opposed to "material") mereology is simply an attempt to lay down the general principles underlying the relationships between an entity and its constituent parts, whatever the nature of the entity.⁷ The symphonic forms are the anagogical individual "parts" of memory while memory is the anagogical "whole." While each symphonic form is revelatory regarding one aspect and function of memory, they work both independently and in unison to allow the operation of memory, which is the whole. Each symphonic form (part) and all symphonic forms (parts) affect memory (the whole) via the behavior they exhibit, which makes the parts known.⁸ It was through the behavioral characteristics of memory that the symphonic forms of memory became clearer to Augustine. Each individual symphonic form explicates the fundamental affordances associated with memory. These fundamental affordances and the symphonic forms

---

3. Tell, "Beyond," 234, 250n4.

4. Tell, "Beyond," 234.

5. Tell, "Beyond," 236n9.

6. Mereology (from the Greek μέρος "part") is the theory of parthood relations: of the relations of part to whole and the relations of part to part within a whole. Its roots can be traced back to the early days of philosophy, beginning with the Presocratic atomists and continuing throughout the writings of Plato (especially the *Parmenides* and the *Thaetetus*), Aristotle (especially *Metaphysics*, but also *Physics*, *Topics*, and *De partibus animalium*). Varzi, "Mereology," 1.

7. Varzi, "Mereology," 4.

8. The philosophical principle of the behavioral mereology of parts affecting the whole is further elucidated in Fong's article. Fong et al., "Behavioral," 1.

comprise the totality of memory. Among the symphonic forms there is an *ordo* of events, a mereological order, a logical sequence that operates in the formation, storage, recollection, and retrieval of memory. As the whole, memory operates within, and conforms to, Augustine's metaphysics of memory(ies) that resides in *memoria*, which is located in the mind, which is in the rational soul. Memory itself is now a "part" of the "whole" of Augustine's metaphysics of memory. The formal analysis of the symphonic forms of memory therefore, sheds light on the part–whole relationship and how memory can operate both within the physical functioning of memory and the metaphysical dynamic where Augustine is searching for God, the *beata vita*, and the answer to his question of how it is that he remembers God.

The operation of memory includes, for example, the individual "parts" of sense perception, learning/teaching, *phantasiae, phantasmata*, recollection, and forgetfulness. All help Augustine in his temporal journey towards the *beata vita* in eternity. Eternity requires the "whole" of memory, or in other words, the completion of memory, composed of its veritable symphonic forms. The memory of creation (*Conf.* XIII) allures Augustine to the acceptance of the Divine and the Word, the incarnate Christ who is a fulfillment of creation and a reminder of God's mercy. Augustine had also learnt of God's mercy through the Psalms as he read about creation and the Creator. He firmly believed that God spoke to him through the Psalms. The Psalms also helped Augustine interpret and give meaning to his past allowing him to have a coherent narrative about his life. Williams explains, "the Psalms is a meaningful narrative structure, a history of the soul. And souls only have a history in conversation with God."[9] The Psalms helped shape memory for Augustine. He saw in the Psalms the narrative of his life but, more significantly, the correlation of his narrative in relation to God and creation. He believed the Psalms were the voice of Christ[10] and that Christ illuminated his personal history through the Psalms. The images perceived through the Psalms formed in Augustine memories of the Divine, creation, and relationship with God. According to Clark, Augustine believed the Psalms were a "prolonged prophecy of the life, passion, resurrection of Christ and a pilgrimage of the Church in dialogue with God."[11] Augustine saw Christ in the Psalms and saw the Psalms as an opportunity to understand more about God and Christ.[12] He also identified with the spiritual history of humanity in the Psalms; it was a reflection of his own

---

9. Williams, "Augustine," 17.
10. Ps 21 [22]. Augustine identifies the words of Christ on the cross in Ps 21.
11. Clark, "St. Augustine's," 91.
12. Clark, "St. Augustine," 91.

spiritual journey, including the emotions he experienced.[13] The Psalms thus became a recollection of the memories of his own spiritual journey and the voice of Christ (*vox Christus*). It could be said that the Psalms also provided future memories of the incarnate Christ and expectations of eternal life for Augustine. The Psalms, as such, assisted in "shaping" Augustine's memories.

Interestingly, the significance of symphonic forms of memory can be illustrated through the singing of the Psalms, an act that spoke to Augustine's soul.[14] Singing required the interaction of the symphonic forms of learning the words of the Psalm, the rhythm of the song, and the meter of the song (time), time, and the sense perception of hearing. The symphonic form of the temporality of memory assisted Augustine in understanding how the present (the start of a word, sentence of a psalm) moved into past memory and the present anticipated future memory of the word not yet completed or spoken. In Augustine's memory, there is a completed whole of the psalm that he sings; Augustine's expectation knows the whole before it is sung.[15] In singing the psalm the expectation found in the memory of the psalm changes in time; as words pass through time, time transcends the words as they pass from future memory, to present, to past memory. The whole in the future becomes parts in the present and then becomes whole again in the past. The whole and parts of a psalm and time reflect the symphonic forms of memory, which are integral to both time and the singing of the Psalms. There is a flowing movement in the singing of a psalm, a perfect (whole) memory that is tightly bonded to the relation of past, present, and future. The "whole" of memory cannot exist without the sum of its "parts," nor can the individual "parts" (symphonic forms) exist in non-relation to the "whole." The individual "parts" can also impact the "whole," including putting a constraint on the "whole," for example, if one stops singing in the middle of the psalm then the future memory of the "whole" psalm is cut off from the first half, which has now moved into the past and become a past memory. In this case, there is no present to the psalm and there is a separation or gulf between past and future where present does not exist. A "part" can interact positively by allowing the individual "parts" (i.e., words) of a psalm to follow sequentially in *ordo* with the future becoming the present and the present moving into the past. The psalm is now a "whole"; on one hand, it becomes a "whole" in the past while still being a "whole" in future memory. On the other hand, the "whole" of the future is an expectant memory in anticipation of singing, and the "whole" of the past is now a

---

13. Clark, "St. Augustine," 92–93.
14. *Conf.* X.33.49.
15. Johnston, "Time," 71.

memory of completion. Singing is an example of a temporal act that cycles backwards and forward and that exhibits architectonic properties in this fluidic movement. Augustine's knowledge of how the individual "parts" and "whole" of the symphonic forms of memory interact with each other enabled him to understand how, for example, the singing of a psalm in time is an activity of the mind, since he can measure time through long and short syllables[16] and an activity of the soul. That activity of the soul is analogous to an image of the whole activity of God in creation.[17] While singing the Psalms, Augustine remembers God, and his soul experiences the fullness of the present in the Divine, and the pull to, and anticipation of, the future towards the *beata vita* in eternity. Through the metaphysics behind the singing of a psalm, the understanding of time (as much as Augustine was able to understand), and the relation of parts to the whole and vice versa, Augustine was able to acquire a much clearer understanding of the operation of memory. Furthermore, the revelatory role of memory and memory images in re-membering God became less opaque, albeit still cloudy.[18] Augustine was, at least, making progressing in understanding how it was that he re-membered God.

Augustine's development of his theory of memory and its symphonic forms had its foundational roots in his theology of creation *ex nihilo*, which undergirded all his theology. Augustine viewed his own creation as memory through the structure and *ordo* of temporal history, a movement through his personal creation, fall, conversion, baptism, to eternal life, in other words, his pilgrimage through his memory and his homecoming as *peregrinus*.[19] Breyfogle posits that Augustine's conversion is the start of "the ordering of memory" and "an understanding of the meaning of his past, and consequently of his present."[20] Creation *ex nihilo* led Augustine to recognize the intimacy of God and his presence with all that he had created, including Augustine himself. The Creator was not impersonal and distant even though there existed an ontological difference between the Creator and his creatures. Soskice asserts that the doctrine of creation *ex nihilo* underwrites human freedom, providence, and the spiritual conviction that God, far from

---

16. *Conf.* XI.27.36.

17. Johnston, "Time," 71.

18. In *Trin.* XV.3.16 explaining 1 Cor 13:12, Augustine describes the meaning of seeing God opaquely through a cloudy mirror. Djuth has an excellent article regarding this topic. Djuth, "Veiled," 89.

19. Sweeney, "God," 686.

20. Breyfogle, "Memory," 217.

being distant, is nearer to a person than their own hands and feet.[21] God overcame the spiritual distance and entered the body to bring it into union with itself via the salvific act of Christ's personal union with humanity and with the physical and the spiritual.[22] Augustine, in seeking God, became cognizant of this intimacy of God (*Conf.* III.6.11). He exclaims, "but you were more inward than my most inward part and higher that the highest element in me" (*interior intimo meo et superior summo meo*).

The architectonic structure behind the location and transiency of memory are exemplified in the community experience of Eucharistic remembrance. Augustine recognized that the Eucharistic sacrament was not only an act of individual remembering but also one of community. His interpretation of the church was Christological, where Christians gathered together into communion with Christ. Augustine writes, "I eat and drink it, and distribute it . . . [Augustine desires] to be satisfied from it together with those who 'eat and are satisfied'" (X.43.70). The ritual of eating bread and drinking wine is a means to remember memory, memory of the incarnate Christ and the mercy of God. Grove comments that in the community experience of the Eucharist, remembering has a location, i.e., within the body of Christ.[23] He goes on to say that the whole Christ prompts individuals to remember that they are forgetful and in this forgetfulness they discover together that they can remember to eat the bread of the Eucharist. Grove writes, "His [Augustine's] congregants' sharing with one another is the mode of staving off forgetfulness."[24] Memory and, in particular, the Eucharistic memory of Christ is the basis of community. This communal remembering is also a memory of time. Milbank describes this as the step-by-step walk through a mystical church-space of collective song in anticipation of the final true location in Jerusalem.[25] Time walks the church community through memory as they experience the passage of time, the remembrance of their eschatological hope, and their journey towards eternity. Remembering is a process that never rests.

The symphonic forms of memory demonstrate that architectonics does not only investigate the structural composition of memory in a purely functionalist manner. Architectonics also plays a significant role in philosophy and theology. It provides information on the relevance and meaning of structure, how parts make a whole (unity), how the whole is made up of

---

21. Soskice, *Naming*, 70.
22. Hochschild, *Memory*, 159.
23. Grove, *Augustine*, 123.
24. Grove, *Augustine*, 123–24.
25. Milbank, "Confession," 53.

individual parts, on relationships, on the role of memory in remembering and knowing God, and the mind of Augustine. It helps one understand, at a deeper level, Augustine, the *peregrinus*.

Arc-hitectonics of Arc

The investigation of Arc has provided several neoteric observations that have unraveled some of the mysteries regarding the operational dynamics of memory. Augustine would have considered the knowledge provided by Arc as *scientia*, a *scientia* that assisted him in his understanding of memory and its function. In this context, Arc's role is foundational to memory and *scientia*. To Augustine, knowledge gained through *scientia* informed *sapientia* when it was not *scientia* that originated from "puffed up" knowledge. Augustine warns of the dangers of bad science in his discussion with Faustus.[26] Augustine clearly saw the importance of *scientia* when temporal knowledge informed *sapientia*. The action of Arc in its role as a memory gene also impacts the metaphysical realization of memory by the soul and its remembrance of God. This to Augustine would have been a case of *scientia* informing *sapientia* and thereby having a role in the "sapiential" realm. Indeed, Augustine would have understood that it is because of the memory of creation and the incarnate Christ that *scientia* and *sapientia* are reconnected in this manner; only in Christ is this possible.[27] I contend that in the same way that Augustine used *scientia* to inform *sapienta*, the biological wisdom (*scientia* or in this case, *biologicum sapientiam*) gained from investigating Arc's role in Augustinian memory also informs *sapienta*.

Augustine always maintained a practical bond between his theological beliefs and *scientia*.[28] Incorporating genetics (via Arc) in order to improve the understanding of memory operations falls into the Augustinian modus operandi of utilizing *scientia* to interrogate memory. Genetics undergirds Augustine's theology of *memoria* and becomes an integral and indistinguishable participant in the holistic deciphering of memory operational mechanisms and of memory itself and consequently, in assisting the soul in remembering God and its origins. The architectonic investigation of Arc's role in memory is informative in five distinct aspects. These are:

---

26. *Conf.* V.3.6–6.11.

27. Gioia discusses the role of *scientia* in Christ and the reconnection of wisdom and science in his book. Gioia, *Theological*, 221.

28. Retief and Cilliers, "St. Augustine," 99.

1. Arc and creation *ex nihilo*
2. Arc and the symphonic forms of memory
3. Arc and the unity of body and soul
4. Arc and temporality
5. Arc, memory, and the Divine

Arc and creation ex nihilo

Arc is a physical manifestation of the Creator's creation *ex nihilo* and therefore is, by definition, a creature. It is iconic in its representational image of creation. Through creation, Arc acquired its conserved nature and architectonic structure via its ancient retrotransposon elements. Arc is operationally defined and constrained by its genomic structure and its regulatory properties as a gene; the molecular organization of the Arc gene enables its specific functional applications. These are the specifics of Arc that the Creator God created to ensure the operational efficacy of Arc in much the same manner as the creation of a human being whose body is designed to be functionally operational in temporality. The genome is the "primordial" starting point from where it acts to promote activation of Arc which then functions within a novel memory neuronal communication system. Arc emerges from the primordial genome in a manner reminiscent of a creature being created from formless matter. Formless matter is completely malleable to God and matter becoming "something" comes from God. Arc, and the "choice" of DNA sequences within the Arc gene, also come from God; the DNA sequences are essential for the successful expression and regulation of Arc (DNA architectonics). The created genome also remembers innately how genes, including Arc, work; the genome and Arc remember their origins analogous to Augustine remembering his own creation. Arc reveals the ongoing work of God in creation as it exquisitely regulates memory formation, storage, recollection, and retrieval. Yet, in all the knowledge regarding Arc, there remains the mystery that resides in its form; the principle of order and source of innate memory that orientates Augustine towards God. This mystery is tethered to creation *ex nihilo*.

Berg and Singer describe a gene as a unit of inherited information.[29] Arc was created to be an information hub with innate knowledge and memory that would be functional in physical memory operations and in the metaphysical ability to recollect the *memoria Dei*. Arc, the creature, through divine illumination operates in facilitating the soul in recalling the *memoria*

---

29. Berg and Singer, *Dealing*, 247.

Dei and remembering its origins. Arc, in this way, participates in overcoming the ontological distance between Augustine and God by unifying the body and soul and their physical and metaphysical dimensions. Further, Arc, the creature, like Augustine, passes through time having experienced past time (their creation), present time (their actions), and future time as Arc is transmitted through one generation to the next moving towards eternity and as Augustine journeys towards eternity. Arc is a transient carrier of historical innate memory but also a gene that acts directed towards a future. Concomitantly, in the present, the regulation and the expression of Arc participates in the creation of a specific memory such as a memory of a place visited, a song, an experience, or a sense perception. Arc, formulates new memories, stores them, and participates in their recollection and retrieval. Time past, present, and future thus converge in Arc and its regulation in genomic memory processes. Further, the anatomical structure of the nervous system and the neuronal network where Arc directs synaptic plasticity is one created and designed by the Creator to accommodate the operation of Arc. For example, the hippocampal formation is richly interconnected with neocortical sites, forming functional networks which include Arc that are important for the encoding and consolidation of new episodic memories.[30] The marvel of Arc is that it participates in multiple mechanisms all involved in memory. Moreover, Arc is an exemplar of the repetition of memory for it goes through the cycle of creation, DNA replication, memory regulation, Arc capsid replication, and eventually death only to be re-created in the next generation and go through this cycle again. Arc thus follows the forward and backward movements through time past, present, and future. Arc, the creature, is a master regulator of memory, memory that is the "bridge to the world outside of ourselves, to ourselves, and to God" as Fredriksen wrote.[31]

Arc and the symphonic forms of memory

The architectonic structure of Arc evokes memory and recalls the relationship that exists between the physical reality and the effects of memory in *memoria* and the mind. Indeed, it is remarkable that Arc dynamics are involved in all aspects of Augustinian memory, including all eight symphonic forms. The versatility of the Arc gene is manifest in each.

---

30. Myrum et al., "'Arc'-hitecture," 9.
31. Fredriksen, "Augustine," 132.

For Augustine, the journey towards God unfolds in a temporal, spatial, and eternal framework.[32] The same can be said of Arc. The location of memory in terms of Arc itself, can be understood as the location of innate memory within the genomic structure of Arc, and indeed, the location of Arc within the human genome. Arc has a spatial orientation within the genome itself as its structure occupies space and operates temporally within that space and the space of the neuronal synapses in the body's nervous system. Arc's regulatory operation occurring within spatial and temporal dimensions is important because the innate memory within provides the soul with the "ability to remember." Arc assists, in a metaphysical sense, the soul in its journey to God and its origin. Arc's ontogenetic properties are such that it not only has built-in mechanisms regarding innate memory but it regulates signals perceived through the external world (i.e., via sense perceptions) and, in doing so, creates memories stored internally in *memoria*. Sensory stimuli perceived through sense perceptions increase excitability in the neuronal synapses and create memories, discerning which are important to store, remember, and finally, retrieve. Memory, for Augustine, was deeply ingrained in sensory experience.[33]

Memory finds its end in relation to God.[34] This is why comprehending the operational dynamics of *memoria* and memory was important to Augustine. Arc participates in this relation to God. The very fact that Arc has been shown to pass on innate memory through multiple generations demonstrates not only that the "ability to remember" exists[35] but also that Arc drives memory towards eternity and thus the end in relation to God. In other words, this "ability to remember" is also a re-memberance of the Divine. Memory drives Augustine towards fulfillment of the *beata vita* where he can find "rest" in God, who is always at rest, the Sabbath rest of the seventh day of creation, the end of temporal memory. Augustine recognizes God as the ultimate fulfillment of his desires and the giver of happiness and peace.[36] Arc, as a participant in the creation and facilitation of memories and the carrier of the ability to remember the *memoria Dei*, helps Augustine remember; Arc acts as a mediator between memory and orientation towards God. Augustine, however, believes that this was not possible without divine illumination; the divine light makes true knowledge of God possible. Accordingly, it can be said that memory is cardinal to the process of divine

---

32. Vaught, *Access*, 14.
33. *Conf.* X.8.12–14.
34. Wu, "'End,'" 15.
35. Chapter 7, n172.
36. *Conf.* II.6.13; X.23.23, XIII.35.50. Shin, "Psalms," 252.

action and Arc, as a facilitator that it is deeply involved in the action of memory recollection and retrieval, also has a cardinal role in divine action. Consequently, both memory and Arc recognize truth. Arc, a veridical agent intricately involved in the mechanics of memory, facilitates the recognition of truth through the innate *memoria Dei* and through learnt memories. Arc, via its creation *ex nihilo* and as a creature, is given power by God in order to perform God's work via memory. Arc is an agent used by God in the orientation of the soul towards him; Arc is given the freedom to interact with the soul. McFarland asserts that this echoes "the intratrinitarian process whereby God the Father gives infinite might to the Son and the Spirit."[37] Memory, Arc, and divine illumination intercalate in Augustine's journey towards God. Augustine knew that the seeking of fulfillment in relation to God, was not an easy task. Arc can be said to engage in the narrowing of the chasm between the corporeal, mutable human being and the incorporeal, immutable God.

Arc and the unity of body and soul

The unity of the body and soul is a central dogma in Augustine's theology of body and soul. Augustine identifies himself as a composite of a soul (*anima*) and a body, where both are ontologically distinct.[38] The soul is better because it animates and gives life to the body, yet it has a necessary relationship with the body; the soul and living body are not antagonistic, but interdependent.[39] Important to note is Augustine's identification of his soul with his memory.[40] The soul's ability to remember via a physical function of the body commands a unity of body (physical) and the soul (metaphysical). There is a participation between corporeal being and the incorporeal soul; however, the incorporeal soul is unlike the body, which is constrained within its physical structure. A parallel can be drawn between the body's physical structure and the constraints of Arc's physical structure. From a physical perspective, Arc provides, to use an Augustinian term, "messengers" to the brain, via neuronal synapses and a neuronal communication pathway, to form and recall memory, including memory of the Divine. The regulation of Arc in genomic memory processes eventuates in a coherent manner where memory recollection is controlled and ordered. The soul remembers the significance of the body's involvement via Arc in memory

---

37. McFarland, "God," 270.
38. *Conf.* X.7.10–11.
39. Copleston, *History*, 79; Vaught, *Access*, 41.
40. *Conf.* X.8.2.

recollection. It is able to "recruit" Arc to understand memory very much analogous to the mind's eye to the soul.[41] The soul, after all, senses through utilizing the body's own senses. However, the soul is not passive but an active agent that operates dynamically, e.g., utilizing Arc to facilitate its ability to remember. Arc, therefore, operates within a metaphysical dimension, but it also functions within its physical expression and regulation to promote remembrance of innate memory. Arc, via memory, reconciles body and soul.

Memory is central to the relationship between the soul and God. Augustine knew of the close connection between the soul and bodily functions in recollection. However, Augustine did state, when he wrote about the soul and the role of bodily functions, that the mechanisms of the human body were beyond his comprehension.[42] Arc helps to clarify, in part, the role of the physical body in the soul's remembrance of God. Arc functions in the unification of the material body and incorporeal soul, the physical and the metaphysical, and the remembrance of God within the rational soul.

Arc and temporality

Arc is an exemplification of physical time involved in memory processes. Arc operates in temporal time, both with regard to its functional responsibilities in the genomic memory process and also in the transmission of Arc from generation to generation, which occurs in physical time and space (spatio-temporal dynamics). The physical time of Arc aligns with both temporal time and eternity.[43] Both the physical structure of Arc itself and its operation of memory processes have an Augustinian past, present, and future. *Arc past* relates to the creation of its genomic sequence with ancient DNA elements. *Arc present* is Arc's expression where there are physical changes in structure that allow operation, and regulation, in the formation, storage, and recollection of memory. *Arc future* is manifest in the formation of future memories and via generational transmission, taking Arc towards eternity and back to its origin. In *Arc future*, Arc remembers how it is expressed and how it provides the soul with the ability to remember. Here is a blending of the physical with the metaphysical; the physical operation of Arc blends into the metaphysical manifestations of memory with time, creation with eternity, and the incarnation with temporality. The past, present, and future converge in the physical time of Arc, and thus, temporality

---

41. *Sol.* I.6.12.
42. *Ep.* 137.8.
43. Figures 7.1, 7.2 (chapter 7).

becomes a function of Arc and its regulation of genomic memory processes. At this point of convergence, Arc touches eternity because in that present moment, memory and time touch eternity. Further, memory is the soul's point of contact with time since memory, in order to function, functions only in the present.[44] According to Smith, Augustine sees eternity as a state or plenitude of being where "has been" and "will be" has no place.[45] He writes,

> Everything is concentrated within a single point, as it were: it is being that fully owns itself, without any scattering or dispersion. And yet it is not homogenous, but structured, if one may use that term; not empty, but perfectly full.

In other words, the point of convergence is the present now. Baker uses the phrase "eternity abides" to describe the convergence within a single point.[46] Memory brings Augustine to this single point (of time) where time past, time present, and time future converge. This is true on all time levels, i.e., eternity, temporal, and physical (exemplified by Arc). Augustine believed that there existed the possibility of participating in eternity in this life, in the present time.[47] Eternity "entered" into can be experienced momentarily in the present temporal moment assisted by memory, time, and even Arc. Augustine experiences this, for example, during his ascent to God at Ostia[48] and his momentary union with Christ in the Eucharist; these experiences were considered by Augustine to be a participation in eternity in present time. Augustine is not only a temporal being but a man in contact with eternity, even in these fugacious moments in time.

Memory, Arc, and time are elegantly intertwined; they cannot exist without each other. There is an architectonic structure to eternity, temporal time, and physical time (exemplified by Arc), albeit this structure is constrained within the bounds of temporality. XIII illustrates the inseparable relationship between memory, time, and creation, and by corollary, even Arc, since Arc is a creation of the Creator. Memory is the basis for the interrelation of the experiences of time and continuity; memory preserves the coherence of any content, including the connection between past, present, and future.[49] Remembering is a movement in time and movement in time is

---

44. Fredriksen, "*Confessions*," 96.
45. Plotinus held this view. Smith, *Cosmos*, 60.
46. Baker, "Augustine," 3.
47. Clemmons, "Time," 15.
48. *Conf.* IX.10.24.
49. Litvin, "Time," 5.

a re-enactment of creation in time, i.e., it is recalling *time* itself. Arc also re-enacts creation as it re-calls its own creation in its passage through time as it slowly moves towards eternity. Re-enactment of time and creation is both physical in construct but metaphysically represented by the rational soul's remembrance of God and its desire to return to its origin. The *historia* of time, memory, and Arc is the temporal dispensation of God's action in time, i.e., the *historia sacra* of Christ. Augustine viewed his life in relation to the *historia sacra*, where structurally creation, the incarnation, and eternity are inseparable from his birth (creation), temporal life (incarnation), and fulfillment of the *beata vita* (eternity). Memories from these moments in time allowed Augustine to re-collect his personal *historia*. More importantly, through the collective action of Arc, time, and these memories, Augustine remembers that God is present in everything that has happened, is happening, and will happen.[50]

Arc illuminates some aspects of time and memory that to Augustine remained paradoxical, time associated with past, present, and future, and how they all exist simultaneously. Chapter 7 posits that the physical time of Arc is intricately woven in relationship with memory and the three cardinal "moments" of time (creation, the incarnation, and eternity), and also temporal time of past, present, and future. This correlation of the unified blending of eternity, temporal time, and physical time may help to unravel Augustine's paradoxical perplexity regarding this aspect of past, present, and future time. It should be noted that if no future existed for Arc, no *Arc future*, then human beings would stagnate or stop becoming.[51] Memories would cease to be formed and there would be no present or future expectation. There are circumstances under which Arc regulation can be severely affected, as evidenced when its functional or temporal profile is altered resulting in either a partial loss or complete loss of memory. Augustine understood the fragilities of memory and forgetfulness.[52] Furthermore, disruption in the degradation of the Arc protein results in deficits in reversal learning strategy.[53] The neuronal activity associated with genomic memory processes is finely regulated by Arc. Arc opens the doorway into the present (creation, recollection, and retrieval of memory) and the future (ability to remember). It allows the body to perceive its senses and the soul to recollect

---

50. Matthews, *Augustine*, 100.

51. Love, "Re-Thinking," 56. Love discusses the concept of the non-becoming of human beings in relation to the genetic understanding of time and the transmission of DNA that enables human beings to open to the possibility of future.

52. *Conf*. X.19.28.

53. Wall, "Temporal," 1129.

the *memoria Dei*. The veracious profundity of the ontogenetic foundation and temporal operation of Arc in memory is striking.

The enigma of memory and time has been made less obscure by Arc. Arc has unveiled molecular pathways of memory's temporal and spatial dimensions that Augustine could only speculate about. Arc, therefore, just like memory, is a central axiom in Augustine's theology of *memoria*.

Arc, memory, and the Divine

The revelatory knowledge regarding memory that Augustine acquired was not solely that from temporal *scientia* or even *sapientia*. Knowledge was revealed to him via divine illumination. Augustine was cognizant that God, through memory and divine illumination, was transforming his soul. God, he knew, gathers (*colligere*) the fragments of his life together and does (*agere*) something. What he does is to make (*facere*) Augustine into a new creation.[54] As a new creation, Augustine reflects (Augustinian interiority) and re-members God. Some of the deeper mysteries of memory were revealed to him, which helped him have a less enigmatic understanding of memory.

God's action is both through a physical realm and a metaphysical dimension where both body and soul are united in participation in God. Russell describes how the outcome of God's activity can be attributed to both nature (physical realm) and God himself.[55] While Russell describes this in the context of quantum physics, the application is the same. The micro-structure of Arc (i.e., its genomic structure and spatial orientation) determines its regulatory processes in the synaptic plasticity of neurons and management of memories. This micro-structure influences the biological properties of Arc and the mechanics of these properties can be deciphered and understood in terms of their operational steps. Arc's role in genomic memory processes is an exemplar of how God is acting through his creation. God enables Arc, his creation, to perform its functional role with regard to memory, i.e., its physical function. God ensures that Arc acts as a regulator in managing memories that not only provide cognizant viability but also act to "prompt" the soul to re-remember the Divine. Consequently, God also enables Arc's metaphysical action; God does not act independently from the physical actions of Arc. God's metaphysical and physical actions regarding memory, and Arc, converge to assist Augustine in his remembrance of God and the incarnate Christ, and in drawing Augustine towards God. Divine illumination was revelatory in this process; however, Augustine was also

---

54. Vaught, *Access*, 53.
55. Russell, "Quantum," 587.

gifted with his intellectual ability, which participated in revelation. References to divine light or illumination are scattered throughout *Confessiones* and the doctrine of divine illumination is implicit in X.[56] Crouse goes so far as to say that the climax of the argument of X is the vision of divine illumination as divine agency.[57] Divine illumination was important in God revealing truth and the Truth to Augustine. Knowledge and wisdom (*sapientia*) revealed by truth allowed Augustine to see how God operated within the natural order, the physical confines of the human body, and the metaphysical dimension of the rational soul. Augustine's search for *sapientia* ushered him to the incarnation for *sapientia* is orientated towards the incarnation.[58] The biological wisdom gained from Arc and its actions regarding memory contributes to *sapientia* and, therefore, to Augustine's remembrance of creation, his origins, and the moment in time when eternity was inserted into temporality. According to Le Blond, the incarnation becomes the path that must be followed; in fact, he writes that it is the submission of one's mind to temporal things, including the incarnation.[59] This certainly was true for Augustine; he not only remembers his origins but also the *historia sacra* of Christ. Augustine's eyes were opened to the inner workings of his soul, mind, and memory.

The act of remembering God is interestingly, and surprisingly, illustrated by a side-by-side comparison of Arc and Noah's ark. Both demonstrate similarities in architectonics and God's action in temporality. This would have delighted Augustine since it would be a case of *scientia* (scientific truth, biological wisdom) standing with the truth of Scripture and not inconsistent with it.[60] *Scientia* and *sapientia* work in unison; this is a foundational principle within architectonics. Divine action through the physical structures of both Arc and the ark and God's divine illumination and resulting action are evident in the re-calling of God's people (Noah) and the soul (Augustine) back to him. Arc is a facilitator of memory in that the soul remembers God and Noah's ark is a facilitator of memory in that Noah remembers God.

It may be thought that Arc is ontogenetically reductionist. In reality, the expression and regulation of Arc is not simply its operational functionality nor its identity as a memory gene. It is not just a structurally aesthetically pleasing gene or even an exquisitely functioning gene. The architectonic

---

56. E.g., *Conf.* IV.15.25; VII.6.8; 10.16; XI.19.25; XIII.16.19.
57. Crouse, "Recurrens," 391.
58. Williams, *Augustine*, 142.
59. Le Blond, *Conversions*, 19.
60. *Gn. Litt.* II.9.21.

structure of Arc has unraveled the multiplicity of layers that facilitate and explain memory and has revealed an architectonic theology regarding Arc's role in memory. Arc may operate in a physical dimension, but it performs metaphysically in assisting the soul in its remembrance of the Divine.

Architectonics of Time and Memory

The start of *Conf.* XI, sets the tone for Augustine's inquiry of time by stating, "Lord, eternity is yours.... [Y]our vision of occurrences in time is not temporally conditioned." Augustine's view of time in temporality is always conditioned by his views of eternity but he acknowledges how precious the "drops of time"[61] are to him. He realizes that time is only time in its temporality because if present time did not pass away into the past, then it would be eternity.[62] Accordingly, Augustine views eternity as the benchmark by which time is investigated. Ayoub writes that this is so because human beings are governed by an unavoidable desire for eternity.[63] Eternity is the teleological trajectory of Augustine's life. He lives in eschatological expectation of the future in hope of achieving the *beata vita*. Ayoub associates future time with an interior reality that is compared to time past, because both exist only inside of human beings.[64] She goes on to say that the future mimics the work of memory (the interior reality of past time) by using another disposition of the soul, which Augustine calls "expectation." The present is the *contuitus* (the sight) of the soul.[65] According to Augustine, all human experience depends on an internal reference, i.e., the soul. According to Gilson, the three divisions of time collide in the present and this is possible only because of the soul.[66] He continues,

> The soul's present is an attention directed both towards that which is yet to be (through anticipation), and towards that which is no more (through memory). The attention of the soul is continuous: it is, so to speak, the point of transition between something anticipated to something remembered.[67]

---

61. *Conf.* XI.2.2.
62. *Conf.* XI.14.17.
63. Ayoub, "Time," 75.
64. Ayoub, "Time," 76.
65. *Conf.* XI.20.26; Ayoub, "Time," 77.
66. Gilson, *Christian*, 281.
67. *Conf.* XI.28.37; Gilson, *Christian*, 281.

Memoria within the soul further defines the soul's internal reference since it is the memories of the past and future memories of anticipation that converge and exist in the present. In X–XIII, Augustine reflects on time, eternity, and creation and how as an embodied, temporal creature he is distended (pulled) across time (*distentio animi*) between recollection and expectation.[68] This is the duration of the attention of the soul, the distention of something internal that pertains to the external temporal reality of the daily routine of Augustine's life. Augustine needs memory to move in time. His memories in the present are recollections of past memories and also memories of future anticipations that perhaps have been experienced in the present. Past memories are called to mind in the present when various aspects of the future are remembered, e.g., union with God as experienced at Ostia and via the Eucharistic memory of Christ's death, also Augustine's journey towards eternity and the fulfillment of the *beata vita*. Memories connect the realities of temporal time with the veridicality of eternity. Christ is the Mediator who gathers Augustine's distended self so that he might follow God *non distentus sed extentus*.[69] Wu writes that, for Augustine, God in Christ, the true living memory of his soul, integrates both past and present, memory and expectation, in an *ordo* that transcends time while remaining *interior intimo meo*, so that in cleaving to God the distended self is integrated.[70] The sequence of time and memory in the past, present, and future is intricately involved in the progression towards eternity where the present is the sight of the soul (*contuitus*) and expectation of the future is the disposition of the soul.[71] Augustine correlates all three tenses of time to the architectonic structure of memory and temporality.

Augustine's understanding of time also relates to the theological implications associated with creation; this can be observed in the recapitulation of time in XIII where Augustine starts out with Gen 1:1. This brings to light the question of Day One of creation having no past, no yesterday. The world was created alongside time, and therefore, there was no time before creation. Consequently, Day One of creation has no past, no yesterday. Augustine declares that it is pointless to ask what God was doing before creation.[72] Associating God with time is not the appropriate way of conceiving of creation; without creation no time can exist. Therefore, Day One of creation is the one situation where time cannot be said to have a past,

---

68. *Conf.* XI.23.30; 26.33; 29.30; Wu, "End," 10.
69. *Conf.* XI.29.39; cf. IX.10.23; Wu, "End," 11.
70. *Conf.* XII.15.22; Wu, "End," 11.
71. *Conf.* XI.20.26. Also, chapter 7.
72. *Conf.* XI.30.40.

present, and future dimension, only a present and a future. Temporality starts at the beginning with an architectonic structure that spans the creation account and that also addresses Augustine the being, his creation, his life, his yearning for God, eternal rest (the *beata vita*), and his memories. Creation does not stand still; it is made up of a sequence of events, of movements that pass away as they arise. There is a fluidic motion to time and structure that is observed in the *historia* of Augustine's life and the *historia sacra* of Christ through creation, incarnation, and eternity. When Augustine describes the seven days of creation in XIII, he develops the place of history. He documents events as the *historia* of things done with regard to God's activity in time. *Historia* allows Augustine to understand the interpretative importance of the temporal dispensation of God's action.[73] In XI, when time is viewed through the lens of Scripture, time is interpreted by way of God's activity in Christ, both in creation and in the incarnation and their subsequent effects.[74] Augustine lives not simply in time but looks to his past for stability and to the future in expectation of experiencing eternity. Augustine argues that memory is extended (stretched out) to "those things which are before" and understanding that "before all times you are eternal Creator of all time."[75] Recollecting what came before transforms memory into hope. Augustine associates the past with creation and the incarnation, the present with the incarnation and death of Christ, and the future with eternal life. Through the incarnation, *in* time and as a human, God liberated human nature to partake in eternity.[76] It is through the *historia sacra* that eternity is witnessed as present in time. In fact, Christ both enters into time and stands motionless in eternity above all time.[77] There is an enduring significance to time because the *historia sacra* expands the understanding and experience of the present time, which always includes the recollection of the memories of God's activity, its continued presence, and the expectation of its culmination.[78] Augustine knows that eternity touches all time but is not competitive with it, and so whether in the past, present, or future of time, eternity allows access to the eternal God. Eternity itself makes this possible by establishing the intimate and transcendent presence of Truth in the soul; human investigation of time depends on eternal Truth, which is

---

73. Clemmons, "Time," 16.
74. Clemmons, "Time," 13.
75. *Conf.* XI.30.40.
76. Clemmons, "Time," 14.
77. Clemmons, "Time," 14.
78. Clemmons, "Time," 16.

always illuminating from within.[79] Temporality conditions every aspect of the created.[80] Yet, it cannot change or fix the course of time. Time is always passing by into the past and ceasing to be whether it be time of the present or of the future. Augustine was cognizant of this. However, he remembered that eternity, simply is.

Theory of Recapitulation: Five Distinct Insights Pertaining to Augustine

The theory of recapitulation is formulated from the findings of my investigations of Augustinian memory and its architectonic structure. This investigation has revealed a complex architectonic structure that breaks down into sub- and sub-sub-structures, each with their own sequence of events and deeper, profound extrapolations and insights into Augustine's theology of *memoria*. The theory of recapitulation identified six distinct categories[81] that have shed light on Augustine's theology of *memoria* but also on Augustine himself and the premise, intention, and interpretation of his writings. Augustine the man can at times seem to be difficult to understand due to his complex personality. He vacillates from the fickle, weak and sickly, sensitive individual who did not hold back in publicly sparring with his opponents, to the strong rhetor, orator, teacher, and intelligent and learned writer. The insights gained from the theory of recapitulation allow for a deeper and intuitive understanding of Augustine. There were five insights that were observed: Augustine's cerebration, Augustine's creation *ex nihilo* theology, Augustine's pedagogy, Augustine's unity of *Confessiones*, and Augustine's recapitulation. Within each, Augustine's theology of creation and theory of memory remain central, as does his journey to know and understand God.

The first insight, Augustine's cerebration, reflects the complex, inner workings of his mind as he sought to know and understand God; this is evident in his writings. Augustine was aware of his "cerebration" compared to some people. He unabashedly and repeatedly referred to "weaker" minds throughout his works and pertinently in *Confessiones*. He states, "to give slower minds..." (XII.4.4), "let him who can, understand this" (XIII.10.11) or "let him who is capable of doing so" (XIII.11.12). Yet, it was this mind that questioned everything, stemming from his desire to gain wisdom and

---

79. Ayoub, "Time," 75.

80. Hannan, *On*, 38.

81. These are: the consummation and the prolegomenon, the architectonic structure of creation, *a* memory and *the* memories, the *beata vita*, temporality and time, the *confessio* of *Confessiones*.

knowledge, from an early age on through the rest of his life, and, particularly as documented in *Confessiones*, his desire to know how it was that he remembered God. It might appear at first that this desire for knowledge of *sapientia*, including how it was that he remembered God, was purely intellectual. Fredriksen asserts that for Augustine the premier role of memory was cognitive; memory was the site of intellectual processes.[82] She describes this in terms of Augustine meaningfully locating himself within time. However, Augustine's intellectual capacity is also evident as he learns and recollects. *Confessiones* X.11.18 describes how "the mind claims the verb *cogitate* for its own province." This he says in the context of the process of learning, whereby thinking ideas that are disorganized are then gathered together in memory. In *Conf.* X.12.19, Augustine asserts that memory contains the innumerable principles and laws of numbers and dimensions. To think of memory in terms of numbers and the law of numbers requires an intellect that is beyond the norm. Augustine asked questions of memory that emanated from a knowledge of multiple disciplines—medical, scientific, mathematical, liberal arts, etc.—which all undergirded his theology and became one discipline, as all participated in his interrogation of *memoria*. Few had the knowledge that Augustine contained within his mind, as demonstrated by his many writings. The other insight regarding his cerebrations was that Augustine always recognized the significance of God's activity and divine illumination in his life. His intellectual search to know and understand God and the memory of God within also had a spiritual component since memory resided in *memoria* in the mind and within the soul. His soul was the gateway to the Divine. He viewed the *historia sacra* as pivotal moments that required recollection of the memories residing in his *memoria* in order to attain union with God. Augustine's cerebrations united the ruminations of his mind with the desires of his soul. Through these cerebrations, Augustine developed a better understanding of *memoria* and how memory worked. He created a sophisticated taxonomy of memory. Many of his works were too advanced to be understood completely or appreciated by his contemporaries.

The second insight, Augustine's creation *ex nihilo* theology was the foundation of all his theology and thought processes. Augustine understood creation *ex nihilo* to be central not only to his theology but also to his own life. Why was this the case? I contend that there are two main reasons for this. The first pertains to why Augustine started to comprehend and expand the theology of creation *ex nihilo*; this was primarily a refutation of Manichaean beliefs. The second, his own yearning and longing to know and

---

82. Fredriksen, "*Confessions*," 96–97.

understand God and how it was that he remembered God. After his conversion, Augustine examined the theology of creation *ex nihilo* more seriously, especially since he firmly believed that the Manichaean beliefs regarding the creation of good and dark (evil) forces were wrong. Augustine, like the early Christians who were his contemporaries, believed in creation *ex nihilo* that held to four tenets nicely summarized by Ge.[83] These are:

1. Creation *ex nihilo* stresses that everything, including matter, is created by God and therefore, intrinsically contingent.

2. Creation *ex nihilo* endorses a radical monotheism, affirming that God is the sole Creator of all that is. Since God is good, all that he creates is good.

3. Creation *ex nihilo* emphasizes the God freely creates all things out of nothing

4. Creation *ex nihilo* stresses a fundamental ontological divide between God and everything else.

These tenets originally developed as a Christian reaction to Hellenism. Creation *ex nihilo* was a riposte to the Greek consensus that from nothing, nothing comes (*ex nihilo nihil fit*); this was considered heretical. The tenets were a corrective to these aspects of Greek philosophy that contradicted biblical teachings or to heretical movements that threatened orthodoxy.[84] Augustine developed this theology of creation *ex nihilo* even further as a direct response to particular Manichaean assertions regarding creation. The Manichaeans believed that absolute evil was completely devoid of goodness and the human body was the natural substance of evil.[85] Here, Augustine develops a unique metaphysics of being, that is, the identification of being with goodness.[86] Augustine writes in *Conf.* VII.5.7, "Here is God and we see what God has created. God is good and is most mightily and incomparably superior to these things. But being God, God created good creatures." Neither the soul nor the body was intrinsically evil for Augustine; they were created *ex nihilo* by the Creator. Nothing in creation can be directly opposed to its Creator, who is himself good. All things are created by God through his goodness, and therefore, existence must be good. Augustine asserts that it is not the body that causes the soul to succumb to its vices but rather the will that is responsible for the soul's vices; the body and soul

---

83. Ge, *Many*, 24–25.
84. Ge, *Many*, 24; Young, "*Creatio*," 139–51.
85. Ge, *Many*, 60.
86. Ge, *Many*, 26.

are good.[87] Creation *ex nihilo* identifies being with goodness; for Augustine the ultimate affirmation of the goodness of creation is a decisive refutation of Manichaeism, and he dissociates himself from the Manichaeans. There are other finer details of Augustine's refutation of Manichaeism that come into play in his development of the theology of creation *ex nihilo*, such as his emphasis on the ontological divide between the Creator and creatures, thereby rejecting pantheism and emanation.[88]

Augustine is amazed at how creation speaks to him. This leads to the second reason for the centrality of creation *ex nihilo* in Augustine's theology and life. Throughout *Confessiones* we see Augustine's yearning and longing to know and understand God, to know how it was he remembered God. Augustine experienced creation speaking out to him of God's presence and thus, his creation *ex nihilo* theology became one that became more defined because of this longing and yearning for truth and the Divine. It is evident that Augustine's yearning and longing to know God is inextricably related to his theology of creation *ex nihilo*. Augustine longing was also a desire to participate in, and achieve union with, God. Augustine defines participation as the relationship between God and creatures. Creatures become chaste, beautiful, good, and wise by participating in God; hence the idea of participation is inseparable from creation *ex nihilo*.[89] There are Platonic doctrinal origins in Augustine's definition of participation; however, he deviates from the Platonic tradition whereby participation describes the relationship between particular things and universal Forms.[90] In the light of creation *ex nihilo*, Augustine described a participation where God is not repressive and exclusive to the creatures but where God embraces, and is in relationship with, his creatures. This participatory ontology is a metaphysical expression of creation *ex nihilo*. Augustine's account in *Conf.* VII (before his conversion) of the beatific vision revealed how embedded creation *ex nihilo* is in participation. The ontological divide between God and Augustine is evident to Augustine; this is a tenet of creation *ex nihilo*. Yet, even at this point prior to his conversion, Augustine is beginning to understand that because of creation *ex nihilo* he is able to be in relationship with God and even participate in the Divine because of God's goodness. It is interesting to note that in his second vision at Ostia, Augustine ascends

---

87. *Civ. Dei.* 19.10.

88. Augustine's creation *ex nihilo* also was a refutation of certain Platonic beliefs, e.g., Plato's assertion that goodness is beyond being. For Augustine, goodness must be ultimately identical to being. Ge, *Many*, 26.

89. Ge, *Many*, 21.

90. Ge, *Many*, 21.

with Monica. Ascension and participation can be communal events not just isolated events.

The third insight pertains to Augustine's pedagogy. *Confessiones* served two purposes for Augustine in terms of pedagogy. First, *Confessiones* was for Augustine a means of remembering and telling his story, and his way of teaching the reader how important memory was in the journey to remember, know, and understand God. He wanted the reader to be aware of the pitfalls on the journey towards fulfillment of the *beata vita*. He wanted them to know the importance of memory and creation *ex nihilo* in that journey. He used narrative, language, the *historia sacra*, and different disciplines. This was the pedagogy he employed. Second, this same pedagogy taught Augustine himself. As he interrogated *memoria* and memory, Augustine discovered more about himself and his ability to remember God. It might be said that *Confessiones* is a book about remembrances, a recollection of Augustine's life and journey towards fulfillment of the *beata vita*. However, Augustine's intellect and writing also allowed him to explore ideas that expanded his knowledge regarding memory and memory mechanisms and further refined the steps of his journey to know and understand God.

The fourth insight is with regard to the unity of *Confessiones*. In *Retractationes* Augustine emphasizes "the thirteen books of my confessions."[91] Clearly, Augustine believed *Confessiones* to be a single volume of thirteen books. The style of writing in the first ten books does differ to the last three, particularly Book XIII. However, when considered in the context of what Augustine was trying to convey, it becomes apparent that all thirteen books are connected. This connectivity is observed in the theory of recapitulation presented in this book. So important is memory and creation *ex nihilo* to Augustine that it not only undergirds his narrative and theology of the preceding twelve books but he also writes a thirteenth book to address creation *ex nihilo* and memory. He firmly believed that God's creation facilitated an awareness of the Divine. Through his understanding of creation *ex nihilo* Augustine believed that God left a remembrance of himself in his soul. This memory of the Divine drew Augustine towards the calling of God. Memory was the means the soul used to remember its origin and embark on a return to its origins. It is in understanding the connection between creation *ex nihilo*, memory, and remembrance of God that the unity of *Confessiones* is confirmed. Further, the unity of *Confessiones* is fortified by the architectonic structure of XIII, which recapitulates I–XII. The style of writing may be different in XIII but it is intimately connected to I–XII.

---

91. *Retr.* 2.6.1.

The fifth insight pertains to Augustine's own recapitulation evident in XIII, which reflects a movement from end to beginning and vice versa. This cyclical pattern observed by Augustine is presented in *Confessiones* as a movement from his own creation to redemption in Christ towards fulfillment of the *beata vita*, and then a return to the beginning again. Recapitulation for Augustine reinforces his belief that God is immutable, incorporeal, infinite, and mysterious, yet this God also reflects eternity. This God sent the incarnate Christ to the world. Christ the Mediator is a recapitulation of creation and of Augustine's memory, for Christ as the second person of the Trinity reveals truth and is the Truth. Augustine recognizes his own mortality and finite limitations and struggles with the earthly torments that besiege him. Nonetheless, God the Creator and Christ the Mediator reveal to Augustine his value as a created creature whom God views as very good and who can be in relationship with the Divine. Creation *ex nihilo* and the incarnation are thus central to Augustine's life in God. Memory is an important and necessary recapitulatory participant as Augustine moves temporally from his creation to redemption to eternity.

Architectonic Structure Supporting Recapitulation

The theory of recapitulation reveals the multiplicity of layers and substructures within Augustinian memory. These are observed throughout *Confessiones*. They are the fibers that weave throughout and the connectors between the physical, metaphysical, and spiritual in Augustine's theology of *memoria*. The elucidation of an architectonic structure was revelatory in that it made memory less enigmatic and, in doing so, allowed for an improved understanding of Augustinian memory and Augustine himself. As memory becomes less enigmatic, the connectors between Augustine's memories of his life and the memory of God's creative act become a unity, a whole. The theory of recapitulation capitalizes on the architectonic structure of memory and its mereological relationships in elucidating XIII as a recapitulation of I–XII. It confirms the unity of individual parts (different motifs within *Confessiones*) to form a whole (*Confessiones* I–XIII). The whole brings to light the parts (Books, motifs) and renders them as parts. This conforms to one of the premises of architectonics, that parts unify to form the whole. Individual memories (*the* memories) comprise the whole of memory (*a* memory). It is my contention that the unity of *Confessiones* is best understood by studying and integrating all the motifs thus providing a holistic, non-reductionist approach; unity cannot be substantiated by one motif alone, one part does not make a whole. Memory must also be investigated in the context of its symphonic forms in order to understand Augustine's metaphysics and theology of *memoria*: memory or memories reside in *memoria*, which resides in the mind, which in turn resides in the soul. *Memoria* is the gateway to the Divine for Augustine. It, along with creation *ex nihilo*, is a key to understanding the architectonic structure that underlies the theory of recapitulation. Architectonics and the theory of recapitulation elaborate on the story of the beginning and end (completion) of memory and Augustine's life journey as he struggles to know, understand, and remember God.

Concluding Remarks

Architectonics is an innovative methodology to investigate and decipher Augustinian memory, and this approach has led to neoteric insights resulting in a less enigmatic, but not purely functionalist, blueprint of Augustine's theology of *memoria*. These prototypical findings regarding the symphonic forms of memory have not been previously published, nor has the association of Arc with Augustinian memory. Architectonics and its subsequent "archaeological excavation" might suggest a "dry" interrogation of *memoria* stripped from any Divine action, metaphysics, or even narrative of Augustine's life. In reality, architectonics, as has been observed, expands this notion and invites a new way of thinking about Augustinian memory. This revised blueprint offers Augustine's readers the same ability to create their own architectonic structure regarding their own remembrances and journey to know and understand God.

The architectonics approach has provided a new and less enigmatic way of thinking about Augustinian memory. In summary, there are four main discoveries in my research of Augustine's theology of *memoria* that consequently encourage a "re-thinking" of Augustinian memory. The first results from the utilization of architectonics to investigate memory. Detailed analysis of the structure of memory formed the basis for my discovery of the structure and sequence of the eight symphonic forms of memory; this is a structure that, to my knowledge, has not been previously delineated. This discovery also supports *Conf.* XIII as a recapitulation of I–XII.

The second finding pertains to the Arc gene and its involvement in memory processes. Arc has never been studied in conjunction with Augustinian memory. The insights gained have allowed for the proposal of a genomic memory mechanism that confers the ability to remember along with its involvement in the operation and regulation of memory processes. Arc, within the architectonic anatomy of memory, is complex yet beautiful in its unique physical structure and exquisite in its regulation and role in memory processes. Moreover, Arc does provide thoughtful insight as to how Augustine might have incorporated twenty-first-century genetic knowledge of medical systems into his interrogations of *memoria* and memory. The inclusion of Arc in researching Augustinian memory resulted in informative and profound novel insights into Augustine's theology of *memoria*. The investigation of the architectonic structure of Arc provides an additional "tool" to understand Augustinian memory.

The third finding involves the architectonics of time and memory, which proposes a model for the simultaneity of the three cardinal "moments" of time (creation, incarnation, eternity), with temporal time (past, present, future), and physical time (illustrated by Arc). One original aspect here is Arc in physical time and how it intercalates with eternity and temporal time.

Finally, I propose a theory of recapitulation where XIII recapitulates I–XII. The same architectonic structure of memory identified in I–XII is present in XIII. This theory of recapitulation is based on the architectonics of memory viewed through creation and other motifs present in *Confessiones*. I contend that the findings elucidated by my research evoke a novel way of thinking about memory and *Confessiones* and proposes a re-thinking of Augustine's theology of *memoria*.

In closing, Augustine's theology is revelatory, insightful, beautiful, and wonderfully complex; a complexity that piqued Augustine's inquisitive mind. His theology of *memoria* is profoundly moving. There is a richness to his intense search for knowledge of the Divine and desire for the *beata vita*. Augustine did encounter aporias and paradoxes that perplexed him and left him without answers; however, he recognized their importance as they evoked a dependence on God every second of his day. This research has provided some insights into these paradoxes and has laid a foundation for future research towards further resolution, assuming God permits these paradoxes to be resolved in the "present now." It is my hope that all the insights and excavated truths presented in this book and my re-thinking of Augustine's theology of *memoria* will provoke and encourage a new way of thinking.

Bibliography

Abdou K., et al. "Synapse-Specific Representation of the Identity of Overlapping Memory Engrams." *Science* 360 (2018) 1227–31.
Ahonen, Marke. *Mental Disorders in Ancient Philosophy*. Dordrecht: Springer, 2014.
Andersen, Birgitte Bo, et al. "A Quantitative Study of the Human Cerebellum with Unbiased Stereological Techniques." *Journal of Comparative Neurology* 326 (1992) 549–60.
Anderson, Gary A., and Markus Bockmuehl, eds. *Creation Ex Nihilo: Origins, Developments, Contemporary Challenges*. Notre Dame: University of Notre Dame Press, 2018.
Anderson, James Francis. *St. Augustine and Being: A Metaphysical Essay*. The Hague: Nijhoff, 1965.
Aquinas, Thomas. *The Summa Theologica of St. Thomas Aquinas, Part 1*. Translated by Fathers of the English Dominican Province, 1952. Reprint, London: Burns Oats & Washbourne, 1927.
Aristotle. *Categories, On Interpretation, Prior Analytics*. Translated by H. P. Cooke and Hugh Tredennick. LCL. Cambridge: Harvard University Press, 1938.
Armstrong, A. Hilary. "St. Augustine and Christian Platonism." In *The Saint Augustine Lecture Series 1966*, 1–31. Villinova, PA: Villanova University, 1967. https://doi.org/10.5840/stauglect19663.
Arnold, Carrie. "Cells Talk in a Language That Looks Like Viruses." *Quanta Magazine* (2018). https://www.quantamagazine.org/cells-talk-in-a-language-that-looks-like-viruses-20180502/.
Ashley, James, et al. "Retrovirus-Like Gag Protein Arc1 Binds RNA and Traffics Across Synaptic Boutons." *Cell* 172 (2018) 262–74.
Asok, Arun, et al. "Molecular Mechanisms of the Memory Trace." *Trends in Neuroscience* 42 (2019) 14–22.
Augustine. *The Catholic and Manichaean Ways of Life*. FoC. Washington, DC: Catholic University of America Press, 1966.
———. *The City of God, vol. 2*. Translated by John Healey, edited by Sir Earnest Barker. 1945. Reprint, London: Dent & Sons, 1957.
———. *The City of God, vol. 6*. Translated by Demetrius B. Zema and Gerald G. Walsh. FoC. 1949. Reprint, Washington, DC: Catholic University of America Press, 1977.
———. *De Civitate Dei, Books I & II*. Edited by P. G. Walsh. Oxford: Oxbow, 2005.
———. *Confessions*. Translated by Henry Chadwick. Oxford: Oxford University Press, 1991.

———. *Contra Academicos; De Beata Vita; De Ordine; De Magistro; De Libero Arbitrio*. Edited by W. M. Green. CCSL XXIX. Brepols Editores Pontificii, 1970.

———. *De Vera Religione*. CSEL. Vienna: Hoelder-Pichler-Tempsky, 1961.

———. *Enarratio in Psalmum 41.9*. PL 36. Edited by J. P. Migne. Paris: Migne, 1844–64.

———. *Expositions of the Psalms 73–98, III/18. The Works of Saint Augustine, A Translation for the 21st Century*. Translated by Maria Boulding, edited by John E. Routelle. Hyde Park, NY: New City, 2002.

———. *The Happy Life*. Translated by Ludwig Schopp. FoC. New York: Catholic University of America Press, 1948.

———. *The Immortality of the Soul; The Magnitude of the Soul; On Music*. FoC. 1977, Reprint, Washington, DC: Catholic University of America Press, 2002.

———. *Letters*. https://www.augustinus.it/latino/lettere/index2.htm.

———. *Letters 1–99*. Translated by Roland Teske, edited by John E. Rotelle. The Works of Saint Augustine, a Translation for the 21st Century. 1990. Reprint, Hyde Park, NY: New City, 2018.

———. *De Musica*. Edited by Martin Jacobsson. Berlin: de Gruyter, 2017.

———. *On Genesis; De Genesi Adversus Manichees; De Genesi as Litteram Liber Imperfectus; De Genesi as Litteram*. Translated by Edmund Hill, edited by John E. Rotelle. FoC. 1990. Reprint, Hyde Park, NY: New City, 2020.

———. *On Music: A New Translation*. Translated by Robert Catesby Taliaferro. FoC 4. Washington, DC: Catholic University of America Press, 1947.

———. *The Retractions*. Translated by Sister Mary Inez Bogan. Washington, DC: Catholic University of America Press, 1968.

———. *Soliloquies: Augustine's Inner Dialogue*. Translated by Kim Paffenroth, edited by John E. Rotelle. Hyde Park, NY: New City, 2000.

———. *The Teacher; The Free Choice of the Will; Grace and Free Will*. Translated by Robert P. Russell. FoC. Washington, DC: Catholic University of America Press, 1968.

———. *The Trinity, De Trinitate*. Translated by Edmund Hill, edited by John E. Rotelle. 2nd ed. 1991. Reprint, Hyde Park, NY: New City, 2015.

Ayoub, Cristiane Negreiros Abbud. "Time, Mirror of the Soul." In *Augustine and Time*, edited by John Doody et al., 73–87. Lanham, MD: Lexington, 2021.

Ayres, Lewis. *Augustine and the Trinity*. Cambridge: Cambridge University Press, 2010.

———. "The Christological Context of the *De Trinitate* XIII: Toward Relocating Books VIII–XV." *AugStud* 29 (1998) 111–39.

Baddeley, A. "Working Memory: Looking Back and Looking Forward." *NRN* 4 (2003) 829–39.

Baker, Jordan. "Augustine, Time, and the Movement of Eternity." *The Other Journal: An Intersection Between Theology and Culture* 31 (2020). https://theotherjournal.com/2020/02/augustine-time-movement-eternity/.

Barry, Daniel N., and Sean Commins. "Temporal Dynamics of Immediate Early Gene Expression During Cellular Consolidation of Spatial Memory." *Behavioural Brain Research* 327 (2017) 44–53.

BBC. "Arc Protein Could be Key to Memory Loss, Says Study." June 9, 2013. https://www.bbc.co.uk/news/health-22811691.

Beagen, Jonathan A, et al. "Three-Dimensional Genome Restructuring Across Timescales of Activity-Induced Neuronal Gene Expression." *NN* 23 (2020) 707–17.

BIBLIOGRAPHY

Beatrice, Pier Franco. "Quosdam Platonicorum Libros: The Platonic Readings of Augustine in Milan." *Vigiliae Christianae* 43 (1989) 248–81.
Berg, Paul, and Maxine Singer. *Dealing with Genes: The Language of Heredity*. Mill Valley, CA: University Science, 1992.
Bergson, Henri. *Creative Evolution*. Translated by Arthur Mitchell. New York: Dover, 1998.
———. *Matter and Memory*. Translated by Nancy Margaret Paul and W. Scott Palmer. New York: Zone, 1994.
———. *Time and Free Will: An Essay on the Immediate Data of Consciousness*. Translated by F. L. Pogson. New York: Harper Torchbooks, 1960.
Bi, G-Q., and M-M. Poo. "Synaptic Modifications in Cultured Hippocampal Neurons: Dependence on Spike Timing, Synaptic Strength, and Postsynaptic Cell Type." *Journal of Neuroscience* 18 (1998) 10464–72.
Bodine, David N. "Retrovirus." NHGRI. https://www.genome.gov/genetics-transcription/Retrovirus.
Boersma, Gerald P. "Augustine on the Beatific Vision as *Ubique Totus*." *Scottish Journal of Theology* 71 (2018) 16–32.
Boldridge, Melissa, et al. "Characterization of the C-Terminal Tail of the Arc Protein." *PLoS ONE* 15.9 (2020) 1–12.
Bonner, Gerald. "Augustine's Conception of Deification." *Theological Studies* 37 (1986) 369–86.
———. "Deificare." In *Augustinus-Lexikon*, vol. 2, edited by Cornelius Mayer. Basel: Schwabe, 1996.
Bourke, Vernon J. *Augustine's Love of Wisdom: An Introspective Philosophy*. West Lafayette, IN: Purdue University Press, 1992.
Bouteneff, Peter C. *Beginnings: Ancient Christian Readings of the Biblical Creation Narratives*. Grand Rapids: Baker Academic, 2008.
Bramham, Clive R., et al. "The Arc of Synaptic Memory." *Experimental Brain Research* 200 (2010) 125–40.
Breyfogle, Todd. "Memory and Imagination in Augustine's *Confessions*." *New Blackfriars* 75.881 (1994) 210–23.
Brown, Peter. *Augustine of Hippo: A Biography*. 45th ed. 1967. Reprint, Oakland, CA: University of California Press, 2000.
Budnik, Vivian, and Travis Thomson. "Structure of an Arc-ane Virus-Like Capsid." *NN* 23 (2020) 153–54.
Burge, Tyler. *Perception, First Form of Mind*. Oxford: Oxford University Press, 2022.
Burke, Kenneth. *The Rhetoric of Religion: Studies in Logology*. Oakland, CA: University of California Press, 1970.
Burleigh, John H. S. *Augustine: Earlier Writings*. Philadelphia: Westminster, 1953.
Callender, Craig. "Time Lost, Time Regained." In *Metaphysics and Cognitive Science*, edited by Alvin I. Goldman and Brian P. McLaughlin, 17–37. Oxford: Oxford University Press, 2019.
Campioni, Matthew R., and Steven Finkbeiner. "Going Retro: Ancient Viral Origins of Cognition." *Neuron* 86 (2015) 346–48.
Caplan, H., trans. *Rhetorica ad Herennium*. Cambridge: Harvard University Press, 1954.

Carr, David. "Phenomenology and Historical Knowledge." In *Phenomenology, Critical Concepts in Philosophy*, vol. 3, edited by Dermot Moran and Lester Embree, 146–58. London: Routledge, 2004.

Carreker, Michael L. "The Integrity of Christ's *Scientia* and *Sapientia* in the Argument of the *De Trinitate* of Augustine." *Studia Patristica* 70 (2013) 265–74.

Cary, Phillip. *Augustine's Invention of the Inner Self: The Legacy of a Christian Platonist*. New York: Oxford University Press, 2000.

———. "Plotinus on the Soul: A Study in the Metaphysics of Knowledge Soul." *AugStud* 36 (2005) 283–85.

Cassel, Jean-Christophe, et al. "From Augustine of Hippo's Memory Systems to Our Modern Taxonomy in Cognitive Psychology and Neuroscience of Memory: A 16-Century Nap of Intuition Before Light of Evidence." *Behavioral Sciences* 3 (2013) 21–41.

Castello-Waldow Tim P., et al. "Hippocampal Neurons with Stable Excitatory Connectivity Become Part of Neuronal Representations." *PLoS Biology* 18.11. e3000928 (2020) 1–23.

Cavadini, John C. "Eucharistic Exegesis in Augustine's Confessions." *AugStud* 41 (2010) 87–108.

———. *Visioning Augustine: Challenges in Contemporary Theology*. Oxford: Wiley Blackwell, 2019.

Cessario, Romanus. *The Godly Image: Christian Satisfaction in Aquinas*. Washington, DC: Catholic University of America Press, 2020.

Chadwick, Henry. *Augustine of Hippo: A Life*. Oxford: Oxford University Press, 2009.

Chaffey, Tim. "An Examination of Augustine's Commentaries on Genesis One and Their Implications on a Modern Theological Controversy." *Answers Research Journal* 4 (2011) 89–101.

Chambers, Nathan J. *Reconsidering Creation Ex Nihilo in Genesis 1*. University Park, PA: Eisenbrauns, 2020.

Chandler, Erin. "The Present Time of Things Past: Julian of Norwich's Appropriation of St. Augustine's Generative Theory of Memory." *Rhetoric Review* 31 (2012) 389–404.

Chen, Janice, et al. "Shared Memories Reveal Shared Structure in Neural Activity Across Individuals." *NN* 20 (2017) 115–25.

Chen, Lingxuan, et al. "The Role of Intrinsic Excitability in the Evolution of Memory: Significance in Memory Allocation, Consolidation, and Updating." *NLM* 173 (2020) 107266. doi:10.1016/j.nlm.2020.107266.

Chen, Tao, et al. "Arc Silence Aggravates Traumatic Neuronal Injury via mGluR1-mediated ER Stress and Necroptosis." *Cell Death and Disease* 11.4 (2020) 1–7.

Chitwood, D. H., and M. C. P. Timmermans. "Small RNAs Are on the Move." *Nature* 467 (2010) 415–19.

Chuang, Y. A., et al. "Rare Mutations and Hypermethylation of the ARC Gene Associated with Schizophrenia." *Schizophrenia Research* 176 (2016) 105–6.

Cicero, Marcus Tullius. *De Orate*. Translated by E. W. Sutton and H. Rackham. Cambridge: Harvard University Press, 1963.

Cilleruelo, L. "La '*Memoria Dei*' Según San Agustín." *Augustinus Magister* 1 (1954) 499–509.

———. "Por qué '*Memoria Dei*?'" *Revue des Études Augustiniennes* 9 (1964) 289–94.

BIBLIOGRAPHY

Cipriani, Nello. "Memory." In *Augustine Through the Ages: An Encyclopedia*, edited by Allan D. Fitzgerald, 553–55. Grand Rapids: Eerdmans, 1999.

Clarke J. R., et al. "Plastic Modifications Induced by Object Recognition Memory Processing." *Proceedings of the National Academy of Sciences of the United States of America* 107 (2010) 2652–57.

Clark, Mary T. *Augustine: Outstanding Christian Thinkers*. Washington, DC: Georgetown University Press, 1994.

———. "St. Augustine's Use of the Psalms." *The Way Supplement* 87 (1996) 91–101. https://www.theway.org.uk/back/s087clark.pdf.

Claussen, M. A. "'Peregrinatio' and 'Peregrini' in Augustine's City of God." *Traditio* 46 (1991) 33–75.

Clayton David F., et al. "The Role of the Genome in Experience-Dependent Plasticity: Extending the Analogy of the Genomic Action Potential." *Proceedings of the National Academy of Sciences* 117 (2019) 23252–60.

Clemmons, Thomas. "Time, Eternity, and History in Augustine's Early Works." In *Augustine and Time*, edited by John Doody et al., 3–20. Lanham, MD: Lexington, 2021.

Cognitive Neuroscience Society. "Identifying Genes Key to Human Memory: Insights from Genetics and Cognitive Neuroscience." *CNS 2017 Press Release*. https://www.cogneurosociety.org/identifying-genes-key-to-human-memory-insights-from-genetics-and-cognitive-neuroscience/.

Conybeare, Catherine. "The Duty of a Teacher: Liminality and *Disciplina* in Augustine's *De Ordine*." In *Augustine and the Disciplines: From Cassiciacum to Confessions*, edited by Karla Pollmann and Mark Vessey, 49–66. Oxford: Oxford University Press, 2005.

Copleston, Frederick. *A History of Philosophy*, vol. 2. London: Burns, Oates & Washbourne, 1950.

Cordaux, Richard., and Mark A. Batzer. "The Impact of Retrotransposons on Human Genome Evolution." *Nature Reviews* 10 (2009) 691–703.

Cottingham, John. "Descartes' I." https://www.youtube.com/watch?v=abVVKe5zObU

Coughlan, M. J. "*Si Fallor Sum* Revisited." *AugStud* 13 (1982) 145–49.

Courcelle, Pierre. *Resherches sur les Confessions de Saint Augustin*. 2nd ed. Paris: de Boccard, 1968.

Coyne, Ryan. *Heidegger's Confession: The Remains of Saint Augustine in Being and Time & Beyond*. Chicago: University of Chicago Press, 2015.

Crosson, Frederick J. "Structure and Meaning in St. Augustine's Confessions." *Proceedings of the American Catholic Philosophical Association* 63 (1989) 84–97.

Crouse, R. D. "*Recurrens in te unum*: The Pattern of St. Augustine's *Confessions*." In *Texte und Untersuchungen zur Geschichte der altchristlichen Literatur*, edited by Elizabeth A. Livingstone, 389–92. Studia Patristica 14. Leuven: Peeters, 1976.

Cunningham, Conor. *Darwin's Pious Idea: Why the Ultra-Darwinists and Creationists Both Get It Wrong*. Grand Rapids: Eerdmans, 2010.

Cunningham, J. G. *From Nicene and Post-Nicene Fathers*. Vol. 1. Edited by Philip Schaff. Buffalo, NY: Christian Literature, 1887.

David, Barry. "Towards Articulating the Unity of Augustine's Confessiones." *Humanities Bulletin* 3 (2020) 45–76.

Day, Cameron., and Jason D. Shepherd. "Arc: Building a Bridge from Viruses to Memory." *Biochemical Journal* 468 (2015) e1–3.

Deichmann, Ute. "Gemmules and the Elements: On Darwin's and Mendel's Concepts and Methods in Heredity." *General Philosophy of Science* 41 (2010) 85–112.

deLacy, Philipp. *On the Doctrines of Hippocrates and Plato, 4,1,2, Second Part: Books VI–IX*. Berlin: Akademie, 2014.

Delbrück, Max. "How Aristotle Discovered DNA." In *Physics and Our World: Reissue of the Proceedings of a Symposium in Honor of Victor F. Weisskof*, edited by Kerson Huang, 129–37. Singapore: World Scientific, 2013.

Di Berardino, Angelo. "Cassiciacum." In *Augustine Through the Ages: An Encyclopedia*, translated by Allan D. Fitzgerald, 135. Grand Rapids: Eerdmans, 1999.

Dickerson, Bradford C., and Howard Eichenbaum. "The Episodic Memory System: Neurocircuitry and Disorders." *Neuropsychopharmacology Review* 35 (2010) 86–104.

Djuth, Marianne. "The Body, Sensation, and the Art of Medicine in Augustine's Early Writings." *Augustiniana* 66 (2016) 63–83.

———. "Veiled and Unveiled Beauty: The Role of the Imagination in Augustine's Esthetics." *Theological Studies* 68 (2007) 77–91.

Dodaro, Robert. "Persona (Non)Grata? Orthodox Readings of Augustine Revisited." The Sheptytsky Institute of Eastern Christian Studies, University of St. Michael's College, University of Toronto, December 3, 2019. https://youtu.be/RMg3gABA6LM.

Dodonova, Svetlana O., et al. "Structure of the Ty3/Gypsy Retrotransposon Capsid and the Evolution of Retroviruses." *Proceedings of the National Academy of Sciences* 116.20 (2019) 10048–57.

Doody, John, et al., eds. *Augustine and Science*. Lanham, MD: Lexington, 2013.

Drever, Matthew. *Image, Identity, and the Forming of the Augustinian Soul*. Oxford: Oxford University Press, 2013.

Dudai, Yadin. "Molecular Bases of Long-Term Memories: A Question of Persistence." *Current Opinion in Neurobiology* 12 (2002) 211–16.

———. "The Neurobiology of Consolidations, or, How Stable Is the Engram?" *ARP* 55 (2004) 51–86.

———. "The Restless Engram: Consolidations Never End." *ARN* 35 (2012) 227–47.

Dumper, Kathryn, et al. "Parts of the Brain Involved in Memory." *PressBooks*. https://opentext.wsu.edu/psych105/chapter/8-3-parts-of-the-brain-involved-in-memory

Dunn, Amy R., and Catherine C. Kaczorowski. "Regulation of Intrinsic Excitability: Roles for Learning and Memory, Aging and Alzheimer's Disease, and Genetic Diversity." *NLM* 164 (2019) 107069, 1–27.

Durling, Robert M. "Platonism and Poetic Form: Augustine's *Confessions*." Public lecture delivered at Princeton University, March 1982.

Ebbinghaus, Herman. *Memory, a Contribution to Experimental Psychology (Über das Gedächtnis)*. Translated by Henry A. Ruger and Clara E. Bussenius. 1885. Reprint, New York: Dover, 1964.

Einchenbaum, Howard. "On the Integration of Space, Time, and Memory." *Neuron* 95 (2017) 1007–18.

Eliot, T. S. "Burnt Norton." In *Four Quartets*. San Diego: Harcourt Brace, 1968.

Encyclopedia Britannica. "Hermann Ebbinghaus." January 20, 2022. https://www.britannica.com/biography/Hermann-Ebbinghaus.

Erlendsson, S., et al. "Structures of Virus-Like Capsids Formed by the Drosophila Neuronal Arc Proteins." *NN* 23 (2020) 172–75.

Falconer, Robert. "Architectonic Theology." *Pharos Theology* 100 (2019) 1–10.

Faur, José. *Golden Doves with Silver Dots: Semiotics and Textuality in Rabbinic Tradition.* Jewish Literature and Culture. Bloomington: Indiana University Press, 1986.

Ferrari, L. C. "Saint Augustine on the Road to Damascus." *AugStud.* 13 (1982) 151–70.

Fila, Michal, et al. "mRNA Trafficking in the Nervous System: A Key Mechanism of the Involvement of Activity-Regulated Cytoskeleton-Associated Protein (Arc) in Synaptic Plasticity." *NP* (2021) 1–12.

Finaert, Guy and F. J. Thonnard, eds. *Oeuvres de Saint Augustin.* Bibliothéque Augustinenne 7. Paris: Desclée de Brouwer, 1947.

Fischer, Petr B. "What's in a Classic? The Unity of Augustine's Confessions." *The Centennial Review of Arts & Science* 2 (1958) 67–80.

Flavell, S. W., and M. E. Greenberg. "Signaling Mechanisms Linking Neuronal Activity to Gene Expression and Plasticity of the Nervous System." *ARN* 31 (2008) 563–90.

Fokas, A. S. "Mathematics, Innate Knowledge, and Neuroscience." Lecture at Harvard University, September 27, 2012.

Foley, Michael P. *Soliloquies.* St. Augustine's Cassiciacum Dialogues 4. New Haven: Yale University Press, 2020.

Fong, Brendan, et al. "Behavioral Mereology: A Modal Logic for Passing Constraints." *EPTCS* 333 (2021) 276–88. https://arxiv.org/abs/2101.10490v1.

Foster, Jonathan K. "Memory: From Sense to Storage." *New Scientist*, November 30, 2011.

Fowler, T., et al. "Regulation of Primary Response Genes." *Molecular Cell* 44 (2011) 348–60.

Fox, Robin Lane. *Augustine: Conversions to Confessions.* New York: Basic, 2015.

Fraser, C. G. et al. "Mathematics." *Encyclopedia Britannica.* https://www.britannica.com/science/mathematics.

Fredriksen, Paula. "Augustine on God and Memory." In *Obliged by Memory: Literature, Religion, Ethics*, edited by Steven T. Katz and Alan Rosen, 131–38. New York: Syracuse University Press, 2006.

———. "The *Confessions* as Autobiography." In *A Companion to Augustine* edited by Mark Vessey, 87–98. Chichester: Wiley & Sons, 2015.

Freed, E. O. "HIV-1 Assembly, Release, and Maturation." *Nature Reviews Microbiology* 13 (2015) 484–96.

Gadamer, Hans-Georg. *Truth and Method.* 2nd rev. ed. Translated by Joel Weinsheimer and Donald G. Marshall. London: Bloomsbury, 2013.

Gallagher, Donald A., and Idella J. Gallagher. "Introduction." In *The Catholic and Manichaean Ways of Life*, xi–xx. FoC 56. Washington, DC: Catholic University of America Press, 1966.

Ge, Yonghua. *The Many and The One.* Lanham, MD: Lexington, 2021.

Geertz, Clifford. *Thick Description: Toward and Interpretive Theory of Culture.* New York: Basic, 1973.

Gershman, Samuel J. "The Molecular Memory Code and Synaptic Plasticity: A Synthesis." *Biosystems* 224 (2023) 1–20.

Ghosh, D., et al. "Molecular Architectonics of DNA for Functional Nanoarchitectures." *Beilstein Nanotechnology* 11 (2020) 124–40.

BIBLIOGRAPHY

Gioia, Luigi. *The Theological Epistemology of Augustine's De Trinitate.* Oxford: Oxford University Press, 2008.

Gilson, Étienne. *The Christian Philosophy of Saint Augustine.* Translated by L. E. M. Lynch. Providence, RI: CLUNY Media, 2020.

Glowasky, Michael. "Naming God: Exodus 3:14–15 in Augustine's *Enarrationes in Psalmos*." *Scrinium* 16 (2020) 177–87.

Goode, T. D., et al. "An Integrated Index: Engrams, Place Cells, and Hippocampal Memory." *Neuron* 107 (2020) 805–20.

Graβhoff, Gerd, and Michael Meyer. "Mapping Memory: Theories in Ancient, Medieval, and Early Modern Philosophy and Medicine." *Journal for Ancient Studies* 6 (2016) 678–702.

Gravitz, Lauren. "The Importance of Forgetting." *Nature* 571 (2019) S12.

Gray, Harry B., et al. *Braving the Elements.* Melville, NY: University Science Books, 1995.

Green, Christopher D. "Where Did the Ventricular Localization of Mental Faculties Come From?" *Journal of the History of Behavioral Sciences* 39 (2003) 131–42.

Greer, Russell. "Architectonics and Style." In *The Centrality of Style*, edited by Mike Duncan and Star Medzerian Vanguri, 71–80. Anderson, SC: Palor, 2013.

Gross, Charlotte. "Augustine's Ambivalence About Temporality: His Two Accounts of Time." *Medieval Philosophy and Theology* 8 (1999) 129–48.

Grove, Kevin. *Augustine on Memory.* Oxford: Oxford University Press, 2021.

Gschwandtner, Christina M. *Marion and Theology.* London: Bloomsbury T&T Clark, 2016.

Guardini, Romano. *The Conversion of Augustine.* Translated by Elenor Briefs. Providence, RI: CLUNY Media, 2020.

Guthrie, Kenneth Sylvan, trans. *Plotinos: Complete Works.* Vol. 1. https://www.gutenberg.org/cache/epub/42930/pg42930-images.html.

Guzowski J. F., et al. "Experience-Dependent Gene Expression in the Rat Hippocampus After Spatial Learning: A Comparison of the Immediate-Early Genes Arc, c-fos, and zif268." *Neuroscience* 21.14 (2001) 5089–98.

Hallin, Erik I., et al. "Structure of Monomeric Full-length Arc Sheds Light on Molecular Flexibility, Protein Interactions, and Functional Modalities." *Journal of Neurochemistry* 147 (2018) 323–40.

Hammond, Carolyn. "Title, Time, and Circumstances of Composition." In *The Cambridge Companion to Augustine's Confessions*, 11–27. Cambridge: Cambridge University Press, 2020.

Hankey, Wayne J. "Self-Knowledge and God as Other in Augustine: Problems for a Postmodern Retrieval." *Bochumer Philosophisches Jahrbuch für Antike und Mittalter* 4 (1999) 83–123.

Hannan, Sean. *On Time, Change, History, and Conversion.* London: Bloomsbury Academic, 2020.

Hantik, Michael P., et al. "Intercellular Communication in the Nervous System Goes Viral." *TM* 44 (2021) 248–59.

Harrison, Carol. *Rethinking Augustine's Early Theology: An Argument for Continuity.* Oxford: Oxford University Press, 2006.

Hashimoto, T., et al. "Collagenous Alzheimer Amyloid Plaque Component Impacts on the Compaction of Amyloid-β plaques." *Acta Neuropathologica Communications* 8.212 (2020) 1–18.

Helm, Paul. "Thinking Eternally." In *Augustine's Confessions: Philosophy in Autobiography*, edited by William E. Mann, 135–54. Oxford: Oxford University Press, 2014.
Hernandez, William Alexander. "St. Augustine on Time." *International Journal of Humanities and Social Sciences* 6.6 (2016) 37–40.
Hill, Edmund. "Forward to Books IX–XIV." In Augustine, *The Trinity*, translated by Edmund Hill. Hyde Park, NY: New City, 1991.
———. *On Genesis*. Edited by John E. Rotelle. Hyde Park, NY: New City, 2002.
———. *The Works of St. Augustine*. Hyde Park, NY: New City, 2002.
Hochschild, Paige E. *Memory in Augustine's Theological Anthropology*. Oxford: Oxford University Press, 2012.
———. "Unity of Memory in *De Musica* VI." In *St. Augustine and His Opponents*, edited by Markus Vinzent, 611–17. SP LXX 18. Leuven: Peeters, 2013.
Hogue, David A. *Remembering the Future: Reimagining the Past: Story, Ritual, and the Human Brain*. Cleveland: Pilgrim, 2003.
Holtmaat, A., and P. Caroni. "Functional and Structural Underpinnings of Neuronal Assembly Formation in Learning." *NN* 19 (2016) 1553–62.
Hopkins, Gerard Manley. "The Blessed Virgin Compared to the Air We Breathe." In *The Poetical Works of Gerard Manley Hopkins*, edited by Norman H. MacKenzie, 151–53. Oxford: Oxford University Press, 1990.
Howell, Kenneth. "How Augustine Reined in Science." *Catholic Answers* (1998) 3–4. https://www.catholic.com/magazine/print-edition/how-augustine-reined-in-science.
The Human Memory. "Memory Processes in the Human Brain." https://human-memory.net/memory-storage/.
———. "Memory Recall and Retrieval System." https://human-memory.net/memory-recall-retrieval/.
Ibraimov, A. I. "Darwin's Gemmules and Adaptation." *Advanced Biology* 8 (2015) 1589–95.
Javelet, Robert. *Image et Ressemblance au XIIe Siècle. De saint Anselme à Alain de Lille*. Paris: Letouzey & Ané, 1967.
Jaynes, Julian. *The Origin of Consciousness in the Breakdown of the Bicameral Mind*. 1976. Reprint, New York: Houghton Mifflin Harcourt, 2000.
Jeong, Yire, et al. "Synaptic Plasticity Dependent Competition Rule Influences Memory Formation." *Nature Communications* 12 (2021) 3915–28.
Jo, Seungkoo. "Aldo Rossi: Architecture and Memory." *Journal of Asian Architecture and Building Engineering* 2 (2003) 231–37.
Johnston, A. M. "Time as a Psalm in Augustine." *Animus* 1 (1996) 68–72.
Kaethler, Andrew T. J. "The (Un)Bounded Peculiarity of Death: The Relational Implication of Temporality in the Theology of Alexander Schmemann and Joseph Ratzinger." *Modern Theology* 32 (2016) 84–99.
Kapur, Shitij, et al. "Neuroanatomical Correlates of Encoding in Episodic Memory: Levels of Processing Effect." *Proceedings of the National Academy of Sciences* 91 (1994) 2009–10.
Karfíková, Lenka. "Memory, Eternity, and Time." In *The Cambridge Companion to Augustine's Confessions*, edited by Tarmo Toom, 175–90. Cambridge: Cambridge University Press, 2020.

BIBLIOGRAPHY

Kavanagh, Denis J. "Answers to Skeptics." In *Saint Augustine, A New Translation*, 85–225. FoC 89.6. 1948. Reprint, Washington, DC: Catholic University of America Press, 2008.

Kedrov, Alexander V., et al. "The Arc Gene: Retroviral Heritage in Cognitive Functions." *Neuroscience & Biobehavioral Reviews* 99 (2019) 275–81.

Keenan, Mary Emily. "Augustine and the Medical Profession." *Transactions and Proceedings of the American Philological Association* 67 (1936) 168–90.

———. "St. Augustine and Biological Science." *Osiris* 7 (1939) 294–97.

Kelly, P., and S. A. Deadwyler. "Experience-Dependent Regulation of the Immediate-Early Gene Arc Differs Across Brain Regions." *Neuroscience* 23.16 (2003) 6443–51.

Kenney, John Peter. *Contemplation and Classical Christianity: A Study in Augustine*. Oxford: Oxford University Press, 2013.

———. "Faith, and Reason." In *The Cambridge Companion to Augustine*, edited by David Vincent Meconi and Eleonore Stump, 275–91. 2nd ed. Cambridge: Cambridge University Press, 2014.

Khan, Amber. "The Master Synaptic Regulator: Activity Regulated Cytoskeleton Associated Protein, Arc, in Normal Aging and Diseases with Cognitive Impairment." PhD diss. The City University of New York, 2019.

Kiefer, Julie. "Surprise: A Virus-Like Protein Is Important for Cognition and Memory." *UNews and Science Daily* (2018). https://unews.utah.edu/surprise-a-virus-like-protein-is-important-for-cognition-and-memory/.

Kirwan, Christopher. "Augustine's Philosophy of Language." In *The Cambridge Companion to Augustine*, edited by Eleonore Stump, and Norman Kretzmann, 186–204. Cambridge: Cambridge University Press, 2001.

Kitamura, Takashi, et al. "Engrams and Circuits Crucial for Systems Consolidation of a Memory." *Science* 356.6333 (2017) 73–78.

Kizilhan, Jan Ilhan, et al. "Transgenerational Transmission of Trauma Across Three Generations of Alevi Kurds." *International Journal of Environmental Research and Public Health* 19 (2022) 81. doi: 10.3390/ijerph19010081.

Klosin, Adam, et al. "Transgenerational Transmission of Environmental Information in *C. elegans*." *Science* 356.6335 (2017) 320–23.

Knotts, Matthew W. "The Inner Word and the Outer Word." In *Augustine and Time*, edited by John Doody et al., 89–105. Lanham, MD: Lexington, 2021.

———. *On Creation, Science, Disenchantment, and the Contours of Being and Knowing*. London: Bloomsbury Academic, 2020.

———. "Space-Time as Gadamerian Prejudice: Augustine on (In)corporeality in *Confessiones* VII." https://www.academia.edu/15030522.

Knuuttila, Simo. "Time and Creation in Augustine." In *The Cambridge Companion to Augustine*, edited by Eleonore Stump and Norman Kretzmann, 103–15. Cambridge: Cambridge University Press, 2001.

Kohut, H. *The Restoration of the Self*. New York: International Universities Press, 1977.

Korb, Erica, and Steven Finkbeiner. "Arc in Synaptic Plasticity: From Gene to Behavior." *TM* 34.11 (2011) 591–98.

Kremerskothen, J., and A. Barnekow. "Human Activity-Regulated Cytoskeleton-Associated Gene (ARC) Maps to Chromosome 8q24." *Chromosome Research* 8.7 (2000) 655.

Kukushkin, Nikolay Vadimovich, and Thomas James Carew. "Memory Takes Time." *Neuron* 95 (2017) 259–79.

BIBLIOGRAPHY

Lamb, Matthew L. "Eternity Creates and Redeems Time: A Key to Augustine's Confessions Within a Theology of History." In *Divine Creation in Ancient, Medieval, and Early Modern Thought: Essays Presented to the Rev'd Dr. Robert D. Crouse*, edited by Michael Treschow et al., 117–40. Leiden: Brill, 2007.

Landgren, S., et al. "A Novel Arc Gene Polymorphism Is Associated Reduced Risk of Alzheimer's Disease." *Journal of Neural Transmission* 119.7 (2012) 833–42.

Landsberg, Paul Louis. "La Conversion de Saint Augustin." *La Vie Spirituelle* 48 (1936) 31–56.

Latta, Corey. *When the Eternal Can Be Met: The Bergsonian Theology of Time in the Works of C. S. Lewis, T. S. Eliot, and W. H. Auden*. Eugene, OR: Pickwick, 2014.

Le Blond, Jean-Marie. *Les Conversions de Saint Augustin*. Paris: Montaigne, 1950.

Lechner, H. A., et al. "100 Years of Consolidation—Remembering Müller and Pilzeckcr." *Learning & Memory* 6 (1999) 77–87.

Lee, Jonathan L. C., et al. "An Update on Memory Reconsolidation Updating." *Trends in Cognitive Science* 21.7 (2017) 531–45.

Leung, How-Wing, et al. "Arc Regulates Transcription of Genes for Plasticity, Excitability, and Alzheimer's Disease." *Biomedicines* 10 (2022) 1946.

Litvin, Tatiana. "Time, Memoria, Creation: Receptions of Augustinism in the Philosophical Theology." *Religions* 13 (2022) 679. doi: 10.3390/rel13080679.

Liu, He, et al. "Forgetting Generates a Novel State that is Reactivatable." *Science Advances* 8.6 (2022) eabi9071.

Liu, Ken. *The Paper Menagerie and Other Stories*. New York: Saga, 2016.

Liu, X., et al. "Inception of a False Memory by Optogenetic Manipulation of a Hippocampal Memory Engram." *Philosophical Transactions of the Royal Society B: Biological Sciences* 369 (2013) 20130142.

Liu, Yongsheng. "A New Perspective on Darwin's Pangenesis." *Biological Review* (2008) 141–49.

Liu, Yonsheng, and Xiuju Li. "Has Darwin's Pangenesis Been Rediscovered?" *BioScience* 64 (2014) 1037–41.

Lo, Y. M., et al. "Presence of Fetal DNA in Maternal Plasma and Serum." *Lancet* 350.9076 (1997) 485–87.

Lobel, Diana. "St. Augustine: The Happy Life of the Soul." In *Philosophies of Happiness*, 145–62. New York: Columbia University Press, 2017.

Locke, John. *An Essay Concerning Human Understanding*. Edited by Roger Woolhouse. London: Penguin, 1997.

Logic Blog. "Logic: A Science and an Art." August 1, 2017. https://logiccurriculum.com/2017/08/01/logic-science-art/.

Lonsdale, Kathleen. "Sir Lawrence Bragg." https://www.britannica.com/biography/Lawrence-Bragg.

Love, Carolyn Jo. "Re-Thinking Anthropomorphism Through a Genetic Philosophy of Time." PhD diss., Loyola University, Chicago, 2014.

Lyotard, Jean-François. *The Confessions of Augustine*. Translated by Richard Beardsworth. Cultural Memory in the Present. Stanford: Stanford University Press, 2000.

Madec, Goulven. "Analyse du 'De Magistro.'" *Revue d'Études Augustiniennes et Patritiques* 21 (1975) 63–71.

———. "L'homme Intérieur Selon Saint Ambriose." In *Ambroise de Milan*, edited by Y-M. Duval, 203–308. Paris: Études Augustiniennes, 1974.

———. "Pour et Contre la *'Memoria Dei.'*" *La Revue d'Études Augustiniennes et Patristiques* 11 (1965) 89–92.

———. *Saint Augustin et la Philosophie: Notes Critique*. Paris: Brepols, 1996.

Manning, Lillian, et al. "St. Augustine's Reflections on Memory and Time and the Current Concept of Subjective Time in Mental Time Travel." *Behavioral Sciences* 3 (2013) 232–43.

Marciniak, Bernard Jaroslaw. "Medical Metaphors in Augustine's Letters." *Vox Patrum* 71 (2019) 373–88.

Marion, Jean-Luc. *In the Self's Place: The Approach of Saint Augustine*. Translated by Jeffrey Kosky. Stanford: Stanford University Press, 2012.

Marrou, Henri-Irenee. *Saint Augustin et la Fin de la Culture Antique*. 4th ed. Paris: De Boccard, 1958.

Martin, Jennifer Newsome. "Memory Matters: Ressourcement Theology's Debt to Henri Bergson." *International Journal of Systematic Theology* 23 (2021) 177–97.

Martin, Josephi. *Sancti Aurelii Augustini; De Doctrina Christiana; De Vera Religione*. CCSL 29. Turnhout: Brepols Editores Pontificii, 1962.

Martinez, M. C., et al. "Memory Traces Compete Under Regimes of Limited Arc Protein Synthesis: Implications for Memory Interference." *Neurobiology of Learning and Memory* 98 (2012) 165–73.

Martins, Rosa Andreia, et al. "Plasticity in the Human Visual Cortex: An Ophthalmology-Based Perspective." *BioMed Research International* 568354 (2013) 1–13.

Marx-Wolf, Heidi. "The Good Physician: Imperial Doctors and Medical Professionalization in Late Antiquity." *SP* 81 (2017) 79–90.

Matin, S., et al. "The Contextual Brain: Implications for Fear Conditioning, Extinction and Psychopathology." *Nature Reviews Neurosciences* 14 (2013) 417–28.

Matthews, Gareth B. *Augustine*. Malden, MA: Blackwell, 2005.

———. "Augustine on Speaking from Memory." *American Philosophical Quarterly* 2 (1955) 157–60.

Mau, William, et al. "The Brain in Motion: How Ensemble Fluidity Drives Memory-Updating and Flexibility." *eLife* 9 (2020) e63550.

Mbagwu, J. P. C., et al. "A Review Article on Einstein Special Theory of Relativity." *International Journal of Theoretical Physics* 10 (2020) 65–71.

McCurry C., et al. "Loss of Arc Renders the Visual Cortex Impervious to the Effects of Sensory Experience or Deprivation." *NN* 13 (2010) 450–7.

McDonald, Glenda Camille. "Concepts and Treatments of Phrenitis in Ancient Medicine." PhD diss., Newcastle University, 2009.

McFarland, Ian. "God, the Father Almighty: A Theological Excursus." *International Journal of Systematic Theollogy* 18 (2016) 259–73.

McKenna, Stephen, trans. *Saint Augustine: The Trinity*. Washington, DC: Catholic University of America Press, 1963.

McMahon, Robert. *Augustine's Prayerful Ascent: An Essay on The Literary Form of the Confessions*. Athens: University of Georgia Press, 1989.

———. *Understanding the Medieval Meditative Ascent: Augustine, Anselm, Boethius, and Dante*. Washington, DC: Catholic University of America Press, 2006.

McTaggart, J. E. "The Unreality of Time." *Mind* 17.68 (1908) 456–74.

Meconi, David Vincent. "The Incarnation and the Role of Participation in St. Augustine's Confessions." *AugStud* 29 (1998) 61–75.

Medina, Luis D., et al. "Neural Correlates of Daily Function: A Pilot Study of the White Matter Retrogenesis Hypothesis and Three Separate Performance-Based Functional Assessments." *Neuropsychology* 35 (2021) 103–10.

Mellor, D. H. *Real Time II*. London: Routledge, 1998.

Menn, Stephen. "The Desire for God and the Aporetic Method in Augustine's Confessions." In *Augustine's Confessions: Philosophy in Autobiography*, edited by William E. Mann, 71–107. Oxford: Oxford University Press, 2014.

Miethe, Terry I. "Augustine's Theory of Sense Knowledge." *Journal of the Evangelical Theological Society* 22 (1979) 257–64.

Milbank, John. "The Confession of Time in Augustine." *Maynooth Philosophical Papers* 10 (2020) 5–56.

Minkowski, Hermann. "Raum und Zeit." In *Jahresbericht der Deutschen Mathematikier-Vereinigung* 18 (1908) 75–88.

Morán, J. "Sobre la '*Memoria Dei*' Augustiniana." *Augustinus* 9 (1964) 205–9.

Morin, Jean-Pascal, et al. "New Insights on Retrieval-Induced and Ongoing Memory Consolidation: Lessons from Arc." *NP* 10 (2015) 1–8.

Mountain, W. J. *Sancti Aurelii Augustini, De Trinitate Libre XV* (Libri XIII–XV). CCSL 50. Turnhout: Brepols Editores Pontificii, 1968.

Mourant, John A. *Saint Augustine on Memory*. Villanova: Villanova University Press, 1980.

Müller, G. E., and A. Pilzecker. *Experimentelle Beiträge zur Lehre vom Gedächtniss. Zeitschrift für Psychologie*. Ergänzungsband. Leipzig: Barth, 1900.

Mutzenbecher, Almut. *Retractationum, Libri II*. CCSL 57. Turnhout: Brepols Editores Pontificii, 1984.

Myrum, Craig, et al. "'Arc'-hitecture of Normal Cognitive Aging." *Ageing Research Reviews* 80 (2022) 1–40.

Nakyam D., et al. "Long-delayed Expression of the Immediate Early Gene Arc/Arg3.1 Refines Neuronal Circuits to Perpetuate Fear Memory." *Neuroscience* 35 (2015) 819–30.

Nash, Ronald H. "Illumination, Divine." In *Augustine Through the Ages: An Encyclopedia*, edited by Allan D. Fitsgerald, 438–40. Grand Rapids: Eerdmans, 2009.

———. *Light of the Mind: St. Augustine's Theory of Knowledge*. Lima, OH: Academic Renewal, 2003.

National Cancer Institute. "Transcription." https://www.cancer.gov/publications/dictionaries/cancer-terms/def/transcription.

National Institutes of Health. "Memory Gene Goes Viral." January 16, 2018. https://www.nih.gov/news-events/news-releases/memory-gene-goes-viral

Naville, M., et al. "Not So Bad After All: Retroviruses and Long Terminal Repeat Retrotransposons as a Source of New Genes in Vertebrates." *Clinical Microbiology and Infection* 22 (2016) 312–23.

Netea, Mihai G., et al. "Innate and Adaptive Immune Memory: An Evolutionary Continuum in the Host's Response to Pathogens." *Cell Host & Microbe* 25 (2019) 13–26.

———. "Trained Immunity: A Memory for Innate Host Defense." *Cell Host & Microbe* 9 (2011) 355–61.

Nielsen, Lau Dalby, et al. "The Capsid Domain of Arc Changes Its Oligomerization Propensity Through Direct Interaction with the NMDA Receptor." *Structure* 27.7 (2019) 1071–81.

BIBLIOGRAPHY

Nikolaienko Oleksii, et al. "Arc Protein: A Flexible Hub for Synaptic Plasticity and Cognition." *Frontiers in Cell and Developmental Biology* 77 (2018) 33–44.

Niño, Andrés G. "Spiritual Exercises in Augustine's Confessions." *Religious Health* 47 (2008) 88–102.

The Noble Prize. "All Nobel Prizes in Physiology or Medicine." https://www.nobelprize.org/prizes/lists/all-nobel-laureates-in-physiology-or-medicine/.

Nordlund, Thomas. "The Physics of Augustine: The Matter of Time, Change, and an Unchanging God." *Religions* 6 (2015) 221–44.

Noyes, Nathaniel C., et al. "Memory Suppressor Genes: Modulating Acquisition, Consolidation, and Forgetting." *Neuron* 109 (2021) 3211–27.

Nunziato, Joshua. "Created to Confess: St. Augustine on Being Material." *Modern Theology* 32 (2016) 361–83.

O'Connell, Robert. "*De Libero Arbitrio* I: Stoicism Revisited." *AugStud*. 1 (1970) 49–68.

———. *Images of Conversion in St. Augustine's Confessions*. New York: Fordham University Press, 1996.

———. "Pre-existence in Augustine's Seventh Letter." *Revue d'Etudes Augustiniennes et Patristiques* 15 (1969) 67–73.

O'Daly, Gerard. "III: Memory in Plotinus and Two Early Texts of St. Augustine." In *Platonism Pagan and Christian: Studies in Plotinus and Augustine*, 461–69. London: Routledge, 2001.

———. *Augustine's Philosophy of the Mind*. London: Duckworth, 1987.

———. "Did St. Augustine Ever Believe in the Soul's Pre-Existence?" *AugStud*. 5 (1974) 227–35.

———. *Platonism Pagan and Christian: Studies in Plotinus and Augustine*. London: Routledge, 2001.

O'Donnell, James J. *Augustine Confessions I: Introduction and Text*. Oxford: Clarendon, 1992.

———. *Augustine Confessions II: Commentary on Books 1–7*. 1992. Reprint, Oxford: Oxford University Press, 2012.

———. *Augustine Confessions III: Commentary on Books 8–13*. Oxford: Oxford University Press, 1992.

———. "St. Augustine." *Encyclopedia Britannica*. https://www.britannica.com/biography/Saint-Augustine.

O'Gorman, Robert T. "Imagination Embodied: The Sacraments Reappropriated." *Religious Education* 111 (2016) 430–46.

O'Meara, John J. *The Young Augustine*. Uxbridge: Alba House, 2001.

O'Neill, Seamus. "Augustine and Boethius, Memory and Eternity." *Analecta Hermeneutica* 6 (2014) 1–20.

O'Toole, Christopher J. *The Philosophy of Creation in the Writings of St. Augustine*. Washington, DC: Catholic University of America Press, 1944.

Oliva, Mirela. "*Das Innere Verbum in Gadamers Hermeneutik*." Hermeneutische Untersuchungen zur Theologie 53. Tübingen: Mohr Siebek, 2009.

Origen. *On First Principles* 3.5.1. In *Beginnings: Ancient Christian Readings of the Biblical Creation Narratives*, translated by Peter C. Bouteneff. Grand Rapids: Baker Academic, 2008.

Ortiz, Jared. *Creation in Augustine's Confessions*. Minneapolis: Fortress, 2016.

———. "Why and How to Read Augustine's *Confessions*." *The Catholic World Report*, August 27, 2024. https://www.catholicworldreport.com/2024/08/27/why-and-how-to-read-augustines-confessions/.

———. *You Made Us for Yourself: Creation in St. Augustine's Confessions*. Minneapolis: Fortress, 2016.

Palop J. J., et al. "Vulnerability of Dentate Granule Cells to Disruption of Arc Expression in Human Amyloid Precursor Protein Transgenic Mice." *Journal of Neuroscience* 25 (2005) 9686–93.

Paolicelli, R. C., et al. "Cell-to-Cell Communication by Extracellular Vesicles: Focus on Microglia." *Journal of Neuroscience* 405 (2019) 148–57.

Park, S., et al. "Elongation Factor 2 and Fragile X Mental Retardation Protein Control the Dynamic Translation of Arc/Arg3.1 Essential for mGluR-LTD." *Neuron* 59 (2008) 70–83.

Park, Wook Joo. "Imagining Divine Beauty: Augustine on *Phantasma*, Lamentation, and Expectation." *Heythrop Journal* 62 (2021) 803–15.

Parker, Rodney Douglas. "The Architectonics of Memory: On Built Form and Built Thought." *Leonardo* 30 (1997) 147–52.

Parsons, Wilfrid. *Saint Augustine, Letters Vol. 1 (1–82)*. FoC. Washington, DC: Catholic University of America Press, 1951.

Pastuzyn, Elissa D., et al. "The Neuronal Gene Arc Encodes a Repurposed Retrotransposon Gag Protein that Mediates Intercellular RNA Transfer." *Cell* 172 (2018) 275–88.

Pegis, Anton C. "The Mind of St. Augustine." *Mediaeval Studies* 6 (1944) 1–61.

Pérez-Cadahía, B., et al. "Activation and Function of Immediate-Early Genes in the Nervous System." *Biochemistry Cell Biology* 89 (2011) 61–73.

Perin, Rodrigo, et al. "A Synaptic Organizing Principle for Cortical Neuronal Groups." *Proceedings of the National Academy of Sciences* 108.13 (2011) 5419–24.

Perri, Trevor. "Bergson's Philosophy of Memory." *Philosophy Compass* 9.12 (2014) 837–47.

Perry, John. "The Problem of the Essential Indexical." *Noûs* 13 (1979) 3–21.

Piette, Charlotte, et al. "Engrams of Fast Learning." *Frontiers in Cellular Neuroscience* 14 (2020) 1–11.

Plath, Niels, et al. "Arc/Arg3.1 Is Essential for the Consolidation of Synaptic Plasticity and Memories." *Neuron* 52 (2006) 437–44.

Plato. *Phaedrus*. Translated by R. Hackforth. Cambridge: Cambridge University Press, 1972.

———. *Phaedo*. Translated by Chris Emlyn-Jones and William Preddy. LCL 36. Cambridge: Harvard University Press, 2017.

Polyn, Sean M., et al. "Category-Specific Cortical Activity Precedes Retrieval During Memory Search." *Science* 310 (2005) 1963–66.

Popa, Tiberiu. "On the (In)consistency of Aristotle's Philosophy of Time." *Society for Ancient Greek Philosophy Newsletter* 379 (2007). https://orb.binghamton.edu/sagp/379.

Popov, N. N., et al. "The Generation of Coding Sequences of Cellular Genome Through Cooption of Viral Genes." *Annals Mechnikov Institute* N4 (2018) 7–14.

Portalié, Eugène. *A Guide to the Thought of Saint Augustine*. Translated by R. Bastian. Chicago: Regnery, 1960.

Pousaz, Lionel. "New Evidence for Innate Knowledge." *EPFL News* (2011). https://actu.epfl.ch/news/new-evidence-for-innate-knowledge-3/.
Proust, Marcel. *In Search of Lost Time*. Translated by C. K. Scott Moncrieff et al. New York: Modern Library, 2003.
Purdy, Daniel L. "The House of Memory: Architectural Technologies of the Self." In *On the Ruins of Babel: Architectural Metaphor in German Thought*, 146–61. Ithaca, NY: Cornell University Press, 2011.
Quintilian. *Institutio Oratoria*. Translated by H. E. Butler. Cambridge: Harvard University Press, 1964.
Ramirez, Steve. "Creating a False Memory in the Hippocampus." *Science* 341.387 (2013) 387–91.
Ramirez-Amaya, V., et al. "Spatial Exploration-induced Arc mRNA and Protein Expression: Evidence for Selective, Network-specific Reactivation." *Neuroscience* 25 (2005) 1761–68.
Rassinier, Jean-Paul. "Le Vocabulaire Médical de Saint Augustin: Approche Quantitative et Qualitative." In *Le Latin Medical La constitution d'un Language Scientifique*, edited by Guy Sabbah et al., 379–95. Saint-Étienne: Université de Saint-Étienne, 1991.
Ratzinger, J. "Awake, and Christ Shall Give You Light!" https://www.vatican.va/liturgical_year/holy-week/2005/documents/holy-week_homily-card-ratzinger_20050326_en.html.
———. *Eschatology, Death and Eternal Life*. 2nd ed.. Edited by Aidan Nichols. Translated by Michael Waldstein. Washington, DC: The Catholic University of America Press, 1988.
———. "Originalitat und Uberlieferung in Augustins Begriff der *Confessio*." *Revue des Études Augustinienne* 3 (1957) 375–92.
Reber, Paul. "What Is the Memory Capacity of the Human Brain?" *Scientific American* 21 (2010) 70.
Reid, Jennifer Karyn. "Patrician and Augustinian Ideas of 'Inner Man.'" *Medieval Latin* 20 (2010) 16–37.
Reid, Shelley Annette. "The First Dispensation of Christ Is Medicinal: Augustine and Roman Medical Culture." PhD diss., University of British Columbia, 2008.
Remizova, Olena. "Architectural Memory and Forms of its Existence." *Architecture and Urbanism* 44 (2020) 97–108.
Retief, Francois P., and Louise Cilliers. "St. Augustine and Medical Science." *Acta Patristica et Byzantina* 21 (2010) 94–101.
Ribot, Theodule-Armand. *Diseases of Memory*. Translated by William Hunnington Smith. New York: Appleton, 1887.
Richards, Blake A., and Paul W. Frankland. "The Persistence and Transience of Memory." *Neuron* 94.6 (2017) 1071–84.
Ricoeur, Paul. *Time and Narrative*. Translated by Kathleen McLaughlin and David Pellauer. Chicago: University of Chicago Press, 1985.
Robinette, Brian D. *The Difference Nothing Makes, Creation, Christ, Contemplation*. Notre Dame: University of Notre Dame Press, 2023.
Rocca, Julius. "Galen and the Ventricular System." *Journal of the History of the Neurosciences* 69 (1997) 227–39.
Röck, Tina. "Time for Ontology? The Role of Ontological Time in Anticipation." *Axioimathes* 29 (2019) 33–47.

Rogers, Timothy. "Beyond Space and Time: Unity and form in Augustine's Confessions." https://www.academia.edu/6047338/.
Rolston III, Holms. "What Is a Gene? From Molecules to Metaphysics." *Theoretical Medicine and Bioethics* 27 (2006) 471–97.
Rose, Steven. *The Making of Memory: From Molecules to Mind*. Rev. ed. London: Vintage, 2003.
Russell, Robert P. "Quantum Physics and the Theology of Non-Interventionist Objective Divine Action." In *The Oxford Handbook of Religion and Science*, edited by Philip Clayton and Zachary Simpson, 579–95. Oxford: Oxford University Press, 2006.
———. *The Teacher, The Free Choice of the Will, Grace and Free Will*. Washington, DC: Catholic University of America Press, 2004.
Sadeghalvad, Mona, et al. "Structure and Function of the Immune System." *Encyclopedia of Infection and Immunity* 1 (2022) 24–38.
Schneider, D., et al. "On the Time Course of Bottom-Up and Top-Down Processes in Selective Visual Attention: An EEG Study." *Psychophysiology* 11 (2012) 1492–503.
Schopp, Ludwig. "The Immortality of the Soul." In *Saint Augustine: A New Translation*, 3–50. FoC. 1947. Reprint, Washington, DC: Catholic University of America Press, 2002.
Séjourné, P. "Les conversions de saint Augustin d'après le 'De Libero Arbitrio.'" *Revue des Sciences Religieuses* 25 (1951) 243–64.
Shen, Helen. "Portrait of a Memory." *Nature* 553 (2018) 146–48.
Shepherd, Jason D. "Arc—An Endogenous Neuronal Retrovirus?" *Seminars in Cell and Developmental Biology* 77 (2018) 73–78.
Shepherd, Jason D., and Mark F. Bear. "New Views of Arc, a Master Regulator of Synaptic Plasticity." *NN* 14 (2011) 279–84.
Shin, Euntaek D. "Psalms for Restless Memory: The Logic of Grace and Rest in Augustine's Confessions." *Scottish Journal of Theology* 75 (2022) 250–61.
Simon, A. K., et al. "Evolution of the Immune System in Humans from Infancy to Old Age." *Proceedings of the Royal Society of London. Series B, Biological Sciences* 282 (2015) 20143085. https://doi.org/10.1098/rspb.2014.3085.
Sinclair Alyssa H., et al. "Prediction Errors Disrupt Hippocampal Representations and Update Episodic Memories." *Proceedings of the National Academy of Sciences* 118.51 (2021) e2117625118, 1–12. https://doi.org/10.1073/pnas.2117625118.
Sipe, Marion. "What Is Innate and Learned Animal Behavior"? *Sciencing*, March 24, 2022. https://www.sciencing.com/innate-learned-animal-behavior-6668264/.
Skalka, Anna Marie. *Discovering Retroviruses: Beacons in the Biosphere*. Cambridge: Harvard University Press, 2018.
Smith, Steven J. "Stunning Details of Brain Connections Revealed." *Science Daily*, November 17, 2020. http://www.sciencedaily.com/releases/2010/11/101117121803.htm.
Smith, William G. "Praetorium." In *Dictionary of Greek and Roman Antiquities*. 2nd ed. London: Murray, 1872.
Smith, Wolfgang. *Cosmos and Transcendence: Breaking Through the Barrier of Scientistic Belief*. Toronto: Sherwood Sugden & Co., 2008.
Solignac, A. "Introduction." In *Les Confessions: Oeuvres de Saint Augustin*, edited by Martin Skutella, v–li. Bibliothèque Augustinienne 13. Paris: Desclée De Brouwer, 1962.
Soskice, Janet. "Aquinas and Augustine on Creation and God as 'Eternal Being.'" *New Blackfriars* 95.1056 (2014) 190–207.

———. *Naming God: Addressing the Divine in Philosophy, Theology, and Scripture*. Cambridge: Cambridge University Press, 2023.

Spengemann, William C. *The Forms of Autobiography*. New Haven: Yale University Press, 1980.

Squire, Larry R. "The Legacy of Patient H. M. for Neuroscience." *Neuron* 61 (2009) 6–9.

Starnes, Colin. "Prolegomena to the Last Three Books" and "The Place and Purpose of the Tenth Book of the Confessions." *Studia Ephemeridis "Augustinianum"* 25 (1987) 95–103.

Stock, Brian. *Augustine the Reader: Meditation, Self-Knowledge, and the Ethics of Interpretation*. Cambridge: Harvard University Press, 1996.

Stuart, Matthew. *Locke's Metaphysics*. Oxford: Oxford University Press, 2013.

Straube, B. "An Overview of the Neuro-cognitive Processes Involved in the Encoding, Consolidation, and Retrieval of True and False Memories." *Behavioral and Brain Functions* 8.35 (2012) 1–10.

Straus, Erwin. "Temporal Horizons." *Phenomenology and the Cognitive Sciences* 17 (2018) 81–89.

Stróżyński, Mateusz. "There Is No Searching for the Self: Self-knowledge in Book Ten of Augustine's *De Trinitate*." *Phronesis* 58 (2013) 280–300.

Stulz, E. "DNA Architectonics: Towards the Next Generation of Bio-inspired Materials." *Chemistry—A European Journal* 18 (2012) 4456–69.

Sweeney, Terence. "God and the Soul: Augustine on the Journey to True Selfhood." *Heythrop Journal* 57 (2016) 678–91.

Tell, Dave. "Beyond Mnemotechnics: Confession and Memory in Augustine Author(s)." *Philosophy and Rhetoric* 39 (2006) 233–53.

Teske, Roland. "Augustine's Philosophy of Memory." In *The Cambridge Companion to Augustine*, edited by Eleonore Stump and Norman Kretzmann, 148–58. Cambridge: Cambridge University Press, 2001.

———. *Paradoxes of Time in Saint Augustine*. Milwaukee: Marquette University Press, 1996.

———. *To Know God and the Soul: Essays on the Thought of St. Augustine*. Washington, DC: Catholic University of America Press, 2008.

———, trans. *Letters*. The Works of Saint Augustine: A Translation for the 21st Century 26. Hyde Park, NY: New City, 2001.

Thumiger, Chiara. *A History of the Mind and Mental Health in Classical Greek Medical Thought*. Cambridge: Cambridge University Press, 2017.

Tonegawa, S., et al. "Memory Engram Storage and Retrieval." *Current Opinion in Neurobiology* 35 (2015) 101–9.

Tóth, Beáta. "Eternity in Time—Time in Eternity: Temporality and the Human Self in the Eschaton." *Irish Theological Quarterly* 84 (2019) 373–91.

Treffert, Darold. "Genetic Memory: How We Know Things We Never Learned." *Scientific American*, January 28, 2015.

Tse, D., et al. "Schema-Dependent Gene Activation and Memory Encoding in Neocortex." *Science* 333 (2011) 891–95.

Tulving, E. "Multiple Memory Systems and Consciousness." *Human Neurobiology* 6 (1987) 67–80.

Tyssowski, K. M., et al. "Different Neuronal Activity Patterns Induce Different Gene Expression Programs." *Neuron* 98 (2018) 530–46.

BIBLIOGRAPHY

UCSF Weill Institute for Neuroscience. "Memory." https://memory.ucsf.edu/symptoms/memory.

Van Fleteren, Frederick. "*Confessiones*." In *Augustine Through the Ages: An Encyclopedia*, edited by Allan D. Fitzgerald, 227–32. Grand Rapids: Eerdmans, 1999.

Van Oort, Johannes. "The End Is Now: Augustine on History and Eschatology." *HTS Teologiese Studies* 68 (2012) 1–7.

Vandermark Lowe, James. "Platonic Recollection and Augustinian Memory." PhD diss., University of Wisconsin-Madison, 1986.

Vannier, Marie-Anne. "*Creatio*," "*Conversio*," "*Formatio*." *Chez S. Augustin*. Friborg: Editions Universitaires, 1991.

Varzi, Achille C. "Mereology." In *The Stanford Encyclopedia of Philosophy*, edited by Edward N. Zalta, 2019. https://plato.stanford.edu/archives/spr2019/entries/mereology/.

Vaught, Carl G. *Access to God in Augustine's Confessions Books X–XIII*. New York: State University of New York Press, 2005.

Vazdarjanova, A., et al. "Spatial Exploration Induces ARC, a Plasticity-Related Immediate-Early Gene, Only in Calcium/Calmodulin-Dependent Protein Kinase II-Positive Principal Excitatory and Inhibitory Neurons of the Rat Forebrain." *Journal of Comparative Neurology* 498 (2006) 317–29.

Venning, Thomas. "Time's Arrow: Albert Einstein's Letters to Michele Besso." https://www.christies.com/features/Einstein-letters-to-Michele-Besso-8422-1.aspx.

Verheijen, Luc. "The *Confessions*: Two Grids of Composition and Meaning." Paper presented at the Patristics, Medieval, and Renaissance Conference, Villanova University, 1989.

Vessey, Mark, ed. *A Companion to Augustine*. Chichester: Wiley & Sons, 2015.

Wall, Mark J., et al. "The Temporal Dynamics of Arc Expression Regulate Cognitive Flexibility." *Neuron* 98 (2018) 1124–32.

Wang, Pengfei, et al. "The Beauty and Utility of DNA Origami." *Chem* 2 (2017) 359–82.

Weigel, Guenther. *De Magistro*. Corpus Scriptorum Ecclesiasticorum Latinorum 76. Wien: Hoelder-Pichler-Tempsky, 1961.

Widom, J. "Structure, Dynamics, and Function of Chromatin in Vitro." *Annual Review of Biophysics* 27 (1998) 285–327.

Williams, Rowan. "Augustine and the Psalms." *Interpretation* 58 (2004) 17–27.

———. *On Augustine*. London: Bloomsbury Continuum, 2016.

Winkler, Klaus. "La Théorie Augustinienne de la mémoire à son point de depart." In *Augustinus Magister*, 1:511–19. Paris: Études Augustiniennes, 1954.

Wiskus, Jessica. "On Music, Order, and Memory: Investigating Augustine's Descriptive Method in *Confessions*." *Open Theology* 6 (2020) 274–87.

———. "On Song, Logos, and the Movement of the Soul: After Plato and Aristotle." *Revista Portuguesa de Filosofia* 74 (2018) 917–34.

Wixted, J. T. "The Psychology and Neuroscience of Forgetting." *ARP* 55 (2004) 235–69.

Wright, Jessica. "Preaching Phrenitis: Augustine's Medicalization of Religious Difference." *Early Christian Studies* 28 (2020) 525–53.

Wu, Abraham S-C. "The 'End' of Memory: Memory, the Porous Self, and the Communion of Saints in Augustine's *Confessions*." *International Journal of Systematic Theology* 26 (2023) 251–73. https://doi.org/10.1111/ijst.12680.

Wu, J., et al. "Arc/Arg3.1 Regulates an Endosomal Pathway Essential for Activity-Dependent Beta-amyloid Generation." *Cell* 147 (2011) 615–28.

Yam, Cheuk Yin, and Anthony Dupont. "A Mind-Centered Approach of '*Imago Dei.*' A Dynamic Construction in Augustine's *De Trinitate* XIV." *Augustiniana* 62 (2012) 7–43.

Yamasaki, Yoshiko. "Off-Line Arc Transcription in Active Ensembles During Fear Memory Retrieval." *European Journal of Neuroscience* 36.10 (2012) 3454–55.

Yap, Ee-Lynn, and Michael E. Greenberg. "Activity-Regulated Transcription: Bridging the Gap Between Neural Activity and Behavior." *Neuron* 100 (2018) 330–48.

Yates, Frances A. *The Art of Memory*. Chicago: University of Chicago Press, 1966.

Yonelinas, A. P., et al. "A Contextual Binding Theory of Episodic Memory: Systems Consolidation Reconsidered." *NRN* 20 (2019) 364–75.

Young, Frances. "'*Creatio Ex Nihilo*': A Context for the Emergence of the Christian Doctrine of Creation." *Scottish Journal of Theology* 44 (1991) 139–51.

Zadbood, A., et al. "How We Transmit Memories to Other Brains: Constructing Shared Neural Representations Via Communication." *Cerebral Cortex* 27.10 (2017) 4988–5000.

Zelikowsky, Moriel, et al. "Contextual Fear Memories Formed in the Absence of the Dorsal Hippocampus Decay Across Time." *Neuroscience* 32.10 (2012) 3393–97.

Zhang, Jiawei. "Basic Neural Units of the Brain: Neurons, Synapses, and Action Potential." *IFM Lab Tutorial Series* 5 (2019) 1–38.

Zhang Jun, et al. "Structure of SARS-CoV-2 Spike Protein." *Current Opinion in Virology* 50 (2021) 173–82.

Zhang, Wenchi, et al. "Structural Basis of Arc Binding to Synaptic Proteins: Implications for Cognitive disease." *Neuron* 86 (2015) 490–500.

Zwart, H. A. E. "In the Beginning Was the Genome: Genomics and the Bi-textuality of Human Existence." *New Bioethics* 24 (2018) 26–43.

Zwollo, Laela. "St. Augustine on the Soul's Divine Experience: *Visio Intellectualis* and *Imago Dei* from Book XII of *De Genesi ad Litteram Libri* XII." *SP* 70 (2013) 88–91.

www.ingramcontent.com/pod-product-compliance
Lightning Source LLC
Chambersburg PA
CBHW021647230426
43668CB00008B/542